THE

RENAISSANCE
IN ITALY

A History

THE
RENAISSANCE
IN ITALY
A History

KENNETH R. BARTLETT

with GILLIAN C. BARTLETT

Hackett Publishing Company, Inc.
Indianapolis/Cambridge

25 24 23 22   2 3 4 5 6 7

For further information, please address
      Hackett Publishing Company, Inc.
      P.O. Box 44937
      Indianapolis, Indiana 46244-0937

      www.hackettpublishing.com

Cover design by E.L. Wilson
Interior design by Laura Clark
Composition by Aptara, Inc.

Library of Congress Cataloging-in-Publication Data

Names: Bartlett, Kenneth R., author. | Bartlett, Gillian C.
Title: The Renaissance in Italy : a history / Kenneth R. Bartlett, with Gillian C. Bartlett.
Description: Indianapolis : Hackett Publishing Company, Inc., [2019] | Includes bibliographical references and index.
Identifiers: LCCN 2019010480 | ISBN 9781624668180 (pbk.) | ISBN 9781624668197 (cloth)
Subjects: LCSH: Renaissance—Italy. | Italy—History—1492–1559—Biography. | Italy—History—1268–1492—Biography.
Classification: LCC DG533 .B29 2019 | DDC 945/.05—dc23
LC record available at https://lccn.loc.gov/2019010480

ACKNOWLEDGMENTS

Those who travel with us to Italy, comment on our video series, and attend our public lectures inspired us to produce a comprehensive but approachable assessment of the Italian Renaissance. This book was long in the making and consequently benefitted from the assistance and encouragement of many others, too numerous to thank individually but nevertheless greatly appreciated.

Our editor at Hackett, Rick Todhunter, deserves our sincere gratitude. His enthusiasm for the project and his appreciation of the special nature of this book provided the encouragement needed to complete such an ambitious task. His colleagues Laura Clark and Liz Wilson proved generously flexible in their production schedule, and their careful reading of the manuscript caught many errors and inconsistencies. Any imperfections that remain are ours alone.

We would also like to recognize the financial support of the Research Committee of Victoria College in the University of Toronto. The constant support and generous grant allowed us to produce a better and more accessible text.

Finally, we would like to dedicate the book to the memory of our mother and mother-in-law, Ethel Edith Cavell Bartlett (1917–2018), who passed away while we were engaged in this project. Her love of books, reading, and travel, and her respect for education and the power of words always served as an inspiration.

Kenneth and Gillian Bartlett
Toronto, March 2019

CONTENTS

INTRODUCTION

The Italian Renaissance has come to occupy an almost mythical place in the imaginations of those who appreciate history, art, or remarkable personalities. Many of the figures who lived in that period are themselves the subject of biographies and narratives that border on hagiography. Michelangelo, Niccolò Machiavelli, Lorenzo the Magnificent, Pope Julius II—these and so many others engender a kind of wonder: How could so many geniuses or exceptional characters be produced by one small territory near the extreme south of Europe at a moment when much of the rest of the continent still labored under the restrictions of the Middle Ages?

This popular understanding of the Italian Renaissance traces its origins as far back as the mid-sixteenth century when Giorgio Vasari wrote of the "Rinascita" (Rebirth) in his *Lives of the Artists* (1550), a series of biographies that describe an ascent of artistic genius from "first lights" to the "divinity" of Michelangelo. In France, Voltaire, foe of the priesthood and luminary of the Enlightenment, praised what he saw as the growing secularism of the Renaissance. The historian Jules Michelet gave us the standard French word to define the period in his monumental *History of France* (1855), characterizing it as a time when society moved away from obscurantist theocracy and monarchism to what he saw as a more enlightened, secular, and progressive era. But it was the nineteenth-century Swiss art historian Jacob Burckhardt, in his *Civilization of the Renaissance in Italy* (1860), who reinforced not only this concept of profound change but also made the significant claim that somehow the Italian Renaissance was the birth of modernity.

Each of these writers can be seen to be channeling for his own present. Vasari, propagandist for the Medici grand dukes that he was, sought to exalt Florentine art and artists to the highest level of perfection. Voltaire's praise of the Renaissance came not so much from a judgment on those historic years themselves as from his personal proscription of the ancien régime, that union of throne and altar that he so deplored. Michelet was seeing encouraging parallels with the rise of mid-nineteenth-century anticlericalism and liberalism. Burckhardt chafed under the moral and social strictures of his deeply Protestant, bourgeois Basel.

The Italian Renaissance, then, was in many ways an entrée into reflections on the contemporary values and hopes of the historians who investigated the period. It became a vehicle for putting contemporary times in context. And so, like these earlier historians, we ask the same questions. Where do so many of the driving principles behind our current Western civilization come from? How did they emerge and how were they defined and developed so that we might use them as tools to unlock our own present and project the future? And to frame the discussion in personalities: Why is it that geniuses such as Leonardo, Raphael, Petrarch, Brunelleschi, Bramante, and Palladio all sustain their towering authority to this day?

This book will reinforce the contention that individuals with access to wealth and power can have a profound influence. They matter. And this explains why the Italian Renaissance is often perceived as elitist. Those who commissioned the works of art, often those who produced them, and many of those who appreciated them were privileged, educated, influential members of the Renaissance "one percent." This is meant in no way to denigrate modern interest in the poor and the marginalized, but merely to say that the enduring ideas and artifacts of the Renaissance arose from a highly rarefied world of sophisticated talent and thought galvanized by individual curiosity and accomplished with practiced skill. And so it is that this book will be an exploration of the Italian Renaissance guided by particular moments and men—and a few remarkable women. It will be a large canvas with broad strokes intended to be seen at a distance for the dynamic sweep of its narrative of ideas and creative genius.

Nevertheless, these individuals must be viewed within their social and economic contexts. Petrarch could not have written without the support of powerful political patrons and the Church. Bruni could not have become the voice of Florentine republican liberty if there were not a great many citizens who believed in such freedom. And Isabella d'Este could not have acquired the reputation of *la prima donna del mondo*—the first lady of the world—if she had not exemplified the qualities valued by her age.

This book will, then, be woven together from the lives and works of those individual men and women who still define the Italian Renaissance in the popular imagination. To begin, we need to start with the figure who identified—even exemplified—what the age was to become in all of its complexity, energy, experimentation, and hope: Francesco Petrarca, or, simply, Petrarch.

PART I

~

The Dawn of Humanism

In his celebrated work *On His Own Ignorance and that of Many Others* (1367) Petrarch made a statement of that most central element in the Renaissance mind: a fascination, almost an obsession, with the human condition and the virtually limitless potential of humanity to attain self-awareness and to create.

> *What is the use, I beseech you, of knowing the nature of quadrupeds, fowl, fish and serpents and not knowing—or even neglecting—man's nature, the purpose for which we were born, and whence and whereto we travel?*[1]

Self-knowledge is a precondition of the modern world, as it assumes the power of human autonomy and agency and a role for individuals in the creation of social, economic, and political structures, independent of a divine plan but inspired by antiquity. And it helps explain why and how the Renaissance developed in the states of the Italian peninsula and subsequently provided a platform—humanism—on which the structure of modern European culture would be raised. In so many ways we can say that it all began with Petrarch.

---

1. Francesco Petrarch, "On His Own Ignorance and that of Many Others," in Ernst Cassirer, Paul Oskar Kristeller, and John Herman Randall Jr., eds., *The Renaissance Philosophy of Man: Petrarca, Valla, Ficino, Pico, Pomponazzi, Vives.* Chicago: University of Chicago Press, 1948. p. 58.

CHAPTER 1

PETRARCH, THE FATHER OF HUMANISM

The year was 1302, and Ser Petracco had just been exiled from his native Florence.[2] He had always been on the side of the Guelfs in the epic European struggle between Guelfs and Ghibellines. But because he had sided with the more liberal White Guelf faction against the vigorously pro-papal Black Guelfs, Ser Petracco was exiled with his family to Arezzo. Consequently, it was there that his famous son, Francesco, was born, rather than in Florence, the city most powerfully associated in the Western imagination with the Renaissance.

The world of Medieval Europe into which Petrarch was born would be unrecognizable to us today. There was no Italy, France, Spain, or Germany as such. Rather, Europe was politically fragmented, a collage of land-based feudal monarchies and nascent city states. Each of these smaller territories looked to one of two main sources of power to affirm its legitimacy: either the authority of the Church as embodied by the bishop of Rome—the Roman Catholic pope—or that of the state in the person of the Holy Roman Emperor. The competing factions were known, respectively, as Guelfs and Ghibellines.[3]

In many ways Florence was an anomaly in Renaissance Italy. As a dynamic republic whose communal institutions survived even the ascendancy of the Medici, it represented an unusual experiment. The more prevalent model of state organization in the peninsula was the lordship or principality—a despotic, top-down governmental structure controlled by individual princes and their families. These principalities had arisen from the chaos after the collapse of Roman civil and military authority and the devastating effects of the barbarian invasions. Territories which had in classical times been part of the vast Roman Empire fragmented into more easily defended jurisdictions defined by the rule of a particular tribe or people.[4]

Communities coalesced around powerful men who could defend them and provide some access to justice. In many instances these men were a species of warlord who commanded large and skilled bands of soldiers, while in other instances the power vacuum resulting from the disintegration of Rome was filled by the local bishop. In order to confirm and legitimize their power, these princes—whether warlord or bishop—sought sovereign recognition from external forces: either the Germanic Holy Roman Emperor or the Roman Catholic pope.

2. For the life of Petrarch, see E. H. Wilkins, *Life of Petrarch*. Chicago and London: University of Chicago Press, 1961; Christopher Celenza, *Petrarch, Everywhere a Wanderer*. London: Reaktion Books, 2017.

3. John Larner, *Italy in the Age of Dante and Petrarch, 1216–1380*. London: Longmans, 1983.

4. Giovanni Tabacco, *The Struggle for Power in Medieval Italy: Structures of Political Rule*, tr. Rosalind Brown Jensen. Cambridge: Cambridge University Press, 1990.

The Germanic Holy Roman Emperors had assumed themselves to be heirs of Roman imperial power after the Roman Empire had collapsed. The papacy disputed this claim, arguing that it was the pope who wielded imperial sovereignty. To support its position, it offered as proof the *Donation of Constantine*, a document declaring that the Emperor Constantine had granted Pope Sylvester (d. 335) rule of the Western empire. The *Donation* was ultimately proven by the humanist philologist Lorenzo Valla (1407–57) to be an eighth-century forgery. But until then—and even afterward—it was accepted and used to validate claims of universal papal power.

These competing claims of pope and emperor were the platform on which the struggle between the papal supporters, or Guelfs, and the imperial allegiance, or Ghibellines, arose. The term "Guelf" derives from a Germanic family who competed for the imperial crown with the support of the pope. This dynasty was the Welfs, which to the Italian ear sounded like "Guelf." The other faction was the Hohenstaufen whose ancestral castle was at Waiblingen. In battle, the Hohenstaufen cried out "Waiblingen, Waiblingen." This was utterly unpronounceable to an Italian tongue, so the name emerged as "Ghibelline."

The Guelf–Ghibelline competition was much more than an abstract duel over the source of political sovereignty in Western Europe: it was the engine that drove centuries of brutal factionalism and warfare throughout Italy. Which side a state supported derived from a complex mix of factors: geography, the social and economic structures in the community, tradition, and pragmatism. For example, if your neighboring enemy was Ghibelline, it was prudent for you to be a Guelf to undermine his authority and seek support and alliances from other Guelf states. A consequence of this checkerboard of allegiances and competition was the opportunity for small territories to sustain their independence, resulting in the mosaic of jurisdictions that characterized the peninsula during the Middle Ages and Renaissance.[5]

The city of Florence in the thirteenth century was dominated by Guelfs. But the grasping ambitions of the ruling pope Boniface VIII dismayed many citizens—among them the poet Dante Alighieri as well as Petrarch's father. A merchant and notary who as a young man had held several prominent political offices, Ser Petracco began to doubt the rightness of the pope's claims to universal dominion in secular as well as spiritual matters, particularly in Florence. He and Dante, who harbored similar views, became allied with a moderate faction called the White Guelfs. But, at the turn of the century, both men were falsely charged with political crimes by the opposing Black Guelfs and forcibly driven into exile. This ignominious circumstance drove them both to switch allegiance, turning to support the imperial cause in hopes that the emperor might restore them to their native Florence.

---

5. Lauro Martines, *Power and Imagination: City-States in Renaissance Italy*. Baltimore: Johns Hopkins University Press, 1988, provides a clear overview of the development of the Italian communes, both signorial and republican.

As a consequence, young Francesco Petrarch absorbed the indignities and uncertainties of exile from the moment of his birth. Even today Italians speak of *campanilismo*—that intense devotion to one's region or town symbolized by the tallest and most prominent building: the campanile, the bell tower of the local church. The Petracco family would have been viewed as outsiders, only temporarily in residence in Arezzo while yearning to return to their native city. Unfortunately, their hopes were shattered by the early death of the emperor Henry VII in Italy in 1313. The death of the emperor meant that there would be little hope of work for Ser Petracco in Italy, and even less hope for a return to Florence.

So it was that young Petrarch suffered the effects of a second exile, this time across the Alps to Avignon where the papal court was currently located. For, ironically, despite his imperial sensibilities, Ser Petracco had secured a position in the papal chancery as a letter writer, or *scriba*.

Petrarch, then, grew up not in his native Tuscany but in the south of what is now France, cut off from his extended kin, his native city, and the bonds of association that gave late Medieval European life so much of its meaning. The result was that Petrarch never felt a close affinity for any one place, with the possible exception of the valley of the river Sorgue, the Vaucluse, near Mont Ventoux, where he constructed a small villa and where he would write some of his finest poetry. He was driven to define his own place in the world; and whatever he was and whatever he possessed he carried with him on his travels. This circumstance was to have profound effects on Petrarch and on the development of the Renaissance.

Because the boy proved precociously intelligent, Ser Petracco sent him to become a lawyer. Petrarch began his training at Montpellier in 1319, but not long after, in 1323, he returned across the Alps to study at the celebrated university in Bologna. Far removed from his father's influence, Petrarch neglected the law. Like so many undergraduates, he proved to be much more interested in a rich social life. And, he was drawn not to the dryness of jurisprudence but to the delights of poetry and ancient literature. In particular, he was engrossed by the orations of Cicero and from there the other, more philosophical writings of that great Roman statesman. It was the clarity and beauty of Cicero's language that inspired Petrarch, as he found it so much more congenial than the Medieval Latin which was the lingua franca of university education across Europe.

Ser Petracco died in 1326. There was only one other son, Petrarch's younger brother, Gherardo, who conveniently decided to become a monk. Petrarch therefore came into the modest patrimony of his family and had sufficient independence to follow his intellectual and personal obsessions, at least for a brief time. His formal studies effectively ended, and he began to seek more pleasure than learning. Indeed, throughout his life Petrarch would have an appetite for pleasures of all kinds, including those of the flesh, as he would produce at least two illegitimate children. This relatively short period of hedonism ended, however, on Holy Friday, 1327, in Avignon in the church of St. Clare. It was then that he saw Laura, who would become his poetic muse and guide him to a more disciplined life. This was the first of the two experiences in Petrarch's life that marked exact moments in the transition from the Medieval to the Renaissance world.

Laura

Some scholars have argued that Petrarch's Laura was Laure (or Laurette) de Noves, a woman married to a local nobleman, Hugues de Sade, and the mother (eventually) of eleven children.[6] It's a plausible and engaging identification. No matter. Because whether Laura really existed is irrelevant. To Petrarch she was the representation of perfect love and beauty, very much in the Medieval courtly love tradition. She was married to someone else; was above his station; was beautiful yet distant, even disdainful; and absolutely unattainable. She was, in other words, the ideal woman.

Having abandoned the law and now having the uplifting inspiration of his pure love for Laura, Petrarch resolved to find a patron. In the Renaissance, the truth of what we like to suppress in our own times was then openly acknowledged: it matters whom you know. A friend from Petrarch's student days at Bologna had been Giacomo Colonna, scion of one of Rome's most eminent families and now a bishop. Writing to Colonna to request his patronage, Petrarch was very fortunate to be recommended by Giacomo to his brother, Giovanni Colonna, a rich and polished member of the Sacred College in Avignon. Cardinal Colonna agreed to serve as Petrarch's patron, and Petrarch was ordained into minor orders, a standing that gave him the perfect blend of status and freedom. He thereby had the authority to perform a variety of lesser clerical functions in the Church and receive income, but he was not precluded from marriage, a union he ultimately chose to avoid despite his taste for women and his fathering of those two illegitimate children.

Petrarch spent much of the 1330s traveling in the service of Cardinal Colonna, including missions to Lobez and Toulouse, Paris, the Netherlands, Ghent, Cologne, and other northern communities. But throughout these travels he remained intensely aware of his Italian heritage and held to an unshakeable belief that those north of the Alps were barbarians and that his own people were the heirs of Roman greatness. It was perhaps this loyalty to the land of his birth that prompted him to write a collection of love poems to Laura in the vernacular, in the language of ordinary life rather than in Latin, that language of the Church and educated Europe.[7]

These poems were a unique form of expression that combined the traditions of southern French troubadour lyrics with classical and religious allusions. In crafting

---

6. Thomas Bergin, ed., *Selected Sonnets, Odes and Letters of Petrarch*. New York: Appleton-Century-Crofts, 1966. p. xii.
7. Victoria Kirkham and Armando Maggi, eds., *Petrarch: A Critical Guide to the Complete Works*. Chicago and London: University of Chicago Press, 2012.

them, Petrarch perfected an entirely new genre of poetry: the sonnet—a poem of fourteen lines in length that observes a rigidly set rhyme scheme. Moreover, these sonnets were written not as isolated expressions of intense emotion but arranged in a deliberate order. In so doing, Petrarch invented the sonnet sequence, a form that the poetry of romantic love would follow for half a millennium, practiced by Shakespeare, Sidney, Spenser, Milton, and an infinite number of lesser poets, continuing even until the mid-nineteenth century and Elizabeth Barrett Browning's *Sonnets from the Portuguese*.

Petrarch's *Canzoniere* (*Songbook*) as he called his collection of love poems to his Laura, attracted enormous fame and resulted in a great moment of theatre, which Petrarch almost certainly stage-managed. He tells us that he was offered the crown of poet laureate both by the University of Paris (the Sorbonne) and by Rome where the ceremony was to be held on the Capitol, presided over by King Robert of Naples and the Senate and people of Rome. Naturally he chose Rome. So, on Easter Sunday 1341 he was duly crowned by the king, enacting a ritual that had not been practiced in a thousand years.

Of course this moment was highly symbolic. In choosing Rome, Petrarch had chosen to reject the scholastic, Medieval culture of the University of Paris, dominated as it was by the faculty of theology. Instead, he favored the recovery of ancient glory symbolized by the Capitoline hill, the ritual center of the ancient city. We should note that it was not Petrarch's love poems, however, that alone attracted this honor. Rather, he had begun an epic poem in the style of Virgil's *Aeneid*, choosing for his subject the exploits of the ancient Republican hero Publius Cornelius Scipio Africanus. Ironically, no one reads this work, *Africa*, today, whereas Petrarch's secular love poetry still resonates.

Petrarch always tempered his love of pagan antiquity with a sincere Christian belief. So, after the ceremony in Rome, he led the assembled crowd to the original, Constantinian basilica of St. Peter where he laid the laurel crown on the altar. Petrarch was indeed enamored of the ancient world and did write that he had been born outside his time; but he was nevertheless a devout Christian, except when his desire for fame and love drove him to compromise his vows and his faith.[8]

The Letters of Cicero

Not long after this celebration, Petrarch experienced the second defining moment of his life: in this case, not one of personal ecstasy, but, rather, one of disillusionment.

From a young age, Petrarch had been interested in ancient texts and had become a disciple of the elegant language of the golden age of Latin authors, writers of the

---

8. Christopher Celenza, *The Intellectual World of the Italian Renaissance*. Cambridge: Cambridge University Press, 2018. pp. 42–43.

first century BC to the second century AD. As a result, it was his habit to spend long hours in scattered libraries looking for manuscripts that were unknown or known only in fragments. The imperative to engage in the search, ransacking monastic repositories and cathedral libraries, and even purchasing manuscripts for his personal collection, arose from the desire both to recover as much ancient knowledge and wisdom as possible and to uncover examples of the intricacies and elegance of mature Latin style. But Petrarch knew that the works he so admired were not the only great texts that had been written in ancient Roman times. He also knew that they had not been produced in a vacuum.[9]

In the late spring of 1345 he was searching for ancient manuscripts in the cathedral library of Verona when he came upon a monumental discovery. There before him were the previously lost letters that Cicero had written to his friend Atticus and to his brother Quintus. To this day Cicero's letters are considered to be among the most reliable and accurate records of the complex political and military events following the assassination of Julius Caesar, really a record of the end of the Roman Republic. They also reflect Cicero's involvement in these events as a leading actor, destroying forever his Medieval reputation as a reclusive and misogynistic Stoic philosopher.[10]

So, how can we explain Petrarch's dissatisfaction when he discovered those previously lost letters of Cicero? Why was Petrarch suddenly disenchanted by his hero? Petrarch tells us himself by writing a letter addressed directly to the ghost of Cicero. In this letter, Petrarch asks the great orator, philosopher, and statesmen why he hadn't abandoned the world of politics to devote himself exclusively to his Stoic writings? Politics surely did not befit such a genius—one educated in the academy Plato himself had founded in Athens half a millennium earlier. Why did Cicero let the desire for power and gain interrupt his calm old age, leading to his murder by the thugs sent by Marc Antony? Cicero's life as an active politician, married with children, and ambitious for personal power and reputation, appeared to Petrarch as unseemly and inappropriate.

Petrarch's intellectual disappointment was soon overshadowed by the immediate and inescapable tragedy of the Black Death. In 1348, Europe was devastated by this virulent pandemic. The rate of mortality varied from place to place, but overall it is generally acknowledged that up to a third of the population of the continent died from this terrible disease. No one was unaffected. Petrarch lost his two great anchors in life: his ideal love, Laura, and his patron, Cardinal Giovanni Colonna. Also taken by the plague was Petrarch's illegitimate son, Giovanni, at the age of twenty-five.

Compounding his melancholy and insecurity now that he was bereft of a benefactor, Petrarch also suffered from papal displeasure. The unsophisticated Avignonese pope,

---

9. Celenza, 2018. pp. 25–28.

10. Francesco Petrarch, "Letter to Marcus Tullius Cicero," in James Harvey Robinson, ed. and tr., *Petrarch: The First Modern Scholar and Man of Letters.* New York: G. P. Putnam, 1898. pp. 249–252.

Innocent VI, grew to see Petrarch as a dangerous man, perhaps even a sorcerer, because of his life of secular seclusion and devotion to pagan authors. To want to be alone, to read Virgil—who was often believed to have had a sorcerer's magical powers of divination—and even simply to write were seen by the pope as symptoms of a pervasive evil desire to master the skills of magic.

Consequently, Petrarch found himself unwanted in Avignon. Despite his advancing years, he agreed to assume the responsibilities of a courtier and diplomat in Milan in the service of the Visconti rulers of the city. In 1353 he took up residence as a guest of Giovanni Visconti, who was both lord (*signore*) and archbishop of the city.[11] Now Petrarch was caught up in the very work that he had chastised Cicero for undertaking in his old age.

Petrarch spent eight years in Milan in the service of despots, first Giovanni Visconti and then his nephew Galeazzo, following Giovanni's death. He was used by the Visconti for important diplomatic work, negotiating treaties and even attending the emperor. But the poet also enjoyed a great deal of comfortable leisure, which he used to write some of his most profound learned works in Latin and continue his *Canzoniere*, his vernacular "songbook," which occupied his imagination from his first sight of Laura in 1327 until the late 1360s.

Throughout his career, Petrarch had never traveled light. Rather, he had always carried with him heavy bundles of his beloved manuscripts and books. By the time he left Milan he was on the cusp of his sixties—a venerable age at the time. And he was ready to organize his legacy. He negotiated a deal with the republic of Venice to donate his precious collection of texts to the basilica of Saint Mark in exchange for a grand residence where he and his daughter, Francesca, and her recently acquired husband could reside. The conditions of the bequest were generous: Petrarch was to have the use of his personal library until his death, and afterwards it was to be maintained intact as a memorial to him.

But Petrarch did not stay long in Venice. Rather, in 1367 he chose to move to the territory of Padua where he enjoyed the sinecure of holding a canonry of the cathedral. He acquired a charming villa just outside of the city in the Euganean Hills, in the village of Arquà (now Arquà Petrarca). It was there that he spent his later years in declining health until his death in 1374.

His passing was loudly mourned by all Italy and Europe. But his library failed to find a home. Despite the fact that his daughter lived there and that he had the support of powerful friends, Petrarch was a foreigner in Venice. And he had made himself even less appealing to the Venetians when he chose to end his years in Padua, a territory which often had a tense relationship with the Venetian republic. Moreover, the appreciation of

---

11. E. H. Wilkins, *Petrarch's Eight Years in Milan*. Cambridge, MA: Medieval Academy of America, 1958.

classical learning had not yet reached the *Serenissima*. As a consequence, the Venetians failed to recognize the value of Petrarch's library. And so, in a terrible loss to posterity, the republic of Venice did not preserve his collection of several hundred manuscripts but allowed it to be dispersed, many volumes now irretrievably lost.

Petrarch in His Own Time

Petrarch's life defines the years in which the ideals of the Renaissance in Italy were developed and institutionalized in the cities of the peninsula. The way he lived it exhibited an attitude and a behavior that would later be seen as presaging the mature civilization of the Italian Renaissance. If we look first at his scholarship and writing, we see a brilliant and influential intellectual breaking away from the received traditions of the Medieval world. It was Petrarch who in so many ways served as the harbinger of Renaissance ideals, because the age in which he lived provided the fertile ground in which these principles would germinate.

Let's first look at the *Canzoniere*. These 366 poems represent a complex, introspective dissection of the emotions, feelings, and thoughts of the poet, expressed in the natural, everyday language of the vernacular and concerned with the love of a woman, Laura. But the poems are not about love or even so much just about Laura: they are focused on Petrarch in love, a statement of the validity and significance of human erotic feeling and its role in animating and engaging the divine spirit. And although she is not in any way a real, flesh-and-blood woman in these poems, Laura still emerges as far more a real woman than does Beatrice in Dante's poetry. What Petrarch is examining is his human emotions and not subjecting them altogether to the divine, angelic projection of an unattainable love.

What about his Latin writings and his letters? Here we see not a brooding and inspired lover but a scholar and publicist using words to define himself in a way closer to the experience of ancient confessional and philosophical literature than the practices of the Middle Ages. Look at what he identified as his magnum opus: an epic poem in Latin about a great Roman republican hero, Scipio Africanus. This in itself would link him to his poetic idol, Virgil, whose *Aeneid* was clearly an inspiration, but it also drives Petrarch away from the Medieval dedication to the era of the classical Roman Empire and toward the time of the Roman Republic.

Petrarch was, in fact, quite ambiguous about his political ideologies and his adherence to any singular creed in government, whether universal or communal. It can be said that he was completely inconsistent, even self-serving in his temporal commitments. But this is probably too harsh a judgment. He was transitional. He was struggling against his Ghibelline, pro-imperial nurturing which had been part of his father's hope of being restored to his native Florence. Furthermore, Petrarch was not a man of action but of words—and words change their focus, even meaning, when the context shifts. Like his father, and like most of us for that matter, Petrarch saw the contours of his life and allegiances change over his long life, and consequently his perspective varied.

Words nevertheless remained important, just as they were to the ancient authors he so admired. Some of his profound belief in the power of language emerged from the writings of Cicero himself or from those parts of Quintilian's (ca. 35–ca. 100 AD) *Education of the Citizen Orator* (*Institutio Oratoria*) known to him. In this work on the training of rhetoricians, Quintilian anticipates Petrarch's belief in the need for the public speaker or writer to be a good person so that his words would reflect this essential virtue. The importance of words—good words—was central to Petrarch's image of himself and his hopes for an improved world.[12]

This raises the question of Petrarch's disappointment when he discovered the previously lost letters of Cicero. Up to that point, Petrarch had thought he knew and understood Cicero well, but his understanding was based on such treatises as *De Senectute* (*On Old Age*) or *De Officiis* (*On Responsibilities*) or even *The Dream of Scipio*, that part of *De Republica* that was known to him. The Cicero whom he had understood from these works was more like the man Petrarch had hoped to be than the flesh and blood Cicero who surfaced in the letters to Atticus. Petrarch himself was not deeply engaged in civic life: like the Cicero he thought he knew, he defined himself as a scholar, a thinker, a writer—not a man of action. After all, he had not held any permanent position in any commune or court; and his role in the Church consisted almost altogether of collecting income from benefices he held as an absentee incumbent. He had even had an opportunity to return to Florence and reclaim his father's property but had refused.

On the other hand, there were inconsistencies and ambiguities. He rejected civic action, but he did spend eight years in Milan in service to the Visconti. Although he wrote in his *Liber Sine Nomine* (*Book Without a Name*)[13] how he detested the morality of the papal court, he was, nevertheless, a cleric of the Church and a servant of the pope in Avignon. He may have been a powerful critic of the Avignonese papacy, but at the same time he accepted benefices from the papacy. In other words, he, like the Cicero he discovered in 1345 through the *Letters to Atticus*, had to function in a context, in the real world, a world he often found imperfect and not worthy of the example of the ancients.[14]

This in no way detracts from his importance. Indeed, it served as an engine for his most important quest: his desire for self-knowledge, a desire acknowledged in a remarkable letter he wrote, the *Letter to Posterity*. This search was driven by his reading of

---

12. See Hans Baron, "Cicero and the Roman Civic Spirit in the Middle Ages and Early Renaissance," *The Bulletin of the John Rylands Library*, 22 (1938), pp. 72–97.

13. Francesco Petrarch, *Petrarch's Book Without a Name (Liber Sine Nomine)*, tr. N. P. Zacour. Toronto: Pontifical Institute of Medieval Studies, 1973.

14. Roberto Weiss, *The Renaissance Discovery of Classical Antiquity*. New York: Humanities Press, 1973.

classical texts, as he sought a world where he could feel content. He noted that his own era "repelled him . . . [He] would have preferred to have been born in any period other than [his] own."[15]

The Problem of Paganism

The language of the ancients appealed to Petrarch. But what about their religion, their beliefs, and their paganism? For all of their virtue and elegance of speech and profundity of thought they were not Christians but pagans! How could a devout fourteenth-century Christian cleric advocate models from a world before Christ? It was his response to this grave and pervasive problem of the disjunction between the Christian and pagan worlds where Petrarch made one of his most profound contributions to modern culture and permitted Christians to deal with the ancient world on its own terms.

Petrarch concluded that the paganism of his ancient Roman heroes was not a great danger to his soul because it was obvious from their writings and the example of how they had conducted their lives that they were good men with useful advice on how to lead an ethical life in this world. Of course they could not assist in his search for salvation; but they could, nevertheless, offer guidance through their moral philosophy—that is, through their advice on ethical behavior.

This uncoupling of the language and moral content of the pagan ancients from the desire for Christian salvation was one of Petrarch's greatest gifts to Western culture and the Italian Renaissance. Previous Christian writers had feared pagan authors: this was true in particular of St. Jerome (ca. 347–420), who was one of the most influential writers of ancient Christianity and the translator of the Bible into Latin. Jerome wrote of a distressing vision in which Christ accused him of being a Ciceronian rather than a Christian. Christ's warning was that the extreme beauty and profound human insight found in classical literature could make us love our life on earth too much and not focus sufficiently on the judgment coming in the next. Jerome's vision sounded confessional alarms in the European psychology for a millennium. Even Petrarch discusses this episode in his *On His Own Ignorance and that of Many Others*.[16]

Petrarch to a great degree solved this problem of the value and efficacy of ancient pagan poetry and prose by arguing that the language alone reflects the inner goodness of those authors. It was simply by an accident of chronology that they had not had the advantage of Christian revelation. To him, these were "justified pagans" who enjoyed a kind of foreknowledge of the Christian dispensation. Because the Christian message itself implied a connection between the words of wise men and their ability to nourish the soul as well as the mind, their work was worthy of study and indeed imitation. The

---

15. Bergin, ed., *Petrarch,* "Letter to Posterity," p. 3.
16. Petrarch, "On His Own Ignorance and that of Many Others," in Cassirer et al., 1948. pp. 47–133.

opening of the Gospel of John in St. Jerome's translation had said that, "In the beginning was the word and the word was with God" (*in principio erat verbum et verbum erat apud Deum*). The prophets of the Old Testament and the pagan sibyls were accorded revelatory knowledge which presaged the coming of Christ; and Petrarch's beloved Virgil in his fourth eclogue foretold the Christian dispensation. So who could deny the value of pagan literature when the signs were so clear?

Petrarch extended this into his adulation of St. Augustine. Like Jerome, Augustine was a doctor of the Church—that is to say, one of the early Christian saints whom theologians regarded as especially authoritative and imbued with the Holy Spirit. Yet Augustine's classical rhetorical education had resulted in beautiful, elegant, and clear Latin prose, and he was deeply influenced by ideas of Neoplatonism and other currents of ancient thought. Moreover, Augustine credited the idea that Virgil in his fourth eclogue had prophesied the coming of Christ, just as did the Erythraean Sibyl. In other words, Petrarch followed the model of his Christian hero, St. Augustine, in bridging the chasm that Christianity had opened between itself and pagan culture. Rather than a chasm, he suggested that there was a continuum: the wisdom and morality of the ancients were to be found in their language, which led to virtue and consequently made them worthy of study.

This revolutionary position emerges most clearly and effectively in Petrarch's late work *On His Own Ignorance and that of Many Others*. This lengthy reply to those of his critics who accused him of showing too much respect for pagan authors and not enough for the Christian scholastics and theologians reads like a vindication of much of Petrarch's intellectual life and a program for the modern world. He not only praises Cicero—and others such as Seneca—for their language, eloquence, and wisdom, but also laments that they did not have the opportunity to know Christ. The implication is that, at least in Cicero's case, conversion would certainly have followed. To Petrarch's mind, it is as a good man with great talents put to the service of his community that Cicero deserves recognition. This in no way compromised Petrarch's sincere Christianity. Quite the opposite. He suggests that it is those who are willfully ignorant of potential moral guidance, regardless of its source, that merit pity, if not opprobrium.[17]

Words to Petrarch were the instruments to externalize the interior self, one's deepest thoughts and beliefs. Consequently, he believed and argued that words must be effective. How can this detract from revealed religion when it reinforces our essential humanity and our unique role in God's plan? Humans are the only creatures with the gift of speech, he argued, and speech reflects the equally unique faculty of reason—that is, the capacity to understand. Humans are also the recipient of God's ultimate gift—that is

---

17. See Charles Trinkaus, *In Our Image Likeness: Humanity and Divinity Italian Humanist Thought.* Chicago: University of Chicago Press, 1970. I, pp. 3–50.

to say, the immortal soul. Thus, to Petrarch, there is an indissoluble connection between speech, reason, and the individual soul.[18]

Cicero, in terms of human gifts, enjoyed great eloquence and wisdom and hence a cultivated soul. Petrarch did acknowledge that Cicero's soul could not be redeemed outside the Christian dispensation. He recognized that Cicero, Seneca, Plato, and the ancients he idolized would always be imperfect because they lacked that central promise of salvation. That said, he believed that their human gifts and the quality of their rational souls are of huge advantage in the things of this world, the moral and ethical decisions all men must make constantly. Here on earth they are reliable and indeed perfect guides. Following the model of his Christian hero, Augustine, Petrarch reminds us of the differences between the City of God and the City of Man: pagan authors can serve as a guide to the latter, whereas only those enlightened by Christian faith can provide an entry into the former.[19]

This division between the human and divine sphere and Petrarch's obsession with self-knowledge and even self-justification reaches its fulfillment in his *Secretum*, or his *Secret Book* (1347–53). Like the *Letter to Posterity* and *On His Own Ignorance and that of Many Others*, the *Secretum* resulted from a desire by Petrarch to insert himself into the company of great men of the past and explain why he is what he is and why he does what he does. It takes the form of three dialogues between two characters—Francesco and St. Augustine—in the presence of Truth. In effect, the *Secretum* is an exploration of Petrarch, the imperfect man, undertaken through debate with his better, Christian self, represented by St. Augustine.[20]

The Invention of the Autonomous Individual

In the *Secretum*, Petrarch admits to his human failings, such as his irrational love for Laura and his dangerous desire for fame, which he knows derives from pride, the deadliest of the sins. For us looking for the beginnings of the Renaissance, this book is central. In the first instance, Petrarch is reviving a genre of psychological autobiography hardly practiced for a thousand years. More important, he uses it to explore his essence, to determine who he believes he is and the motives for his actions and thoughts.

This element of self-investigation through words constitutes a kind of early Renaissance logotherapy through which Petrarch is both studying and defining his unique

---

18. Gur Zak, *Petrarch's Humanism and the Care of the Self*. Cambridge: Cambridge University Press, 2010.
19. Celenza, 2018. p. 27.
20. Carol Quillen, *The Secret by Francesco Petrarch*. Boston: Bedford/St. Martin's, 2003; W. H. Draper, *Petrarch's Secret, or the Soul's Conflict with Passion* (*Three Dialogues Between Himself and St. Augustine*). CreateSpace Independent Publishing Platform, 2015. Reprint of 1911 edition; H. Baron, *Petrarch's Secretum: Its Making and Its Meaning*. Cambridge, MA: Medieval Academy of America, 1985.

persona, his essential character of which he is very much aware. He does it by the act of writing, the recording of words. He is an active agent in this exercise, making himself emerge from his words as someone who has a great deal of control over his own self, actions, and life. He is hardly a passive vessel filled by other's expectations; and he is certainly not merely an actor in a great drama written by God as in the Medieval model. No. He is Francesco and he has free will, despite his bondage by love and fame. His desire for self-knowledge can elucidate the contours of his life on earth, how others see him, and how posterity will remember him.

In other words, Petrarch is admitting that he is creating himself, his own persona and his own legacy. He is a consciously self-created individual in a world in which human action is the consequence of human agency, informed by good thoughts and knowledge, clarified through good words, which will direct him to what is truly morally good, just, and right. But he equally confesses to being challenged by those very human failings of fleshly passion (both youthful lust and his love for Laura) and his vanity, that sin of pride, which he knows to be the greatest threat to his Christian soul.

Petrarch is the harbinger of a revolution, one in which human action and thought on earth is fully validated, at least in terms of the terrestrial world, the result of reason guided by the words and virtue of others. In some ways Petrarch has created the modern conception of the self-actualized individual, a man who has made himself who he is on earth, fashioning both his conception of himself for himself and, perhaps even more significantly, for others.

Petrarch of course did more to cement his consciously fashioned self in the eyes of posterity than write letters to the past and future or examine his character in a psychological dialogue. He ensured that there would be something like a coherent record of his life through his correspondence. It is probable that Petrarch was thinking of his own discovery of Cicero's *Letters to Atticus* in 1345, the book that caused him so much discomfort, when he decided to edit his own letters into volumes.[21] They fall into two main collections, his *Litterae Familiares*, that is the letters he wrote to friends, and his *Seniles*, letters from later in his life, his old age.

Although the full collection contains almost five hundred entries, it is obvious that Petrarch engaged in a good deal of editing to ensure that there appeared more coherence in his thought, more consistent eloquence in his language, and more continuity in his beliefs. These letters do form much of what we know of the poet, including the most famous examples, those that are really literary constructions, such as his *Letter to Posterity* and his *Ascent of Mount Ventoux*. Petrarch was hardly the first public figure to attempt to control his legacy; but he was the first one to do so since antiquity who was not a prince or a prelate.

---

21. David Thompson, ed., *Petrarch: A Humanist Among Princes.* New York: Harper & Row, 1971. pp. 60 and n. 1.

Humanism

What the life and work of Petrarch was defining was a new way of interpreting the human condition. It was a vision based on knowledge of ancient literature, a belief in individual human agency on earth, and acceptance of the validity of individual human experience. This belief system and cultural model developed into what became known as human-ism.[22] The term itself was derived in the early Renaissance from student slang: professors of the *studia humanitatis*, the liberal arts, were known as *humanisti*; and, the disciplines that constituted humane letters (*litterae humaniores*) were poetry, rhetoric, history, and ethics, the tools needed for the understanding of the human condition. Petrarch was not only one of humanism's earliest practitioners but also one of its primary prophets. In this system, each person had the capacity to create or re-create him- or herself based upon a set of principles acknowledged as virtuous.[23]

This belief in the efficacy of ancient knowledge and wisdom, the power of clear speech and writing to investigate human experience, and a secular acceptance of the ability of individuals to fulfill their potential would find a home in Petrarch's ancestral city of Florence. It developed into not only a guide for life but also a kind of elite ideology based on Latin and Greek literature, rhetoric, the celebration of the individual personality, and the principle of self-determination. Christian salvation still mattered of course: God was still omnipotent. But the condition of man on earth was something that could be eluci-dated and, indeed, guided by pagan knowledge.[24]

---

22. Ronald Witt, *In the Footsteps of the Ancients: The Origins of Humanism from Lovato to Bruni.* Leiden: Brill Academic Publishing, 2000.
23. Robert Black, *Humanism and Education in Renaissance Italy: Tradition and Innovation in Latin Schools from the Twelfth to the Fifteenth Century.* Cambridge: Cambridge University Press, 2001.
24. Albert Rabil Jr., ed., *Renaissance Humanism, Volume 1: Foundations, Forms, and Legacy.* Phila-delphia: University of Pennsylvania Press, 1988; Charles G. Nauert Jr., *Humanism and the Culture of Renaissance Europe.* Cambridge: Cambridge University Press, 2006.

**Illus. 1.1 Contemporary Portrait of Petrarch by Altichiero
in the Basilica of St. Anthony in Padua.**

This portrait by Altichiero for the Chapel of St. James in the Basilica of St. Anthony (*Santo*) in Padua was likely conceived during Petrarch's life, about 1372. It is extremely likely that Altichiero (Altichiero da Verona, also known as Aldighieri da Zevio, ca. 1330–90) knew Petrarch personally from the court of Francesco I da Carrara (1325–93), lord of Padua, who was the poet's friend and patron; indeed, it was Francesco who gave Petrarch his villa at Arquà.

This fresco is consequently among the most reliable portraits of the poet. Among others, it illustrates the fame that Petrarch had achieved and how rulers such as Francesco saw the poet as an ornament to his city. Padua was in fact a center of early humanist scholarship, where the writing of classical Latin, the growing cult of the individual, and the central of role of antiquity played a significant role, especially as the city was believed to have been founded by the legendary counsellor to King Priam, Antenor, fleeing like Aeneas from Troy. This legend, then, provides a parallel foundation myth to Aeneas as the founder of Rome and hence merits an equal place in the humanist cultural geography.

Illus. 1.2 Francesco Petrarca's Tomb at Arquà Petrarca. Veneto, Italy.

Petrarch died early on July 19, 1374. Four years before, he had taken up permanent residence at Arquà (now Arquà Petrarca) in the Euganean Hills outside of Padua, in a little villa which had been granted to him by Francesco da Carrara, the lord of Padua. He had been joined by his illegitimate daughter, Francesca, and her family, with whom he had previously lived in Venice. Initially he was buried in the parish church of Arquà but six years later, in 1380, this elegant tomb, constructed of pink marble from Verona, was erected outside the church, paid for by the poet's son-in-law Francescuolo da Brossano. The construction is interesting because it reflects the design of the so-called tomb of Antenor, the legendary Trojan who founded the city. Even in death Petrarch was to be surrounded by classical literature and antiquity.

The subsequent history of the grave becomes tangled in our own times. In 2004 the tomb was opened so that forensic pathologists might make a model of the poet's face from his skull. The skull, however, was in fragments and when analyzed it was discovered not be the poet's but the skull of a woman who had died about a century before Petrarch. The general belief is that the professor of anatomy from the University of Padua who had opened the tomb in the late nineteenth century took the skull as a tribute to the poet and replaced it with another. Despite a universal call throughout Italy to return the original skull, no one has come forward.

Illus. 1.3 Andrea di Bonaiuto (1346–79), *Allegory of the Active and Triumphant Church and of the Dominican Order,* **1365. Fresco, Spanish Chapel, Basilica of Santa Maria Novella, Florence.**

This fresco celebrates the victory of the earthly church—the Church Militant—through a variety of instruments. These include an acceptance of hierarchy, the conversion of heretics; the practice of preaching, disputation, pilgrimage, and faith; as well as the cultivation of learning and art. Fulfilment of the obligations of the faith in life was said to lead to the Church Triumphant in paradise.

The influence of Petrarch and his ideas in Florence is evidenced by his portrait on the right in the upper register of the fresco. He is in the company of contemporary painters, such as Cimabue, Taddeo Gaddi, Giotto, and Simone Martini, as well as his muse, Laura, and his friend, Giovanni Boccaccio, whose Neapolitan muse, Fiammetta, also appears.

In the lower register, the man in white with the hood is most likely a pilgrim and certainly an English knight, as he wears the Order of the Garter on his left leg. The dogs are common symbols of the Dominican Order, a clever pun on their name: *Domini Canes,* or hounds of the Lord.

The church that serves as the backdrop for this iconographic scene is traditionally identified as the cathedral of Florence, Santa Maria del Fiore, although the identification is hardly precise and is rather more fanciful than exact. That said, Arnolfo di Cambio, the architect of the cathedral (as well as the Palazzo della Signoria) is portrayed in the fresco; and Andrea di Bonaiuto was one of the artists engaged in planning for the duomo. Consequently, the image probably represents early designs for the church, including the plan for a dome almost seventy years before Brunelleschi raised the famous symbol of the city over the crossing of the transept and nave of the cathedral.

The site of the fresco, the Spanish Chapel, only received its current name during the period of the Medici Grand Duchy in the sixteenth century. Duke Cosimo I assigned its use to his Spanish Neapolitan wife, Eleanora di Toledo, and her largely Spanish household. It was originally built as the burial chapel of the patrician Guidalotti family but soon after became the Chapter House for the Dominican Monastery.

CHAPTER 2
LEONARDO BRUNI AND CIVIC HUMANISM

Petrarch had never put down deep roots anywhere. He was always a wandering scholar with no fixed moorings, especially after the deaths of Laura and Giovanni Colonna. The ideas about the role of classical antiquity, the power of language, and the central role of the autonomous individual were developed for his own comfort and self-knowledge. It was only when these principles were introduced into the fertile soil of the Florentine republic that his ideas bore fruit, applied not to individuals alone but to the collective of the community.

Petrarch himself never returned to Florence, but his disciples, Giovanni Boccaccio and, later, Coluccio Salutati, domesticated Petrarch's thinking in Florence and served as the vanguard for Leonardo Bruni. Bruni, the man who ultimately connected Petrarch's ideals to the dynamic principles of Florentine republican liberty, served as chancellor of Florence between 1427 and 1444. It was he who institutionalized a perspective that was to characterize Renaissance Florence and provide the engine for its dynamic sense of self-confidence and creativity. The example of his life and the power of his writing made him the voice of a second wave of humanism—civic humanism—and help to explain the remarkable explosion of genius in fifteenth-century Florence. But we must begin, first, with Boccaccio.[1]

Giovanni Boccaccio

The intellectual and cultural movement that Petrarch began was continued by those who saw that his ideas and work applied not just to him but also to others who shared his rejection of the style and theocentric worldview of the Middle Ages. In particular, Petrarch's contemporary, friend, and fellow Florentine, Giovanni Boccaccio (d. 1375), also born to exiles outside the city, adopted many of his attitudes, especially Petrarch's commitment to ancient literature and human agency.[2]

Like Petrarch, Boccaccio was a major literary figure, the author of a book that is popular to this day—the *Decameron*—a collection of one hundred tales told over ten days by a group of young Florentine men and women fleeing the Black Death of 1348–49. Unlike Petrarch, however, Boccaccio accepted an offer to return to Florence to teach at the university, something Petrarch refused to do. As a result, it was through Boccaccio's

---

1. James Hankins, ed., *Renaissance Civic Humanism: Reappraisals and Reflections*. Cambridge: Cambridge University Press, 2000.
2. Victoria Kirkham, Michael Sherberg, and Janet Levarie Smarr, eds., *Boccaccio: A Critical Guide to the Complete Works*. Chicago: University of Chicago Press, 2013.

example, lectures, and writing that so many of the principles Petrarch was developing ultimately entered the city.[3]

It was a perfect moment for these ideas to germinate in the fertile minds of the Florentine patrician elite. The city was rich, having established a continent-wide market for high-quality woolen cloth, and the resulting profits from this trade permitted the wealthy merchant class to engage in banking. So it was that Florence became the economic engine of the thirteenth and fourteenth centuries, with its golden florin (first minted in 1252) the standard currency for international trade. It was also the leading Guelf city in north-central Italy, meaning that lucrative papal contracts and banking arrangements added to the city's wealth and influence.[4] Finally, through a bourgeois coup d'état in 1293 (known as the Ordinances of Justice) Florence had emerged as a guild republic. It was ruled by its mercantile elite who governed the city to fulfill their economic ambitions and to ensure that the state would not fall under the control of a tyrant.[5]

The terrible events of war, plague, and economic dislocation experienced in the calamitous mid-fourteenth century in Europe had an equally devastating effect on Florence. In particular, there was the failure of the great Florentine banks of the Bardi and Peruzzi families in the 1340s. The cause of this failure was enough to alarm any international banker. Rather than honor his enormous debts to the Bardi and Peruzzi, Edward III of England had chosen to renege on his huge loans from their firms. He then compounded the injury by confiscating their substantial properties in England and exiling them from his kingdom.

But Florence rebounded and in addressing the problems of financial instability and plague, the city became even stronger. The financial disaster galvanized the merchants in control of the city to institute a novel form of public finance, the *Monte*. In 1343 all the accumulated public debt was combined into a single account against which shares were issued, with a guaranteed rate of return. This brilliant invention was one of the first broadly based experiments in public state financing. It had the effect not only of servicing the public debt but also of drawing those with any amount of surplus capital into the workings of the affairs of the republic. Power was already very widely distributed in the republican constitution. But introducing a mechanism that offered investors influence on all political decisions made the city a dynamic laboratory for social, political, and economic experimentation.[6]

The traditions of the Middle Ages had long proscribed social mobility—the rapid movement from one social class into another. Equally vilified was usury—the taking of

3. Celenza, 2018. pp. 32–43.

4. Richard A. Goldthwaite, *The Economy of Renaissance Florence*. Baltimore: Johns Hopkins University Press, 2011.

5. Gaetano Salvemini, *Magnati e popolani in Firenze dal 1280 al 1295*. Florence: Carnesecchi e figli, 1899. pp. 385–95.

6. Carlo M. Cipolla, *The Monetary Policy of Fourteenth Century Florence* (Publications of the UCLA Center for Medieval and Renaissance Studies, 17). Berkeley and Los Angeles: UCLA Press, 1982.

interest on loans, no matter how minimal. But these proscriptions were unattractive to republican Florentines as they did not reflect the reality of their lives. In a republic run by merchants, social mobility was now possible. And those newly enriched and empowered guildsmen needed a justification for their new and often spectacular wealth.[7]

There had to be a means of validating the rewards of a secular life spent in commerce and public service for these nouveaux riches. They were wealthy and enjoyed power, but they were not nobles typically privileged through an ancient name alone. They followed a secular path in their educations and professions. They married and established families. In short, they also challenged the Medieval view of the superiority of the contemplative, celibate life of a monk, devoted to prayer and poverty. The attraction of the example set by St. Francis of Assisi was always still there for certain devoted Christians. But a different ideology was needed to get this new mercantile elite through their dark nights of the soul.

In searching for a new ideal to meet their requirements, the mercantile elite identified Petrarch's ideas as attractive and useful. Petrarch's discovery of Cicero's *Letters to Atticus* might have given the poet some misgivings, but to the patricians of Florence, this new, politically engaged Cicero was the model they had been searching for. Cicero was a republican like them. He had risen from the equestrian to the senatorial order in Rome—an example of social mobility. And, he had grown wealthy. True, he had trained in the academy founded by Plato in Athens and continued to write philosophical works. But he was also a lawyer for whom effective language was a wonderful and elegant tool. He married and sired children and served the state. Indeed, he met his death because of his continuing opposition to Marc Antony after the assassination of Julius Caesar: he had principles and scruples. In short, the Cicero to whom Petrarch wrote his letter in despair over these very characteristics was the Cicero who met the needs of the Florentine elite at a critical moment, and he had been rediscovered and made available by Petrarch.[8]

The message for Florentine merchants was that a secular education and a secular life, then, did not necessarily make one's ascent to heaven more difficult. Rather, it offered different paths, and these paths could also be followed with integrity, virtue, and pride. Furthermore, in choosing a secular life, a man would be able to serve not only his own soul but also the well-being—especially the earthly well-being—of his fellow citizens. Petrarch had written that words are indices of the soul and that we can help the souls of others through words as well as deeds. Florentines realized that they could make the world a better place for the city as a whole in similar ways.[9]

---

7. This was equally illustrated in bricks and mortar as the city grew with new private and public buildings adding to the reputation of the city. See Richard A. Goldthwaite, *The Building of Renaissance Florence: An Economic and Social History*. Baltimore: Johns Hopkins University Press, 1980. pp. 29–113.

8. Celenza, 2018. pp. 44–63.

9. Gene A. Brucker, *The Civic World of Early Renaissance Florence*. Princeton: Princeton University Press, 2016.

Coluccio Salutati

Petrarch died in 1374; his friend Boccaccio in 1375. But at that critical moment the ideas that Petrarch had been developing fused with the dynamic mercantile republic of Florence in the person of his disciple, Coluccio Salutati (d. 1406). In 1375 Salutati was appointed to the highest nonelective position in Florence, that of chancellor of the republic, with responsibility for all the public correspondence and administrative structures of government. There is no real modern equivalent to this position, though it might help to think of Salutati as head of the civil service.[10]

Salutati had engaged in a correspondence with Petrarch and had followed him in his classical studies and acquisition of manuscripts. In fact, he had amassed his own significant private library of ancient authors. He sought to perfect his Latinity so that it reflected the elegance of the age of Cicero. He also started to learn Greek, in part simply to augment his classical education but also because Cicero himself knew the language and its rich literature. Ultimately Salutati failed to master Greek, but he did ensure that others would have this opportunity by arranging the employment at the Florentine university of a professor of Greek, the celebrated Byzantine scholar Manuel Chrysoloras (d. 1415).

Salutati was also a professional bureaucrat, trained as a notary and experienced in administration. It was his well-paid appointments in the commune that allowed him to lead a secular life and support a family (in fact, he married twice) while still enjoying the fruits of his scholarship. And he articulated his principles through his work.

This was no more apparent than when Florence was threatened by Giangaleazzo Visconti, the duke of Milan (1351–1402). Visconti was an ambitious ruler, having come to power by treacherously overthrowing his own uncle and then proceeding to conquer one by one neighboring city-states in the Po Valley. But he had even bigger dreams, as he was intent on uniting all of northern Italy under his rule, with particular aspirations for Florence and Bologna.

The Florentines were hard pressed at the time. But, Salutati realized that defense could come from words as well as arms. He became the spokesman for the ideal of republican liberty, defining Florence as a fortress against the tyrannical ambitions of enemies such as Visconti. He rallied Florentines against Milan so powerfully that the duke once remarked that a letter of Salutati's was worth a hundred soldiers in the field. The threat to Florence was very real, and although there were great losses on both sides, Visconti was widely assumed to be winning. But fate intervened when the duke was felled by a fever late in 1402. Squabbling erupted among his heirs. The quest for northern domination collapsed, and Florence was saved from tyranny.

---

10. Ronald G. Witt, *Hercules at the Crossroads: The Life, Works, and Thought of Coluccio Salutati.* Durham: Duke University Press, 1983.

Despite his commitment to classical learning, polished Latin, and the value of humanistic studies, Salutati, like Petrarch, retained many of the old values reflective of the Middle Ages.[11] He was a devout Christian, one who continued to see the monastic, contemplative life as superior—at least for those who could sustain it.[12] And he believed, as had Aristotle, Dante, and Petrarch's father, that monarchy was the ideal form of government if practiced correctly. He was, then, a transitional figure who managed to transmit so many of the ideals and practices of Petrarch into the heart of the Florentine *polis* but did so in a way that was not revolutionary but transformative.[13]

It could be said that Salutati's greatest contribution was simply the example of his own life, work, and voice, but he also extended his patronage to other young men who wished to be scholars familiar with ancient texts and furnished with a powerful Latin style while remaining in the world, marrying, and earning a living. Florence was exploding with new wealth and opportunities, and Salutati was able to expand the appointments in the chancellor's office by hiring young men who could live their ideals. Consequently, around the chancellor there grew a coterie of classically educated young men, intent on public service and eager for recognition and advancement. These men read like a *Who's Who* of early-fifteenth-century humanistic studies including figures like Niccolò de' Niccoli (d. 1437), a wealthy heir to a mercantile Florentine family who chose to neglect political activity in favor of book collecting and scholarship and Poggio Bracciolini (d. 1459) who eventually succeeded Salutati as chancellor after a distinguished career at the papal court.

Leonardo Bruni

Of all of those in Salutati's circle of young, classically trained, and carefully tutored youth, none had as much talent and would come to embody the second stage of Renaissance humanism more than Leonardo Bruni. Bruni was not even a Florentine by birth but came from Arezzo—where Petrarch had been born—a town in Tuscany that came under Florentine dominion in 1385, when Bruni was fifteen. His father was a successful grain merchant who, like Dante and Petrarch's father, was arrested during the internecine Guelf–Ghibelline struggles that characterized Tuscany for so many years.

After a thorough education in Latin, Bruni moved to Florence to attend university, some time soon after 1390. His studies began with the traditional curriculum in the liberal arts followed by four years of studying law. But it was his admission into the coterie

---

11. Trinkaus, 1970. I, pp. 51–102.
12. Coluccio Salutati, *On the World and Religious Life*, tr. Tina Marshall, intro. Ronald G. Witt. Cambridge MA: Harvard University Press. The I Tatti Renaissance Library, 62, 2014. For the influence of the Church Fathers and Christianity in general on early humanist thought, see Trinkaus, 1970.
13. Stefano U. Baldassarri, ed., *Coluccio Salutati: Political Writings*, tr. Rolf Bagemihl. Cambridge, MA: Harvard University Press, The I Tatti Renaissance Library 64, 2014. This translation contains the text of *On Tyranny* (*De Tyranno*), as well as several important letters.

of gifted young scholars around Salutati that set Bruni apart and moved him away from the practice of law to the study of classical languages and literature for their own sake. By 1398 he had begun studying Greek with Chrysoloras and proved to be a brilliant linguist. After only two years of close study, Bruni began his celebrated career as a translator, making the surviving corpus of Greek literature available to the Latin West.[14]

His first translations indicate his growing commitment to the ideals of the ancient world. They also helped nurture what ultimately became his lifelong belief in the special role of Florence as a beacon of republican liberty in a dangerous world of tyrants. He produced a version of Xenophon's *On Tyranny* as well as a translation of a work of St. Basil the Great (d. 379), a patristic Greek theologian and doctor of the Church who had famously encouraged young men to study the pagan Greek authors as a prelude to their Christian learning.[15]

Bruni's translation of St. Basil's work directly challenged the growing hostility of some traditional churchmen, especially Dominicans, to the rising interest in the study of antiquity. They feared its seductive qualities and pagan content. Bruni was a traditional Christian, but he also saw how the movement begun by Petrarch and sustained by Boccaccio and Salutati enriched the minds and culture of educated Italians. Petrarch had shown those pagans to have often been good and virtuous men, so Bruni used the words of St. Basil, one of the most influential Greek doctors of the Church, to rebuke obscurantist polemics, much as Petrarch had done in *On His Own Ignorance and that of Many Others.*

It was also at the very beginning of the fifteenth century that Bruni began to compose original works that would reflect his attachment to Florence and to the person and circle of Coluccio Salutati. His *Dialogues to Pietro Paolo Vergerio of Istria* were written at two different times: the first book about 1401, the second about 1405. These were discussions ostensibly held in the circle of Salutati in which the scholars compared the virtues of vernacular and ancient authors—of those who wrote in modern Italian versus those who had been writing in ancient Latin.[16]

Hans Baron, in a fundamental book of Renaissance scholarship, *The Crisis of the Early Italian Renaissance* (1966),[17] has argued that the perspective of Bruni and the expectations of his audience changed between the composition of the first and second

14. David Thompson, Gordon Griffiths, and James Hankins eds. and tr. *Humanism of Leonardo Bruni: Selected Texts.* New York: Renaissance Society of America, 1987.

15. St. Basil's letter to young men (*Ad Adolescentes*) was translated by Bruni between 1400 and 1403. See James Hankins, "The Dates of Leonardo Bruni's Later Works (1437–1443)," in *Studi medievali e umanistici,* 6 (2007). p. 6.

16. Stefano Baldassari, ed. *Dialogi ad Petrum Paulum Histrum.* Florence: Olschki, 1994. Studi e Testi: Istituto Nazionale di Studi sul Rinascimento. For a discussion of the *Dialoghi,* see Celenza, 2018. pp. 97–103.

17. Hans Baron, *The Crisis of the Early Italian Renaissance,* rev. ed. Princeton: Princeton University Press, 1966.

books. Baron detected a change from a more traditional perspective, such as that exemplified by Salutati, to a new, more active and civically engaged attitude toward the community. He cited in particular the fact that Florence was singled out for special praise because of the freedom of its citizens, which could enable them to confront and vanquish any attempt to impose a tyranny.

In part this shift in perspective, if there is one, can be attributed to contemporary events arising from the territorial ambitions of Giangaleazzo Visconti, the duke of Milan, who was so admiring of the power of Salutati's pen. Baron called this new perspective of active political engagement and the service of the scholar to the community "civic humanism," thereby expressing a complex of ideas in one efficient term. First, it encompasses this new way of seeing the relationship between the citizen and the community. Then there is the role of engaged publicists in defining civic freedom and encouraging its defense. And, finally, the term implies a regard for the virtue of the ancients in suggesting that the republic of Florence was the new Athens or the new Rome.

The civic humanism of Leonardo Bruni was powerfully reinforced by his writing of the *Laudatio Urbis Florentinae* (*Praise of the City of Florence*) some time between 1401 and 1403. This oration reflects both Bruni's skill at Greek studies and the Renaissance respect for modeling new work on ancient texts. In fact, this extended oration is a close translation of Aelius Aristides's (d. 181 AD) *Panathenaicus* (*Praise of the City of Athens*). Today we would call it outright plagiarism. But there is method in this translation: Bruni is making a direct comparison of Athens—the ancient center of democracy, freedom, and culture—with Florence. And he is simultaneously offering a formal panegyric to celebrate the victory of Florence over Milan in 1402.[18]

The ambitions of the duke of Milan to unite much of north-central Italy under his rule had come very close to success. Only Florence had refused to yield and expected a brutal attack, fighting against overwhelming odds. Florence was saved, perhaps only by Visconti's death. Publicists like Bruni did not attribute this salvation to divine intervention, as earlier historians would have done. Instead they argued that the city's commitment to republican freedom had been such that Florence could never have been conquered. The text of the *Laudatio*, like most panegyrics, is full of absurdities, such as the statement that Florence had never fought a war of aggression and only intervened when freedom was at stake. This is not just rhetoric: it is propaganda, designed to focus the mind of the listener or reader on the essential quality of Florence, which was its leadership in Italy of all those who valued freedom.

The *Laudatio* and the *Dialogues* did not succeed in getting Bruni a position in Florence, however. Rather, as a result of a recommendation from Poggio Bracciolini, his friend from the circle of Salutati, Bruni entered the papal curia in Rome in 1405 as a secretary.

---

18. Leonardo Bruni, "Panegyric to the City of Florence," tr. Benjamin G. Kohl, in Benjamin G. Kohl and Ronald G. Witt, eds., *The Earthly Republic: Italian Humanists on Government and Society*. Philadelphia: University of Pennsylvania Press, 1978.

This was a dramatic time for the Roman pontiff, as it corresponded to the last decade of the Great Schism when two popes, one in Avignon and one in Rome—and later a third elected in 1409 in Pisa—all claimed to be the legitimate successor to St. Peter. It was a time when Bruni's rhetorical skill and his ability to take historical example and precedent and use them as powerful tools in advancing the cause of his employer had great effect, arguing the papal position against not only the other claimants to St. Peter's authority but also their supporters, such as the king of Naples.

When the anti-pope John XXIII, the last of the four popes he served, was deposed in 1414 as part of the movement to resolve the Schism, Bruni left the curia and returned to Florence. He apparently was either too tainted by his work for a disreputable anti-pope or lacked the deep interest to become involved in the Council of Constance that would eventually reunite the Church under a single pope, Martin V, in 1417. Martin had offered Bruni a senior position, if he returned to the papal curia, but Bruni declined. He had decided to become a Florentine and live in the city whose Renaissance character he would help shape profoundly.

Bruni was now leading a rich civic life in Florence. He had married a woman from a Florentine patrician family much younger than he and had sired a son. He had brought a considerable fortune to Florence, as the anti-pope had been kind to him. And Florence, recognizing his value, granted him both citizenship and exemption from taxation—a perk that would help him keep his fortune intact as well as keep him tied to the city—a perk that not even the most eloquent civil servant today could imagine or aspire to!

Bruni was by this time respected and wealthy, a husband and father, and a productive scholar whose service to the republic was recognized as both useful and an ornament to the city. He was a convincing apologist for the secular, classically inspired values of the Florentine patriciate into which he was now a new recruit. Ultimately, as the historian of Florence, he would recast its traditions, mythology, and past to reflect his profound belief that the glory of the city resided in its commitment to republican freedom and that it was consequently the legitimate heir of the Roman Republic and the Greek *polis*.

His major works in these years are interesting in their content. He translated the pseudo-Aristotelian *Economics* with a commentary in 1420 to argue for the legitimate, indeed meritorious, place for wealth in the community, refuting powerfully the still-lingering belief in the sanctity of Franciscan poverty and simplicity.[19] A great city needed wealthy men, he argued, so that it could grow more beautiful through building and patronage, more socially compassionate through charity, and more secure through the ability to hire and equip armies. He also wrote a new biography of his—and Petrarch's— hero, Cicero. This *New Cicero* (*Cicero Novus*) of 1413 didn't use the traditional ancient biographies as sources. Rather, it was based on newly discovered ancient sources. And, instead of confirming Petrarch's disappointment on discovering Cicero's letters to

---

19. Hankins, 2007. p. 7; Hans Baron, "Franciscan Poverty and Civic Wealth as Factors in the Rise of Humanistic Thought," *Speculum*, 13 (1938), pp. 1–37.

Atticus, it praised those very things that Petrarch had so abhorred: Cicero's marriage, his service to the state, his labor as a lawyer and an author, and his highly principled animosity to Marc Antony.

Bruni also did the same for Dante. Boccaccio, in an earlier *Life of Dante*, had attacked the poet for his conjugal life, his political activity, and his refusal to simply write poetry and practice contemplation. In contrast, Bruni's shorter *Life* (1436)[20] took the opposite view, praising rather than condemning those elements, suggesting that the poet was great because he served his community, his political faction, and his family as much as because he loved poetry and the divine Beatrice. In so many ways, as Hans Baron has argued, Bruni set Cicero and Dante on a new civic altar as the secular saints of a new order of political engagement, classical scholarship, and public virtue.

Bruni's History of Florence

It was in his magisterial *History of the Florentine People* that Bruni marked out a place for himself in the pantheon of Renaissance Italian thought and writing, as well as in the development of modern historiography.[21] His large history, written over an extended period, takes up the theme that had been guiding him since his early days in the circle of Salutati: the special place of Florence in Italy as the exemplar of republican liberty and freedom.

To accomplish this, he reviewed the traditional sources for the foundation of the city and discarded them as myth. In their place, he erected a new myth, but one for which he added evidence and which suited what must be seen as a genre of propaganda. Bruni proved that Florence was not founded by Caesar and thrived under the Empire, as was generally believed, but was a republican foundation. Consequently, he argued, its love of freedom was native to its very historical DNA. Florence was not rebuilt by the emperor Charlemagne as had been believed, and its traditional connection to the pope was not as central as thought, if only because when the papacy challenged the freedom of the commune, Florence rejected that alliance.

Bruni's *History* is an assertion of how Florence was born in liberty and had spent all of its existence extending and protecting that freedom. The city was chosen not by God, popes, or emperors for its special mission but by history itself to preserve and exemplify the strengths and security that arose from freedom. The style of his argument is derived from the rhetorical elements found in Livy, with imaginary speeches put into the mouths of great figures from the past. But the *History* is more than just another classical exercise: it is a statement of the miraculous nature of the Florentine state, the virtue and strength

---

20. Leonardo Bruni, "The Life of Dante," in F. Bassetti-Sani, ed., *The Earliest Lives of Dante*. New York: Frederick Ungar, 1963. pp. 82–94.

21. Leonardo Bruni, *History of the Florentine People*, tr. James Hankins. Cambridge, MA: Harvard University Press, 3 vols., 2003–2007, The I Tatti Renaissance Library.

of its people, and the powerful engine of liberty which invariably drives the community to accomplish great deeds.

Bruni's wealth, fame, writing, and commitment to the city resulted in his becoming chancellor of the republic in 1427, filling the same position that his mentor, Salutati, had enjoyed when the youthful Bruni was a student in the city. He had now reached the pinnacle of power and influence, and his reputation was acknowledged throughout Europe. His contributions to Greek studies, philology, history, and rhetoric had made him wealthy and universally respected.

At the time of his death in 1444, Bruni was honored by universal acclamation with a great tomb by Bernardo Rossellino, which can still be seen in the basilica of Santa Croce in Florence.

Illus. 2.1 Bernardo Rossellino, *Tomb Monument of Leonardo Bruni* (1444–1447). Basilica of Santa Croce, Florence.

In the effigy that graces Bruni's memorial, he is depicted lying on his bier, surrounded by the images of both ancient and Christian iconography and holding on his chest a copy of his *History of Florence*. His epitaph states what everyone must have felt on that cold January day of 1444:

> *Since Leonardo departed this life, History is mourning, Eloquence is mute, and it is said that the Muses, both Greek and Latin, could not restrain their tears.*

The famous epitaph was composed by Bruni's successor as chancellor, Carlo Marsuppini. The original Latin reads: *Postquam Leonardus e vita migravit*

> *Historia luget; eloquentia muta est*
> *Ferturque musas tum Graecas tum*
> *Latinas lacrimas tenere non potuisse.*

Illus. 2.2 *A View of Florence in the Fifteenth Century.*
Catena map. Museo di Firenze Com'Era, Florence.

This view of Florence was made about 1480 and indicates how little the city has changed since the Renaissance. By the time of Salutati, Florence had become one of Italy's largest and richest cities, although it had yet to fully recover from the demographic catastrophe of the Black Death of 1348–49, the event that provides the frame for Giovanni Boccaccio's *Decameron*. The city had not reached the new walls constructed just before the plague struck and indeed would never regain its population until modern times.

As a result of the Ordinances of Justice (1293), the private towers of the great families had to be pulled down to a regulated height. The result was that the urban topography was defined by the towers of the churches and those of the commune, such as the Bargello (1250) and Palazzo della Signoria (1299, now the Palazzo Vecchio). This symbolized that power as represented in towers was henceforth in the collective authority of the commune and the Christian citizens of the city and no longer the private prerogative of military force and lawlessness.

Illus. 2.3 The Marzocco. In front of the Palazzo della Signoria, or Palazzo Vecchio.

The Marzocco is the symbol of the Florentine republic, even if it was later appropriated by the Medici monarchy in the sixteenth century. It represents one of the lion "protectors" of the city and consequently holds a shield with the *Giglio*, or lily of Florence, another traditional symbol of the city.

The beginnings of the role of the Marzocco, like so many things Florentine, are encrusted with myth. What is certain, however, is that the republic did keep live lions in cages, originally located on the Piazza San Giovanni, near the baptistery and cathedral. This might provide a clue to the name, as the baptistery was believed to have been in ancient times a Roman temple to Mars (it is in fact a Romanesque building) so the name of the god in Latin, Mars, or Italian, Marte, might well have been the root of the Marzocco.

The earliest legend concerning the lion dates from the late twelfth century. In this fanciful narrative, one of the live lions broke free of its cage in front of the old cathedral, Santa Reparata, and carried off a baby from its mother's arms. Her cries elicited pity from the lion who returned to deposit the infant unharmed in front of her. The spin was that the lion would always protect and watch over the citizens of Florence.

Whether the story was pure legend or an embellishment of a real event, the importance of the lions grew. After the Ordinances of Justice of 1293, the republic commissioned Arnolfo di Cambio to design a huge new cathedral (the current building, Santa Maria del Fiore) and a town hall, the Palazzo della Signoria (now Palazzo Vecchio). The work on the cathedral required moving the lions, so they were relocated to the new secular space of civic authority near the Piazza della Signoria. When the building was completed, the site of the cages was behind the Palazzo in a street to this day named the Via dei Leoni, the street of the lions. To sustain the symbolic role of protector of the city, the Signoria commissioned in 1377 a gray sandstone (*pietra serena*) image of a lion, now sadly lost, for the Palazzo: this represented the republic's first commission of a secular sculpture. It was placed on the *Ringhiera*, the external extension of the palace, a space that connected with the sacred role of government that resided in the Palazzo. Ambassadors were received, the population addressed, and priors announced on the outdoor raised dais that faced the huge public square of the Piazza della Signoria.

In about 1420 the Signoria ordered its most famous sculptor, Donatello, to make another image of a lion holding the *Giglio* shield. Initially it stood in front of Pope Martin V's apartments in Santa Maria Novella as a statement to the pope that Florence would protect its liberty, despite its Guelf allegiance. Afterwards, it was moved to the *Ringhiera*, replacing the earlier image. The Marzocco we see there today is a copy, the original having been moved to the Bargello in the nineteenth century.

The creation of the Medici monarchy in 1530 saw the grand dukes of Florence assume the tradition, indeed expand it, despite the fact that the republican defenders of the city against the Medici in 1529–30 were called *I Marzoccheschi*, the men of the Marzocco. Under Grand Duke Cosimo I (1537–74), there were twenty-four live lions in their cages behind the Palazzo Vecchio, but they were moved in 1550 to an open space near the Medici monastery of San Marco to make room for the Vasari's Uffizi. It was only in 1770, during the reign of that most enlightened Grand Duke Pietro Leopoldo of Habsburg–Lorraine, that the ancient practice of keeping live lions to symbolize the protection of the city was abandoned. By then, however, the symbol had spread everywhere Florentine authority held power, not unlike the symbolism of the lion of St. Mark for Venice.

Illus. 2.4 Coluccio Salutati (1331–1406), *Immagine che ritrae Coluccio Salutati, proveniente da un codice della Biblioteca Laurenziana a Firenze* **(an image that portrays Coluccio Salutati, taken from a manuscript in the Laurentian Library in Florence).**

Salutati was an early admirer of Petrarch, with whom he corresponded and whose dedication to elegant, Ciceronian Latin he shared. Unlike Petrarch, however, he trained as a notary and practiced his art in several important positions, including the papal curia and as chancellor of the republic of Lucca. In 1375 he achieved his greatest appointment: the post of chancellor of Florence, an exalted position he would hold until his death more than thirty years later. He also married and had children, living the domestic life scorned by Petrarch and Boccaccio as inappropriate for scholars.

Like Petrarch, he was obsessed with recovering the heritage of antiquity, amassing in his lifetime a huge library, one of the largest in Europe, containing more than eight hundred manuscripts. In his search for lost classical texts he found the *Litterae Familiares* of Cicero, the letters written by the Roman statesmen to his friends. Whereas Petrarch recoiled against his discovery of the letters to Atticus in 1345, letters that indicated how deeply involved in public affairs his hero had been, Salutati rejoiced in the additional evidence of Cicero's commitment to the Roman Republic.

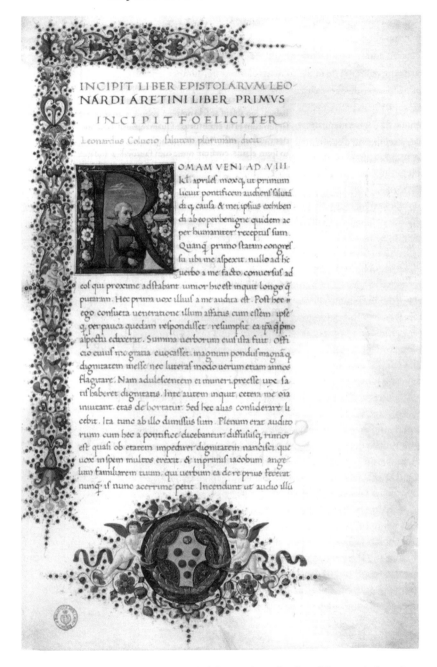

Illus. 2.5 Gherardo di Giovanni del Fora, in *Epistolae di leonardo bruni*, biblioteca medicea laurenziana, pluteo 52.6 f 1r. (1450s–1470s).

This page of a manuscript in the Laurentian Library (*Biblioteca Laurenziana*) in Florence, written just after the death of Leonard Bruni, carries a letter from Bruni to his mentor, Coluccio Salutati, as well as a small, probably fanciful, portrait of the author in the decorated initial. What is most significant about this manuscript page is the handwriting, so different from the heavily abbreviated Medieval "gothic" script. Not only did the Renaissance humanists beginning with Petrarch seek to change the written style of the contents of literature, but they also planned to create a new form of writing to carry that new, elegant, classically correct material.

Again, the initiative begins with Petrarch. As he aged, he had increasing difficulty reading the gothic script of his manuscripts, so he asked his friends to send him texts in "*litterae rotondae*," the easily deciphered, clear writing popular among certain scribes in northern Italy. Salutati's disciple and Bruni's colleague, Poggio Bracciolini, together with his friend, the bibliophile, scholar, and Salutati acolyte, Niccolò de' Niccoli, identified a script that they believed was ancient Roman writing from some extremely old manuscripts. It wasn't Roman, in fact, but Caroline Minuscule, the writing developed at the court and scriptorium of the emperor Charlemagne in the late eighth and ninth centuries. It was beautiful, very easily read, and could be written quickly. So, they adopted it and transformed it into humanist script, a true "*felix culpa*" or "lucky mistake." The script was so popular that when printing was introduced into Florence in the 1470s this handwriting of Niccoli and Bracciolini was chosen as the typeface for the new invention: thus was born our "*italic*" type, still in use and still elegant and easy to read.

Illus. 2.6 Masolino (Masolino da Panicale), *The Healing of Tabitha*, **1420s. Brancacci Chapel.**

This fresco by Masolino in the Brancacci Chapel in the church of Santa Maria del Carmine, illustrates how Petrarch's concepts of the validity of human experience on earth, individual agency, and the intimate relationship between the human and divine all took root in Florence by the mid-1420s. The images in this scene—part of a larger program of the Miracles of St. Peter in the chapel—reflect how episodes from the Acts of the Apostles illustrate not only the miracles of the early Church but also the environment of Masolino's Florence.

The painter joins two separate stories that occurred in different places at different times to describe a vision of dramatic human action and divine power. On the left is portrayed St. Peter healing the lame man in Jerusalem (Acts 3: 1–10), and on the right is the raising of Tabitha (Acts 9: 36–43), which occurred in Joppa. The event on the left is very focused, without a large audience, and establishes a connection on a very personal level between the lame man and the saint. The raising of Tabitha, however, is a piece of dramatic theatre in which the dead Tabitha, having been summoned back to life, becomes the focus for the family members and widows whom St. Peter had called to witness the miracle. There is a collective emotional intensity, but one created by each individual's sense of wonder at what has just happened.

The figures all enjoy a human scale, with correct anatomy and natural gestures and posture. Each is painted as an individual character, displaying different responses to the event. The perspective is perfect, and the distances of objects and figures from one another are carefully drawn to provide a reflection of what the eye would have seen if present at the moment of the miracle. But it is the detail of the figures not in the biblical story that most engages us: the depiction of the Renaissance city of Florence. Contemporary humanity is shown in the two wealthy dandies walking together but placed so that they link the composition of the two scenes. They pay no attention to the saint; their minds and certainly their conversation are on the things of this world, not seeing the miraculous in their midst. They are discrete personalities, symbolic of a successful secular life, outside the lives of the poor. Their presence almost constitutes a statement that the ideals of Franciscan, even apostolic, poverty are no longer requisite for salvation. Wealth can aid in the succor of the poor and can provide the community with protection, government, work, and justice. The active life and the accumulation of experience and wealth can help build a better city.

Equally, the streetscape is a schematized view of 1420s Florence, with all of its bourgeois, domestic quality. The fine houses in the background tell of the pleasures of this life: songbirds in cages, pet monkeys, clean laundry, and social cohesion. A mother takes out her child, followed for the sake of propriety and tradition by a loyal servant. The loggia beside which the cripple begs is indicative of the fusion of public and private space that animates Renaissance cities; and the view down the side street shows the wooden enclosed balconies illegally added to existing buildings to increase space. These were forbidden because they often collapsed and blocked sunshine on the street, but space was so expensive that they were still built. All citizens, regardless of wealth, form the community portrayed here in a fresco which is almost an allegory of civic humanist thought, painted just prior to Leonardo Bruni's election as chancellor of Florence in 1427.

PART II

———

Florence: The Humanist Republic

The rise of the Medici changed the nature of humanism in Florence but only gradually over time. Cosimo de'Medici, *il Vecchio*, was a great patron of art and culture and had a humanist's appreciation of its value. He institutionalized the traditions by following the practice of using competitions for important commissions, even serving on the selection committees himself. And the examples of his palace and its decoration and his interest in Platonism and Neoplatonism place him convincingly in the community of humanist patrons. His son, Piero, continued this pattern, working initially with his father and then in his own right to continue the cultural experimentation that animated Florence. But it was Cosimo's grandson, Lorenzo the Magnificent, who fulfilled so much of humanism's potential as both the celebration of the human spirit and genius while simultaneously establishing the circle around Lorenzo—in effect a Medici court—as the arbiters of taste and scholarship.

It was in part a reaction against this increasingly esoteric culture of Neoplatonic thought and complex iconography that assisted in the rise of Savonarola. Few men, even the richest or cleverest patricians, could compete with the coterie around Lorenzo in the last decade of his life. Those of simple faith began to see humanism as a pagan alternative to the traditions of Florentine piety; and ideological republicans interpreted Lorenzo's patronage as more the glorification of a prince than an ornament to the city. The theocratic experiment of Savonarola constituted a kind of anti-humanism, a sign of how deeply humanist ideas had infused the culture of the republic. With the fall of Savonarola and the rise of the republic of Soderini, humanism returned, but chastened. Machiavelli illustrates how humanist republican principles still obtained in Florence, although now with a more focused and inherently political agenda.

CHAPTER 3
THE RISE OF THE MEDICI IN FLORENCE

Even before the time of Salutati's and Bruni's chancellorships, elements of self-confidence, republican freedom, and human dignity were apparent in Florentine government. The constitution of the city was essentially that of a guild republic in which membership in one of the twenty-one guilds allowed a citizen to hold public office. In effect this meant that those with property who paid taxes and who employed others held a monopoly of authority within the city.

Inside the guild system there were levels of power. The seven major guilds (*arti maggiori*) were essentially mercantile and professional cartels organized by the richest and most influential citizens such as the bankers, notaries, and wool merchants. The fourteen lesser guilds (*arti minori*) were comprised of the less influential craftsmen such as the blacksmiths, innkeepers, and vintners. Those outside the guild system—in particular the working poor—had no influence whatsoever over the machinery of government.[1]

The Struggle for Power

The crises of the 1340s, such as the collapse of the Bardi and Peruzzi banks and the Black Death, had strained the republican constitution almost to its limit and threatened the extinction of that republican freedom so important to Salutati and Bruni. A scheme was engineered in 1342 by the most conservative and reactionary of the patricians who suggested "temporarily" subverting the guild republic by inviting a lord (*signore*) to rule the city and address its problems.[2]

To be sure, this was not the first time this mechanism had been used to address crises in unstable times. In fact, the first experiments in such "temporary" tyranny had occurred in 1313 when King Robert of Naples, the leader of the Italian Guelfs, was offered the lordship. Then in 1325 the offer was extended to Robert's son, Charles of Calabria. Such submissions had put Florence in danger of becoming an extraterritorial appendage of Naples, a condition which would have certainly foreclosed the promise of the Renaissance. But, happily, King Robert was too busy to care about ruling the city, and his son, Charles of Calabria, conveniently died. Florence was lucky in its escape.

It was equally lucky in the desperate arrangements of 1342. The French nobleman invited to be *signore*, Walter of Brienne, duke of Athens, started to behave like an

---

1. The best comprehensive history of Renaissance Florence is John M. Najemy, *A History of Florence, 1200–1575*. Oxford: Blackwell, 2006.
2. For a discussion of the republic before 1348, see Marvin Becker, *Florence in Transition*, vol. 1. Baltimore: Johns Hopkins University Press, 1967.

actual tyrant, turning his one-year contract with the city into a lordship for life.[3] He was expelled by a popular revolt in 1343, a consequence that both discredited the old, reactionary, self-serving aristocrats who had imported Walter and encouraged a new republican zeal and engagement in the operation of the state. A more broadly based government was introduced that reflected the large numbers and importance of the lesser as well as greater guilds. By allowing the lesser guildsmen access to office in proportion to their membership, the city thrived and took on a renewed energy and unity. It was this government, for example, that adopted the *Monte* in 1343, thus addressing the needs of all the political, property-owning classes.

Unfortunately, this happy situation did not last, the disintegration ironically beginning in the year Coluccio Salutati was chosen as chancellor. A war against the papacy—the so-called War of the Eight Saints (1375–78)—was disastrous to Florentine banking and the wool industry. Using its spiritual weapons, the papacy declared Florence to be an enemy of the Church, forbidding trade with the city and permitting foreigners to seize Florentine property. The result was depressed wages and unemployment among the thousands of *ciompi*, or wool workers, in the city.

The *ciompi* labored under often terrible conditions in the combing and stretching sheds and the dyeing factories necessary to the wool trade. They worked with hazardous dyes and breathed in woolen particles suspended in the air of their unventilated workrooms. Not surprisingly, they died young and poor. In good times their wages were above subsistence level, a situation that often attracted more unskilled laborers from the countryside. In bad times, they often starved or were compelled to assume loans at high interest or even forced to return to their rural villages, often leaving behind their wives and children with insufficient funds to eat and live.

In 1378 the *ciompi* revolted, manipulated by some unscrupulous patricians intent on humbling their enemies. Initially the revolt was a success, with three new *ciompi* guilds added to the seven major and fourteen minor guilds. The omnibus *Guild of the People of God (Arte del popolo di Dio)* permitted for the first time men without property—men who paid no tax and who employed no one—to sit in the highest councils of the state, even up to the office of prior, one of the committee of nine officials who collectively formed the executive of the republic.

Galvanized by this challenge to their monopoly on power, the traditional property-owning guildsmen worked together to suppress the revolt and the *ciompi* guilds, executing their leaders and invoking an even harsher regime in the factories and sheds. The lesser guildsmen, whose wealth was concentrated in their shops and whose ability to pay higher wages in hard times was limited, effectively ceded the influence they had acquired

---

3. Giovanni Villani, *The Final Book of Giovanni Villani's New Chronicle*, tr. Matthew Thomas Sneider. Kalamazoo: Western Michigan University–Medieval Institute Publications, 2016. pp. 25–26.

after 1343 to the more powerful greater guildsmen. For them, security was more important than an equitable access to power.[4]

Civic Humanism under the Albizzi Oligarchy

Thus, an oligarchy emerged in Florence by the early 1380s comprised of the rich patricians—the bankers, leading merchants in the wool industry, judges and notaries, professional men, and long-distance traders. It was an oligarchy initially well-managed by the Albizzi family. Its leader, Maso degli Albizzi, was effective in protecting Florentine interests, expanding Florentine territory, and working against the ambitions of Giangaleazzo Visconti, the duke of Milan. In 1385 Florence had acquired Arezzo, and in 1406 the capture of Pisa finally gave Florence a seaport. Equally, however, the oligarchs ruthlessly crushed their opponents by means of confiscation of property, exile, and even execution. A difficult war against Lucca and the more limited abilities of Maso's son, Rinaldo, resulted in growing opposition to an oligarchy that was increasingly arrogant and restrictive.

One of the ironic observations to be made about Florence under the Albizzi oligarchy is that it corresponded exactly with the beginnings of humanism and civic humanism.[5] As we have seen, Salutati was chancellor from 1375 until his death in 1406. And Leonardo Bruni was resident in the city from 1415 and elected as chancellor in 1427, the very years when the oligarchy was at its most oppressive. How can we reconcile the development of a sense of republican virtue and an ideology of civic engagement guided by the principles of antiquity with what was in fact something of an odious regime?

The answer lies, it can be argued, in the divorce of ideology from the reality of factional politics, especially in the context of military success and economic experimentation. After the suppression of the *ciompi* regime, there was an element of cohesion and stability in Florence that permitted new ideas to percolate. To their advantage, these ideas were initially abstract in their formulation and only actualized near the end of the oligarchy.

Furthermore, some of the policies of the communal government after the 1380s reinforced what would become Bruni's historical revisionism. For example, the War of the Eight Saints (1375–78) against the Avignonese papacy was offered as evidence that Florence stood up for her self-interest even in the face of hostility from the papacy, the leader of Guelf Europe, a traditional ally. Then the long and difficult wars against Giangaleazzo Visconti allowed the civic humanist belief in republican virtue and independence to shine, illustrating how Florence would never submit to tyranny, regardless of the odds: it would be the Italian bulwark against tyranny.

---

4. For the Ciompi Revolt, see Gene Brucker, "The Revolt of the Ciompi," in Nicolai Rubinstein, ed., *Florentine Studies: Politics and Society in Renaissance Florence*. London: Faber & Faber, 1968.
5. Becker, 1967, vol. 2. pp. 25–92.

The death of Giangaleazzo in 1402 consequently seemed like a reprieve, not through divine intervention but as a consequence of that history of opposing tyranny and oppression that Bruni and others defined as the essence of the Florentine character. Similarly, the acquisition of Arezzo and especially the addition of Pisa to the Florentine state seemed again like rewards for a people who exemplified virtue. The commune continued to thrive, and the putative cause of this success was its adherence to republican values and freedom. In other words, the myth of Florence as the center of freedom and ancient virtue was reinforced by these events. Spokesmen like Salutati and Bruni could write what they did because the evidence seemed to be in their favor.

Of course these humanist statesmen ignored the shrinking of the political class during the oligarchy and the extraconstitutional and often illegal means it employed to destroy its enemies. Myth and political reality are often mutually exclusive. So long as Florence was successful in expanding its territories and defeating its enemies, then the myth and humanist ideology would trump the actual reality of politics as practiced. As we have seen, Bruni himself succumbed to this deception in his propagandistic *Laudatio Florentinae Urbis* (*Panegyric to the City of Florence*).

That said, not all was oppressive or reactionary during the Albizzi oligarchy. Especially during its last decade, a rising self-confidence and willingness to experiment yielded some remarkable innovations. In 1425, the republic instituted a second *Monte*, this one the *Monte delle doti*, or state dowry fund. Its purpose was to ease the increasingly onerous financial burden involved in finding suitable husbands for female children.[6]

When a girl was born, her father was encouraged to make payments into this fund so that it could accrue interest at a guaranteed rate until the girl was about fifteen—the usual age to begin arranging a marriage. The returned principal and interest were to serve as the basis of the girl's dowry, allowing her to marry honorably. But this *Monte delle doti* was also designed to be self-financing, because if the girl died (and the rates of child mortality were horrendous), only the principal would be returned to the family, thus allowing the interest to fund the marriage portions of those girls who survived.

Two years later, in 1427, the commune instituted a form of wealth tax, known as the *catasto*, which was intended to be fair and effective. All citizens were required to self-assess in a particularly modern manner, listing their assets and liabilities.[7] This experiment in state building presupposed the actual participation of the population. Although the *catasto* arose from the necessity of paying the enormous cost of the lengthy wars with Milan, it was a novel and remarkably modern response to state financing, not unlike the *Monte* of a century earlier.

---

6. Anthony Molho, *Marriage Alliance in Late Medieval Florence*. Cambridge, MA: Harvard University Press, 1994. Harvard Historical Studies (Book 114).
7. David V. Herlihy and Christiane Klapisch-Zuber, *Tuscans and Their Families: A Study of the Florentine Catasto of 1427*. New Haven: Yale University Press, 1989. Yale Series in Economic and Financial History; Giovanni Ciappelli, *Fisco e società a Firenze nel Rinascimento. Studi e testi del Rinascimento europeo* 36. Rome: Edizioni di Storia e Letteratura, 2009.

These innovations were truly remarkable as they reflected a sense of community and a belief that the state could be used as an instrument to improve the lives of its citizens—even to the point of becoming a partner in one of the most intimate events of family life: the marriage of a child. These policies also reflected a movement away from the idealized Christian practice of personal charity toward a civic sense of mutual responsibility of all citizens to be facilitated by the commune. In short, the modern concept of the state was being formed. It is not an accident that the first iterations of the word for that concept of the state—*lo stato*—appeared in Italian during the Renaissance.

The Florentine republic, then, in the years beginning with Salutati's rise to the chancellorship came to be not just a place where the ideas of Petrarch, Salutati, and Bruni were generated and discussed: it was the place that experimented with mechanisms to actualize these principles. That these years corresponded to the age of oligarchy is largely irrelevant because the ideas generated by humanists, particularly civic humanists, had a theatre in which they could be developed and ultimately rehearsed and played. Florence served as a real laboratory for ideas in community, statecraft, finance, and propaganda, creating an environment that encouraged experimentation and invested citizens with a self-confident notion of their own individuality and the imperative to live it and make it known to others.

The Culture of Republican Liberty and Civic Humanism

Leonardo Bruni was in many ways the voice of the maturing Renaissance in Florence under the oligarchy and for the first decade of the hegemony of Cosimo de'Medici.[8] During those years in the city after Bruni's return from the papal curia, there was an extraordinary blossoming of a new intellectual and cultural order.[9] Just consider the major moments of Renaissance art and architecture completed or commissioned during those years, years which connected the period of oligarchy with the Medici ascendency.

For example, Filippo Brunelleschi's splendid and almost miraculous dome on the cathedral was commissioned in 1419 and completed in 1436. Cosimo de'Medici had been Brunelleschi's strongest supporter during the competition between Brunelleschi and Lorenzo Ghiberti. However, Ghiberti later won the commission for the third (east) set of doors for the baptistery in 1425, bronze portals that Michelangelo would later describe as worthy to be the gates of paradise.

Masaccio's *Trinity* fresco in Santa Maria Novella was painted in that same year of 1425; and Masaccio and Masolino's Brancacci Chapel in Santa Maria del Carmine was

---

8. Vespasiano da Bisticci, a Florentine stationer, wrote the biographies of his most celebrated clients, including Bruni and Poggio. See Vespasiano da Bisticci, *Renaissance Princes, Popes and Prelates*, tr. W. G. and E. W. Waters. New York: Harper & Row, 1963. pp. 358–69 for Bruni and pp. 351–58 for Poggio.

9. For a general assessment of recent scholarship on civic humanism and republicanism in Florence, see Hankins, 2000.

begun, only to be left incomplete in 1427. Donatello sculpted his celebrated bronze *David* in about 1430 and his splendid *Annunciation* in Santa Croce about 1437. There was his *cantoria* (choir gallery screen) for the cathedral and his decoration of the old sacristy of San Lorenzo. Fra Angelico was painting the cells of the monastery of San Marco and in 1439 completed his brilliant San Marco altarpiece. Michelozzo's Palazzo Medici (now Medici-Riccardi) was commissioned in 1444, the year of Bruni's death. In cultural theory, Leon Battista Alberti's treatise *On Painting* (*Della Pittura*) was written in 1435.

This list represents only the most celebrated of the works and events produced in those remarkable years of Bruni's ascendancy. It is, then, a tribute to Leonardo Bruni that his final residence in Florence witnessed the efflorescence of art, architecture, and learning. It was also, it can be maintained, that these things occurred in part *because* of him.

In proving to his receptive readers that Florence was a special city with a unique past and a sacred duty to create beauty and protect freedom, Bruni was providing the intellectual and cultural motivation for the fulfillment of that prophetic mission. By telling the citizens of Florence that they were set apart by that mission and had in the past accomplished great things, Bruni was giving the city a degree of self-confidence that allowed for, indeed demanded, such achievements. By popularizing Petrarch's principles of self-exploration, clarity of expression, and the validation of human experience on earth, Bruni was encouraging artists and writers to investigate themselves and their fellow men.

Human experience was now given a new vocabulary, based on sight, interpretation, and understanding, that made the city and, in fact, the universe a more comprehensible place, available to all through their common faculties of sight. The rich but obscure allegories and hieratic style of the Middle Ages and the learned but abstruse theological structures of scholasticism gave way to a true humanism, a set of ideals, skills, and principles that encouraged and permitted man to know himself. Revived ancient tags, such as *Man is the measure of all things* and *Man can do anything he wills*, challenged the Medieval worldview in which men and women were merely actors in a divine script. There was now agency and the means to externalize that agency through shared experience illustrated in art or precisely expressed in elegant language.

This was no more apparent than in the revival of portraiture. The Medieval practice of identifying people through abstract symbols was abandoned, and again, as in ancient times, portraits reflected the actual physiognomy of individuals and revealed their characters. The portrait bust, a genre not practiced since antiquity, was reborn during Bruni's time, and the understanding of geometric linear perspective, discovered and codified by Donatello and Brunelleschi and popularized by Alberti during those years, provided artists with the tool to create three-dimensional images on two-dimensional planes. Art could accurately, then, reflect what the eye sees, whether the shape and demeanor of men and women or the distance between them or the isolation of objects through exact geometric clarity.

Petrarch, later reinforced by Salutati and especially by Bruni, believed that speech was the reflection of the soul and of human reason. Good words resulted from good men with good thoughts and ideas. By extension, these products made humans quasi-divine because humans alone possess speech, reason, and souls, so there must be an association among them. Moreover, it was part of the duty of good men—Christian men—to make clear what is good and so to avoid what is evil or merely incorrect. Cicero had shown through his words that he had the qualities of a good man, despite his paganism. So, for Christians in a Christian city, how much more important these principles had to be and how much more effectively they needed to be imparted to all.[10]

Thus for the intelligentsia in Florence there was no longer a divorce between ancient, pagan learning and the Christian dispensation; there was, rather, a kind of fusion in which two forms of virtue—the human and the divine—would merge to guide people to a better experience in this life and an easier ascent to the next. In this exaltation of the human spirit, art, architecture, and literature could help.

Leonardo Bruni, by giving the educated patricians of Florence the confidence and the mission to achieve great things, created an environment in which genius could flourish and in which experimentation in different ways to accomplish this mission might occur. Florence became a laboratory in which artists, writers, and even political leaders tried to fulfill their unique talents, in part simply because they believed they could. The city was redefined through Bruni's *History* as a place in which freedom of thought and experimentation constituted part of their tradition of republican freedom and part of the mission of the city to become the new Athens or the new Rome.

Florence was to be the cutting edge, the forefront of new ideas. It was to be beautiful, like Athens or Rome, to reflect its role as a beacon of hope and freedom. And, it was to be active in the creation of a new order of freedom and stability in an unstable world. In many ways Florence produced the successive generations of geniuses and that huge explosion in art, architecture, and thought because its citizens believed that they could accomplish great things and because they consequently felt the obligation to do so.[11]

Cosimo de'Medici, il Vecchio

One of the Albizzi oligarchy's most feared opponents was Cosimo de'Medici, the head of the Medici bank and a man held in great respect by all classes of citizen. Cosimo wasn't from a long-standing aristocratic family. Rather, he was a new man (*novus civis*) whose family appeared to have come to Florence from the Mugello, the comparatively poor, northern region of Tuscany, in about the 1230s. It was Cosimo's father, Giovanni di Bicci

---

10. Celenza, 2018. pp. 59–63.
11. For a broad discussion of the interaction among social history, space, art, and architecture, see Roger J. Crum and John T. Paoletti, eds. *Renaissance Florence: A Social History*. Cambridge: Cambridge University Press, 2006.

de'Medici, who founded the family fortunes. He established a bank that made great prof-its from papal contracts and from the rights to mine the alum needed in the processing of cloth. By the end of his life in 1429, Giovanni di Bicci was one of the wealthiest men in Florence and had set a course for his son.[12]

Fearing the breadth and depth of his support, his wealth, and his abilities, the Albizzi arrested Cosimo on trumped-up charges of treason and exiled him in 1433. This act, however, sparked the reaction the oligarchs had most feared: a popular revolt. The Albizzi supporters were driven into exile, their palaces were burned, and their property appropriated. Cosimo was recalled in 1434. And thus began the extended period of the Medici hegemony.

Cosimo was a gifted businessman and a skilled political operator. His return to Florence as a consequence of the expulsion of the oligarchs meant that he could have assumed a more prominent role in the rule of the city. But Cosimo was in essence a committed republican, and he consequently left the structure of the constitution intact. He realized that offending the jealousies and ambitions of his fellow patricians would be counterproductive, if not dangerous. And, he was mindful of the fact that he had risen to prominence not only because of his wealth but also through the support of the lesser guildsmen and those disadvantaged by the Albizzi regime. Equally, however, he was very much aware of the dangers of factionalism and the difficulty of sustaining a coherent policy of any kind in a republic where the executive was a committee of nine men who held office for only two months, ineligible to return as priors for three years.

Once in power in 1434, Cosimo allowed all the offices of state to continue as they had, with wide rotation of men in office and committees and councils debating and occa-sionally determining policy. He himself held only those posts to which he was elected, and he was scrupulous to appear not to wield undue influence in those positions, even if everyone knew his real power was immense. He achieved this by assuming control of what to many seemed a minor committee—the *Accoppiatori*—the committee which determined who was eligible for office. By controlling who sat on the *Accoppiatori*, Cosimo ensured that he could always have a majority of supporters in government.

As a result, the Medici faction controlled the entire operation of the state, but in a subtle, opaque, less abrasive manner than under the Albizzi. The sensibilities of the proud and ambitious—and very fractious—political classes in Florence were conse-quently largely unprovoked, and Cosimo was regarded as having made the republic operate more efficiently and coherently than previously. Certainly there was opposition, but during his lifetime the anti-Medicean faction never succeeded in seriously threaten-ing the regime.

---

12. Dale Kent, *The Rise of the Medici: Faction in Florence, 1426–1434*. New York: Oxford University Press, 1978.

Cosimo, moreover, knew how to use the theatre of life.[13] He dressed like a sober, learned patrician, often affecting the red robes of a physician as a pun on his name (*medico* means *physician* in Italian) so as not to stand out as vainglorious. He walked through the city unattended and behaved like a good citizen, humbly accepting office if elected but making no outward show of extraordinary power. He used his vast wealth to help the public finances in difficult times. He did not take money from communal resources or from subject territories; on the contrary, he made up fiscal shortfalls from his own resources. He married his two legitimate children to leading Florentine patrician families, rather than to noble dynasties outside the city as might have been expected.[14]

Part of Cosimo's success and an explicit goal of his policy was to ensure that Florence sustained peace. War is expensive and unpredictable, and this was especially true in Florence where wars were waged by professional mercenary armies. The long period of engagement against Milan had strained every financial instrument available to the city, while the inconclusive war with Lucca added even more pressure, a pressure that had ultimately brought down the oligarchs. So Cosimo sensibly sought peace.

In this pursuit he had an unlikely ally: Francesco Sforza, the new duke of Milan who, like Cosimo, was an upstart strongman. Cosimo and Francesco made common cause, and the results were wonderful both for their respective cities and for Italy as a whole. In 1454 Cosimo and Francesco negotiated the Peace of Lodi that recognized five major powers in the peninsula—Venice, Milan, Florence, the Papal States, and Naples—and agreed to their enjoying protected spheres of influence. The following year, the Italian League was formed, designed to protect Italy from invasions from across the Alps. Thus, forty years of relative peace and calm descended on the peninsula, allowing the Italian Renaissance, already well established in Florence, to spread and put down deep roots in other centers where local variations could add to the experimental and searching quality of this fundamental moment in European culture.

Cosimo, Patron of the Arts

Not only was Cosimo a brilliant politician, but he was also one of Renaissance Italy's most generous and astute patrons of art and culture.[15] He was a true Maecenas who realized that art could not only bring personal honor and recognition but could also benefit his city by making it a renowned place of artistic and cultural excellence.[16] His patronage

---

13. For Vespasiano's life of Cosimo, see da Bisticci, 1963. pp. 213–34.

14. For an astute contemporary assessment of Cosimo, see Aeneas Silvius Piccolomini (Pius II), *Commentaries*, eds. M. Meserve and M. Simonetta. Cambridge MA: Harvard University Press, 2004. I, pp. 314–19.

15. E. H. Gombrich, "The Early Medici as Patrons of Art," in E. F. Jacob, ed., *Italian Renaissance Studies*. London: Faber and Faber, 1960. pp. 279–311.

16. Michael Levey, *Florence, A Portrait*. Cambridge MA: Harvard University Press, 1996. pp. 77–205.

connected his person, his family, and the city in a profound way, and it was accomplished consciously and with both discretion and taste. Consequently, throughout his life he used his vast wealth to adorn public buildings and commissioned works of art that could be appreciated by many.[17]

His family church, the basilica of San Lorenzo, was a major recipient of Cosimo's patronage. A papal dispensation permitted the Medici to place their coat of arms in the church, so it came to honor not only St. Lawrence but also the Medici themselves. Cosimo continued the decoration of Brunelleschi's old sacristy (1421–28), commissioning Donatello for the work. It was to be a kind of Medici shrine, designed to hold the tombs of Cosimo's family, though Cosimo himself would be buried in the church proper.

The nearby Dominican monastery of San Marco also benefitted from Cosimo's wealth and sincere piety. After the Dominicans took possession of the much older complex in 1435, Cosimo was approached to fund its rebuilding. He accepted the responsibility in 1437 and commissioned his personal architect, Michelozzo, to build a dignified and restrained cloister, while the artist-monk Fra Angelico was asked to fresco the walls of the dormitories.

Fra Angelico was both a Dominican of San Marco and one of the most brilliant of that first generation of Florentine artists who turned the abstractions of humanist thought into visible programs. Even the most jaded visitor was reminded of the transcendent power of faith, painting, and the beauty of human form when encountering Fra Angelico's *Annunciation* near the entrance to the monastic dormitories, while the artist's San Marco altarpiece remains one of the most moving panels of its generation. Cosimo kept a cell—also painted by Fra Angelico—for his own use when the affairs of state or his religious concerns required a respite from responsibility.

The quantity and quality of Cosimo's patronage is remarkable. Donatello crafted his *David* for Cosimo's palace, producing the first freestanding male nude since antiquity. In doing so he exalted the dignity of the human body that reinforced Petrarch's belief in the validity of human experience on earth. Donatello also fashioned for Cosimo *Judith and Holofernes*—a symbol of virtue and steadfast dedication to freedom and civic duty that can be seen as turning the ideology of Bruni into a powerful artistic statement. Completed in the year of Cosimo's death, Donatello's bronze was initially installed in the garden of the Medici palace. But because its statement of freedom and sacrifice made it a symbol of the republic itself, it was moved after the expulsion of the Medici in 1494 to the ring outside the Palazzo della Signoria where it would later share space with an even more famous republican symbol, Michelangelo's *David*.[18]

---

17. Dale Kent, *Cosimo de' Medici and the Florentine Renaissance: The Patron's Oeuvre*. New Haven: Yale University Press, 2000; to place Cosimo in context, see Richard A. Goldthwaite, *Wealth and the Demand for Art in Italy, 1300–1600*. Baltimore: Johns Hopkins University Press, 1993.

18. Francis Ames-Lewis, *The Early Medici and Their Artists*. London: Birkbeck College University of London, 1995.

Cosimo was also dedicated to learning and books, acquiring an exceptional private library which he greatly expanded on the death of one of his circle, Niccolò de' Niccoli. The latter had accumulated substantial debts which Cosimo repaid, taking in exchange Niccoli's library of precious manuscripts. The merged collections formed the nucleus of what is today the Laurentian Library at San Lorenzo. This collection, now housed in a building adjacent to the Medici church of San Lorenzo in a space designed by Michelangelo, was always intended to be a public library, open to any scholar who needed to consult its remarkable holdings. In fact, all of Florence became a place of humanist and artistic pilgrimage, with scholars traveling to use the libraries of ancient texts, and with artists, sculptors, and architects attracted to the models and workshops of the finest practitioners in Italy. Cosimo made it possible and saw his gift as more for his city than for himself.

Perhaps his only egregious manifestation of pride was the construction of his enormous palace, Palazzo Medici (now Medici-Riccardi) between 1444 and 1459. But, even here, it can be argued that he was using his wealth to adorn his city with a splendid building. It stood both as a reflection of Cosimo's patronage and the center of his political faction. Until this day the huge building merits respect, if not affection. But that is true only of the powerful exterior: the courtyard inside is elegant and even delicate, permitting light to enter the huge building from the center as well as the exterior.

To this very day, the highlight of a visit to the palazzo is the chapel painted by Benozzo Gozzoli (1459). It illustrates the *Journey of the Magi*—a subject of special interest to the Medici as they were devotees of the biblical three kings, traditionally enrolling their young men in the Florentine confraternity dedicated to the kings' honor. But, as much as the fresco is based on the biblical story, it is also very much a portrait of Cosimo's contemporary world and of his greatest triumph. The landscape in the background is an idealized representation of Tuscan rural life and features a view of one of the Medici villas. In the procession can be found stylized portraits of Cosimo's family and a portrait of the artist himself. Even more important, many of the exotically dressed and bearded men in the procession represent the Byzantine imperial court and orthodox hierarchy— Cosimo's personal guests in 1439 during the Council of Florence.

The great ecumenical Council of the Church had been called to unite the Latin and Eastern Orthodox Churches in order to galvanize European support for the Byzantine Empire, then under peril from the Ottomans. Originally summoned to Ferrara, the Council was moved to Florence where it met from 1438–39, a change of venue occasioned by plague and Cosimo's offer of substantial financial support. In fact, Cosimo hosted some of the imperial party in his own palace, and in commissioning the Benozzo Gozzoli fresco, recorded the event and his role in it for all time. Because it has hardly changed in the centuries since, a visit to this chapel is a journey back through time to meet Cosimo, his family, and distinguished international guests.

Attending the Council, in addition to the emperor himself, were the patriarch of Constantinople, seventeen metropolitans (bishops), and more than seven hundred theologians, scholars, courtiers, and servants. They brought with them celebrated scholars, such as John Bessarion, who stayed in Italy, ultimately rising to the rank of cardinal in the Latin Church, and who carried with him a large library of Greek works that would later constitute the foundation of the Marciana library in Venice. Also among the luminaries was Georgius Gemistus Plethon, whose discussions of Plato would develop into the informal Platonic Academy.[19]

Neoplatonism

The connection with Constantinople, therefore, went beyond diplomacy and hospitality. Plethon, together with many other Greeks in the imperial or patriarchal entourage, was interested in Neoplatonism. This was a philosophical system of exceptionally abstract ideas based on Plato that had developed in Alexandria in the early years of the Christian era through writers such as Plotinus. Neoplatonism in turn influenced Christian theology as it was being articulated, especially in the Orthodox world, through men such as Clement of Alexandria and Origen.

Especially attractive to the Florentines were the texts of the obscure writer identified somewhat awkwardly as "Pseudo-Dionysius the Areopagite." His commentary on such matters as the celestial hierarchy of angels added a mystical element to the Florentine iteration of Neoplatonism. So too did the *Hermetic Books*, at the time thought to be the writings of one Hermes Trismegistus who was associated with the Egyptian and Greek gods of writing and magic, Hermes and Thoth. In these texts were found—in addition to more familiar topics such as the training of priests—spiritual elements such as incantations, sacred rituals, and spells.

These complex ideas held such a great attraction for Cosimo that he engaged Marsilio Ficino, the son of his personal physician, to translate this literature into Latin. Though the scope of the task was monumental—the translation of all of the works of Plato as well as the *Hermetic Books*—Marsilio was a man of astounding intellectual and linguistic ability. In 1462, Cosimo set him up in his villa at Careggi, on the outskirts of Florence, and Ficino got to work on the project. It did not see completion until well after Cosimo's death, but it signaled the birth of the Platonic Academy, a loose association of philosophers, poets, artists, and learned patricians that would have such an influence under Lorenzo de'Medici, Cosimo's grandson.[20]

---

19. James Hankins, *Plato in the Italian Renaissance*. Leiden and New York: E. J. Brill, 1994. I, pp. 27–101; 265–359.
20. Celenza, 2018. pp. 241–63.

Cosimo, Pater Patriae

Cosimo died in 1464, lauded at his death by Florentines as *Pater Patriae*, the father of his people, an epithet that appears to this day on his tomb in front of the altar in San Lorenzo. This honor was appropriate as it was the same accorded to great Romans of the ancient republic including the general Marcus Furius Camillus; Marcus Tullius Cicero; and, significantly, both Julius Caesar and his nephew Augustus, generally acknowledged as the first of the Roman emperors.[21]

Again, in Florence, the connection between good men, words, and deeds, and the example of these great Roman statesmen was reinforced. The ancient honor of *Pater Patriae* was a title that prophetically connected the great age of the republic with the age of imperial authority. It seemed indeed that Florence had become the new Rome and the Medici dynasty the transition from guild republic to dynastic principality.

---

21. Cosimo's generosity, wisdom, and patronage were all recognized during his lifetime, especially by those who benefitted from them. See especially the ca.1456 dialogue by Timoteo Maffei, *On the Magnificence of Cosimo dè'Medici of Florence against [his] Detractors*, in Peter Howard, ed., *Creating Magnificence in Renaissance Florence*. Toronto: Centre for Reformation and Renaissance Studies, 2012. pp. 142–43.

Illus. 3.1 Giorgio Vasari (1511–78), *Partenza di Cosimo il Vecchio per l'esilio* (*Cosimo goes into exile between allegories of Prudence and Fortitude,* 1433), 1556–58. Fresco, Palazzo Vecchio, Florence.

The Medici had a genius for using history and art as propaganda, amply illustrated by this sixteenth-century fresco painted by Giorgio Vasari for the autocratic Cosimo I. The fresco decorates a wall in the Palazzo della Signoria which by then had become the Palazzo Vecchio, the building that was once the proud seat of the Florentine republic, but which by the 1550s had been symbolically transformed into Cosimo's personal palace. The Palazzo della Signoria was renamed Palazzo Vecchio in the 1550s to distinguish it from Cosimo's subsequent residence, Palazzo Pitti, on the opposite side of the Arno.

The fresco portrays the 1433 exile of Cosimo *il Vecchio*, who is shown being guided by the personified figures of Prudence and Fortitude with the silhouette of Florence in the background. One hundred years earlier, this event was seen as the spark which led to the ultimate victory of republican ideals in Florence: Cosimo *il Vecchio* had been popularly viewed as a politician of integrity fighting against oligarchic authority, and the perceived injustice of his exile resulted in the expulsion of the oligarchic régime in 1434.

But in Vasari's hands and in the context of Cosimo I's private palace, this pivotal event no longer celebrates republican values. Rather, it has been transformed into a dynastic celebration of the Medici family and the virtues his autocratic namesake shares with the first Cosimo.

Illus. 3.2 Giorgio Vasari (with Marco Marchetti), *Filippo Brunelleschi and Lorenzo Ghiberti Present a Model of San Lorenzo to Cosimo il Vecchio.*

This fresco of about 1560 in the Room of Cosimo *il Vecchio* in the Palazzo Vecchio illustrates how the Medici in the period of the monarchy linked their rule to the patronage, beneficence, and taste of Cosimo (d. 1464). It portrays the two great architects with the model of the church that Cosimo rebuilt for his family, as it stands just behind the Medici palace. Brunelleschi had already worked on the church for Cosimo's father, Giovanni di Bicci de'Medici, creating the old sacristy as a burial chapel. On the right, workers are constructing the basilica, reflecting the industriousness of the Florentines and the benefits of Medici patronage. Behind Cosimo is the sculptor Donatello whose bronze *David* Cosimo commissioned in the late 1430s.

Illus. 3.3 Palazzo Medici-Riccardi, Florence.

Ten years after his triumphant return to Florence in 1434, Cosimo commissioned the architect Michelozzo Michelozzi (1396–72) to build a grand new palace, a home suitable to his wealth and position but sufficiently understated so as not to excite the jealously of the notoriously fractious and proud Florentine elite. The story is told how Cosimo first turned for his palace to the architectural genius Filippo Brunelleschi, who had constructed the dome of the cathedral as well as the family's old sacristy at San Lorenzo. But Cosimo rejected Brunelleschi's plans as too grand for a simple citizen. Looking at the huge mass of the palace that still stands on the Via Cavour (then the Via Larga), we can only imagine how grand Brunelleschi's project must have been!

In 1659 the Medici, now ruling as grand dukes of Tuscany and living in the Palazzo Pitti, sold the palace to Marchese Gabbriele Riccardi. The new owners made some substantial changes to reflect the baroque taste then fashionable, especially the addition of a sumptuous ballroom painted by Luca Giordano (1680).

Illus. 3.4 *Journey of the Magi,* **1459–61. Palazzo Medici Chapel, Florence.**

Benozzo Gozzoli's narrative tells the story of the Journey of the Magi, the three kings who followed the star to the birth of Christ. This theme was so very appropriate, as the oriental costumes of the kings would allow for rich decoration and exotic wardrobes and would permit the Medici to appear in exalted company. Also, the Medici were patrons of a religious confraternity devoted to the Magi, which held an actual procession through the city each year, so the association was personal and linked the images to Florence, as did the rather stylized landscape of Tuscany in the background.

There were three themes represented, all important to the Medici, Florence, the Church and Christendom. The first was the celebration of the 1439 Council of Florence, a conference held to unite the Eastern Orthodox Church with the Western Latin Church. There arrived in Florence the Byzantine emperor, John VII Paleologus (who appears as Balthazar in rich costume and a gold crown); the Patriarch Joseph of Constantinople (as the elderly Melchior, with a long white beard); and Caspar, the youngest, who is a stylized young (he was ten years old at the time) Lorenzo de'Medici in white and gold, who represents the future of the dynasty. Many portraits appear in the procession, including other prominent members of the Medici family, such as Piero the Gouty and Cosimo, Lorenzo's brother Giuliano (who was six); family friends, such as Marsilio Ficino; and Florentine patricians, Orthodox bishops, and courtiers. There is also a self-portrait of Benozzo himself, looking out of his painting, with his name on his hat, in case the viewer doesn't recognize him.

Benozzo is also alluding to the then Pope Pius II's 1459 call for a new crusade to recover the Holy Land and Constantinople from the Turks—to whom it had fallen in 1453. The procession looks like a crusade, composed of Christians from both Churches and carrying treasure to confront the Muslims.

Finally, the fresco cycle links the upstart, bourgeois Medici with the ruling dynasties of Italy. Portraits of Sigismondo Malatesta of Rimini and of the future young Duke Galeazzo Maria Sforza of Milan appear among other hereditary rulers who have now admitted the Medici as their equals.

**Illus. 3.5 Cosimo de'Medici's cell in the Monastery
of San Marco, painted by Fra Angelico.**

Cosimo de'Medici, *il Vecchio*, was a sincerely devout Christian. When he needed time for reflection or meditation he retired for a few days to his private cell in the monastery of San Marco. Because of his position as patron of the convent, Cosimo's cell—cell number 39 at the end of a very long corridor—had two rooms rather than the traditional single unit.

His cell was also exquisitely decorated. The Dominican monk Fra Angelico had been given the commission to fresco the walls of the monastery, and naturally he chose topics of particular interest to Cosimo when decorating his cell. The first room portrayed the martyrdom of Cosimo's patron saints, Saints Cosmas and Damian. Obviously, Cosimo was named for Saint Cosmas, but there was another, subtler connection: these two Arab martyrs were also physicians, or *medici* in Italian, a pun on the family name. In the inner, private cell, Angelico painted a moving image of the *Man of Sorrows* for Cosimo's contemplation. Above that was the narrative of the *Adoration of the Magi* (1441–42), again a subtle reference to the Medici. The family had a personal devotion to the Magi, whose confraternity they joined and whose annual procession through the city they supported.

As well as coming here for private devotion, Cosimo sometimes used his cell for appropriate diplomatic events. In fact, he even received Pope Eugene IV in these rooms during the pope's residence in the city for the Council of Florence.

CHAPTER 4
THE MEDICI DYNASTY

There was no clearer indication of how Cosimo had made the Medici the recognized leading family in Florence than in his succession. Supported by a substantial portion of the political classes, Cosimo's son Piero was acclaimed as his successor to lead the dominant political faction. However, although Piero had enjoyed a humanist education and was personally cultivated, he tragically lacked his father's skill in keeping the allegiance of the jealous and fractious Florentine patriciate.[1]

Besides not having his father's remarkable political skills, Piero had been raised more as a prince than as a republican magistrate and banker. And he was unwell, suffering from gout most of his life—hence his unfortunate nickname of Piero the Gouty (Piero *il Gottoso*). His illness restricted his mobility, which meant that his father's practice of posing as an average, if well-respected citizen was beyond Piero's capacity. He was not seen walking the streets among Florentines, and rich and powerful men were forced to attend on him in the Medici palace, a royal affectation that offended the sensibilities of the wealthy citizens who saw the Medici only as the first family among equals at best. Under Piero, the Medici lost their public face and with it much of their sometimes grudging acceptance.

Consequently, the five years of Piero's rule were not very successful, becoming ever more unstable as time passed. A major plot against the family was narrowly averted, and growing dissatisfaction promised only more conspiracies and political maneuvering.[2] So when Piero died in 1469, he was not greatly mourned as his father had been. Rather, the eyes of the entire city were now on his son and heir, the twenty-year-old Lorenzo, whose many talents and powerful personality would eventually identify him as *il Magnifico*, an honorific well deserved.[3]

Like Piero, Lorenzo had also been raised as a prince, with the most celebrated humanists of Florence as his tutors. His mother, Lucrezia Tornabuoni, came from a great Florentine patrician clan.[4] And Piero had arranged for Lorenzo to marry a daughter of the ancient Roman magnate family of the Orsini. In terms of social standing, this union brought another level of nobility to the Medici, tainted as they were by trade:

---

1. See Nicolai Rubinstein, *The Government of Florence under the Medici (1434 to 1494)*. Oxford: Clarendon Press, 1966.
2. For a contemporary record of the plot against Piero, see Luca Landucci, *A Florentine Diary from 1450 to 1516*, tr. Alicia de Rosen Jervis. London: J. M. Dent and Sons, 1927. p. 8.
3. Francis W. Kent, *Princely Citizen: Lorenzo de'Medici and Renaissance Florence*, ed. Carolyn James. Turnhout, Belgium: Brepols, 2013.
4. Maria Grazia Pernis and Laurie Schneider Adams, *Lucrezia Tornabuoni de'Medici and the Medici Family in the Fifteenth Century*. Bern and New York: Peter Lang, 2006.

in many parts of Europe, a feudal, warrior nobility still monopolized social prestige. Although it was less than a perfect match—Lorenzo and his wife had very little in common—it produced a large family of ten children to ensure Medici power in future generations.

Besides these princely aspects of his upbringing, Lorenzo also had practical training in diplomacy and statecraft occasioned by his having to represent his gouty father on embassies and in receiving important visitors.[5] But unlike his father, he enjoyed a great natural intelligence, a gift for poetry and for friendship, and a common touch that endeared him to the lower classes of the city. Naturally there were early mistakes in his rule. One error in particular was his failure to control a mercenary army that viciously sacked the Tuscan town of Volterra in 1472 after it had revolted against Florentine rule. Still, in Lorenzo's twenty-five years in power, that brutal attack was something of an anomaly.

Lorenzo de'Medici, il Magnifico

Like his grandfather, Cosimo *il Vecchio,* Lorenzo was one of the Italian Renaissance's greatest patrons of culture. He himself had an indisputable eye for excellence. He recognized the genius of Michelangelo, for example, when the artist was still a youth and invited him to live in the Medici palace. This was not mere hospitality: Lorenzo encouraged the young genius to study his antiquities under their curator, Bertoldo di Giovanni (1420–91), thus schooling him in the classical arts. The results are fully visible in Michelangelo's work before Lorenzo's death, especially the *Battle of the Centaurs* and the *Virgin of the Steps.*

The list of important painters, sculptors, and architects Lorenzo patronized, often on a lavish scale, is remarkable. Andrea Verrocchio, for example, was engaged in 1469 to decorate the burial places of Lorenzo's father, Piero de'Medici, and his uncle, Giovanni, in the family church of San Lorenzo. That same artist produced two bronzes for Lorenzo's villa at Careggi as well, quite likely the *Putto Holding a Fish* and most certainly the iconic *David.* Similarly, for the decoration of his Volterran villa of La Spedaletto, Lorenzo commissioned Sandro Botticelli, Filippino Lippi, Perugino, and Domenico Ghirlandaio to fresco the walls in 1487, although, tragically, those works have since been lost.

Lorenzo also had a personal, amateur interest in architecture and worked with his favorite builder, Giuliano Giamberti (da Sangallo), to create classically inspired buildings. In particular, in 1488 Giuliano was engaged to design a monastery near the gate of San Gallo in Florence. Lorenzo, who might have had an actual hand in the planning, noted that this talented man would thereafter be known as "da Sangallo"; that is, recognized from and forever associated with this building. So it was that Lorenzo provided the

---

5. Nicolai Rubinstein, "Lorenzo de'Medici: The Formation of his Statecraft," in Gian Carlo Garfagnini, ed., *Lorenzo de'Medici: Studi.* Florence: Olschki, 1992. Istituto nazionale di studi sul Rinascimento, Studi e testi, 27. pp. 41–66.

celebrated architect with the name by which he and his extended family of architects is known to this day. In addition, the wonderful villa at Poggio a Caiano was influenced by Lorenzo's interventions with that same Giuliano da Sangallo.

Furthermore, the growing coterie around Lorenzo—reminiscent, to be sure, of a princely court—and the respect accorded to him, together with the very real appreciation for his knowledge and taste, resulted in a great many indirect commissions. Patricians interested in acquiring paintings or sculpture or building a new palace or chapel would ask his advice, and he would very specifically nominate one of those artists whom he himself had patronized and who would bring fame to his city. Similarly, bodies such as guilds or confraternities would seek guidance from Lorenzo, and he would happily comply.

His style of patronage was quite different from his grandfather's inasmuch as his interest included a virtual obsession with small, exquisite objects of great rarity, often of ancient provenance and considerable intrinsic value. These cabinet pieces are still to be seen in part in the Gabinetto degli argenti in the Palazzo Pitti (Galleria Palatina). A few of these objects are incised with his name (LAVR. MED.), reflecting his sense of personal ownership. The acquisition of these *objets de vertu* required a complex network of agents and suppliers, men who could enrich themselves and Florence's patrimony by feeding Lorenzo's appetite for rarity and beauty.[6] Taking his patronage and collecting together, then, it is not incorrect to speak of a Laurentian age in Florence, informed not only by Lorenzo's great gifts but also by his commitment to humanism and the recovery of ancient models in art, building, and thought.[7]

He also saw the diplomatic power of art. For example, Lorenzo encouraged the young Leonardo da Vinci to leave Florence to work for Lodovico *il Moro*, the regent of Milan, in 1482. Lorenzo was somewhat wary of the staggeringly brilliant, charming, and handsome young Leonardo. After all, the painter had been denounced on two occasions for sodomy, one of which also implicated a relation of Lorenzo's mother's great patrician clan, the Tornabuoni. So by supporting Leonardo's translation to Milan, furnished with gifts for Lodovico, Lorenzo accomplished two goals. He not only ensured that Leonardo was safely away from the temptations of Florence but also earned the gratitude of Lodovico, an ally whom Lorenzo needed to keep close.[8]

In literature and thought, Lorenzo was again both a discerning patron and a capable poet himself. His range was remarkable: from moving religious poetry to obscene carnival songs.[9] His close friend and the tutor to his sons was Angelo Poliziano, one of

6. See Laurie Fusco and Gino Corti, *Lorenzo de'Medici, Collector of Antiquities: Collector and Antiquarian.* Cambridge: Cambridge University Press, 2006.

7. Levey, 1996. pp. 209–35.

8. Walter Isaacson, *Leonardo Da Vinci.* New York: Simon and Schuster, 2017. pp. 68–72, 91–96.

9. Lorenzo de'Medici, *The Complete Literary Works of Lorenzo de'Medici,* ed. and tr. Guido A. Guarino. New York: Italica Press, 2015. Italica Press Medieval & Renaissance Texts; Maurice Bowra, "Songs of Dance and Carnival," in Jacob, 1960. pp. 328–53.

the fifteenth century's greatest vernacular poets, famed for both modernizing poetry and singing the virtues and brilliance of the Medici. If Botticelli was the painter of Lorenzo—creating the portraits of his family and circle and celebrating his love of classical antiquity and humanist ideas—then Poliziano was his poet. Whether he was writing of the jousts occasioned by Lorenzo's marriage to Clarice Orsini[10] or translating Greek or Latin texts or writing his own Latin poem *Manto*, or merely serving as the tutor to Lorenzo's sons, Poliziano used the polished, elegant, and mature humanism of Lorenzo's age to celebrate his patron and the city he greatly loved.

But there were other poets as well, including the anticlerical wit, Luigi Pulci. Pulci's *Morgante Maggiore* hilariously burlesques the epic tradition to the delight of audiences even to this day. The poet Gentile Becchi (d. 1497), the bishop of Arezzo, had been Lorenzo's tutor but was also one of the most accomplished Latin stylists of the age, writing letters and poetry of great elegance. He was also an active member of the informal Platonic Academy, sharing his deep classical—and religious—knowledge with those, like Pulci,[11] who were less devout.

Cristoforo Landino (d. 1498), who held the chair of poetry and rhetoric at the Florentine university, was also the official state secretary in recognition of his Latinity. He had also studied Greek and authored a large number of commentaries on classical authors, such as Virgil and Pliny, and even Dante. He produced several volumes of poetry and delivered a famous lecture series on Petrarch, reinforcing the role of that early founder of humanism with the city of his ancestors. Landino, too, was an active participant in the Platonic Academy under Lorenzo.

In philosophy Lorenzo was drawn, like his grandfather Cosimo, to Neoplatonic ideas. He saw this Florentine version of Plato's and Plotinus's thought as an ennobling vision, one which could assist in an individual's rise up that ladder of perfection, ascending to the level of angels. The group that had formed around Marsilio Ficino at the Medici villa at Careggi after 1462 grew to include painters like Botticelli and Michelangelo, poets like Poliziano, and philosophers such as Gentile de'Becchi and Cristoforo Landino.

Finally, there was the enigmatic character of Giovanni Pico, count of Mirandola. Pico had passed the rule of his tiny principality near Modena to others in his youth so that he could devote himself to philosophy and writing. Called to Florence by Lorenzo, the young man proved to be a polymath, learning not only Latin and Greek but also Hebrew, Arabic, Chaldean, and Aramaic. He believed in the Unity of Truth, holding that all religions and philosophies participate in some aspects of divine truth, so by knowing

---

10. The best translation of *Le Stanze per la giostra* is Angelo Poliziano, *The Stanze of Angelo Poliziano*, tr. David L. Quint. Philadelphia: Penn State University Press, 2005.

11. It is significant that Pulci's *Morgante Maggiore* was specifically mentioned as a book to be burned by followers of Savonarola during the Burning of the Vanities during carnival in 1497. See Landucci, 1927. p. 130.

as much as possible, men on earth could ascend that Platonic ladder and learn to avoid mundane contagion.

These ideas developed most perfectly in Pico's *Oration on the Dignity of Man*, a work that stressed the free will of men to determine where on that continuum between the lowest and highest forms of existence they would reside.[12] This was the Platonic Academy, and Lorenzo gave it vitality and patronage and was himself an active participant in its discussions, celebrating the birthday of Plato each seventh of November as a great feast day.

Although an important contribution to Western thought, the Neoplatonism of Laurentian Florence would later have disturbing implications. This highly cerebral and abstruse system of philosophy divorced the elite around the Medici from those with more traditional views. The Platonic Academy became a kind of metaphor for the distancing of the circle of Lorenzo from his fellow citizens, those hard-headed businessmen, conventional Christians, or simple workers who had little interest in or understanding of the Unity of Truth. This was a situation on which the enemies of the Medici would later capitalize.[13]

The Pazzi Conspiracy

Thus, Lorenzo's patronage of culture and his wide popularity in Florence hid somewhat the changing situation in the city and in Italy as a whole. Lorenzo, despite his great gifts—or perhaps because of them—had no interest whatsoever in the practical affairs of the Medici family bank, leaving its operation to trusted but often incompetent or corrupt agents: indeed, the bank almost failed during his time.[14] This consequent loss of income drove Lorenzo to bad decisions, some of which would have disastrous consequences.

For example, while his grandfather Cosimo had used the Medici family fortune to support the republic, Lorenzo, in a selfish reversal, used money from the state dowry fund (*Monte delle doti*) to subsidize his own projects and even style of life. He also retroactively changed a law of inheritance so that the ancient and rich Pazzi family—antagonists of his regime—would not benefit from additional wealth. This provided another of the many grudges the Pazzi and a few other old oligarchic families continued to hold against the Medici. As a result, once Lorenzo had antagonized Pope Sixtus IV della

12. Giovanni Pico della Mirandola, *Oration on the Dignity of Man: A New Translation and Commentary*, eds. Francesco Borghesi, Michael Papio, and Massimo Riva. Cambridge: Cambridge University Press, 2012.

13. Celenza, 2018. pp. 264–87; 313–71.

14. Raymond De Roover, *The Medici Bank: Its Organization, Management, Operations, and Decline*. Whitefish, MT: Literary Licensing, 2011.

Rovere, a conspiracy was hatched not simply to overthrow the Medici but to murder them.[15]

Pope Sixtus IV (1471–84) was in many ways a truly great successor to St. Peter. He was responsible for the building and decoration of the Sistine Chapel, whose vault would later—under his nephew, Julius II—be painted by Michelangelo. He built the first bridge over the Tiber since antiquity (Ponte Sisto), re-founded the Vatican Library, and instituted what would become the Capitoline Museum, the first public museum since antiquity.

However, Sixtus IV was also obsessed with his della Rovere and Riario relations. This crime of papal nepotism was not unique to Sixtus, but he carried it to dangerous new levels. He gave his often-worthless nephews the richest sees in the Church, including the archbishopric of Florence, as well as cardinals' hats. And, he wanted to establish his secular nephews as princes, ruling small territories in the States of the Church.

It was Sixtus's desire to make his nephew Girolamo Riario the ruler of the town of Imola that began the Pazzi Conspiracy against the Medici in earnest. Imola was a strategic town commanding the routes of Florentine trade and one not far from the frontiers of the Florentine state. When asked, Lorenzo refused to lend the money necessary for Riario and the pope to capture the town, despite the traditional role of the Medici bank in papal fiscal policy. Angered, Pope Sixtus transferred the papal accounts to the Pazzi bank, well aware that they were enemies of the Medici. So, the plot was hatched in the early spring of 1478 to rid the city entirely of Lorenzo's faction.

The conspiracy required that both Lorenzo and his younger brother, Giuliano, be present together, unarmed, and unsuspecting. The assassination was planned for Holy Friday in the cathedral of Florence during mass, with the bell signaling the Elevation of the Host as the cue to strike. When informed of these sacrilegious details, the professional assassin engaged to strike Lorenzo withdrew, despite the fact that Pope Sixtus had given absolution in advance should anything violent occur. His place was taken by an amateur—a mere priest. The result was that the Pazzi conspirators succeeded only in murdering Giuliano. Lorenzo was wounded, but not mortally, and brought into the sacristy by his companions for his protection.

Undaunted, the Pazzi and their followers then rode through the street shouting *libertà—liberty!*—while a delegation of leading conspirators went to the Palazzo della Signoria to demand the resignation of Medici supporters. The delegation consisted not only of members of the old oligarchic families but also the archbishop of Pisa, another enemy of Lorenzo's. The group demanded to be admitted to the palace to address the priors, and admitted they were—but the door was bolted behind them to lock them in.

---

15. Lauro Martines, *April Blood: Florence and the Plot Against the Medici.* Oxford: Oxford University Press, 2004, which remains the best account of the conspiracy; Harold Acton, *The Pazzi Conspiracy: The Plot Against the Medici.* New York: Thames and Hudson, 1979.

Meanwhile, as Pazzi supporters rode through the city with their shouts of *liberty*, they were rebuffed with calls of *palle*, the rallying cry of the Medici faction (literally, "balls," referring to the six orbs on the Medici coat of arms). Once the officials in the Palazzo della Signoria realized what had happened—that Giuliano was dead and Lorenzo's fate unknown—they tied ropes around the necks of the Pazzi delegation and threw them from the windows, including even the archbishop of Pisa.

Seeing that the plot had badly miscarried, the Pazzi supporters immediately fled the city, but many were captured and killed, their palaces burned, and their property looted. The emergence of Lorenzo and his friends from the cathedral sacristy gave welcome reassurance to Florentine citizens that the Medici would continue to rule, though there was great sadness over the death of Giuliano, who had been one of the most popular young men in the city. He was handsome, raffish, charming, and exuberant, an antidote to Lorenzo's dignified reserve. But, his place in history was assured. Although he was unaware of it at the time of his murder, one of his mistresses was carrying his child. This was the boy who would grow up to be elected Pope Clement VII in 1523.[16]

The Consequences of Failure

The failure of the plot infuriated Sixtus IV. On the pretext that the Florentines had killed an archbishop and hence attacked the inviolability of the hierarchy of the Church, the pope demanded that his vassal, the king of Naples, gather an army to attack Florence and its territory. King Ferrante of Naples had no real animosity toward Lorenzo. But because he was illegitimate and required at least the tacit acceptance of the papacy for his rule, King Ferrante had no choice but to obey. Florence was hardly prepared for war in 1478, and the papal army quickly and brutally reached the territories of the city.

The war was not against Florence, according to the pope. Rather, he declared that it was against Lorenzo and the Medici clan, so he demanded that Lorenzo be handed over to the Church for judgment. But the Florentines adamantly refused. If there was ever need for proof of how deeply the Medici were embedded in Florentine government and society and the immense popularity of Lorenzo, this decision on the part of the entire city to protect him against the pope is evidence undeniable.

The War of the Pazzi Conspiracy lasted until 1480 and ended only through another heroic act and personal intervention of Lorenzo de'Medici. In the face of the desperate situation in the city, starving and cut off from its trade, Lorenzo secretly sailed to Naples, the very capital of the kingdom ravaging his territory. His intention was to convince King Ferrante that it was not in the king's interest to see the papacy and the Riario family triumphant.

---

16. There is a contemporary account of the events of the Pazzi Conspiracy by Angelo Poliziano, *The Pazzi Conspiracy* (*Pactianae coniurationis commentarium*), tr. Elizabeth Welles, in Kohl and Witt, 1978. pp. 305–22.

It is easy to overdramatize this moment of personal diplomacy. Lorenzo was a master diplomat, with significant experience navigating the dangerous world of Italian politics. In this case, he had prudently sent signals of his intentions prior to embarking, and Ferrante had even sent a ship for him. Regardless, it was a gamble, because with Lorenzo out of the city, it would have been easier for his internal enemies to disrupt or overthrow his faction, especially given the suffering of the city as a result of the war. Lorenzo stayed with the king for many weeks arguing his case until he won over Ferrante, convincing him to abandon the pope's war against Florence. Lorenzo's gamble had worked. He and Florence were saved.

The separate peace between Florence and Naples again enraged the pope, but there was now little he could do. In a second feat of diplomacy, Lorenzo smoothed relations with Sixtus by allowing, in 1480, the most talented of his Tuscan painters to go to Rome to decorate the pope's new Sistine chapel. Ghirlandaio, Botticelli, and Cosimo Rosselli all traveled to the holy city, together with Pietro Perugino from Umbria. In little over a year the walls of that new and iconic papal chapel were frescoed with paintings that mollified the pope at that time and astonish us to this day.

In many ways Lorenzo and the Medici emerged more powerful in the city as a result of the Pazzi Conspiracy. Nevertheless, those events also changed the situation both for Florence and for the Medici.

Lorenzo's Retreat

Lorenzo had greatly loved his brother, and Giuliano's death resulted in an element of sadness that shadowed Lorenzo until his death. The conspiracy had happened with no advance warning, and a Medici had been murdered in the cathedral. Now wary, Lorenzo began to travel through the city with an armed retinue, completely changing the pacific and collegial nature of the Medici hegemony. Moreover, he began acting more like a prince, in part occasioned by the financial damage caused by the war and in part because he realized that it might have been his openness and republican gestures that had allowed the Pazzi to work their plot.

To ensure Medici control in the Signoria, Lorenzo made a major change in the constitution. He instituted a powerful council that assumed the role of the older councils—the Council of Seventy. This body was to have wide legislative power, and its initial membership was nominated by Lorenzo. Any vacancies would be filled by the Council itself. The Medici, then, were transforming themselves from republican factional leaders to princes in all but name.

Lorenzo also went to some lengths to extend and solidify his family's power and future outside of Florence as well as within. His eldest son, Piero, a rash young man lacking in judgment, was still recognized as Lorenzo's heir. He was married to a relation of his Orsini mother to cement the connection with the old military nobility of Rome.

His second son, Giovanni, was put in the Church, with an appointment as a cardinal at the uncanonical age of seventeen. The intention was first to bring Medici influence into the center of the Church in Rome and second to prepare the rich and cultivated boy for the possibility of one day becoming pope. This dream was realized as Giovanni de'Medici was elected in 1513 as Pope Leo X, at the unheard-of age of thirty-seven.

Lorenzo even sacrificed one of his daughters, marrying her to Franceschetto, a son of the fabulously wealthy Pope Innocent VIII Cybo. Franceschetto was well known as a loutish wastrel. But the diplomatic connection with the Cybo pope was too important to allow paternal affection to interfere: Lorenzo had to consider the future of his entire dynasty and his city. This was a particularly significant opportunity because Innocent was not very interested in the administration of the Church. Consequently, power and access to much wealth devolved to Florentine cardinals and agents who were recommended to the Holy See by the Medici, now connected by marriage to the pope.

The last years of Lorenzo's life were not as glorious and splendid as those of his youth. Certainly, Botticelli continued to paint allegories of the Medici's success, such as *Pallas and the Centaur,* representing the events of the Pazzi Conspiracy. Poliziano continued to write poetry and serve Lorenzo. The Platonic Academy still met. And this was the period in which the young Michelangelo was patronized by Lorenzo. However, the environment in Florence and indeed in all of Italy was growing increasingly unstable.

The Death of Lorenzo il Magnifico

In the city a fiery Dominican monk, Girolamo Savonarola, the prior of San Marco, was preaching to huge crowds on the coming Apocalypse. Not only poorer citizens were attracted to his gloomy message and powerful sermons, but also some wealthy patricians found spiritual renewal in his presence. Intellectuals, such as Botticelli and Pico della Mirandola, were converted, with Pico even giving away his fortune and undertaking holy orders as a Dominican. Still others saw in Savonarola a useful tool to use against the Medici hegemony.

The situation in Italy and Europe was also changing, with a son of Francesco Sforza, Lodovico *il Moro,* assuming rule of Milan after the assassination of his brother, the duke. The end of the Hundred Years War in northern Europe allowed the cloth industry in the Low Countries to rebound and challenge Florentine domination of the market. New banking houses were able to concentrate capital and reap profits previously accessible only to the Italians. And, with the end of the war, the restless and ambitious power of the kingdom of France began to posture on the European stage, especially in Italy where the young Charles VIII had dynastic claims on Naples.

It was under these clouds of instability and danger that Lorenzo de'Medici, the Magnificent, died in 1492 at the young age of forty-three. With his death and the accession of his limited son, Piero, not only Medici but also Italian fortunes as a whole began to decline. The age of Lorenzo de'Medici had shown the potential of humanist princi-ples of liberty and the deeply held belief in Florentine exceptionalism. Certainly, the Medici regime had elements of tyranny, and these became more prominent after 1480. However, to most citizens of the city living under Lorenzo, it appeared that genius and freedom seemed to operate in ways unknown in other Italian states.

It may have been an illusion, but illusions have the power to inspire. And the efflo-rescence of culture, the cult of the individual, and the belief in human dignity that the years of Lorenzo's ascendancy witnessed continue to excite the imagination and exalt the human spirit.

Illus. 4.1 Andrea Verrocchio (?), Terracotta Bust of Lorenzo de'Medici, *il Magnifico*. Fifteenth- or sixteenth-century copy of the wax original, National Gallery of Art, Washington, DC.

This lifelike terracotta bust of Lorenzo de'Medici, *il Magnifico*, was made from a model produced by Andrea Verrocchio in 1478. The purpose of the original was to serve as the exemplar for wax votive images distributed throughout the city to Medici supporters in thanks for his surviving the Pazzi Conspiracy of Easter 1478. The original life-size wax image made by Verrocchio was created to be the center of a public celebration of thanksgiving; it was even dressed in the blood-stained clothes that Lorenzo was wearing when attacked in the cathedral, an attack that took the life of his younger brother, Giuliano.

This portrait bust is probably the closest surviving representation of the real Lorenzo de'Medici. Its detail is remarkable, including the five o'clock shadow of a beard and an unflattering, realistic reproduction of his prominent nose. It also carries, like all Medici images, an element of propaganda. Lorenzo is dressed in the sober but fine clothes of a Florentine patrician with nothing that even suggests that he claimed to be anything more. The Pazzi had formed their conspiracy with the Riario nephew of Pope Sixtus IV out of jealousy. The sculpture indicates that the plot was without justification and consequently an act of vicious personal treachery rather than an attempt to assassinate a tyrant.

Illus. 4.2 Sandro Botticelli, *Pallas and the Centaur*, ca. 1482. Uffizi, Florence.

This painting by Botticelli likely dates from 1482–83. Although several interpretations have been offered for its mythological and iconographical meaning, it is almost certainly an allegory of the events of the Pazzi Conspiracy and the subsequent war with the papacy and Naples that ensued (1478–80). It consequently represents another example of Medici patronage of great art as personal and dynastic propaganda.

The figure on the right represents Pallas Athena (Minerva in the Roman pantheon), goddess of wisdom, carrying a pike indicating a willingness to fight if required. Her dress links the figure directly to Lorenzo, as it is embroidered with the three intertwined rings, one of his personal *imprese*, or symbols. The laurel that encircles her represents the crown of victory as well as a pun on Lorenzo's given name, giving it double significance. She has captured and tamed the Centaur, shown by her grasping the hair of this half-man half-horse mythological creature which represents the dual nature of man: capable of reason but often driven by animal instincts. The expression on the Centaur is that of submission, reinforced by his removing one hand from his bow. The ruined classical structure behind him makes reference to the traditional symbol for the advent of a new dispensation. Finally, the composition which creates a circular "window" between the two figures focuses on a ship at sea: this was the ship sent by Ferrante of Naples to take Lorenzo to his capital to negotiate an end to the hostilities that resulted from the failed attempt by the Pazzi and the Riario to murder Lorenzo.

Illus. 4.3 Cosimo Rosselli (1439–1507), Detail of *The Procession of the Miracle of the Chalice*, 1481–86. Church of Sant'Ambrogio (Saint Ambrose), Florence.

In Renaissance Florence the past and present and the miraculous and the human merge. This fresco by Cosimo Rosselli (1439–1507) in the Chapel of the Miracle of the Chalice in the church of Sant'Ambrogio (Saint Ambrose), Florence, is a detail of a larger narrative of a procession of 1340 throughout the city. In 1230 the priest of this ancient church failed to wipe the chalice of remains of wine left after the eucharist. The next morning he found it full of blood. As a result of this miracle reinforcing the sacrament and real presence, the chalice was revered. In 1340 there was a religious procession carrying the chalice to ask for an end to a plague then ravaging the city: the plague duly subsided.

    Rosselli was a close friend of Benozzo Gozzoli and a contemporary of Botticelli and Ghirlandaio and consequently close to the center of Florentine culture under the Medici. He used the opportunity offered by this commission to populate the procession with his contemporaries. Besides a self-portrait, Rosselli depicts three members of the intellectual "court" around Lorenzo de'Medici. Shown here is Angelo Poliziano at the right. Poliziano was the brilliant poet and classicist who was tutor to the sons of Lorenzo. In the center is the handsome polymath Count Giovanni Pico della Mirandola, a friend of Lorenzo's and a leading member of the Platonic Academy, like his intimate friend, Poliziano. The figure on the left is not easily identified. One suggestion is Leon Battista Alberti, the architectural and artistic theorist, but it might also be a movement through time once again, with the representation of Marsilio Ficino, the founder of the Platonic Academy and translator of Plato. At the time the fresco was painted, Ficino was an old man, but his evergreen presence in the company of his two youthful associates would be appropriate and would form a link between the patronage of Cosimo de'Medici with his grandson, Lorenzo.

The significance of the fresco could again relate to Lorenzo's diplomacy in ending the suffering caused by the War of the Pazzi Conspiracy (1478–80), just as the chalice had ended the plague.

CHAPTER 5

THE CHALLENGE OF SAVONAROLA

B efore we enter into a discussion of the period in Florence dominated by the Dominican monk Girolamo Savonarola, we need to investigate how his extraordinary rise to power happened: how an apocalyptic, ascetic preacher from Ferrara—he was not even Florentine—came to power in the city that had produced the highest expressions of Renaissance culture and thought and had been managed by the House of Medici for sixty years. So, let's return to the moment of Lorenzo the Magnificent's death on April 8, 1492.

Piero de' Medici il Sfortunato

It is hard to imagine two personalities more distant than those of Lorenzo and his eldest son, Piero, who was the same age as his father had been—twenty—when he was thrust into power. Despite a superb humanist education under the leading lights of the Florentine cultural aristocracy, Piero was neither intellectually gifted, curious, nor astute. His earlier youth was characterized by brawling and public skirmishes that his family cleverly—and at some expense—covered up in hopes that he would mature. It is a testament to his father's honesty and insight that he once described his eldest son and heir as a fool.

It was, perhaps, in part because of his lack of natural ability and his sense of being excluded from the esoteric culture around his father that Piero grew to be a surly, distrustful braggart. Nevertheless, despite the general recognition of his personality and abilities, there was never any question but that he would succeed Lorenzo. If the Medici were to sustain what really amounts to a republican political dynasty in control of Florence, the heir had to be Piero: there was no one else. Consequently, on Lorenzo's death a delegation of *Palleschi*—that is, members of the Medici faction—went to Piero and had him confirmed in his father's offices and dignities.

It did not take long before Piero's weaknesses and limitations became undeniable, first to his faction, then to the Signoria, and finally to the population at large. His paranoia resulted in his believing that anyone who opposed or even questioned his authority or policies was a conspirator. He drew his circle of advisors ever smaller and, whenever possible, avoided employing members of the great families who enjoyed a power base of their own. Rather, Piero preferred to surround himself with those who depended on his largesse and were thereby bound to him. Consequently, men from minor guilds or, even more inappropriately, members of Piero's own household, were given important positions or dignities at the expense of those substantial citizens and hitherto loyal Medici supporters who believed such favors belonged to them.

In a display of impolitic arrogance, Piero also required that ranking officials of the state come to his private palace on the Via Larga rather than meet with them at the Palazzo della Signoria. His haughty disregard for others grew to the point of alienating even members of his own family. Altogether, there was a growing sense that Piero not only saw himself as an uncrowned prince but intended to establish a monarchical regime, a concept that was anathema to Florentine republican political culture.

These problems were all magnified by the growing crisis of 1493–94. Before the end of 1493 it was becoming increasingly evident that the king of France, Charles VIII, intended to invade Italy to claim the crown of Naples. In this he was encouraged by the regent of Milan, Lodovico Sforza, *il Moro*. Despite Florence's traditional friendship with France and its now long-standing diplomatic ties to Milan, Piero temporized, failing to offer either support or resistance to the prospect of a French invasion. This inaction was perhaps the worst possible option for Florence, as Tuscany was obviously on the route of the French army as it marched toward Naples and because it distanced the Medici from the assured support of Milan.[1]

The invasion was launched in 1494, and by the fall the enormous French army was at the borders of Florentine territory. Only then did Piero panic. Attempting to rehearse the brilliant diplomacy of his father during the War of the Pazzi Conspiracy some fourteen years earlier, Piero went privately, with just a few retainers, to the camp of Charles VIII. In no mood to honor or even humor Piero and Florence, the French king made extraordinary demands: in return for not laying waste to Florence and the surrounding countryside, Charles demanded a large subsidy, control of the perimeter fortresses around Tuscany, and the ports of Pisa and Livorno. Finally, in the ultimate humiliation, Charles demanded that he and his army be permitted to enter Florence in effect as conquerors and leave a garrison in the city. In return all Piero received was the promise of an alliance and support for his dynasty. Fool and coward that he was, he capitulated totally.[2]

When the Signoria, the political elite, and the general population learned of this deal, there was fury in the city. Piero had not received any authority from the republican Signoria to negotiate on the city's behalf. His ceding of Florence's defenses was disastrous. Even more crushing was the loss of Pisa. Pisa had only been acquired at the beginning of the century after years of conflict. It was Florence's sole access to the sea and lucrative maritime trade, and so its loss was a blow both to commerce and civic pride. It was totally understandable, then, that on his return to Florence on the eighth of November 1494, Piero's entourage was greeted by showers of mud and shouts of revolt.

---

1. For a detailed discussion of the political and military events, see Michael Mallett and Christine Shaw, *The Italian Wars, 1494–1559: War, State and Society in Early Modern Europe*. New York: Pearson, 2012. pp. 22–25.
2. Luca Landucci describes Piero's political and diplomatic failures and the Medici's expulsion from Florence in his diary. See Landucci, 1927. pp. 58–64.

The Rise of Savonarola

One of the reasons that the wider population of Florence had so turned against the Medici was the growing influence of Savonarola.[3] There is no doubt but that Savonarola had a remarkable intelligence and an ascetic's desire to forsake all of the sins of the flesh. As a youth, he had entered a Dominican monastery in Bologna, stating in a letter to his father that he wanted to escape the sinfulness of the world and become a "knight of Christ." He later proved himself a fine scholar when he entered the University of Bologna where he studied theology, logic, and philosophy. After only one year he was deemed worthy of ordination and became a priest.

Despite his rapid rise, Savonarola was always uncompromising in his vituperative condemnation of what he saw as the sins and abuses in the Church. As a result, he found himself in conflict with the hierarchy of the Dominicans, including his superior who was to become the General of the Order. He was consequently sent to Florence, to the convent of San Marco, in 1482 as a teacher of novices. But this was the period of Lorenzo de'Medici's ascendency and the apogee of humanist culture in the city. Savonarola's Ferrarese accent, gloomy predictions, and ineffectual sermons found little traction.

He left Florence and served as an itinerant preacher. His sermons were becoming ever more apocalyptic, blending the Italian prophetic tradition with his own view of the sinfulness of mankind and the Church, sins for which he declared God would exact exemplary and terrible punishment. Some of these prophecies arose from the twelfth-century Calabrian abbot Joachim of Fiore (d. 1202) whose reading of the Book of Revelation provided millenarian insight into divine intentions and methods. Savonarola believed that the Joachimite third order—that of the Holy Ghost—was at hand. This was the period in which the Church would be cleansed by the righteous and a time of Christian peace and brotherhood would descend. And it seems that Savonarola felt called upon to be part of that process.[4]

It might appear incongruous that these apocalyptic messages found fertile soil in Florence in 1490 during the last years of Lorenzo's life or that Savonarola returned to the city at all, given his less than successful earlier residence at San Marco. But in some ways Florence—and Italy—had changed, and in others Florence was receptive to the friar's message.

---

3. For the career and influence of Savonarola, see Lauro Martines, *Fire in the City: Savonarola and the Struggle for the Soul of Renaissance Florence.* Oxford and New York: Oxford University Press, 2007; Donald Weinstein, *Savonarola: The Rise and Fall of a Renaissance Prophet.* New Haven: Yale University Press, 2011; and by the same author the still useful, *Savonarola and Florence: Prophecy and Patriotism in the Renaissance.* Princeton: Princeton University Press, 1970; and Lorenzo Polizzotto, *The Elect Nation: the Savonarolan Movement in Florence, 1494–1545.* Oxford: Clarendon Press, 1994.
4. For the kinds of mystical prophecies with political implications circulating in Florence, see S. Baldassari and A. Saiber, eds., *Images of Quattrocento Florence.* New Haven: Yale University Press, 2000. pp. 236–37.

It was Lorenzo's close friend, the philosopher and polymath Count Giovanni Pico della Mirandola, who encouraged him to appoint Savonarola prior of San Marco, despite the reticence of the Dominicans. At the time, Pico was experiencing something of a spiritual conversion. He believed that Savonarola could be a salutary voice in Florence, and perhaps in particular for Lorenzo who had become somewhat morose because of illness and dismay at the character of his son and heir. Moreover, Florence had enjoyed a very long tradition of exceptionalism. Leonardo Bruni, for example, had thought it to be the new Rome or Athens, mandated to be a beacon of republican freedom for all Italy and obliged to save the freedom of its citizens. It was therefore not a great leap to see Florence as the New Jerusalem, an example of the ideal godly community with the responsibility of cleansing the Church and practicing Christian virtue, thus fulfilling the Joachimite prophecy.

Furthermore, the high culture of Laurentian Florence, with its elaborate symbols, Neoplatonic references, and classical learning, was not something many citizens of any social class could acquire or even appreciate. True, members of the political elite were often trained in the classical humanism of the fifteenth century with knowledge of ancient texts and good Latin style and perhaps some Greek. But the majority were also merchants, hard-headed guildsmen whose first responsibility was to build the family's wealth and reputation through success in business and political office.

Beneath them, the mass of disenfranchised citizens and even the great majority of lesser guildsmen were not troubled by the finer points of humanism. On the contrary, they were concerned with more practical issues like how to earn enough to allow them to lead respectable lives or even just survive in a city with a cyclical economy and expensive food and rents. They were traditional, devout Christians whose own hopes for the future were invested in the next world rather than this. They were told by their own preachers, especially the radical Franciscans (*Fraticelli*), that they would merit heaven because of their poverty and suffering while their bosses and the rich in general would have great difficulty entering Paradise. These elite, they were told, were more likely to be consigned to the fires of hell as punishment for their vanity, arrogance, and lack of charity than to get past St. Peter at the gates to heaven.[5]

So Savonarola's message fell on receptive ears, and this attraction grew as Lorenzo's life drew to a close. The Dominican attacked many of the fundamental aspects of Laurentian civilization: love of the pagan classics, human reason and agency, and secular art and culture. He also appealed to many of those who were alienated from the dominant ideas of the Platonic Academy and the sophisticated world of late fifteenth-century humanism. The poor and women, excluded from all aspects of government and marginalized by society, were especially sensitive to the friar's sermons. His use of the prophetic tradition

---

5. Savonarola stated constantly that faith was the only solution to the problems of humanity and that concern for this world would lead to God's anger. See Girolamo Savonarola, *The Triumph of the Cross*, ed. and tr. John Proctor. London: Sands and Company, 1901. pp. 51–54.

intersected brilliantly in both their popular intellectual heritage and their hope for the future. In addition, greater guildsmen and those hostile to the Medici hegemony saw an instrument that could be used to effect a rupture between the Medici and the city they had controlled for more than half a century.

Savonarola's sermons were so heavily attended that he had to move from San Marco to the cathedral to accommodate the faithful. Despite attempts to co-opt his popularity, the Dominican remained resolutely in opposition to the Medici and Florentine culture and the established hierarchy of the Church. Nevertheless, as Lorenzo lay dying he still summoned Savonarola to deliver extreme unction, following a tradition that these last rites be performed by the prior of San Marco. There are two versions of what occurred, both from otherwise reliable sources. In one, Savonarola acted like any priest at the deathbed of a Christian; in the other he heard confession but followed this by asking whether all of the sins of Lorenzo had been confessed, including that of having stolen the liberty of his city. In this version—which is largely apocryphal and intended as propaganda—Lorenzo did not answer but turned his face to the wall and was not granted absolution.[6]

The manifold failures of Lorenzo's son Piero increased the reputation and authority of Savonarola after 1492, the year of Lorenzo's death. In this Savonarola was strongly aided by the content of his sermons, which had been transformed into prophecies. He said that a scourge would be sent to chastise the Church and Italy to begin the process that would lead to the second coming of Christ, ideas very much in the Joachimite tradition. This would be a new Cyrus, a new Charlemagne who would cleanse Italy and then lead a crusade to liberate the Holy Land from the Muslims. Of course, that scourge would be the French king Charles VIII who harbored some of these fantasies himself.[7]

The success of these prophetic sermons attracted a broader audience than those left outside the culture, society, and simple faith of Laurentian Florence. Anti-Medicean patricians and politicians began to see Savonarola as the vehicle by which they might dislodge the Medici from power, especially given the weakness and incapacity of Piero. Open discussion of the expulsion of the Medici was heard throughout the city, advocated by all classes, including those in the Palazzo della Signoria. With Savonarola's moral authority, this might be more easily accomplished.

---

6. Maurice Rowdon, *Lorenzo the Magnificent*. Chicago: Regnery, 1974. pp. 216–20.

7. As early as December 1494 Savonarola was preaching against vice and the moral regeneration of Florence, with oblique references to the need to fill the political vacuum left by the Medici with virtue and godliness. See Girolamo Savonarola, "Aggeus [Haggai, a prophetic book of Hebrew and Christian texts] Sermon," December 14, 1494, in Girolamo Savonarola, *Selected Writings of Girolamo Savonarola on Religion and Politics, 1490–1498*, ed. and tr. A. Borelli and M. Passaro. New Haven: Yale University Press, 2006. pp. 157–58.

The Expulsion of Piero de'Medici

Within days after Piero's disastrous return from negotiating privately with Charles VIII, the Medici were expelled from Florence. Piero, his family, and servants were treated with open hostility that soon degenerated into violence which saw the death of at least one member of the family. Recognizing that he had no support in the city and no immediate hope of military intervention to keep him in his position, he fled Florence like a coward, followed by the rest of his immediate family. The Palazzo Medici, so beautifully filled with treasures by Cosimo, Piero the Gouty, and Lorenzo, was looted, with its contents stolen or destroyed. A price was put on Piero's head and on that of Giovanni as well, despite its red hat: if caught the Medici brothers were to be returned dead or alive. The regime of Medici rule begun by Cosimo *il Vecchio* sixty years before was now over.[8]

Although a great many of the political class had turned against Piero after his capitulation to Charles VIII, there were temporizers, men whose careers depended on Medici patronage or who were not willing to enter into formal opposition until it was absolutely clear that Piero would not return. Moreover, the anti-Medicean opposition was hardly a singular faction. There were those who wanted a return to a restricted government of great patrician clans as during the oligarchy: *governo stretto*. On the other hand, there were those who wanted a broadly based republic with as much representation as possible for the lesser guildsmen and others who had been excluded from power: *governo largo*. Both factions, however, saw the need for action to ensure that Piero would not prevail and to deal with the crisis of a French army outside the city demanding a triumphal entry into Florence, an army led by a king who had given his word to support Medici rule.

In mid-November, another delegation was sent to Charles in an attempt to undo the damage that Piero had wrought. Among the leaders of the delegation was Savonarola, who used the opportunity to praise Charles as the New Cyrus who was a divine agent in the regeneration of the Church and the faith, as well as the scourge of sin, luxury, and idolatry in Italy. Although Charles responded well to this flattery, he was still intent on maintaining his control of Pisa and the Tuscan fortresses; and he still expected a triumphal entry. This humiliation could not be avoided. Hopeful that the French would not occupy their city, the citizens decorated it with French symbols and the royal arms. The king was celebrated with pageants, installations, and even a Latin oration at the cathedral by Marsilio Ficino. Nevertheless, the French advance party had already begun to mark houses and spaces for billeting soldiers, while Charles himself took up residence in the now-empty Medici Palace.

No occupying army is truly welcomed by its hosts, and this was true in Florence where brawls developed, despite the initial show of friendship. Moreover, Charles demanded the return of Piero, whose rule he had promised to protect. Naturally, the

---

8. For an eyewitness description of the expulsion of the Medici, see Landucci, 1927. pp. 60–72.

Florentines refused to even consider this demand. This led to the famous exchange between the French king and the patrician Piero Capponi in which an exasperated Charles said all he had to do was blow upon his trumpets to get his way, to which Capponi replied that if the trumpets sounded, the Florentines would ring their bells, meaning that the city would fight.

Ultimately, subduing Florence was not to the advantage of the French, as their prize was Naples. So, Savonarola and a delegation worked out a deal with Charles. The king promised to recognize Florence as a French ally and thus not to garrison the city. He also changed from "demand" to "advice" his proposal that the Medici be restored to power. However, the price of the concessions was considerable. The French would receive a huge subsidy (120,000 florins) and keep military control of the perimeter fortresses, despite Charles having officially recognized Florentine sovereignty over these sites. Moreover, Charles refused to assist in the recovery of Pisa, which had reasserted its independence following Piero's craven capitulation. So, it was under these conditions that on November 28, 1494, Charles and his army left Florentine territory.

Savonarola had by then established his position as a spokesman for Florence and a leading voice in the city. He had, however, no status, because as a priest and a foreigner he could not hold public office. Indeed, he was not even permitted to engage in political action because of these constraints. But the times were extreme. The Medici instruments of control, the councils dominated by the *Palleschi*, were abolished, and there seemed to be a movement toward a broadly based republican regime, a position supported by Savonarola.[9] The power vacuum that emerged had to be filled and quickly, given the danger of the times and the divisions in the city.[10]

---

9. Girolamo Savonarola, "A Treatise on Florentine Government," in Baldassari and Saiber, eds., 2000. pp. 252–65.
10. Nicolai Rubinstein, "Politics and Constitution in Florence at the End of the Fifteenth Century," in Jacob, 1960. pp. 148–83.

Illus. 5.1 Sefano Galletti (1832–1905), *Statue of*
Savonarola, **1875. Piazza Savonarola, Ferrara.**

Galletti's statue of Savonarola was placed near the Este Castle in Ferrara, the birthplace of the fiery Dominican, in the nineteenth century. It captures the fervor of the preacher but also provides a contemporary commentary on the tense relationship between the secular Italian state and the Church after the kingdom's capture of Rome in 1870. Savonarola's anti-papal sermons resonated in the nineteenth century as potently as they had in the fifteenth. These later statues, such as the figures of Cola di Rienzo and Giordano Bruno in Rome, suggested powerful links between the events of the Italian Renaissance and the Risorgimento, the project of Italian unification. The memory of the Renaissance remained strong and such symbols served to connect two glorious moments of Italian history in the minds of patriotic Italians. Galletti significantly was also given the commission to cast the large bronze statue of Camillo Benso di Cavour, the first prime minister of a united Italy, which anchors the eponymous piazza in Rome near the papal palace.

Illus. 5.2 Giuseppe Bezzuoli (1784–1855), *Entry of Charles*
VIII into Florence, **1829. Palazzo Pitti, Florence.**

Piero de'Medici's capitulation to the French king Charles VIII resulted in the expulsion of the Medici in November 1494. A subsequent embassy from Florence, in which Savonarola was a spokesman, attempted to undo some of the more humiliating terms demanded by the French. These negotiations were only marginally successful. Charles entered Florence as a conqueror, his lance unsheathed, but with a parade of only ten thousand soldiers out of an army of forty thousand.

CHAPTER 6
SAVONAROLA IN POWER

The authority of Savonarola among the political classes arose from his steadfast hostility to the Medici and his success in negotiating with the French, but he was still viewed with suspicion by the great families because of his advocacy for the poor and disenfranchised. He sounded cautious and reasonable when he recommended reconciliation with former Medici supporters and that there be no reprisals against them. But soon after he made his political position very clear in a sermon addressed to the male citizens of Florence in which he praised the Venetian constitution and its Great Council as vehicles for cohesion and stability.[1] Although there had been a long tradition of Florentine praise of Venice as an ideal republic, it was universally accepted that Savonarola was advocating a *governo largo* with the widest representation. It was equally believed that such a government would be the least likely to accept the return of the Medici.

The message was clearly heard because the committee charged with drafting a new constitution for Florence finally reported in December of 1494: the model chosen was very much that of Venice. There was established a Great Council, whose five hundred members were elected from a pool of more than three thousand potential councilors. This extensive list of eligible candidates ensured that there could be no return to oligarchy because of the impossibility of manipulating such numbers.[2]

The Council of Five Hundred

The Council of Five Hundred required a massive new space be constructed in the Palazzo della Signoria. After all, five hundred men had to be accommodated at one time in a single room. Simone del Pollaiuolo, known as *il Cronaca*, was charged with engineering the chamber on the second floor of the Palazzo. It was to be unimpeded by supporting pillars yet match in width and length the great Sala del Maggior Consiglio in the Palazzo Ducale in Venice. To achieve this, Cronaca had to strengthen the piers on the ground floor, massive supports still visible to tourists climbing the grand staircase to the grand sala above.

The room was completed by the beginning of 1496 when it welcomed the first iteration of the new, broadly based Council. Savonarola himself was by law not able to hold office. But this did not mean he had no influence. On the contrary, he advised a group of

---

1. The sermon of December 14, 1494 in the cathedral is described in some detail by Landucci in his diary: Landucci, 1927. p. 76. A further sermon on December 28 is noted on page 78.
2. Savonarola drafted models of a theocratic republic for Florence: Girolamo Savonarola, "Selections from a Draft Constitution for Florence," in R. N. Watkins, ed., *Humanism and Republican Liberty*. Columbia: University of South Carolina Press, 1978. pp. 253–60.

loyal followers who became pejoratively known as *Piagnoni*, "snivellers," because of their tendency to cry at the friar's sermons. (More politely they were called *Frateschi*, that is, "followers of the friar.") The elected officials among them constituted the public voice of the friar and usually took direction from him in San Marco. It was a mixed group, but many of its leaders were true believers who accepted Savonarola's prophecies that Christ was now king of Florence, acting through him, and that He had promised the greatest riches and power to Florence once the city had been morally renovated. This was to be the first stage of the cleansing of the Church in preparation for the Second Coming.[3]

In addition to those among the *Piagnoni* who were true believers, there were those who cynically saw Savonarola as a means of keeping the Medici out of Florence forever and a way to ensure that the republic did not degenerate into an oligarchy managed by great families as it had been before Cosimo de'Medici took power. These were pragmatic politicians committed to a *governo largo*, and Savonarola's authority was clearly the best way to guarantee it, at least for the immediate present.

Opposed to the *Piagnoni* party were the *Arrabbiati*, the "rabid dogs" or those hot with anger. This, too, was a portmanteau and pejorative category, consisting in part of great patricians who desired a return to a *governo stretto* in which they would hold power at the expense of lesser guildsmen and their poorer colleagues. Many of these heard Savonarola's message as too reminiscent of the leaders of the 1378 *Ciompi* Revolt to be comfortable. And there were also many young patricians, angry at Savonarola's fulminations against state brothels, gaming tables, and Carnival.

Another powerful group of opponents were traditional Catholics loyal to the clerical hierarchy and nervous about the effects the friar's sermons would have on economic relations with the Church. Indeed, Savonarola's sermons were becoming ever more political and directed frequently against the Borgia pope, Alexander VI. Often these traditional Catholics had connections with the Franciscans who had lost followers and revenue because of the ascendancy of the Dominican Savonarola and consequently stirred up opposition.

Finally, there were the unrepentant—if discreet—*Palleschi*. These were the Medici supporters who had to choose their words and actions carefully and not appear to advocate the return of Piero, making them often silent in a council dominated by those who had exulted at his expulsion.

---

3. This is stated clearly in Landucci's description of the April 1, 1495, sermon in which Savonarola swore that he had received the information directly from the Virgin Mary. Landucci, 1927. p. 85. See also Girolamo Bieniveni's *piagnone laude* "Live in Our Hearts, O Florence (*Viva nei nostri cuori, O Florentia*). Bieniveni (1453–1542) had been an intimate of Lorenzo's circle, a poet and musician and a friend of Pico della Mirandola. But he was converted to Savonarola's cause and later translated his sermons into Italian. "Long Live Christ, Your King, O Florence/May He live in our hearts . . . /You will become more powerful and glorious/Than you ever were . . ." in Savonarola, 2006, p. 159.

Florence as the New Jerusalem

There followed a moral renovation of the city under Savonarola's influence that was the cause of some rejoicing but also much anger, and, in some instances, terror. The Council of Five Hundred ordered the closing of the state brothels, for example, a move that was not universally popular because of the late age of marriage of Florentine patricians. But it was the legislation against homosexuals that was particularly harsh. The practice of male same-sex relations had a long tradition in Florence and seemed to be condoned by the humanists whose Greek texts could be used to illustrate its acceptance.[4] This the Dominican attacked with the fury of a celibate ascetic puritan. Burning or stoning was his preferred punishment; but, fortunately, neither was actively applied. Leonardo da Vinci, twice accused of this crime at the time of Lorenzo, must have been happy to have left for Milan before the regime of Savonarola: future generations certainly celebrate that good fortune.

Given Savonarola's influence with the Signoria, Jews also suffered from his vigorous and uncompromising anti-Semitism. As in almost all Italian cities, Jews were restricted in Florence in the professions they were allowed to practice. As a consequence, Florentine Jews operated the small pawnbroking shops that catered to the poor. These were the only recourse for those *ciompi* whose property consisted of their clothes or wool-working tools. But Savonarola denounced the Jews as not only the killers of Christ but also the bloodsuckers of the poor. In order to put their shops out of business, he established in late 1495 the *Monte di Pietà*, a communally sponsored small loan and pawnbroking institution. He also asked the Signoria to expel the Jews from Florence, and the Signoria complied by passing a law, although that law was never physically enforced. Those Jews who left did so out of their own accord, driven by fear rather than by compulsion, and the expulsion law itself was repealed in 1496.[5]

Savonarola's obsession with turning Florence into the local version of the Heavenly Jerusalem was all encompassing. He was not content with railing against sin, luxury, pagan leaning, vice, and the lack of piety from the pulpit. Nor was he content just to see the brothels and gambling dens closed and homosexuals and Jews persecuted by the authorities. No, Savonarola wanted the city cleansed of its collective sin as represented by the material manifestations of its fallen state. He wished to destroy every object of art, every book, every item of clothing, every artifact that represented human vanity. It was completely inconsequential to him that these objects constituted some of the treasures of Western civilization. Such considerations were irrelevant to a man who saw the things of this world as worthy only of contempt and anything that took the human mind and spirit away from contemplation of God as inherently evil. To change the culture

---

4. See Michael Rocke, *Forbidden Friendships: Homosexuality and Male Culture in Renaissance Florence*. Oxford: Oxford University Press, 1996.
5. For a contemporary description of the actions against the Jews, see Piero Parenti, *Storia Fiorentina* in Savonarola, 2006. pp. 239–40.

of Renaissance Italian humanism and Laurentian cultural sophistication, Savonarola needed a cadre of disciples ready to do his bidding: his choice was to use the children of the *Piagnoni*.

It is so often remarked that only the most repressive regimes give power to children, and the example of Florence under Savonarola seems to support that assertion. Young boys, pledged by their devout parents, were organized into Bands of Hope. With their hair cut unfashionably short and often dressed like angels, they led religious processions, many of which superseded the traditional festivals like Carnival. They were assigned to break up gambling parties; accost women whom they thought dressed too immodestly; and, most famously, canvass the city demanding that Florentines surrender their Vanities for destruction in massive bonfires. [6]

To Savonarola and his disciples Vanities constituted anything that might direct the owner toward sin or away from God. Thus, many pagan authors, including Ovid and Catullus; vernacular writers who were deemed immoral, such as Boccaccio; false hair; mirrors; cosmetics; musical instruments and scores; and even secular art were tossed into the flames. The artistic genius Sandro Botticelli was said to have actually destroyed some of his own pictures. There is no firm evidence of this travesty, but it is, however, extremely likely as Botticelli did become a fervent follower of Savonarola. Certainly his contemporary Lorenzo di Credi contributed his own art to the fires. What we do know is that a great deal of precious material was destroyed in what came to be known as the Burning of the Vanities.

Savonarola did not invent the practice of destroying material deemed sinful or immoral. Earlier in the century the celebrated preacher Bernardino of Siena had begun the tradition; Savonarola merely perfected and expanded it. The first instance was the celebration of Lent in 1495. To replace the lascivious traditions of Carnival, Savonarola instituted religious processions, led by the Bands of Hope singing hymns. The truly contrite were invited to contribute to these processions objects that might lead to sinful thoughts or actions, material that would be burned. The most dramatic burning took place during the 1497 Carnival, when a huge consignment of Vanities was amassed and carried to the Piazza della Signoria to be offered to the flames. On seeing the value of so much of the material, it is said that the more practical than devout Venetian ambassador offered to purchase the lot for a good price. Savonarola undoubtedly remarked that the wages of sin are paid in a different coin and then ostentatiously burned the pyre of Vanities to the pious rejoicing of the Bands of Hope and his followers.[7]

This moment perhaps represented the apogee of Savonarola's influence in Florence. The decline in his influence in the city resulted from circumstances both within and

---

6. Landucci, 1927. pp. 101–4 records these events in detail.
7. Pseudo–Fra Pacifico Burlamacchi, *Vita del Beato Hieronimo Savonarola*, in Savonarola, 2006. pp. 345–48. See also Landucci, 1927. p. 130.

outside his control. First, in foreign affairs, Savonarola proved to be a disaster, after his initial success in negotiating with Charles VIII. Despite the powerful pressures put on Florence by its former ally Milan and by the papacy to abandon the French alliance and make common cause with the other Italian states to defend the peninsula, Savonarola refused. To some extent he had reduced his flexibility through his claims that Charles had been a divine instrument sent to cleanse the Church and prepare Italy for a great crusade and the consequent Second Coming. To join his enemies now would be unthinkable.

But Charles had to a degree abandoned Florence. The port of Pisa was not returned to Florence but allowed to recover its independence, not only a humiliation but an economic threat. This problem led Savonarola to play his card of divine agent on earth. In his sermons he claimed that God had given him Pisa and it would be returned to Florence. But there seemed to be no consummation of this promise, as Pisa remained in armed opposition to Florentine demands. By preaching of his divine gift of Pisa, Savonarola undermined his role as prophet. And it is a universal truth that prophets should not promise what they cannot deliver.

The Fall of Savonarola

The loss of Pisa was only one danger to Florentine trade. Savonarola's increasingly scurrilous attacks on the papacy and the person of Pope Alexander VI undermined the important banking connections with Rome and the Church. They also caused many traditional Catholics to feel they had to choose between the Dominican prior of San Marco and the successor to St. Peter, Christ's vicar on earth. Pope Alexander was losing patience with Savonarola both because of his refusal to abandon the French alliance and because of his anti-papal sermons.

In October of 1495 the pope had issued a demand that Savonarola stop his preaching. At first the renegade priest obeyed, but Savonarola's silence was temporary: he resumed his inflammatory sermons again the next year.[8] Trying a new approach, the exasperated Alexander summoned the friar to Rome in order to explain himself. Savonarola knew the likely consequences of making that trip, so he pleaded illness, despite a veiled promise that he would be given a cardinal's hat if he reconsidered. Instead, in an act of arrogant defiance, Savonarola sent the pope a printed copy of his sermons and prophecies, perhaps as an attempt to indicate that it would be unwise for the Church to move against God's chosen prophet. So, in June 1497 he was excommunicated and ordered, once again, to be silent.[9]

---

8. Savonarola's late apologetic letters and treatises are recorded in Girolamo Savonarola, *Apologetic Writings*, tr. M. Michèle Mulchahey. The I Tatti Renaissance Library, 68. Cambridge, MA: Harvard University Press, 2015.

9. Landucci, 1927. pp. 122–23.

This ban also worked for a time, but by the end of the year Savonarola resumed saying mass, despite his excommunication.[10] And in the following February of 1498 he not only said mass but also resumed his preaching against the sins of the Church and its papal head. Because of the drama of this standoff between pope and prophet the cathedral was jammed with both the faithful and the curious. It was clearly a situation that could not last and would likely be resolved in a cataclysmic manner.

Sensing Savonarola's growing weakness, groups of well-born young men, joined by a number of common street thugs, all furious at the loss of their pleasures, formed gangs called *compagnacci* to disrupt the sermons of the friar and his disciples and to sow instability in the city.[11] Street violence became common: Florence appeared increasingly less like the New Jerusalem and was hardly prepared for Christ's return. Many in the city began to distance themselves from Savonarola. In fact, as time had somewhat erased the memory of their failures, a great many citizens of all classes began to regret the expulsion of the Medici, remembering not the idiocy of Piero but the civility and stability of his father's rule.

This nostalgia for the Medici led to a conspiracy that the friar's faction handled extremely badly. Piero de'Medici, in the company of a small band of armed men, returned to the gates of the city in April 1497. This seemed like a pointless challenge, until it was learned that there were Medici supporters from old patrician clans who had worked with him and his faction to rehabilitate him in a desire to expel Savonarola and dismantle the *governo largo*. Although in 1494 Savonarola had counseled a policy of leniency toward the *Palleschi* and a policy of reconciliation, now, when the five leaders of the plot were identified, they were tried and sentenced to death.[12]

The new constitution, written under the friar's influence, specifically gave condemned prisoners the right to appeal their executions directly to the Council of Five Hundred. However, the leader of the *Piagnoni*, Francesco Valori, made a powerful speech in that same Council denouncing the Medici conspirators. He argued that they had forfeited that right of appeal and thus their pleas should be denied. Valori carried the vote, and the men were put to death without appeal. This harsh decision, which was universally believed to have been approved by Savonarola, alienated many in the Council. So, too, it offended a great many members of the old noble clans who identified with the class if not the politics of those who were executed.

Then the papacy issued an ultimatum. Savonarola had proved contumacious in continuing to preach and say mass, despite being under a sentence of excommunication. The pope threatened that if he was not silenced immediately, Florence would be placed under

---

10. Savonarola responded to his excommunication in a sermon of February 11, 1498; Girolamo Savonarola, "Sermon of February 11, 1498," in *A Guide to Righteous Living and Other Works*, tr. and ed. K. Eisenbichler. Toronto: CRRS, 2003. pp. 149–76.

11. Landucci,1927. p. 131.

12. The conspirators were from the most prominent patrician families in Florence, including the Tornabuoni, Pucci, del Nero, Ridolfi, Dell'Antella, and de'Medici. Landucci, 1927. p. 125.

an interdict. This would mean that the mercantile and diplomatic ambitions of Florence abroad would be compromised at a time when the economy was already in shambles, the city isolated, and harvests reduced because of incessant rain, causing a substantial increase in the price of food. Despite opposition from the *Piagnoni*, the Signoria voted to silence Savonarola.[13]

The friar did not stop his political meddling, however, as he continued to meet and advise his faction at San Marco. True, he did stop preaching and celebrating the Eucharist. Nevertheless, the show of official opposition to Savonarola and the loss of his pulpit—the primary source of his power—galvanized his enemies who had grown in numbers and resolve. And, not only the secular opposition, the *Arrabbiati*, was emboldened, but also the friar's religious foes, the Franciscans, set out to challenge his authority.

The Franciscans had lost a great deal of money as donations had moved to the Dominicans under Savonarola. Even their traditional role as the disciples of St. Francis, the *poverello* (poor little one), to speak for the poor and women and to preach on their behalf had been compromised. So, seizing the initiative the Franciscans responded with the only spiritual weapon they had: a challenge to Savonarola to an Ordeal by Fire to determine definitively whether he was indeed a divine agent and prophet. Savonarola had no choice but to accept. So, in this city of humanist thought, republican freedom, and human agency, a city of practical and pragmatic merchants and bankers, an Ordeal by Fire was arranged for the Piazza della Signoria on April 7, 1498. The date was in its own ways prophetic because it was the day on which Charles VIII of France died.

The event turned out to be as strange as the supremacy of the Dominican himself. When the parties of three Dominicans and three Franciscans arrived, challenged to walk through a bed of flaming coals, there were arguments over precedence, costume, order, and many other trivialities, all within sight of the population of the city who had emerged to watch this superstitious theatre. Then God indeed seemed to speak: a violent rainstorm extinguished the flames so there could be no Ordeal.

The assembled population was disappointed, and Savonarola's credibility as God's prophet plummeted. Reasonable questions were openly asked: If he had God's ear why did Savonarola not return Pisa as he said he had the power to do? Why had the weather of 1497–98 turned so brutal, to the point that there were food shortages and bread riots and much suffering among the poor, whom Savonarola said he championed before God? Why did the pope excommunicate him, if he was a truly religious leader? And why had civil order begun to break down, with dissension, hatred, and anger dividing the city? Sensing the evaporation of Savonarola's authority, the emboldened *Arrabbiati*, *compagnacci*, and solid patrician guildsmen, clearly exasperated by this absurd situation and fortuitously holding a majority in the Signoria, acted decisively.[14]

---

13. Landucci, 1927. p. 132.
14. Landucci, 1927. pp. 134–38.

Arrest, Trial, and Execution

The day following the abortive Ordeal by Fire, Palm Sunday, April 8, 1498, a gang of *compagnacci* rioted around the palace of Francesco Valori, the *Piagnoni* leader who had demanded the immediate execution of the five pro-Medici conspirators in contravention of the law. Valori's wife made the fatal mistake of going to a window to investigate the commotion and was killed by a crossbow bolt to the head. Even his children and their nurse were wounded. Francesco had been taken from his house by men sent to offer him protective custody, but he never made it. Surrounded by a gang of *compagnacci*, he was separated from his guards and struck by a blow to the head with a pike. His body was then stabbed repeatedly by the patrician leaders of the mob, those who had kinsmen among the executed pro-Medici conspirators. The young patricians then withdrew, leaving Valori's bloodied body to be stripped by the street thugs who fought over the fine clothing.

Valori's murder happened prophetically near the church of San Procolo, in which the family had its burial chapel; and, ironically, it was the Franciscans who took charge of the corpse of this man who had been the most powerful spokesman of Savonarola's faction. Criminal and terrible as this event was, it seemed to have satisfied the bloodlust and the thirst for revenge of the *compagnacci*, so the other prominent *Piagnoni* who had also been identified for mob violence managed to escape the anger and vengeance of the gangs.

Nevertheless, at the same time a large mob laid siege to San Marco, demanding the surrender of Savonarola. The prior and two of his closest Dominican acolytes were arrested and taken to the Palazzo della Signoria where they were subjected to examination by torture. During this ordeal Savonarola confessed that his prophecies had not come from God and that he had contravened the law and custom of Florence by engaging in political activity. A party of inquisitors empowered by Rome also examined the friar. Their verdict matched the Florentine decision. Savonarola was declared a contumacious heretic. As a result, he was surrendered to the secular arm of government for execution.[15]

The effect of Savonarola's retraction of his belief in his own divine mission and prophecies deflated his followers, except for the most fanatical. The response of the apothecary Luca Landucci, a moderate supporter of the friar's mission, is exemplary. He wrote in his diary:

> . . . he whom we held to be a prophet confessed that he was no prophet, and that he had not received from God the things he had preached; and he confessed that many things that had occurred during the course of his preaching were contrary to what he had given us to understand. I was present when this protocol was read,

---

15. Landucci, 1927. pp. 142–44.

and I marveled, feeling utterly dumbfounded with surprise. My heart was grieved to see such an edifice fall to the ground as it had been founded on a lie. Florence had been expecting a New Jerusalem, from which would issue just laws and splendour and an example of righteous life, and to see the renovation of the Church, the conversion of unbelievers, and the consolation of the righteous. I felt that everything was exactly contrary . . .[16]

The execution of Savonarola on May 23, 1498, ended the Florentine experiment with theocratic government he had inspired. It did not, however, end that return to *governo largo*, as the Council of Five Hundred continued to meet and a new, dynamic, but very secular regime replaced the tensions between *Arrabbiati* and *Piagnoni*. Nor did his death end the threat to Florentine independence. The struggle between the great powers of the Habsburgs and Valois largely played out in Italy and resulted eventually in the return of the Medici in 1512. Thankfully this was not in the person of Piero, who had conveniently drowned while retreating with a French army, but through his brother, Giuliano.

The remarkable events of the years between 1494 and 1498 were momentous for Florence and for Italy, which effectively had lost its independence as a consequence of the French invasions. In some ways the rise of Savonarola might be attributed to the power vacuum caused by the expulsion of Piero, leaving no internal alternative within the city because of the success of the Medici in destroying or co-opting their opponents. There was also the instability of the times, the consequence of dynastic intrigue in Milan, and Borgia ambitions in Rome and the States of the Church.

But there was also the recognition that Savonarola played into Florentines' confident belief in their exceptionalism, defined by humanists like Salutati and Bruni but open to reinterpretation by preachers like Savonarola who privileged the New Jerusalem over the New Rome or Athens. He also mined a deep alienation felt by many Florentines who were excluded from the esoteric humanist court culture of Lorenzo the Magnificent and whose piety allowed for little interest in Neoplatonism or pagan classics. These citizens had been conditioned by a prophetic tradition of apocalyptic narratives that were part of their religious and cultural experience. Savonarola filled the vacuum with a message that was familiar and indeed comforting. He was, then, not so much an anomaly as a re-figuration of stories already known, with a message eagerly embraced, one that remains sufficiently attractive that even today there are usually red roses on the site of his execution in the Piazza della Signoria.

---

16. Landucci, 1927. p. 139.

Illus. 6.1 Filippo Dolciati (1443–1519), *The Execution of Girolamo Savonarola*, 1498. Museo di San Marco, Florence.

The execution of Girolamo Savonarola on May 23, 1498, ended the career of the apocalyptic Dominican. He and two of his chief monastic supporters were first hanged and then their bodies publicly burned, as this image shows. After the bodies had been fully consumed by flames, the ashes were collected and thrown into the Arno to ensure that no "relics" of the Dominican could be collected and used by the still numerous *Piagnoni* who continued to believe in the message of the prophet. And, in a symbolic but cathartic act, the bell of San Marco was carried from its tower into the streets and publicly flogged.

Nevertheless, the friar's memory remained potent, particularly in the convent of San Marco, the center of Savonarolan ideology. Cosimo I, the first hereditary duke of Florence, was moved to expel the intransigent occupants and replace them with more amenable monks. The story goes that Cosimo rode up to San Marco and summoned the prior, asking loudly, "Who founded your convent?" "Cosimo *il Vecchio*," replied the prior. To this Cosimo snarled, "Well now Cosimo *il duca* (Cosimo the duke) is shutting you down." Nevertheless, the suppression was never complete.

**Illus. 6.2 Sandro Botticelli, *The Mystic Nativity*,
ca.1500. National Gallery, London.**

This painting illustrates how one of the Medici's favorite painters, Sandro Botticelli, fell under the
influence of Savonarola and how he sustained that devotion to the apocalyptic Dominican even

after his execution. It is a complex mystical study of one of Savonarola's central millenarian sermons, delivered on Assumption Day, and refers to his *Compendium of Revelations* (1495). Its date is also important, as 1500 marks a millennial moment for those who accepted Savonarola's belief that the apocalypse was at hand ("in the half-time after the time").

At the top of the picture is an inscription in Greek that reads: "This picture, at the end of the year 1500, in the troubles of Italy, I, Alessandro, in the half-time after the time, painted, according to the eleventh [chapter] of Saint John [*The Book of Revelation*], in the second woe of the Apocalypse, during the release of the devil for three-and-a-half years; then he shall be bound in the twelfth [chapter] and we shall see [him buried] as in this picture" (NGL).

Botticelli abandons his control of perspective to create a world beyond human perception and populates the heavens with dancing angels who carry (now largely illegible) banners with the twelve divine attributes of the Virgin Mary. In the lower register there are seven devils retreating to hell and angels in an embrace signifying Peace on Earth to Men of Good Will, as the banderole rehearses. The picture is consequently both elegantly engaging and iconographically disturbing. It illustrates the power of Savonarola's apocalyptic vision and how it entered the cultural world of Florence through the mediation of even those most intimate with the intellectual and artistic environment of Lorenzo *il Magnifico*'s circle.

CHAPTER 7
THE AGE OF NICCOLÒ MACHIAVELLI

A mong the most influential Renaissance figures, Niccolò Machiavelli (1469–1527) is one of the few to have become a concept—his name being synonymous in popular culture with a crafty and calculating if not ruthless exercise of power. But this is a profound misreading of and disservice to a great political thinker, historian, and writer.[1]

Niccolò could count among his ancestors thirteen Machiavelli who had held the post of *Gonfaloniere di Giustizia* (Standardbearer of Justice). In this, the highest elected office in the Florentine republic, his forebears had been responsible for maintaining public order and controlling internal security forces. One could almost say that politics was in his DNA. So, too, was humanism, insofar as his father, Bernardo, a lawyer, was a passionate student of Latin and collector of classical texts. As a consequence, young Niccolò was born into a household predisposed to political service and classical learning.

When he turned seven, he was placed with a series of private tutors to learn Latin and arithmetic. Thus prepared, he entered the University of Florence (the *Studio Fiorentino*) that was located at the time in Pisa. There he gained a solid grounding in the core humanist subjects of rhetoric, grammar, poetry, and moral philosophy. Some evidence exists to suggest that he participated in the circle of the younger Medici under the patronage of Lorenzo. There are also reports that he was a popular young man, known for his wit and companionship that extended beyond humanist coteries into the brothels and gambling dens of the city.

Second Chancellor

At barely twenty-nine years of age, Niccolò Machiavelli secured his first public appointment. He was confirmed in the prestigious post of second chancellor on June 19, 1498, just weeks after the trial and execution of Savonarola. Machiavelli seemed neither to have suffered under the friar's policies nor embraced them. His celebrated remark on the Dominican's fall was simply that it illustrated the fate of prophets without power. From Machiavelli's point of view, Savonarola's failure to confront his enemies and use force to

---

1. There is an enormous bibliography on Machiavelli and his work. See the massive annotated bibliography compiled by Silvia Ruffo-Fiore of work prior to 1990: Silvia Ruffo-Fiore, ed., *Niccolo Machiavelli: An Annotated Bibliography of Modern Criticism and Scholarship.* New York: Greenwood Press, 1990. The best general biography of Machiavelli remains Maurizio Viroli, *Niccolo's Smile: A Biography of Machiavelli*, tr. Antony Shugaar. New York: Hill and Wang, 2002. The best short introduction to his major works is Quentin Skinner, *Machiavelli: A Very Short Introduction.* Oxford: Oxford University Press, 2002.

keep order in the city and intimidate his opponents outside its walls was the direct cause of his downfall. Obviously, the young Machiavelli was a keen observer even then.

As second chancellor, Machiavelli was charged with oversight of the government's correspondence, in particular but not exclusively in the matter of domestic affairs. It was a tumultuous time in which to begin a political career. The expulsion of the Medici in 1494 and the arrest and execution of Savonarola in 1498 had not ended the debate among the various factions seeking control of Florence. In the summer of 1498 there were still *Palleschi* plotting the return of the Medici, patricians from rich and ancient families attempting to subvert the broadly based *governo largo* constitution established under the influence of Savonarola in hopes of a return to oligarchy. There were as well those who might not have sympathized with the Dominican's belief that Florence was a theocracy, the New Jerusalem, but did embrace his popular republican political order, represented by the Council of Five Hundred. In the chaotic aftermath of Savonarola's fall, it was this latter group that remained in control.

Nevertheless, the dangerous economic context of Savonarola's fall remained. There was still insufficient food for the poor, and the continuing campaign to recapture Pisa was devouring enormous amounts of communal cash to pay mercenaries. Machiavelli's first term in office was spent in almost continuous negotiations with the various condottieri whom Florence hired to retake the port. His abilities were so evident in these negotiations with men not known for loyalty or subtlety that he became known as a shrewd negotiator and was confirmed in his office when his first term expired. It was widely recognized that Machiavelli was a very useful official of the republic and hence worthy of a diplomatic appointment. When that appointment came, it proved to be the most challenging posting of the time: he was to travel to the court of the king of France, Louis XII, whose designs on Italy were adding to the instability of the peninsula, but whose assistance in recovering Pisa was seen by the Signoria as crucial.

Machiavelli Abroad

This first important diplomatic assignment in 1500 to the court of Louis XII was both an opportunity and an education for the young man. Machiavelli had never before been away from Tuscany, and the distance between France and Florence meant he would need to act independently. He was also forced to shift his vision from his own narrow Florentine perspective and experience to the view of Florence held by others, especially from across the Alps. It became obvious to him that Italian affairs were being determined by foreigners, with little consultation with or even concern for the particular interests of Florence. The most he could get from the French was a grudging reaffirmation of the agreement to help capture Pisa, provided that the Florentines bore the full cost.[2]

---

2. For Machiavelli's diplomatic reports see Niccolò Machiavelli, *Diplomatic Missions (1498–1527)*, tr. Christian Detmold. CreateSpace Independent Publishing Platform, 2015. The letters and reports from France comprise pages 40–101.

Machiavelli also appreciated for the first time that Florentine liberty came at a high price. Dynastic monarchies like that of Louis XII could act decisively and quickly and sustain policies over a long period. In a republic like Florence, this was impossible, with the result, Machiavelli feared, that his city would never be able to sustain its freedom and its republican virtue. The cumbersome electoral procedures, short terms of office, and a briefly elected executive that consisted of a committee of nine men meant that quick decisions and sustained policy were almost impossible. Add to this the contempt with which the French nobility and crown looked at a state that paid mercenaries to defend itself, and it became clear to Machiavelli that Florence would have to adopt some of the methods of the "barbarians"—a term of contempt that he and many other Italians used for northern Europeans—even at the expense of some measure of republican freedom.

Machiavelli spent six months in France but returned at the beginning of 1501 to ensure his re-election to his post and to impose some order on his own chaotic personal affairs. He also re-entered Florentine political life with his perspective and experience greatly expanded. Where once he had viewed the world through the narrow lens of Florence, he now had a wider vision, one which allowed for entertaining ideas that he, like most fervent republicans, would have once dismissed as tyrannical.

This fresh willingness to investigate other ways of governing Florence and finding allies was further reinforced in 1501 with Machiavelli's diplomatic posting as Florentine resident with Cesare Borgia. Cesare, the son of Pope Alexander VI, was using the authority of the papacy and his own ruthlessly violent strategies to construct a powerful, centralized Borgia state carved out of the States of the Church. What Machiavelli observed on this occasion was an Italian—actually an Italianate Spaniard—behaving in a way analogous to the French and the Aragonese. That is, Cesare acted with self-serving ruthlessness, vigor, and determination. It was during this first short embassy that Machiavelli conceived the central character for his most famous work, *The Prince*: his protagonist, Duke Valentino. The character's name may seem ironic, but it has nothing to do with lovers and valentines. Rather, it was derived from the French duchy, the Valentinois, which Cesare had received through his marriage to a French princess, arranged by his father the pope and Louis XII (whose earlier marriage the pope had conveniently annulled).[3]

In his negotiations with Cesare, Machiavelli was required to listen to proposals and advice, which he must have found uncongenial, especially the Borgia's suggestion that Florence recall the Medici, advice which mirrored what Machiavelli had heard in France. Only through a prince, he was told, could Florence manage these dangerous times when quick action and steely resolve were required. He was told that a prince could impose internal order on the traditionally divided and fractious republic and crush any factional stasis. Distasteful as the prospect might have appeared, it seems that this external perspective gained traction within the city. True, the Medici themselves were not recalled,

---

3. Machiavelli, 2015. See pp. 102–89 for the letters and reports from his mission to Cesare Borgia.

but in 1502 Piero Soderini was made gonfaloniere for life, in effect a republican prince, a doge for Florence.[4] And Machiavelli was his primary political operative.

Piero Soderini: Gonfaloniere for Life

In so many ways Soderini was an ideal person to guide Florence at this dangerous time. His father, Tommaso, had been a supporter of the Medici and was personally close to Lorenzo. On the other hand, his brother Paolo Antonio had been a leading *Piagnone* politician, close to Savonarola. Still another brother, Francesco, was bishop of Volterra and one of Machiavelli's colleagues in diplomatic work, including his mission to Cesare Borgia. Francesco would be made a cardinal in 1503 as a reward for his support of Louis XII and Julius II. Consequently, Soderini's family connections alone gave him wide credibility.[5] Moreover, he enjoyed a great deal of political and diplomatic experience, having first been elected a prior of the republic in 1481 and then named ambassador to Charles VIII of France in 1493. He was a familiar of Piero de'Medici but with the expulsion of the Medici in 1494 had been able to rehabilitate himself as a dedicated republican statesman.

Soderini was a judicious, cautious, honest, and patriotic leader of Florence, holding office for ten years during a very unstable period in Italian affairs. For this he deserves enormous credit. It was under his government that Pisa was finally recovered in 1509; and he was successful in reforming Florentine finances and other areas of public policy, including the formation of a citizen militia to reduce the republic's reliance on mercenaries. His diplomacy was successful in maintaining Florentine independence and territory, a complicated task in a peninsula fragmented by the competing powers of France and Spain and the warlike policies of Julius II during the War of the League of Cambrai. In short, there is much to admire in Piero Soderini.

On the other hand, he was often overly cautious, and he steadfastly refused to abandon the traditional French alliance, even when it was becoming evident that the Spanish would be the dominant power in the peninsula. He lacked charisma and to a degree lacked imagination. He did not enjoy the gifts of deep insight or muscular leadership. Still, he was a gifted administrator who had the ability and good sense to recognize and employ talent. This was particularly the case with Machiavelli.

The Traveling Diplomat

By 1502, then, it appeared that Machiavelli's career was secure and his future bright. He married at that time, effecting a match with Marietta Corsini, a woman from a solid patrician clan, wealthier than the Machiavelli and with excellent political and social

---

4. Luca Landucci describes his election on September 22, 1502. See Landucci, 1927. p. 200.

5. For the Soderini family, especially their relations with the Medici, see Paula C. Clarke, *The Soderini and the Medici: Power and Patronage in Fifteenth-Century Florence*. Oxford: Clarendon Press, 1991.

connections: there was no better indicator of his rosy future. It was a typical patrician union: it was certainly an arranged match, and Niccolò appeared to be indifferent to his wife, although not to women in general as his pleasure with mistresses and prostitutes was well known. He later wrote a humorous novella, called *Belfagor*, in which Satan sends a devil, Belfagor, to earth to discover why so many men consigned to Hell blamed their marriages for their fall. At the close of the novella and after experiencing the matrimonial state himself, Belfagor begs Satan to let him return because Hell is so much more peaceful than marriage.

Certainly, Machiavelli spent many months in Soderini's service traveling far from Florence and his family. In 1502, he was dispatched on a second embassy to Cesare Borgia, who was now duke of the Romagna ruling from Urbino. Cesare had captured a great number of small principalities through horrendous violence and brutality and deceit and was now turning his attentions toward the acquisition of Florence from whom he demanded tribute. But, the unexpected death in 1503 of Cesare's father, Pope Alexander, meant that Cesare's power base had evaporated.[6]

To help protect Florentine interests, the Signoria ordered Machiavelli's first visit to Rome. The election of the new pope was fraught with intrigue. The conclave elected Pius III to succeed Alexander, but Pius lived less than a month, with many believing that he had been poisoned. The next conclave saw Cesare's ambitions outmaneuvered by his father's worst enemy, Cardinal della Rovere, who was elected in 1503 as Julius II, the *papa terribile*. In the face of these high-stakes negotiations, there was little Machiavelli could actually accomplish for the republic while in Rome. But it is obvious that he enjoyed his time exploring the ancient ruins; engaging in learned discussions with newly made friends; and, doubtlessly, enjoying the celebrated courtesans of the city. Despite the fact that at the time he set out, his wife, Marietta, was nearing the end of her second pregnancy and soon after gave birth to a son, and despite complaints from members of the Signoria that he was neglecting his duties, Niccolò extended his visit to Rome by some weeks. It is sometimes hard to remember that the author of *The Prince* was not a dour manipulator but a charming bon vivant.

The election of Julius II resulted in Machiavelli's return to Florence, only to be posted back to France to witness the signing of the Treaty of Lyon between the French and Aragonese. The posting afforded him sufficient leisure to begin his first major literary/historical work, *La Prima Decennale* (*The First Decade*),[7] a verse chronicle covering the decade following the French invasions. In some ways the chronicle is a valediction to Machiavelli's hopes that Cesare Borgia would reverse the humiliation of Italy: the poet reflects on how this humiliation will, alas, continue unless a powerful, determined, and

---

6. Landucci, 1927. pp. 196–208.
7. Corrado Vivanti, ed., *Niccolò Machiavelli, Opere*. Torino: Einaudi-Gallimard, Biblioteca Della Pleiade, 1997. Online edition http://machiavelli.letteraturaoperaomnia.org/machiavelli_decen nale_primo.html.

ruthless Italian should arise to unite the divided states of the peninsula and drive out the barbarians.

Back in Florence, Machiavelli became involved in the recapture of Pisa. Unwilling to risk a military assault and with the costs of mercenary warfare unpalatable to the cash-strapped Signoria, Soderini was convinced to try an extraordinary scheme: the digging of a canal to divert the Arno away from Pisa, destroying its commerce and to a degree its protection. The genius behind this bold scheme was Leonardo da Vinci.[8] It is probable that Machiavelli had met Leonardo in the company of Cesare Borgia, for whom he worked as a military engineer for a brief time.[9] The diversion of the river proved a monumental failure and a great expense because the Florentines provided insufficient men and money to dig the channel to the necessary depth—a depth that Leonardo had mathematically determined.

Pisa may have been saved from Leonardo's genius but not from the dangerously shifting currents of the Italian Wars, occasioned by the power of the barbarians, especially when the interests of ambitious Italian states were willing to turn against their fellows to further their own ends. The War of the League of Cambrai, consisting among other combatants of Louis XII, the Emperor Maximilian, and the king of Spain (Ferdinand of Aragon) encouraged by Pope Julius II, made war on Venice, perhaps the most powerful of the Italian states able to resist the barbarians. Florence did not participate actively in the League but did provide substantial subsidies to the French and Habsburgs.

A lucky consequence of the war was the Florentine recapture of Pisa. The city had been blockaded for some time, and its fields ravaged by Florentine troops. Now without allies and starving, Pisa capitulated and sent an embassy to the Palazzo della Signoria to sign its surrender. This easy victory made the militia that Machiavelli had equipped and trained in his new post of secretary to the war office unnecessary. He had hoped to restore some of the ancient Roman sense of vigor and civic virtue through this citizen army, raised mostly from the rougher rural districts of the *contado*. At this point it was not needed; and when it was, it hardly fulfilled Machiavelli's dreams.

Diplomatic Failure

Soderini sent Machiavelli back to France in the fall of 1511 to assure Louis XII of Florence's continued alliance, despite recognizing that this was hardly the French king's main concern.[10] Nevertheless, Louis should have been impressed, as this loyalty proved a fleeting and dangerous continuation of a policy that Florence had followed from the time of the Medici. Pope Julius II and Ferdinand of Aragon had realized that dismem-

---

8. Martin Kemp, *Leonardo da Vinci: The Marvellous Works of Nature and Man*. Oxford: Oxford University Press, 2006. p. 219.
9. Kemp, 2006. p. 208.
10. Machiavelli, 2015. pp. 257–90.

bering Venice had left the north of Italy prey to the French, so the pope raised a Holy League to "drive out the barbarians," that is, the French: the Spanish and Swiss now seemed at least temporarily rehabilitated. Louis's clever response, supported by a group of rebel cardinals, was to try to decapitate the alliance by calling a Council of the Church to depose Julius and elect a more malleable French or Spanish pope. It was proposed that the Council meet at Pisa, now once again Florentine territory.

In a decision of the utmost foolishness, Soderini agreed to this, even though he must have realized that the calling of a Council would infuriate the *papa terribile*, who was known to pursue revenge without pity. What drove this policy was likely personal. Just before, there had been a plot against Soderini's life by a patrician who was a Medici supporter, and soon after evidence emerged indicating that Pope Julius was in support of the plot. Although the proof was hardly conclusive, Soderini and perhaps his faction felt that the pope was in favor of the restoration of the Medici, especially given the prominence of Lorenzo's son Giovanni de'Medici at the papal court. Nevertheless, Soderini's decision to host a council at Pisa whose aim was to depose Julius was a disastrous miscalculation.

Julius responded first with threats and then later with the imposition of an interdict on Florence, prohibiting religious services in the city.[11] Intimidated, Soderini assigned Machiavelli the impossible tasks of convincing Louis XII to abandon the idea of a Council and then trying to stop the rebel cardinals from entering Florentine territory. Although Louis gave Florence a month's grace, he was determined that the Council was to proceed. At the same time, Florence found itself completely dependent on the French to protect its territory from the large and experienced Spanish army marching north led by the viceroy of Naples. A miracle did almost save the situation when the French decisively defeated the Spanish at Ravenna, slaughtering much of their army. But, as Machiavelli would later recount, malevolent Fortune again intervened. Killed in the battle was the brilliant French general Gaston de Foix, and his death took away both the strategy and energy of the French pursuit of the Spaniards. So, despite its losses and its hunger, the remnants of the Spanish force marched into Tuscany, their wages ominously paid by Cardinal de'Medici. A demand was made for tribute and the restoration of the Medici family to power or the army would attack. Soderini, again foolishly and against all sensible advice, refused.

The tough, experienced Spanish army moved against the city. Machiavelli had arrayed his militia to defend Florentine territory at Prato, a town some dozen miles outside Florence. But, despite the fact that they outnumbered the enemy and had the advantage of protective walls, despite their years of training and shiny new steel breastplates, and despite the lack of Spanish siege equipment, it took very little for the Spanish veterans to put the militia to flight, sack and ravage Prato, and advance on Florence itself.

---

11. The best analysis of Julius's policies and machinations is Christine Shaw, *Julius II: The Warrior Pope*. Oxford: Blackwell, 1993.

Realizing at the end of August 1512 that his days in Florence were numbered, Soderini fled the city in panic, leaving behind him a collapsed regime. There was a brief attempt at electing another gonfaloniere for life while welcoming the Medici back as mere private citizens, but this quickly failed. So *Palleschi*, together with the Spanish and papal forces, re-established Medici rule in the person of Lorenzo's third son, Giuliano. The Council of Five Hundred and the other republican magistracies that had arisen since 1494 were abolished and a special committee, or *balìa*, of *Palleschi* assumed authority. Machiavelli, as Soderini's puppet, was relieved of all his positions, one of only two officials so punished by the new regime.

But the situation grew much worse for Machiavelli. He was arrested in February of 1513, suspected of conspiracy against the Medici: apparently his name had been discovered on a list of sympathizers created by a patrician conspirator against Giuliano. Although there was no evidence that he was an active member of the conspiracy, he was thrown into a cell and tortured. The leaders of the plot were beheaded, and Machiavelli had every reason to believe that his would soon be lost.

Ironically, it was a great event in the history of the Medici family that secured Machiavelli's release after three weeks of terrible suffering and fear. In March of 1513, Lorenzo's second son, Giovanni, was elected pope as Leo X. The city, now sincerely jubilant and wishing to advertise its new Medici allegiance, broke into a frenzy of rejoicing. Part of this was a general amnesty, including the release of Machiavelli from his prison cell. He was free but without income or respect, barred from the Palazzo della Signoria, and suspected by many in the new power structure. Unable to afford to live in Florence, Machiavelli and his family left for their small farm near San Casciano from which he could see the towers and dome of his beloved city. It was here in this rural exile that he would produce two of the most important texts of the later Italian Renaissance: *The Prince* and *The Discourses on Livy*.[12]

The Prince *and* The Discourses on Livy

The Prince arose from a correspondence with one of Machiavelli's friends from Soderini's regime, but one who was acceptable to the Medici: Francesco Vettori. In the spring and summer of 1513 Machiavelli began considering the implications of the political and military situation in which Italy found itself, so he composed a short treatise on the nature of the state, a work that would become *The Prince*. The letter to Vettori informing him of this work is perhaps the most famous piece of private correspondence in Italian.

> *In the morning I get up with the sun and walk to a woodlot I am harvesting where I spend a couple of hours reviewing yesterday's work and pass the time with the woodcutters who are always ready to complain about their own or their neighbors' misfortunes.*

---

12. David Wooton, ed. and tr., *Machiavelli, Selected Political Writings*. Indianapolis: Hackett Publishing Company, 1994. The complete text of the *Discourses*, together with *The Prince*.

I go from the woodlot to a spring and from there to my bird snare, always traveling with a book—Dante, Petrarch, or a minor poet like Tibullus, Ovid, or another. As I read of their loves and passions, I am reminded of my own, and this reverie gives me some brief pleasure. I continue walking along the road to the inn, where I talk with the travelers who pass through, asking for news from where they came. In this way I find out what is happening and observe the many and varied interests and tastes of men.

By then it is time for dinner. Together with my family I eat whatever food my small property provides. After eating, it is back to the inn where I find the innkeeper, often the butcher, miller, and a couple of kiln owners; and with these companions I slip into rusticity for the rest of the day, playing cards or backgammon. Our games trigger a thousand arguments and endless name calling, even though we only argue over pennies. Still, they can hear us shouting as far as San Casciano. Afflicted with such vermin I keep my mind active and let the ignominy of my fate take its course, content to be driven down this road if only to see if Fortune blushes with shame.

In the evening I return home and go into my study. Before entering I strip off my clothes, dirty and dusty from the day's work, and change into my courtier's robes. Then, appropriately attired, I enter the courts of the Ancients, and they receive me as a friend. I dine on the food that is for me alone and for which I was born. I am not afraid to ask them what motivated their actions, and they graciously answer me. For the next four hours I know no boredom, forget my troubles, no longer fear poverty or even death. I am completely immersed in their company.

Dante says that we forget what we have heard if we do not write it down, so I have transcribed everything useful from my conversations with the Ancients, composing a little book, De Principatibus, *in which I delve into my thoughts on the subject, investigating what a principality is, the forms they take, and how they are won, kept, and lost. And, if you have enjoyed any of my trifles, you should like this one; and it should be well received by a prince, especially a new one. Thus, I have dedicated it to his Magnificence Giuliano (de'Medici).*[13]

The lessons of this short book were not to Machiavelli an abstract study of political theory but a specific response to a critical moment in 1513. Its theme was one that he had identified as Savonarola's fatal weakness: ambition not matched by force. Italy was too divided, with the rulers of every state looking not to drive out the barbarians collectively but to seek their own best interests. Only a figure capable of imposing—or inspiring—unity, armed with both a powerful military, ideally formed by citizen soldiers, and possessed of an iron will and ruthlessness that equaled the brutality and power of the northerners, could save Italy from the barbarians.

---

13. Letter of Machiavelli to Francesco Vettori, December 10, 1513. Niccolò Machiavelli, *Opere*, ed. M. Bonfantini. Milan: Ricciardi Editore, 1954. *Lettere XI.* Accessed through Progetto Manuzio electronic edition, 2003. My translation.

From his experience, Machiavelli suggests that Cesare Borgia (Duke Valentino) came closest to achieving this, but he was undone by Fortune. Indeed, if there is a transcendent idea in *The Prince* it is that human power and ingenuity, or in Italian *virtù*, regardless how skilled and ruthless, will forever be in a struggle with Fortune (*Fortuna*), whose intervention will always be unpredictable. Despite his abilities, Cesare was dependent on his father, the pope, whose unexpected death in 1503 robbed him of his authority; and, ill himself, Cesare was unable to fully exploit his advantages over his enemies.

The Prince is Machiavelli at his aphoristic and concentrated best. The book, which was never printed in his lifetime, was regarded as shocking because it put into writing what every statesman and commander knows, although rarely vocalizes: success requires force, violence, ruthlessness, infidelity, and steely resolve. As Machiavelli notes, to pursue what *ought* to be done rather than what *must* be done is to court disaster. Nevertheless, although he remarks on the instability and lack of resolution in republics, we must remember that he served the Florentine republic for his entire career until its demise. And, despite his praise of ruthless princes, he concludes the final chapter of *The Prince*, "The Exhortation to Liberate Italy from the Barbarians," with a quote from Petrarch's poem *Italia Mia* because, humanist republican that he is at his core, he believes that in the Italian breast the Roman heart is still beating.

Machiavelli's more thoughtful, abstract investigation of politics, the *Discourses on Livy*, constitutes an analysis of Florentine politics in three books under the camouflage of a commentary on the Roman historian Titus Livius. What emerges are the causes of the failure of Soderini's republic. Some of these repeat those mentioned in *The Prince*, like the failure to build a citizen army, the lack of resolute policy, and the inherent instability of republics. Others point to what he sees as the root cause of these failures. In particular, there is the lack of ancient Roman civic virtue, the enervated weakness of the political class more concerned with luxury and wealth than the success of the republic. And the passivity of Christianity concerns him, compared to the Roman civil religion. What is needed, then, is a man on horseback, a prince, who can restore the lost *virtù* of Florence. But once the job is done, he should then retire and let the regenerated republic regain its freedom.

Finale

Machiavelli wrote a great deal more; he was a prolific and talented writer in a great many genres: plays, stories, letters, verse, among others. He was also an historian. From the time of Leonardo Bruni, the chancellors of Florence had the responsibility of continuing the history of the city up to their own time; but Machiavelli's *History of Florence and the Affairs of Italy* is different, as was everything he wrote.

In 1520 Cardinal Giulio de'Medici, the cousin of Pope Leo X, and the future Pope Clement VII, commissioned Machiavelli to write a new history of the city, not in his role as ruler of the city but as governor of the university. It was also a task that might end the constant importuning from the unemployed (and hence poor) former official of Soderini's regime. It is great history, especially given Machiavelli's constraints. He obviously could not offend the Medici, but he also had to adhere to his understanding of why events turned out as they did. Consequently, he moved away from traditional models by not beginning where other chancellors had left off but by returning to the foundations of the republic, although most of the material deals with the time closest to his own experience.

By 1525 he had taken the story up to the death of Lorenzo de'Medici in 1492, and there it ends, despite his deep knowledge of and experience with the events that followed. Praising Lorenzo was easier than confronting the failures of his son; and Machiavelli could focus on foreign affairs which were not only his own interest but a field in which the Medici excelled. The dramatic conclusion of *History of Florence and the Affairs of Italy*, in which lightning strikes the cupola of the cathedral at the moment of Lorenzo's death, marked a kind of celestial caesura in the city's history and destiny. As Machiavelli observed, evil followed Lorenzo's death, germinated by a cascade of events that culminated in the French invasion of Italy and the ruin of the state system that the Medici had so well managed.[14]

Machiavelli's work had little influence in his lifetime. He never regained favor, and his life after 1512 must be seen as a kind of exile from his true loves: Florence, political action, and diplomacy. He could, however, still write, and the result is an insight into his age that few others could equal. He died in June of 1527, just weeks after the Imperial army began their horrible Sack of Rome. Consequently, he did not live long enough to include this unspeakable event in his analysis of the decline and humiliation of Italy. It would be left to his contemporary and fellow Florentine, Francesco Guicciardini, to incorporate the Sack into the melancholy story of Italy after 1494.

---

14. Niccolo Machiavelli, *History of Florence and of the Affairs of Italy from the Earliest Times to the Death of Lorenzo the Magnificent.* New York and London: W. Walter Dunne, 1901. Book VIII, chapter VII. No pagination. https://ebooks.adelaide.edu.au/m/machiavelli/niccolo/m149h/index .html. "... [T]he highest pinnacle of the church of Santa Reparata [the old name for the cathedral, Santa Maria del fiore] was struck with lightning, and great part of it thrown down, to the terror and amazement of everyone. The citizens and all the princes of Italy mourned for him, and sent their ambassadors to Florence, to condole with the city on the occasion; and the justness of their grief was shortly after apparent; for being deprived of his counsel, his survivors were unable either to satisfy or restrain the ambition of Lodovico Sforza, tutor to the duke of Milan; and hence, soon after the death of Lorenzo, those evil plants began to germinate, which in a little time ruined Italy, and continue to keep her in desolation."

Illus. 7.1 Peter Paul Rubens (1577–1640), *The Battle of Anghiari*
*(detail after Leonardo da Vinci)***, 1603. Louvre, France.**

Although the diversion of the Arno may have proven a monumental failure and a great expense, it appeared that Machiavelli and Leonardo had developed a friendship. Certainly it was through the second chancellor that Leonardo was given the prestigious commission, together with Michelangelo, to paint the walls of the Room of the Five Hundred with famous Florentine victories.

Leonardo's charge was to depict the Battle of Anghiari. Unfortunately, just as he had done with *The Last Supper* in Milan, the artist insisted on using an experimental fresco technique and unstable materials, and consequently the fresco was lost. The wall was soon covered by a work of Giorgio Vasari, but a cryptic inscription (*cerca trova*—look and find) implies that the later painter did not destroy the vestigial work of Leonardo but left it protected behind his own fresco.

Even while it was being painted, Leonardo's work was recognized as a masterpiece, an opinion shared by later artists. This drawing by Rubens based on an earlier engraving shows only a detail of the monumental fresco—*The Battle of the Standard*—but nevertheless conveys the magnificence of what has been lost.

**Illus. 7.2 Giovanni Stradano, *The Siege of Florence 1529–30*,
1556–62. Palazzo Vecchio, Florence.**

This fresco of the 1529–30 siege of Florence is in the Room of Clement VII in the Palazzo Vecchio. It was painted between 1556 and 1562 by the Fleming Jan Van der Straet (1523–1605) who Italianized his name to Giovanni Stradano while working in Florence for the Medici. The Sack of Rome in 1527 had resulted in the second expulsion of the Medici and the renewal of the republic; but, after peace had been made between Pope Clement VII de'Medici and Charles V, a campaign to restore the Medici was planned.

The city was determined to resist the attack, and Michelangelo was made the chief architect of the city's defenses. Young, idealistic republicans volunteered for the militia, but the cause was hopeless. So, in August of 1530 the city capitulated, and the Medici returned in the person of Duke Alessandro de'Medici (assassinated in 1537), an illegitimate son perhaps of the pope himself and one of Florence's most distasteful rulers. Stradano's fresco tells the story from the Medici perspective. There are no scenes of violence; the countryside is lush and the city intact. The Goddess of Victory dominates the central lower register of the fresco, holding an olive branch in her right hand, symbolizing the peace that was about to descend. The reality, however, was very different: republican leaders were exiled or executed in reprisals, and the institutions and symbols of the republic were forever abolished.

PART III

Princes, Patronage, and Power

Petrarch descended from a Florentine family; and humanism found a natural and supportive environment in Florence. Coluccio Salutati and Leonardo Bruni were chancellors of Florence and developed the concept of civic humanism in the environment of the guild republic. Moreover, the revival of art and architecture inspired by ancient models and the classical tradition first emerged in the context of the Tuscan city. But it would be an error to assume that the Renaissance was a uniquely Florentine phenomenon. Indeed, one of the great strengths of humanism in Italy was its adaptability and its ability to galvanize disparate societies, informed by very different experiences, traditions, and histories from those we investigated in Florence.[1]

In principalities, where the ruler was the source of patronage and power, humanism shifted from a focus on models from the republican period of ancient Rome to referencing archetypes from the later period of the Roman Empire. Many of these principalities were ruled by professional mercenaries. It may seem odd to us, but wars in Medieval and Renaissance Italy were fought not by citizen militias but by professional mercenary bands. Their leaders were the condottieri—whose name derived from the Italian word for "contract." The condottieri who organized these contract armies were sometimes petty nobles who collected gangs of skilled thugs to rent to the highest bidder, but more often they were the rulers of small states that required additional income to augment their poor patrimony.[2]

---

1. For the artistic culture of the Italian Renaissance principalities see Charles M. Rosenberg, *The Court Cities of Northern Italy: Milan, Parma, Piacenza, Mantua, Ferrara, Bologna, Urbino, Pesaro, and Rimini*. Artistic Centers of the Italian Renaissance Series. Cambridge: Cambridge University Press, 2010.
2. See Michael Mallett, *Mercenaries and their Masters: Warfare in Renaissance Italy*. Barnsley, UK: Pen and Sword, 2009.

The practice of arms was considered an appropriate profession for these minor princes and gave an added insurance for their people against the aggression of others. And so the provision of mercenary bands came to characterize the culture of the ruling dynasties of several important states. As a counterpoint, the humanist patronage of art and learning and the reputation and honor that came from this largesse were equally valued as ornaments to the state and its ruler, and a powerful instrument of social currency.[3] In fact, all of the petty condottieri princes in the peninsula during the Renaissance used the patronage of art and culture as a means to establish their right to rule and to add some dignity to their positions: after all, many had come to power through unsavory means such as violence and usurpation. These princes also understood that artistic patronage was war by other means, so they worked to establish reputations and an aura of magnificence that almost rivaled success on the battlefield.

---

3. See Michael Baxandall, *Painting and Experience in Fifteenth-Century Italy*. Oxford: Oxford University Press, 1988.

CHAPTER 8

THE VIPERS OF MILAN

The duchy of Milan—frequent foe, sometime friend of the Florentine republic—was located in northern Italy on the rich Lombard plain. This region is irrigated by the longest river in Italy—the River Po—which to this day provides fertile land for agriculture, supporting populous, rich, and inventive communities.[4]

The huge city of Milan was a great and influential metropolis from ancient times. It was a leading Roman city, ultimately becoming capital of the Western empire after 286 AD. Milan had an equally celebrated religious history, marked by the Emperor Constantine's momentous *Edict of Milan* (313) that granted freedom of religion to Christians. St. Augustine was famously converted to Christianity while in the city: his baptism was administered by another great doctor of the Church, St. Ambrose (bishop 374–97 AD), who held the see of Milan.

After the fall of Rome, Milan's position on the flat plain of Lombardy attracted waves of invaders from across the Alps. It was destroyed by the Ostrogoths and soon after taken by the Germanic tribe of the Longobardi (Longbeards). In fact, it was from the Longobardi that the territory of Lombardy derives its name. Charlemagne captured the city in 744, declaring himself the Lombard king. Thus, Lombardy was absorbed into the Holy Roman Empire and the emperor became its source of sovereignty. Consequently, it was traditionally a Ghibelline state.

Yet despite its imperial status, Milan was a leader of the Lombard League formed in 1167 against the emperor Frederick Barbarossa. It was through this strategic alliance that Milan was able to secure its freedom as an independent commune. However, this independence led, as in so many Italian communes, to factional warfare, especially between the powerful rival families who sought to rule the territory as despots. Ultimately, the Visconti, a Ghibelline clan who enjoyed the support of the emperor, triumphed. So it was that in 1311 the Emperor Henry VII made the Visconti *signori* of the city.[5]

---

4. For detailed information beginning with Giangaleazzo Visconti, see *Il Ducato Visconteo e la Repubblica Ambrosiana (1392–1450)*. Storia di Milano. Vol. 6. Milan: Fondazione Treccani degli Alfieri, 1955.

5. The best political history of Renaissance Milan is Jane Black, *Absolutism in Renaissance Milan: Plenitude of Power under the Visconti and the Sforza 1329–1535*. Oxford: Oxford University Press, 2009. See also, Andrea Gamberini ed., *A Companion to Late Medieval and Early Modern Milan: The Distinctive Features of an Italian State*. Leiden: Brill Academic Publishing, 2014. Brill's Companions to European History, 7. There also remains the now almost century-old Dorothy Erskine Muir, *A History of Milan Under the Visconti*. London: Methuen, 1924.

Petrarch in Milan

In the late spring of 1353, Petrarch chose to move from his beloved "harbor" in the gentle forests of the Vaucluse in France in order to escape what he saw as the dissipation and disarray of the papal court at Avignon. He determined to return to his native Italy, though to which part he did not know. Although he had received a formal invitation to settle in Florence, he found it difficult to forgive the republic for the exile of his parents, despite the fact that he had a wide circle of friends there. He had sent scouts out in the months before his departure to assess the current situation in cities as widespread as Parma, Rome, Mantua, and Padua. But, when he crossed from France into Italy through the Montgenèvre Pass, he still had no idea as to where he would settle, where he would find a new harbor where he could devote himself undisturbed to his reading and writing. All he knew for certain was that he intended to "dwell forever" in his homeland of Italy: "Land far nobler than noble climes, / More fertile and more fair than all the rest."[6]

And so he arrived in Milan, accompanied by his precious books and his collection of ancient Roman coins, his servants, and his horses.[7] The city he entered was an energetic, thriving metropolis. The surplus produce from the fruitful Lombard plain had encouraged a surge in population, and that population in turn serviced highly profitable enterprises. These included the massive armaments industry famed for its production of high-quality weaponry and armor; and there was, as well, the increasingly lucrative manufacture of woolen textiles, made possible by the considerable flocks nurtured in the city's countryside. The infrastructure was robust, canals having been dug for irrigation and transportation, making Milan one of the wonders of the continent by the time of Petrarch's arrival.[8]

As befitted his status and fame, Petrarch immediately sought an audience with Giovanni Visconti, who was not only lord of the city and all of Lombardy but also Milan's archbishop. Perhaps to Petrarch's surprise—most certainly to the surprise of his Florentine friends—Giovanni extended an extraordinarily generous invitation to the scholar, offering him housing, a living, and the promise of solitude. No demands would be made upon him beyond those he chose to accept.

As a result, there was considerable consternation among Petrarch's friends when he agreed to lodge in the urban roar of Milan. Boccaccio, outraged and bitterly resentful, charged Petrarch with disloyalty to Florence and chastised him for serving a restless tyrant, an archbishop who had suffered several excommunications and seldom said Mass. Milan was Florence's implacable enemy. And, after all, it was only two years before that Petrarch had written negatively and vehemently about the "tyrant" Visconti. Others in Florence and Mantua were equally incredulous of his decision, as they might well have been, given Petrarch's own declared distaste for city life:

---

6. Thompson, 1971. p. 127.
7. Wilkins, 1958. pp. 3–12.
8. Patrizia Mainoni, "The Economy of Renaissance Milan," in Gamberini, 2014. pp. 118–41.

So I, from my earliest years such a lover of solitude and of the woods, labor now at a more advanced age in cities and amidst the hateful multitude; and I find it unpleasant."[9]

Nevertheless, Petrarch had been offered something unique—honor and security without having to perform onerous duties of state unless he personally chose to be involved. Consequently, he lived in Milan for eight years—longer than he had ever resided anywhere continuously, even in his beloved Vaucluse, and he served not only the remarkable Giovanni Visconti but also his nephew Galeazzo after Giovanni's death. Moreover, while Petrarch had been granted freedom to remain uninvolved in political matters, he did in fact help bring peace between Venice and Genoa when the Genoese asked for support from the Milanese.[10]

Petrarch also traveled to Paris and Prague on behalf of the Visconti. But he never hesitated to refuse to serve where he thought the cause was compromised—especially when he was approached to visit Avignon as a Milanese envoy. This was an offer wisely avoided as Petrarch had recently written some of the most scandalous invectives against the papal court in his *Book Without a Name (Liber Sine Nomine)*.

Indeed, it was in Milan that Petrarch worked on some of his most important writing. He continued his wide correspondence and wrote part of his *Secretum* and *Africa* and other material, all the result of his honorable service at the Visconti court. During his years in Milan Petrarch thus succeeded in raising his reputation as a writer and poet even beyond his already lofty fame, and, at the same time, by his very presence, raised the reputation of a city previously not widely celebrated for its culture.[11]

The Rise of Giangaleazzo Visconti

The death of Archbishop and *signore* Giovanni Visconti in 1354 resulted in his territories being inherited jointly by his three nephews: Bernabò, Matteo, and Galeazzo. Of these Bernabò was the most significant, as he immediately assumed rule of Milan where he soon became known for cruelty and oppression of his subjects. Matteo outdid him, practicing viciousness so extreme that Galeazzo, although himself showing a talent for elaborate methods of torture, conspired with Bernabò to murder Matteo in 1355.

The territory was then divided between the two remaining nephews, with Bernabò controlling Milan and Galeazzo, the more polished brother, establishing his court at Pavia. There he briefly assumed the sponsorship of Petrarch, continuing his late uncle's patronage, before the poet accepted a residence in Venice in 1362. He also founded the University of Pavia (1361) as well as constructed the imposing Visconti castle in that

---

9. Gamberini, 2014. p. 131.
10. Gamberini, 2014. pp. 53–60.
11. For a comprehensive study of Milan's patterns of cultural patronage and production, see Evelyn Welch, *Art and Authority in Renaissance Milan*. New Haven: Yale University Press, 1996.

city (1363). He was devout enough to undertake a pilgrimage to Jerusalem and was recognized for his cultivated and diplomatic personality. These were characteristics surprisingly unusual in the famously violent and tyrannical Visconti.

In some ways the greatest contribution made by Galeazzo was siring his only son, Giangaleazzo Visconti. When Galeazzo died in 1378, he left his territories entirely to Giangaleazzo.[12] Nevertheless, Bernabò in Milan wished to reunite the Visconti patrimony under his own family and immediately began to plot the death of his nephew. He thought this would not be difficult as Giangaleazzo had a reputation for quiet, scholarly, and pious living, rather than the traditional Visconti cruel despotism; indeed, he was an avid collector of manuscripts and lover of books.

But Giangaleazzo was also a brilliant Renaissance prince and one who had the measure of his uncle. In 1385, having heard rumors of a plot against his life from Milan, Giangaleazzo invited Bernabò and his two eldest sons to visit his territory. Not fearing anything from the man they despised, uncle and cousins went openly, only to be arrested and thrown into a dungeon where all three were summarily poisoned. Giangaleazzo then moved quickly to consolidate all the Visconti territory under his personal rule and move his court to Milan as *signore* of all Lombardy. Then in 1395 he purchased the title of "duke" from the Holy Roman Empire, thus making him the first duke of Milan.

Not content with consolidating the Visconti properties, Giangaleazzo then began to extend his state by force of arms, his ambition being to create a huge northern Italian monarchy dependent on Milan. He conquered Verona, Vicenza, Padua, and the greater part of the March of Treviso, before moving his armies relentlessly south toward Tuscany. In 1399 he acquired the lordships of Pisa and Siena, and in 1400 of Perugia and Assisi in Umbria. Finally, in 1401–2 he annexed Lucca and Bologna, the latter being a strategic prize as it controlled the passes through the Apennines. Still, it was the conquest of Florence that was critical to Giangaleazzo's ambition. But in September of 1402, only months after taking Bologna and just as he planned to mass his armies against the republic, Giangaleazzo fell ill and died of fever. So it was that Florence was saved; and it also forever allowed the voices of the Florentine republican humanists to be in the ascendant, relegating Giangaleazzo to the circle of tyrants and despots, unable to breach the wall of freedom that Florence had erected.[13]

We have seen that Florence's refusal to yield resulted in the development of civic humanism and the republican ideal of freedom as later defined by its chancellor Leonardo Bruni.[14] Florence was also defended by the rhetoric of the contemporary chancellor, Coluccio Salutati, whose missives were famously seen by Giangaleazzo as the equivalent of one hundred troops in the field. Giangaleazzo was described by the Florentines

---

12. D. M. Bueno de Mesquita, *Giangaleazzo Visconti, Duke of Milan (1351–1402): A Study in the Political Career of an Italian Despot.* Cambridge: Cambridge University Press, 2011.

13. Baron, 1966. pp. 3–38.

14. See Chapter 2, pp. 25–28.

as the Viper of Milan, an allusion to the Visconti arms of a serpent devouring a naked baby. He was associated with tyranny and despotism and the despoiling of weaker states. To Florence he was pure evil and the greatest threat to the liberty of the city and indeed all Italy. We must, however, look beneath this humanist republican propaganda created in Florence by those masters of rhetoric and invective in the chancery. What was the real Giangaleazzo like?

Certainly Giangaleazzo, like all the Visconti, could be ruthless: he did, after all, murder his uncle and cousins, even if they planned to do the same to him. But he was very different from the almost psychopathic Bernabò. Above all, he was a serious scholar and patron. The Visconti Castle in Pavia was largely completed during his reign and held much of his celebrated library, one of the most important in Italy. It was an enormous collection of manuscripts of classical authors and scientific works, subjects which were of great interest to him. He patronized the University of Pavia, endowing it with books, and he brought the famous Byzantine scholar Manuel Chrysoloras to teach Greek in Milan, broadening the humanist curriculum available in the city.[15]

To the modern eye, however, perhaps his greatest work was the construction of two exceptional churches. To this day visitors admire the exquisite Certosa of Pavia, commissioned in 1396. Renowned as one of the finest structures of the Italian Renaissance, this monastic complex rises exuberantly in its rural setting, an entrancing confection of spires and filigree in white stone. Even more famous is the Italian Gothic Duomo in Milan. Although commissioned prior to Giangaleazzo's assumption of power and not finished until two centuries later, this enduring symbol of the city was largely conceived by Giangaleazzo, who vigorously supported its construction and influenced its design.[16]

Giangaleazzo was demonstrably a great patron, but he could be so only because he was also an exceptional administrator. He encouraged his senior officials to study economics and other subjects necessary for a well-ordered duchy, and, as a consequence of this training and his oversight, the treasury expanded despite the demands of war. Giangaleazzo also introduced widespread measures in public health to combat communicable disease, especially the plague—an infection that had in large part precipitated Petrarch's ultimate departure from Milan. Quarantine was required for the ill, and medical services were provided. In the matter of communication, Giangaleazzo established a postal service for public and private letters, with up to one hundred riders servicing a

---

15. For Giangaleazzo's patronage of manuscripts and learning, see Edith W. Kirsch, *Five Illuminated Manuscripts of Giangaleazzo Visconti*. Philadelphia: Penn State University Press, 1991; Kay Sutton, "Giangaleazzo Visconti as Patron: A Prayer Book Illuminated by Pietro da Pavia," *Apollo: The International Magazine of Arts*, 372 (1993), pp. 89–96; Giovannino De'Grassi and workshop, *The Visconti Hours (Biblioteca Nazionale Centrale di Firenze)*, intro. by Millard Meiss and Edith Kirsch. New York: George Braziller, 1972.

16. For a history in English of the building produced by the 600-year-old organization of the Fabrica, see Angelo Ciceri, *The Duomo of Milan*. Milan: Veneranda Fabbrica of the Duomo of Milan, 1965.

complex system of delivery. He had canals dug and extended for inland transportation and irrigation. He also paved the streets of the city and built arcades.

It is important, then, that we not simply accept the Florentine assault on Gianga-leazzo as the Viper of Milan—the vicious tyrant and destroyer of the liberty of free cities. He was in his own way a humanist prince, but one who saw the monarchy of the Roman Empire as superior to the chaotic rule of the republic.[17] The little known and admittedly minor humanists at his court, such as Uberto Decembrio of Pavia, offer another view.[18] But none had the ability or genius of Salutati or Bruni. Thus, their pedestrian accounts have been obscured by the more attractive propaganda of the Florentines.

Gian Maria Visconti

During his reign, Giangaleazzo had despaired of an heir. He realized the need to cement his dynasty through his line, but for a time his duchess seemed unable to produce the required son. Consequently, following long-practiced Italian tradition, he appealed to the Virgin Mary to intercede. While doing so he also rather zealously promised to dedi-cate to her any boy duly conceived as appropriate recognition of her divine intervention.

His prayers worked. A boy, Gian Maria (r. 1402–12), was born and this heir was followed soon after by the spare—another son, Filippo Maria. But this fecundity posed a dilemma for Giangaleazzo: he had promised any son to the Virgin, but he could hardly undo her good work and assign the boy to a position in the Church. So instead he can-nily honored the Blessed Virgin by assigning both sons her name, hence the curious union of the traditionally male names "Gian" (an abbreviation of Giovanni, or John) and Filippo (Philip) with the feminine "Maria."

With the death of Giangaleazzo came the death of his great dream of a united Italy through a Milanese empire. His subject territories declared again their independence while his family struggled for hegemony. His son, the depraved thirteen-year-old Gian Maria, was declared duke but under the regency of his mother, Caterina Visconti, who also happened to be her husband's first cousin. Perhaps as a result of this inbreeding, Gian Maria grew ever more bizarre, famed for loving his large pack of dogs more than any human. Indeed, the rumor was spread that he trained the animals to eat human flesh—his favorite form of execution being to feed prisoners to the dogs. It was said that he hunted in the city at night, letting his dogs tear apart and devour anyone they caught after the curfew. If he thought they were at all disloyal, he would murder his subjects in large numbers—or merely if it suited his capricious whim.

---

17. Albert Rabil, "Humanism in Milan," in Rabil, 1988. pp. 235–63.

18. James Hankins, "A Manuscript of Plato's Republic in the Translation of Chrysoloras and Uberto Decembrio with Annotations of Guarino Veronese (*Reg. Lat. 1131*)," Part 1: "Chrysol-oras, Uberto Decembrio, and the Translation of the Republic," in James Hankins, John Monfasani, and Frederick Purnell Jr., eds., *Supplementum Festivum: Studies in Honor of Paul Oskar Kristeller.* Binghamton, NY: Medieval and Renaissance Texts and Studies, 1987: pp. 149–61.

Gian Maria's mother, Giangaleazzo's widow, was the only rational restraint over the young duke, but she soon proved unable to control her son. A violent mercenary captain played upon Gian Maria's cruelty and gained his trust to the point that Gian Maria dispatched his mother to a dungeon where she was poisoned in 1404. This condottiere, Facino Cane ("cane" means "dog" in Italian), then declared himself regent and protector of the unstable young duke. The nobles of the city both feared for their lives and for Milan under the obviously insane young man. When Facino Cane fortuitously fell ill in 1412 and was consequently unavailable to protect his ward, conspirators assassinated Gian Maria as he was about to enter a church. He had no heirs, so the duchy passed to his equally strange brother, Filippo Maria Visconti, in 1412.

Filippo Maria Visconti

The world of violent, lethal madness surrounding the court of Milan after the death of the remarkable duke Giangaleazzo affected everyone, but had a particularly unfortunate influence on Duke Gian Maria's brother, Filippo Maria (r. 1412–47). Often sent away from court, perhaps for his own safety, Filippo Maria had grown up to be a paranoid, cruel, and superstitious young man. However, unlike his brother he was crafty, highly intelligent, and devoted to the expansion of Milan and the glory of the city.[19]

After the assassination of his brother, Filippo ordered the brutal torture and death of the conspirators, not only to punish their assault on the sacred person of a legitimate duke but also to send a warning to other malcontents who might plot against him. He then married (in 1412) Beatrice Lascaris, the much older widow of the condottiere Facino Cane. This allowed Filippo Maria to recover not only the immense fortune that Cane had acquired in the Visconti's service, but also his highly professional army.

This marriage was not to last, in part because Beatrice seemed unable to produce an heir but also—perhaps conveniently—because the paranoid duke believed her to be unfaithful. The duchess was arrested and tortured together with one of her pages whose sin was apparently that of sitting too close to his mistress in her bedroom. Under torture the young man confessed to a crime he certainly did not commit, resulting in his and Beatrice's execution. Because he believed that they must have aided the liaison, Filippo had the duchess's ladies-in-waiting killed at the same time. Subsequently, Filippo Maria married the daughter of the duke of Savoy, a more appropriate consort for a reigning duke of Milan, and one who could ensure her father's support in his military ambitions in the north of Italy. Yet he was equally afraid of her infidelity, so he locked her up with only female attendants.

---

19. For Filippo Maria's biography, see Gigliola Soldi Rondinini, "Filippo Maria Visconti, duca di Milano," in *Dizionario Biografico degli Italiani*. Vol. 47. Rome: Istituto della Enciclopedia Italiana, 1997.

Filippo Maria's paranoia extended well beyond marital jealousy. He was afraid of sharp objects of any kind, of thunderstorms—from which he would cower in a protected space—and of strangers, even once refusing to meet the Holy Roman Emperor. He never slept in the same room on consecutive nights and often switched quarters several times in a single night, fearing being murdered in his sleep. However, his choice of rooms became increasingly reduced, as his size made it impossible to squeeze through some castle doors with any dignity. It seems that Filippo Maria, in seclusion with his counselors, astrologers, and magicians, ate continuously to the point of becoming grossly obese. Exquisitely aware of his own ugliness (courtiers were forbidden to mention his appearance), he still hoped for an heir before his death. No one under any circumstances was allowed to say the word "death," and ill members of the court had to be instantly removed so that no one would die in his proximity.

The duke's subjects never saw him, as his paranoia drove him to lock himself deep in his castles, seldom to emerge. No one in his service was ever permitted to stand at a window out of fear that some signal might be sent. A complex relay of vehicles was always ready to move the duke to another palace or castle in his dominions—by road or canal—and the vehicles were contrived in such a way that the duke would never be seen or have to exit his cabin or carriage in public. None of his counsellors was given a complete file; rather, information was distributed among many so that the pieces could only be put together in Filippo Maria's presence.

Clearly, as an individual Filippo Maria was a strange character inviting dismay and possibly contempt. But, as a duke of Milan who reigned for thirty-five years, he was in actuality quite brilliant. His diplomatic skill was remarkable for a recluse. He managed alliances with Naples, whose king he once briefly held as a respected captive, and Savoy, whose duke became his father-in-law and, curiously, served as the anti-pope Felix V with Milanese support. His armies were somewhat successful in his attempt to reassemble the state his father had once controlled, recapturing Parma and Piacenza, although he lost contests with Florence and Venice, both of which recognized the dangers of Milanese ambitions. Filippo was also a gifted administrator, bringing order and a rather oppressive stability to the Milanese state. And it is he who is recognized as the founder of the important silk industry in the city.

But it was as a patron of humanism and art that this odd man should be most praised. The duke himself was both learned and cultivated, reading widely in classical texts as well as chivalric romances. Wanting to rival the other brilliant courts of northern Italy, he brought the celebrated rhetorician and grammarian Gasparino Barzizza to Milan in 1418 to open a humanist school that for decades trained scholars in the new classical Latin style for which he was famous. Barzizza's method of teaching the writing of classical Latin was so influential that he is recognized as the stylist behind so many of his pupils—Leon Battista Alberti, among them—and his textbook on the writing of letters became the first book ever printed in France. In appreciation of his rhetorical skill, Filippo Maria appointed Barzizza as the orator of his court.[20]

Filippo Maria also patronized Pier Candido Decembrio, the more famous son of his father's humanist servant, Uberto Decembrio. Filippo Maria appointed him his secretary and used him for diplomatic work as well.[21] But his most important commission was the completion of the *Aeneid* of Vergil, not out of humanist ambition but because the Visconti believed that they were directly descended from Aeneas. Pier Candido also made a great many translations from the Greek, including texts by Plato, Xenophon, and Aristotle, as well as using classical sources to argue in favor of monarchy over republicanism. But for our purposes, Pier Candido's most significant contribution was his biography of his master, Filippo Maria, written immediately after the duke's death and the source of much of our intimate knowledge of that strange man's life.[22]

Pier Candido had already, significantly, produced a biography of Petrarch (*Vita Francesci Petrarchae*), but his inspiration for his *Vita di Filippo Maria Visconti* was Suetonius's *Lives of the Twelve Caesars*, hence the somewhat tabloid detail. It is, like so many humanist histories, an attempt to use an ancient Latin model for contemporary events; and in the case of Filippo Maria, the model of Suetonius is certainly appropriate.[23]

Filippo also brought artists to his court. Pisanello created a medal of Filippo Maria, for example, which likely flattered him, at least in full profile. But what is oddly the most enduring monument of artistic patronage of this duke is the tarot deck. For throughout his life, in addition to being afflicted with pathological paranoia, Filippo Maria was also addicted to and firmly believed in magicians and astrologers. In 1424–25, the court painter Michelino da Besozzo produced the first ever example of a tarot deck—the eponymous "Michelino Deck"—to celebrate both the duke's love of card games and his superstitious personality.[24]

---

20. Guido Martellotti, "Gasparino Barzizza," in *Dante e Boccaccio e altri scrittori dall'Umanesimo al Romanticismo*. Florence: Leo S. Olschki, 1983. pp. 468–78.

21. Cynthia Munro Pyle, "Pier Candido Decembrio and Rome," in *Milan and Lombardy in the Renaissance: Essays in Cultural History*. Rome: La Fenice, Istituto di filologia moderna, Università degli studi di Parma, testi e studi, nuova serie, studi, 1, 1997. pp. 31–44.

22. Gary Ianziti, "Pier Candido Decembrio and the Beginnings of Humanist Historiography in Visconti Milan," in Nicholas Scott Baker and Brian Jeffrey Maxson, eds., *After Civic Humanism: Learning and Politics in Renaissance Italy*. Toronto: University of Toronto Press, 2015. pp. 153–72. See also Marianne Pade, "Guarino at Ferrara in the 1430s: Pier Candido Decembrio's *Comparatione di Cesare e d'Alexandro*," in Marianne Pade, ed., *The Reception of Plutarch's Lives in Fifteenth-Century Italy*. 2 vols. Copenhagen: Museum Tusculanum, 2007. I, pp. 251–54.

23. Pier Candido Decembrio, *Vita di Filippo Maria Visconti*, ed. Elio Bartolini. Milan: Adelphi Edizioni, 1983.

24. The significance of astrology at the Milanese court beginning with Filippo Maria's daughter Bianca is authoritatively illustrated in Monica Azzolini, *The Duke and the Stars: Astrology and Politics in Renaissance Milan*. I Tatti Studies in Italian Renaissance History. Cambridge, MA: Harvard University Press, 2013.

This first-ever example of the tarot was almost certainly created in celebration of the birth of Filippo's natural daughter, Bianca, and the "triumphs" (*trionfi*) that attended that event. For despite the fact that he was a slave to their schedules, the magicians whom Filippo Maria consulted daily ultimately failed to facilitate his most important desire— that he be able to sire a legitimate heir. Bianca was merely the illegitimate daughter of one of his mistresses. Despite his extraordinary efforts, he lacked the son who would continue the main line of the Visconti dynasty.

This last Visconti duke of Milan, then, was a curious mixture of brilliance and strangeness. It must be remembered that the humanist recovery of classical antiquity brought to light not only the exempla of great men accomplishing great deeds but also the more sordid aspects of the lives of the ancient Roman emperors, such as those depicted in Suetonius. In choosing to place Filippo Maria in the company of Tiberius, Pier Candido Decembrio is illustrating the power of classical models to illuminate the present and proving once more the intellectual and cultural authority of all aspects of the ancient world represented by humanism.

Illus. 8.1 Ambrogio da Fossano, known as il Bergognone (d. ca. 1522),
Duke Giangaleazzo Visconti with his three sons, presents a model
of the Certosa di Pavia to the Virgin. **Certosa, Pavia.**

This fresco by il Bergognone illustrates the duke, Giangaleazzo Visconti, fulfilling his votive oath to the Virgin Mary but painted from 1492–95 during the reign of Lodovico Sforza, *il Moro*. The presence of Giangaleazzo's sons is significant because his oath was made to the Virgin to build a great church and monastery dedicated to her if the duchess should bring forth a male heir. The dynastic brutality of the Visconti required a secure succession, and Giangaleazzo's wife had suffered miscarriages. This later fresco, then, is a narrative of how the Virgin honored the duke's prayer for sons, as they are portrayed on the Virgin's left, the same side as her son, Jesus. The model of the church to her right represents the transaction of the votive supplication. The dynastic element is central because the church was to be the Visconti burial chapel; and, in fact, Giangaleazzo (d. 1402) is buried in the right transept in a splendid tomb by Gian Cristoforo Romano, surmounted by a similar image of the Virgin and Child. This commission of Duke Lodovico Sforza reinforces the dynastic continuity between the two families of Visconti and Sforza.

CHAPTER 9

MILAN TRIUMPHANT

The death of Filippo Maria Visconti signaled the extinction of the main branch of his dynasty. The duke had produced only one child: an illegitimate daughter, Bianca, whom he had married to his leading condottiere, Francesco di Muzio. Called "Sforza" because of his bodily strength, Francesco was himself the son of a condottiere who had been ennobled by the king of Naples for his service. Francesco's union with Bianca succeeded doubly in linking his ambitions to the fate of the Visconti for she brought with her as dowry the control of several Lombard towns. In effect, Francesco Sforza's army had become the paranoid old duke's army, even though Sforza had earlier fought against Milan and despite Filippo Maria's lingering distrust of his new son-in-law.

The people of Milan, having endured the cruelty and unpredictability of the last two Visconti dukes, did not want another tyrant as their ruler. Thus, in 1447, soon after Filippo Maria's death, they proclaimed a republic, one made sacred by invoking the memory of St. Ambrose, the city's saintly patron. However, this Ambrosian Republic was in direct contravention of Filippo Maria's will which named the king of Naples as his chosen successor. Furthermore, the Holy Roman Emperor, who was Milan's feudal overlord, refused to recognize this claim of popular sovereignty and independence and threatened war to ensure that his own candidate would be proclaimed as duke. To add more danger to this precarious situation, neighboring Italian states, especially Venice, looked to take advantage of Milan's weakness and instability to seize territory.

Consequently, the Ambrosian Republic engaged Francesco Sforza to protect the city and the new regime. He was able to bring some measure of stability to the situation, but then was dismissed in a most ignominious fashion. Motivated in equal parts by anger and ambition, Sforza used this occasion to declare his own rule of the city, citing his status as the husband of Bianca, the last Visconti's only child. Sforza's tough, experienced mercenary army then laid siege to the city, until in 1450 Milan was starved into submission. The city gates were opened, and Sforza's troops, in a politically astute act of generosity, distributed bread to the people. With armed soldiers posted in highly visible places, he then demanded from the senate the rule of the city. It was summarily granted. Francesco Sforza was proclaimed duke, despite the protestations of the emperor and the resentment of the republicans.[1]

---

1. Although over a century old (1907), Cecilia Ady, *A History of Milan under the Sforza*, CreateSpace Independent Publishing Platform, 2015, is still available in a reprint edition.

Francesco Sforza's Rule

The distrust and anger felt toward the new duke and dynasty quickly dissipated, however, as his rule proved strong, capable, and effective. He ran the state as he ran his army—with skill, organizational genius, discipline, and authority. Stability returned to the city, and it appeared that a new golden age had dawned in Milan. This was especially so as Francesco wisely sought a policy of peace and security rather than adventurism and war, despite his profession.

He built upon the administrative procedures Filippo Maria had put in place but made them far more efficient. The laws he passed and taxation he assessed were fair, even if sometimes severe, and his officials were controlled and monitored. Well-established industries, such as armaments and sericulture, thrived, and the canal network begun under the Visconti was extended. A new hospital (Ospedale Maggiore) was constructed and public buildings refurbished or new structures built. Of these the most important was the imposing Castello Sforzesco, a new ducal palace begun in 1450 to replace the Visconti castle destroyed during the Ambrosian Republic.

The Castello was a huge, intimidating fortress in the center of the city, part pleasure palace and part condottiere fortress designed to protect the duke while at the same time advertising his power and wealth to his people. It stands to this day as homage to this first Sforza ruler. As a burial chapel for his family, Francesco commissioned the construction of the convent of Santa Maria delle Grazie, with the Milanese Guiniforte Solari as architect. This church, completed in 1469, with its deep connections to the ruling family, would continue to be expanded and decorated by his son Lodovico turning it into a symbol of the Renaissance in Milan, and eventually the site of Leonardo's *Last Supper*.

Although he was a professional soldier, Francesco was also interested in books and literature. He expanded the great library that Giangaleazzo had begun in Pavia and honored scholars and artists at his court. His court poet was the arrogant and intemperate[2] but very learned and gifted humanist Francesco Filelfo, a servant Francesco had inherited from Filippo Maria Visconti. As court poet Filelfo had the responsibility of writing works in praise of his patron. In Filelfo's case, this reached the level of an epic poem—the *Sforziad*—based on the life of Francesco Sforza and modeled somewhat on the *Aeneid*; in this epic, Francesco was cast in the succession of Aeneas and Augustus.[3]

This epic eventually ran to almost thirteen thousand lines but was still never completed. Nevertheless, it illustrates how humanism was manifested in the princely courts, despite its being practiced far from the traditions of Florence and the republicanism of Leonardo Bruni. Here humanism was in praise of the Roman Empire and the majestic stability of Augustus and the good emperors: the devotion to classical learning and style

---

2. This established reputation has been challenged as the consequence of the invectives of his detractors. See Diana Robin, "Reassessment of the Character of Francesco Filelfo," *Renaissance Quarterly* 36 (1983), pp. 202–24.

3. Diana Robin, *Filelfo in Milan: Writings 1451–1477*. Princeton: Princeton University Press, 1991.

remained, but the emphasis shifted from the pristine and virtuous republic to the strong, gifted, and powerful prince who brought peace, order, and stability and who left a city of marble after having inherited one of brick.

In fact, Filelfo was deeply read in the classics, both Latin and Greek. He had studied in Constantinople where he married the great-niece of Manuel Chrysoloras and served the Venetians in the Byzantine capital and later the Byzantine emperor himself. Odes, occasional poems, and flattering prose all streamed from his pen, in a brilliant, fluid, but somewhat sycophantic style. Overall, Filelfo was a very famous scholar and poet and Francesco Sforza's court was given luster by his presence.

The Peace of Lodi

Of all Francesco's successes, however, it was his alliance with Cosimo de'Medici and his negotiation of the Peace of Lodi in 1454 that made the greatest difference to Italy and indirectly to Renaissance culture. For it was through this peace that the rulers of the peninsula could develop and enjoy patronage in an age of stability and calm.

From the time he assumed power, Sforza was nevertheless endangered on his throne, as he ruled without the recognition of the emperor, who claimed Milan as his fief. Naples, whose king had been Filippo Maria's choice as his successor, equally obstinately refused to accept the new dynasty on the grounds its authority had been acquired by force. Venice was also anxious to expand its territory at Milan's expense. Internally, Sforza's support among the people of his city was not yet fully established. In these circumstances, the best solution was to avoid or limit war by defining spheres of influence for the five great Italian powers: Venice, Milan, Florence, the States of the Church, and Naples.

As a parvenu ruler, Francesco had much in common with Cosimo de'Medici in Florence, a man who also needed peace to secure his hold on power. Ironically, Cosimo had once employed Francesco's army against Milan in the 1430s so these men understood each other and the situation in the peninsula very well. The signing of the Peace of Lodi in 1454 gave everyone involved the security to follow their own policies in some measure of safety and without the prospect of expending the huge amounts of cash required by mercenary warfare.

The next year, 1455, the peace was expanded by the signatories into the Italian League, which promised a collective security to all of Italy against foreign intervention. If any of the designated Italian states were to be attacked from outside the peninsula, the others would rally to its defense. This was a treaty much to the advantage of Milan, given its geographical position and international borders. To the north was the Holy Roman Empire whose leader was Francesco's implacable enemy. To the west lay France where the French duke of Orleans, the grandson of Valentina, the daughter of Giangaleazzo Visconti, also claimed the duchy of Milan.

The years from 1455 to Francesco's death in 1466 consequently saw a period of calm prosperity throughout the peninsula and in Milan in particular. The duke grew in such estimation of his people that he was greatly mourned in his passing. Happily, he seemed to have ensured a peaceful succession as he and Bianca had produced eight children, including a son and heir, and several spares who could take that boy's place if required. Francesco's younger son Ascanio would rise in the Church to the Sacred College and come close to the papacy, thus offering another measure of stability. His daughter Ippolita wed Alfonso II, king of Naples, neutralizing the threat that Filippo Maria's will had caused. Unfortunately, the curse of Milan seems to have held. As with the Visconti, the Sforza dynasty was fated to see good dukes alternate with evil rulers.

Galeazzo Maria Sforza

Galeazzo Maria (r. 1466–76) was the eldest son of Francesco Sforza and Bianca Visconti.[4] He was educated largely by Filelfo who attempted to instill a love of literature and culture in the young man, even to the point that his father intervened and reminded the court humanist that he was training a future prince and not a poet. It appears that there was little danger of the boy becoming a humanist himself, however, although he was noted for enjoying a fine talent for extemporaneous speaking. He also was a great lover of music and later brought a number of Flemish composers to his court and his chapel.[5] That said, the two compelling interests of this extremely complex personality were gambling and women. He was also exceptionally greedy for other men's property and cruel in the best Visconti tradition, a trait he exhibited often in the torture and execution of those who had offended him or broken the law.

Galeazzo was twenty-two when his father died, and he was declared, through both public approbation and pragmatic acknowledgment of his descent, to be the duke of Milan. Nevertheless, his mother, Bianca, remained a powerful influence at court, attempting to control some of his voracious appetites, desires that seemed to intensify with age. Consequently, he began to distance his mother from his rule, eventually suggesting she leave Milan and return to her territory of Cremona, which had been her father's settlement as her dowry on her marriage to Francesco Sforza. She acquiesced, but did, however, return for her son's wedding in 1468, despite being warned against the journey. After the wedding feast and during her return to Cremona, she fell ill en route and died. Much of Italy and a great many in Milan believed that she had been poisoned on the order of Galeazzo Maria, her son, as their estrangement had led to her seeking allies among Milan's enemies.

---

4. Gregory Lubkin, *A Renaissance Court: Milan under Galeazzo Maria Sforza*. Berkeley and Los Angeles: University of California Press, 1994.
5. L. Matthews and P. Merkley, *Music and Patronage in the Sforza Court*. Turnhout, Belgium: Brepols, 1999.

Whether or not that murder was planned by the duke, with the death of his mother his actions and personality became ever more unstable. His cruelty increased to the point that he often personally participated in torture. His greed expanded, as he capriciously confiscated the properties of his nobles if they appealed to him, and he demanded that they gamble for high stakes, knowing the dangers if they should win. But it was his obsessive lechery that caused the greatest distress. Seeing a pretty young woman at court, he would demand she be sent to him or he would arrange it directly himself, debauching the wives, sisters, and daughters of his courtiers. These were the practices that led to his assassination.

Three young men of the noblest Milanese families, all of whom had places at court, conspired to rid their city of the tyrant. In this they were coached by their tutor, a humanist who filled them with stories of Brutus and Cassius and other classical tyrannicides in their lessons. This humanist, Cola Montano, had been famously humiliated by the duke and publicly whipped, an act he swore never to forgive. Of the three conspirators, one was avenging his young sister whose virginity had been taken by the duke; another was avenging his family's loss of substantial property, illegally alienated by Galeazzo Maria; and the third was a committed ideological republican, distraught that the noble experiment of the Ambrosian Republic had failed and trusting that the death of the Sforza would rekindle republican virtue in his city. In fact, all three conspirators were convinced that the entire population—regardless of rank—would rise against the Sforza once news of the duke's assassination became known. They believed that everyone hated him as much as they did. Sadly, they were mistaken.

The plot was set for the day after Christmas when it was universally known that the duke would attend mass at the church of St. Stephen, as was traditional. The assassins waited by the door and in unison stabbed Galeazzo, killing him immediately. One conspirator was slain at the scene, as he unfortunately tripped over the long trains of the court ladies who had already taken their seats near the altar. The others were apprehended soon after, with one killed on sight and the other brought to the prisons to endure unspeakable torture. Nevertheless, he achieved immortality for his heroic dying declaration in Latin, "My death is painful, but my fame shall be everlasting (*mors acerba, fama perpetua*)"—a humanist even unto death.[6]

What did not happen was a popular revolt. On the contrary, the citizenry was appalled, expressing horror and fury at the duke's death. Although lecherous, cruel, and greedy at court, he was not seen as such by most of the common people. He had supported agriculture and the city's industries, as well as bringing music to Milan, together with a narcissistic sense of pomp and glory appreciated by the lower orders. His entry into Florence, for example, had been so magnificent that it was talked about for years

---

6. Those famous words now even provide the subtitle for a popular Italian historical narrative, Ernesto Speroni, *Congiura. Mors acerba, fama perpetua*. Milan: Lampi di Stampa, 2006.

afterward. And, his love of tennis and his skill at hunting and cards gave the still young duke a raffish reputation that many admired.

Nevertheless, the assassination of Galeazzo Maria Sforza in 1476 was ultimately a positive act as it resulted in the rise of his brother, Lodovico, who would bring Milan to the pinnacle of its fame and glory.

The Regency of Lodovico il Moro

Giangaleazzo Sforza (r. 1476–94), the eldest legitimate son of the murdered Galeazzo Maria, was only seven when his father was assassinated. As a result, the next years saw a divisive struggle for the regency. On one side was, most prominently, his mother, the duchess Bona of Savoy. In opposition was his uncle Lodovico, the fourth son of Francesco Sforza, popularly called *il Moro*—the Moor—a reference to both his swarthy complexion and his middle name of "Mauro."[7]

Lodovico did not have an easy road to power, however, as his early attempt to supplant the dowager duchess ended in his brief exile. He managed to orchestrate his return and outmaneuvered Bona of Savoy, in part by arranging the execution of her gifted minister and confidant Francesco (Cicco) Simonetta, through a false charge of treason in 1480, despite Simonetta's brilliant and loyal service to the Sforza from before the time of their ascent to power. In the aftermath, Bona of Savoy was required to quit Milan, with the effect of removing Lodovico's most formidable rival. Thus, by 1481 Ludovico was triumphant, and he began to assume the duties of regent of Milan, still acting, he claimed, only in his nephew's name.

Lodovico proved a skillful ruler and master diplomat. He supported the expansion of Milanese industries, such as armaments, but also extended the network of canals and supported agriculture and animal husbandry to provide sufficient food for his territory. Silkworm cultivation and the manufacture of silken textiles developed into an increasingly important source of wealth, employing up to twenty thousand workers.

In 1488 Lodovico arranged for his nephew, the duke, to marry his first cousin, the granddaughter of both the king of Naples and Francesco Sforza, Isabella of Aragon. This sealed an even closer alliance between the two states at a moment when the situation in Italy was becoming unstable, in part because of fear of an ambitious Venice and the possibility of a French invasion. Similarly, Lodovico maintained a warm relationship with Lorenzo de'Medici, sustained since the War of the Pazzi Conspiracy, in which Lodovico had intervened to assist Lorenzo in his overtures to Naples. And, the papacy was massaged by Lodovico's extremely talented brother Ascanio Sforza, who was a powerful cardinal in the Sacred College and one who assisted in the elevation of Alexander VI Borgia in 1492.

---

7. Gino Benzoni, "Lodovico Sforza, detto il Moro, duca di Milano," in *Dizionario Biografico degli Italiani*. Vol. 66. Rome: Istituto della Enciclopedia Italiana, 2006.

In 1491 Lodovico brought his greatest prize to Milan: Beatrice d'Este, his fifteen-year-old bride. She was the daughter of Ercole I, duke of Ferrara, and sister to the celebrated Isabella d'Este, Marchioness of Mantua. Like her sister, she enjoyed a brilliant classical education and was vivacious and charming, traits that compensated to a degree for Lodovico's rather austere character. In 1493 Beatrice gave birth to a son, Massimiliano, who would in time briefly succeed to the duchy, as would his slightly younger brother Francesco (b. 1495).[8]

These two sons raised the stakes in Lodovico's precarious position as regent for his nephew, who was now reaching the age of majority. Moreover, the young duchess's family in Naples was becoming ambitious for her husband to assume rule of Milan in his own name. Isabella of Aragon had as early as 1492 implored her grandfather, Ferdinand (Ferrante) of Naples, to demand that Lodovico relinquish his power to the legitimate duke. Ferdinand died in 1494 and the new king of Naples, Alfonso II, despite his close family connections to the Sforza, was no longer content with the Milanese alliance and began to negotiate with Pope Alexander VI, another Spaniard, to pressure Lodovico to yield the regency and form a joint defense against the French threat.[9]

Lodovico began a diplomatic campaign to maintain his power in 1492–93. He made an overture to Venice, the ambitious neighbor he had previously distrusted. And he encouraged Charles VIII of France to press his claim to the Neapolitan throne. If Charles could neutralize the duchess's Aragonese family, then Lodovico would be in a strong position to seize the crown and secure his son as his successor to protect his family from the anger of his nephew and his ambitious Neapolitan duchess. To ensure success, Lodovico approached the Holy Roman Emperor Maximilian, who was technically the overlord of Milan. Always short of money, Maximilian happily accepted an enormous sum of cash and Lodovico's niece, Bianca, the sister of the legitimate duke, as his wife. In return, he invoked his imperial authority and declared Lodovico to be the duke should his nephew prematurely die, despite Giangaleazzo and Isabella having had a son, Francesco, who should have been the next in line to the throne.

The French invasions of 1494 brought all these issues into play under a prevailing climate of shifting alliances fueled by raw personal ambition. For example, even though Lodovico had encouraged the French king's ambitions, Charles VIII had not treated him as the de facto ruler. Instead, Charles had pointedly emphasized the legitimacy of the young duke by visiting him in person. Charles was also probably aware of the deal Lodovico had made with the Emperor Maximilian and was sensitive to the power play

8. Julia Cartwright Ady's 1905 biography of Beatrice remains largely available and remarkably still engaging: *Beatrice d'Este, Duchess of Milan, 1475–1497: A Study of the Renaissance*. London: J. M. Dent & Co., 1905. There is a more recent Italian biography in the *Le Vite* series: Silvia Alberti de Mazzeri, *Beatrice d'Este duchessa di Milano*. Santarcangelo di Romagna: Rusconi, 1986.

9. David Abulafia, ed., *The French Descent into Renaissance Italy, 1494–95: Antecedents and Effects*. Aldershot, UK: Ashgate, 1995.

between France and the empire that it implied. The situation was further complicated by the ambitions of the king's cousin, the duke of Orleans, who had a claim to Milan through the Visconti line.[10]

Lodovico il Moro, *Duke of Milan*

Mere days after Charles had promised Giangaleazzo his support, the legitimate young duke died at Pavia in October of 1494. The circumstances were, to say the least, suspicious. Word was put out that the young man had died of sexual excess, but it was universally believed that he had been poisoned on Lodovico's orders, a belief corroborated by at least one physician who inspected the body.

At the time of Giangaleazzo's passing, Lodovico had been accompanying Charles on the king's journey southward toward Naples. On hearing the news, he rapidly returned to Milan to press his claim to the dukedom, a claim he had so carefully prepared through his agreement with the Emperor Maximilian. For his part, King Charles knew that there was little he could do to prevent Lodovico's elevation. Furthermore, Charles certainly did not want a hostile Milan behind him during his progress south. So, he congratulated Lodovico on his succession to the throne, but only in the most perfunctory way.

Lodovico, however, recognized the ambivalence of Charles's recognition of his rule and on seeing the ease with which Charles conquered Naples, the new duke became as wary of Charles as were the other powers of Italy. He switched allegiance and joined the league formed by Venice to drive out the French. And at Fornovo in Lombardy in 1495, a Milanese army defeated the French as they were returning to France.

The new duke of Milan had redeemed himself in Italian eyes, winning honor and respect, and was no longer seen as a tool of Charles's policy. His reputation was rehabilitated and the rumors about his dubious route to the throne became secondary to his defense of Italian independence. Therefore, it seemed by 1495 that Lodovico had played a brilliant hand: he was duke both de facto and now de jure; he had secured his dynasty and he had defeated the invading French, winning praise and showing military prowess, adding to his already powerful reputation as a patron of culture and a diplomat. Even Charles VIII of France forgave his treachery, needing the Milanese alliance as security for future incursions.

Then, when all seemed secure in Milan, personal tragedy struck. At the very beginning of 1497, Lodovico's immensely popular wife, Beatrice d'Este, died in childbirth. She was only twenty-one years old. The court believed that she was melancholy from the duke's many infidelities with his mistresses; but the reality was that Lodovico, who adored his wife, was devastated. Consequently, he spent weeks in solitary prayer and despair just at the moment when decisive action was needed. The dilemma arose from another untimely death. In April of 1498 Charles VIII of France was at Amboise.

---

10. See Mallett and Shaw, 2012.

Unfortunately, he ran forcefully into a low lintel while racing to see a tennis match. Later that afternoon he fell into a coma from which he never recovered, dying early the next morning. He was only twenty-eight.

Charles VIII had no living male issue, so the crown passed to his cousin, who became Louis XII. This cousin was that very duke of Orleans who had tried in 1494 to press his claim to Milan through his Visconti antecedents. Consequently, in ascending to the throne of France he simultaneously asserted his claim to the crown of Milan. Lodovico's brinkmanship and clever diplomatic maneuvering was coming undone. Disaster had merely been postponed.

In 1498, the French, under Louis XII, invaded Italy once again, but this time bound for Milan, not Naples. Despite his victory over the French at Fornovo in 1495, the other major states of Italy saw no compelling reason to anger the French by coming to Lodovico's aid, especially as the situation in Italy was becoming increasingly dangerous because of the desire of various states to capitalize on the instability. The papacy and Naples remained hostile, and Venice wanted to take advantage of Milanese weakness to continue its expansion into the peninsula, including northern Lombardy. Florence was in turmoil as a result of the expulsion of the Medici and the rise of Savonarola, whose policy was zealously pro-French, an alliance that was maintained even after the fall of the Dominican in the spring of 1498. Milan, then, stood alone against the powerful French army, bereft of allies.

It was no surprise, then, that the city fell to Louis in 1499. However, Lodovico managed to escape to the court of his nephew by marriage, the Emperor Maximilian. Equipped with a mercenary army, Lodovico returned to Milan in 1500 and managed to retake the city but not his sumptuously decorated palace, the fortified Castello Sforzesco. Instead, he moved his military base to Novara, just over thirty miles from Milan. Louis XII marched on Novara with his forces and besieged the town. Lodovico was defeated, betrayed by his own Swiss mercenaries who refused to fight their own countrymen employed by the French. According to tradition, Lodovico was handed to the French by a Swiss soldier, Hans Turmann, who was bribed to do so but was later executed for his treachery by his fellow Swiss mercenaries.

Louis was at once harsh and benevolent to Lodovico. The duke was not granted an audience with the king, despite his pleas and the intervention of other rulers who referenced the rules of chivalry. But, taken to France as a prisoner, Lodovico was lodged eventually in the Chateau of Loches, where he was accorded a great deal of freedom and kept in a manner respectful of his rank; Louis even sent his own physician to him when he was ill. However, in 1508, Lodovico attempted to escape. This misadventure, occurring at a decisive moment of European history when the War of the League of Cambrai had just begun, forced Louis to place the deposed duke in a subterranean dungeon, relieved of all pleasures and comforts, even his books. It was there in May 1508 that he died, soon after his abortive plan to escape.

Leonardo da Vinci in Milan

As with so many of the Renaissance princes of Italy, Lodovico recognized the value of patronage. Some of his commissions were the continuation of earlier projects, such as work on the splendid gothic cathedral begun by Giangaleazzo Visconti.[11] And, naturally, there were the necessary but elegant additions to the city's public buildings and churches.[12] Already resident in Milan was Donato Bramante from Urbino who had come to the city probably sometime after 1474 and he may have been given commissions as early as 1476 by the dowager duchess Bona and Duke Giangaleazzo. He was certainly involved in the building of Santa Maria Presso San Satiro, where his illusionistic choir (1482–86) remains a tour de force, the brilliant response to a very restricted site. He designed the cloisters of Sant'Ambrogio and contributed to the Great Hospital.

But it was Bramante's enlarging of Santa Maria delle Grazie (1492–96) that was perhaps his most important legacy in the city. He was called upon by Lodovico to build the transept and choir of the church, which had been completed in 1469 by Guiniforte Solari on the order of Francesco Sforza. This was not only an important commission for Bramante but it was also a statement by Lodovico that this was now the dynastic church in the city. His tomb was to be set in the space created by Bramante; so, after her early death, Beatrice d'Este was buried there to await her husband. As with so many of the artists and scholars at the Sforza court, Bramante fled the city at the time of the French invasion of 1499 and went to Rome where he would become the architect of St. Peter's basilica and the huge addition to the apostolic palace commanded by Julius II, the Cortile del Belvedere.

However, of all the artists surrounding Lodovico none had the reputation of Leonardo da Vinci. When Lorenzo de'Medici first encouraged the artist to leave Florence and work for Lodovico, he was doing Leonardo a great favor.[13] The abstract world of Laurentian Florence with its love of Neoplatonic thought and esoteric humanist discussion did not suit Leonardo well. He was, rather, a gifted empiricist, who, as the illegitimate son of a provincial notary, lacked formal training in the polished traditions of humanism. Leonardo liked to say that his education was from nature, not books. When he wrote to offer his services to Lodovico, he described himself as a jack of all cultural trades: a musician—which he very much was, a military engineer, and an artist.

During the sixteen years he served at the court in Milan, Leonardo produced some of his most celebrated works. *Lady with an Ermine*—his portrait of Lodovico's mistress, Cecilia Gallerani—is universally recognized as a masterpiece of brilliant technique and

11. Serena Romano, "Milan (and Lombardy): Art and Architecture, 1277–1535," in Gamberini, 2014. pp. 214–47.

12. Alison Cole, "Local Expertise and Foreign Talent: Milan and Pavia Under Lodovico il Moro," *Italian Renaissance Courts: Art, Pleasure and Power*. London: Lawrence King, 2016. pp. 200–51.

13. Luke Syson, *Leonardo da Vinci: Painter at the Court of Milan*. London: National Gallery London, 2011.

insight. His *Virgin of the Rocks* (of which there are two versions—one in the Louvre and one in the National Gallery in London) was commissioned by a Milanese confraternity; and his *Last Supper* in the refectory of the monastery of Santa Maria delle Grazie remains one of Western culture's most remarkable creations, despite its poor state of conservation.

The difficulty was that the brothers commissioned Leonardo to paint the *Last Supper* in fresco, a technique he had never before practiced. It soon became apparent that it was a totally unsuitable medium for him. Leonardo had invented and become famous for his "sfumato"—the misty effect of blending line and color in his paintings that is most famously observed in the Mona Lisa's eyes. This technique was achieved by layering glazes one on top of the other and through constant retouching. Fresco, on the other hand, requires swift execution because the paints are absorbed deeply into rapidly drying wet plaster. Ever inventive, Leonardo developed a different technique for painting the refectory wall, mixing pitch, mastic, and clay to apply to the surface so that the color would not be absorbed immediately and he could work slowly. Unfortunately, the experiment did not work, and *The Last Supper* had begun to flake off the wall even during Leonardo's lifetime. Yet even though some of the figures are now barely discernible, the masterpiece still strikes awe in viewers to this day.[14]

Like all court artists, Leonardo had other responsibilities, some of which were hardly worthy of a great genius but which Leonardo seemed to accomplish with his usual skill. For example, he was charged with organizing the celebrations surrounding the wedding of Lodovico and Beatrice d'Este in January 1491—an enormously complicated affair because it was a double wedding also honoring the marriage of Beatrice's brother, Alfonso d'Este, to Lodovico's niece, Anna.[15]

Events like these were important opportunities for Leonardo to shine at court. He was a splendid composer and musician who played a lyre that he had himself crafted in the shape of a horse's head. He was devastatingly handsome, dressed beautifully in the latest fashion, and was utterly charming with women. Because of his sexual orientation, he had no carnal interest in them, so his charm and attentions were welcomed by everyone, including the husbands and fathers of ladies whose flirtations might otherwise have elicited aggressive jealousy.

Lodovico also employed Leonardo as his personal interior decorator, having him paint at least two rooms in the Castello Sforzesco. The only one that survives is the celebrated *sala delle asse* or "room of the wooden planks," a reference to the wooden wall paneling that had earlier been installed to make the room temperature more comfortable. Leonardo's decorative scheme reflects his lifelong apprenticeship to nature, as the

---

14. Kemp, 2006. pp. 177–86.
15. See Elvira Garbero Zorzi, "Court Spectacle," in Sergio Bertelli, ed., *Italian Renaissance Courts*, trs. M. Fitton and G. Culverwell. London: Sidgwick and Jackson, 1986. pp. 157–58. Leonardo's designs for the *giostra-torneo* became ideal exemplars of this kind of extravagant spectacle.

intertwined and knotted boughs and leaves rising from trunks in the corners create a brilliant canopy on the ceiling. In his notebooks we can see Leonardo experimenting with these woven branches, creating perfectly balanced knots to decorate the duke's private space.[16]

Leonardo began recording his thoughts, observations, experiments, and drawing in these notebooks beginning as early as 1478. A unique insight into the mind of a genius and the working technique of an important artist, they contain thousands of pages of text and drawings inscribed in Leonardo's unique, left-handed mirror writing, despite the artist being perfectly ambidextrous and quite capable of normal script. We are fortunate to still have many of these notebooks, and their survival is the consequence of Leonardo's time in Milan and his employment of an aristocratic apprentice, one Francesco Melzi (ca. 1491–1570). Melzi was brought into Leonardo's household in Milan after the artist had met his father, a military engineer and officer at the Sforza court. The boy later did become a painter, which was unusual for one of his rank. It was perhaps because of his chosen profession, his status, and his loyalty verging on hero worship that Leonardo made him the beneficiary of the notebooks after his death in 1519.

Melzi devoted himself to preserving his master's work for the fifty years he outlived Leonardo, housing and caring for them in his family villa which is still owned by the Melzi dukes. He compiled *The Treatise on Painting*, a collection and distillation of Leonardo's scattered writings on art. He also indexed some of the voluminous writings of his teacher. Unfortunately, Melzi's son Orazio was completely disinterested in the notebooks that had been his father's passion and allowed them to be dispersed. But by then they were safe for posterity.[17]

It was also in Milan that Leonardo began the serious study of anatomy, filling his notebooks with the finest anatomical drawings until Vesalius. His intention, he said, was to write a textbook on anatomy, particularly on the body in motion. But like so much of what Leonardo planned, he never wrote it. He did, however, pursue another obsession—geometry—which he studied with Fra Luca Pacioli, the most famous mathematician of his age.

Both the artist and monk, who shared a house for some time in Milan, were fascinated by geometry and what it could do to elucidate hidden mysteries and inform the human condition. They worked together on Pacioli's book *The Divine Proportion*. Also known as the Golden Section, this was believed to be the perfect ratio, creating a natural sense of harmony and completion, whether in a building, a painting, or a mathematical proposition. For this book Leonardo invented and engraved the images of the skeletonic solids, which allowed all sides of a geometric form to be viewed simultaneously. Similarly, Leonardo's Vitruvian Man solves a problem set by the ancient Roman architect

---

16. For a detailed discussion of this remarkable space, see Kemp, 2006. pp. 167–76.
17. Jean Paul Richter, ed. *The Notebooks of Leonardo Da Vinci*, 2 vols. Mineola, NY: Dover, 1970 (reprint of 1883 edition).

Vitruvius by placing the human figure in both a square and a circle, showing the extension of the limbs in what is one of the most famous drawings in the world.[18]

Unfortunately, there is actually very little of Leonardo's work that was ever finished or survives. One sad example is the official monument to Francesco Sforza, Lodovico's father, that he was commissioned to design not long after he came to the city. It was to be a great horse which, if it had ever been cast, would have been the largest bronze sculpture ever made. The project engaged Leonardo for sixteen years, and his drawings, both artistic and technical, reveal his flexible genius. But, the fall of the city to the French in 1499 was the end of Sforza patronage: Leonardo's maquette for his *Gran Cavallo*, or Great Horse, was used by French archers for target practice, and Lodovico had been compelled to use the seventy tons of bronze collected for its casting to make cannons instead.[19]

---

18. For the Vitruvian Man, see Kemp, 2006. pp. 96–97; for Leonardo's collaboration with Luca Pacioli, see Kemp, 2006. pp. 130–34, 308–9 et passim.
19. Kemp, 2006. pp. 190–97; 201–3.

Illus. 9.1 Leonardo da Vinci, *The Lady with an Ermine (Portrait of Cecilia Gallerani)*. Wawel Castle, Krakow.

Leonardo, as court painter to Lodovico *il Moro*, regent of Milan, was commissioned to paint his beautiful mistress, Cecilia Gallerani (1473–1536), in about 1489, before she gave birth to Lodovico's natural son in 1491. Cecilia was an extremely accomplished woman: a poet, musician, and scholar who spoke perfect Latin. She presided over a kind of literary and philosophical salon in the ducal palace that was frequented by Leonardo. The portrait is pure brilliance, as it captures the moment when the woman's attention has been caught by something, possibly the entry of

Lodovico into her room. The ermine represents both purity because of its white coat and ducal rank. In addition, it references Lodovico's induction into the Neapolitan Order of the Ermine the year before.

Literature did not have the same luster in Milan as painting. The court poet Bernardo Bellincioni (d. 1492) was a bit of a hack, and largely forgotten. He had migrated around Italy looking for a suitable patron, moving from Florence to Mantua (1483) where he spent time at the court of the Gonzaga before leaving for Milan two years later. He, like Leonardo, had the duty to provide material for entertainments: scripts for masques and festivals, poems for particular occasions, and humorous burlesques and satires to lighten the tone of the duke's chambers, as Lodovico was known to be grave and austere in demeanor. Bellincioni is important, however, because of his connection to Leonardo. We only know that Leonardo's subject for the *Lady with an Ermine* is Cecilia Gallerani because the panel is described in one of Bellincioni's poems where the sitter is identified. No one reads Bellincioni today, except for that one poem, and not because of its genius but because it solves one of Leonardo's mysteries.

Illus. 9.2 Leonardo da Vinci (1452–1519), *John the Baptist,* **1513–16. Louvre, Paris.**

Leonardo spent longer in Milan than anywhere else in his adult life. It was there that he established the only two lasting relationships in his life, both with young men who began as apprentices but became intimate members of the artist's household. One, Francesco Melzi (ca. 1491–ca. 1570), was the son of a nobleman at the Sforza court. Leonardo met the young man about 1505, but he likely did not enter Leonardo's household until 1508. He stayed with Leonardo until the end of the painter's life; was with him when he died; and was bequeathed his notebooks, a gift that ensured their survival. His relationship with Leonardo appeared filial rather than romantic.

The same cannot be said for Gian Giacomo Caprotti da Oreno, universally known as Salai (1480–1524). This young boy of low birth became an intimate of Leonardo in 1490 when he was about ten, living with the painter until his last year in France. Salai means "little dirty one," or "little devil," and comes from the Arabic but through that satirical epic masterpiece from the circle of Lorenzo de'Medici, Luigi Pulci's *Morgante Maggiore*. Salai was a thief and a liar but Leonardo forgave him everything because he was beautiful, with curly hair and a beguiling smile, as can be seen in this painting of John the Baptist, for which Leonardo is said to have used him as the saint's model, a suggestion reinforced by some preliminary drawings that bear a very close resemblance to Leonardo's images of his beloved Salai. It also explains the extremely erotic nature of this image of a figure more commonly associated with asceticism and chastity, as Salome was to discover.

Illus. 9.3.a Jacopo de'Barbari (?), *Portrait of Luca Pacioli* (1445–1517) with a student (Guidobaldo da Montefeltro?), ca. 1500. Palazzo di Capodimonte, Farnese Collection, Naples.

Luca Bartolommeo de'Pacioli (ca. 1447–1517) was a Franciscan monk who was the most celebrated mathematician of his age. Born in Borgo San Sepolcro, Tuscany, he studied in Rome, where he lived with Leon Battista Alberti, and then taught in Perugia, ultimately holding the chair in mathematics in the studio (1477–80). He spent some years in Urbino where he was tutor to Guidobaldo da Montefeltro (to whom the friar's *Summa de mathematica* is dedicated) and came to know Piero della Francesca whose work in mathematics was to influence his own, resulting in charges of plagiarism by Vasari.

In 1497 Pacioli traveled to Milan at the invitation of Lodovico *il Moro* and established a close relationship with Leonardo da Vinci, with whom he lived until they were both driven from the city by the French in 1499. It was during those years that he collaborated with Leonardo to produce the influential *De Divina Proportione (On the Golden Section)*, a work which Leonardo illustrated and for which he invented the skeletonic solid—images of geometric figures in which every side was visible. In return Pacioli taught Leonardo mathematics and geometry. The work, printed in Venice in 1509, was hugely influential among not only mathematicians but also among artists and architects.

This celebrated portrait (ca.1500), often attributed to Jacopo de'Barbari (d. ca. 1516), portrays Pacioli in his Franciscan habit illustrating a geometric theorem to an anonymous student who has improbably been identified as Guidobaldo da Montefeltro. His left hand indicates a passage in Euclid, and the tools of mathematics appear on his desk. A rhombicuboctahedron (a convex solid of eighteen squares and eight triangles) dominates the left upper register of the picture.

Illus. 9.3.b Piero della Francesca, *Madonna and Child with Saints*
(*The Montefeltro or Brera Altarpi*ece), ca. 1472. Brera, Milan.

The influence of Pacioli cannot be overstated. His mathematical texts, especially his *De Divina Proportione*, had wide circulation; and his translation of Piero's work into Italian raised the profile of the painter among the practitioners of mathematics. Indeed, Pacioli appears in Piero's *The Montefeltro Altarpiece* as St. Peter Martyr (the figure on the right in the back row with the head wound, the sign of the saint's martyrdom, above the kneeling figure of Duke Federigo da Montefeltro of Urbino).

CHAPTER 10
MANTUA AND THE AGE OF THE GONZAGA

L eonardo da Vinci may have found a patron and a home in Milan at the service of the
Sforza, but he was sought after in other, smaller principalities. They, too, wanted to
use his fame as a way of embellishing the reputation of their prince and dynasty. In the
example of the remarkable Isabella d'Este, marchioness of Mantua and the wife of Francesco Gonzaga, patronage and cultivation reached an international level of renown.[1]

Indeed, Isabella in her lifetime became known as *la prima donna del mondo*—first
lady of the world. As befit her ambition and taste, she systematically sought the most
accomplished contemporary artists to portray her. So, when Leonardo passed through
Mantua on his way to Venice in 1499, she had him sketch her in profile as preparation
for a fully executed portrait. Although she pestered him to complete the commission, as
was typical with him, he never did. The drawing—now in the Louvre—is nevertheless
considered one of Leonardo's finest portraits, the only one he ever treated with color.

The Gonzaga and Mantegna

Patronage requires money, and the city of Mantua was well situated to produce the necessary wealth. Mantua had not been an important town in Roman times, despite its reputation as the birthplace of the poet Virgil. But it grew in significance under the Lombards,
in particular because of its control of the routes used for trade along the river Po. This
allowed Mantua to exact tolls—not unlike any modern highway authority—on the cargo
carried through its territory. In addition to being situated in a fertile valley crossed by
lucrative river routes, Mantua enjoyed another advantage—that of being an eminently
defensible site. With the river Mincio on one side and natural or artificial lakes on the others, as well as a dense expanse of marshland, its topography made direct attack difficult.

The connection between the House of Gonzaga and the city of Mantua is old. It also
began through an act of treachery and a program of extraordinary violence. In 1328 Luigi
Gonzaga was a leading noble under the Bonacolsi, the family that at the time ruled over
the city under the protection of the Holy Roman Emperor. Gonzaga was podestà of the
city but was not content to obey the Bonacolsi in this secondary role. Consequently, he
made an arrangement with the ruler of Verona, Cangrande della Scala, to borrow an army
to overthrow the Bonacolsi and rule in their place. The coup was successful, with the Bonacolsi family and their supporters murdered in the city. The Gonzaga cut out their hearts

---

1. For a discussion of Gonzaga patronage, see Barbara Furlotti and Guido Rebecchini, *The Art of
Mantua: Power and Patronage in the Renaissance*. Los Angeles: The J. Paul Getty Museum, 2008. A
general and accessible history of Mantua and the Gonzaga is Kate Simon, *A Renaissance Tapestry:
The Gonzaga of Mantua*. New York: Harper & Row, 1988.

and nailed them, still warm, to the doors of their palaces to indicate who was now in charge. In the face of such incontrovertible evidence, the Gonzaga dynasty was firmly launched.

The Gonzaga ascent to totalitarian power could not be more different from the comparatively gentle rise of the Medici dynasty in republican Florence. But, in one critical way, the two regimes were similar: they were equal in their estimation and understanding of the importance of art and culture. In the Renaissance, in this age of patronage, the Gonzaga stood out both for the quality and quantity of their patronage over a very long period of time, indeed almost to the end of the dynasty itself.[2]

The first of the Gonzaga to earn a European-wide reputation for patronage was Lodovico III (1412–78). His father had purchased the title of marquis from the emperor, so Lodovico ruled as a prince in name, not merely as a *signore* or lord. He was also married to the emperor's daughter Barbara of Brandenburg. But, it was not his exploits in imperial politics or his reputation on the battlefield for which Lodovico is remembered; rather, he is best known for his patronage of the artist Andrea Mantegna, who painted a lasting image of Lodovico's family in the so-called *Camera degli Sposi*, or "Room of the Betrothed," in the marquis's palace.[3]

Mantegna, born about 1431 in Vicenza, served his apprenticeship in the Veneto where remnants of his earliest masterpiece, the Ovetari Chapel in the church of the Eremitani in Padua, can be found. The church was bombed in 1944, and most of the cycle was lost, but what remains reflects his masterful control of perspective and a genius for narrative. Lodovico convinced Mantegna to become court artist in Mantua in 1460, offering a huge salary as enticement. After all, there was no tradition of major painting among the Gonzaga that might encourage Mantegna to come: he was to be the first celebrated artist to serve the family.[4]

Mantegna's depiction of Lodovico and Barbara's family in that cycle in the *Camera degli Sposi*, painted between 1465 and 1474, represents not only a wonderful example of group portraiture but also an almost intimate view of the prince's personal life. His children and even his dogs surround him as the narrative of the scene unfolds. In the first panel, Lodovico is depicted sitting with his family as his secretary brings him an important letter. This letter captures the attention of the marchioness who gazes at the exchange, ignoring the attempt by her young daughter to gain her attention. Also present are the Gonzaga dwarves, here depicted as the important members of the household that they were. These little people were not the objects of derision but the esteemed companions of children: they were adults with judgment who could play with the children without intimidating them.

---

2. "The Art of Diplomacy: Mantua and the Gonzaga," in Cole, 2016. pp. 164–99.

3. The *Camera degli Sposi* in the Castello di San Giorgio is a later name; at the time it was simply called the *Camera Picta*, or painted room.

4. Keith Christiansen, *Andrea Mantegna, Padua and Mantua*. New York: George Braziller, 2000; Giorgio Vasari, *The Lives of the Painters, Sculptors and Architects*, tr. Gaston De Vere. New York, Knopf, 1996. I, pp. 557–64.

Elsewhere in the room there is the image of the marquis Lodovico outside a stylized view of Rome. It depicts Lodovico's encounter with his younger son who had just been raised to the Sacred College as a cardinal—a memorable moment in the family's fortunes. In the scene there also appears the Holy Roman Emperor and the king of Denmark, putting Lodovico in very good company indeed. But the humanist program is most blatantly displayed in the trompe l'oeil ceiling. Up there a painted oculus inhabited by exotic birds and *putti* completes the scene amidst roundels of the "good" emperors of Imperial Rome.

What is remarkable about this space is the very domesticity of the images. The letter the marquis is receiving at the start of the narrative is the announcement that his son is to be a cardinal, while the meeting scene outside Rome is the consummation of the family's dignity and aspirations. Lodovico is in the company of an emperor and a king, and his son may one day be pope. If this were a modern family, such triumphs would be recorded on Facebook. But this dynastic success story is told with charm and brilliance by a court painter. Mantegna left his own image by a door, hidden in the decoration that features a plaque held by *putti* to say that this work of his is meant as a mark of gratitude for the patronage he has received from the prince.[5]

After the death of Lodovico in 1478, Mantegna traveled for a time to Rome to paint for Pope Innocent VIII. He had already acquired an obsession with ancient Rome, and he used the opportunity to study the monuments and remains of that ancient civilization closely. It was likely he began his famous *Triumphs of Caesar* there, only to complete the series of nine panels back in Mantua where he continued to work until his death. These images of Julius Caesar are among the first depictions of antiquity that systematically attempt to reproduce the actual costumes, practices, and objects of the ancient world correctly. It is almost as though Petrarch's desire to recover the ancient world through letters and texts has been fulfilled visually in this remarkable series, completed more than a century later.

On his death in 1506, Mantegna was buried at his own request in Mantua's church of Sant'Andrea. The church was—and still is—famed for containing the highly venerated relic of the most precious blood of Christ. According to legend, St. Longinus, the centurion who administered the merciful coup de grace to Christ on the cross, collected the blood that flowed from Jesus's wound. Longinus then traveled to Italy and buried the blood-filled chalice in Mantua. In 1049 a priest had a dream as to where the blood was to be found, started to dig, and miraculously found it. In 1053 the Church recognized its authenticity, and from that time since it has been an attraction for pilgrims—a major source of revenue for the Church.

But Mantegna's desire to be buried in this location rested more on Sant'Andrea's architecture than on its sacred associations, for the church was the most classical structure in Mantua.[6] The building itself was an older foundation of the early fifteenth century,

---

5. Michele Cordaro, ed. *Mantegna's Camera degli Sposi*. Milan: Electa, 1993.
6. Eugene J. Johnson, *S. Andrea in Mantua: The Building History*. University Park: Pennsylvania State University Press, 1975.

but only the original bell tower survived. Wisely Lodovico III, in another inspired acqui-sition of artistic genius, had brought Leon Battista Alberti from Florence in 1462 to undertake the redesign of the church. The degree of sophistication of the Gonzaga court is reflected clearly in this choice of the most celebrated humanist theorist on architec-ture and painting of his age.[7] It connects this minor principality with the great humanist center of Florence at the time of the Medici and brings Mantua right into the center of Renaissance culture.

Leon Battista Alberti was a theorist of both painting and architecture, and his trea-tise *De Re Aedificatoria Libri Decem* (*Ten Books on the Art of Building,* ca.1452) was the codification of the classical style in architecture.[8] His Rucellai Palace in Florence turned these abstract principles into an actual building that was enormously influential in the second half of the century. In Sant'Andrea, Alberti used ancient architectural vocabulary to link the Gonzaga with two good emperors of Imperial Rome. The façade of the church is inspired by the Arch of Titus, an emperor renowned for being just and merciful. The vaulted interior aptly quotes the basilica of Maxentius and Constantine—the latter the emperor who recognized the central role of Christianity. For artistic patronage and pro-paganda, Alberti's work was a stroke of genius. As a consequence, Mantua is still a place of pilgrimage not only because of the most precious blood venerated by the faithful but also for the church Alberti constructed to house it.[9]

It is appropriate that the careers of the two great classicists should come together in Mantua. Alberti became the Vitruvius of his age and his classical church a fitting envi-ronment for the tomb of Mantegna, that most classical of painters. Mantegna was buried in a small side chapel that he began decorating a few years before his death. A true perfec-tionist, he purchased the open plot of land just outside the chapel window and donated it to the church. His only condition was that the land never be developed or built upon. So it was that he ensured his tomb would be forever illuminated by natural daylight.

Isabella d'Este

The next great moment of Gonzaga patronage was the second quarter of the sixteenth century with the ascendancy of the incomparable Isabella d'Este.[10] Born in 1474, Isabella was the eldest daughter of Duke Ercole of Ferrara and Eleanora of Naples. As she

7. Anthony Grafton, *Leon Battista Alberti: Master Builder of the Italian Renaissance.* Cambridge, MA: Harvard University Press, 2002.

8. Leon Battista Alberti, *On the Art of Building in Ten Books,* tr. Joseph Rykwert, Neil Leach, and Robert Tavernor. Cambridge, MA: MIT Press, 1991.

9. Hanno-Walter Kruft, *A History of Architectural Theory.* New York: Princeton Architectural Press, 1996. pp. 41–72.

10. Lorenzo Bonoldi, *Isabella d'Este: A Renaissance Woman,* tr. Clark Lawrence. Rimini, Italy: Guaraldi/Engramma, 2015; Raffaele Tamalio, "Isabella d'Este, marchesa di Mantova," in *Dizion-ario Biografico degli Italiani.* Vol. 62. Rome: Istituto della Enciclopedia Italiana, 2004.

proved brilliantly precocious from a young age, her parents employed the finest tutors in classical studies, encouraging her humanist learning to the point that she had a superb command of Greek and Latin and could recite passages of classical authors to the court and visiting dignitaries. She was also a gifted musician and had a sense of style and elegance that attracted the attention of everyone who met her.

At the age of six she was betrothed to Francesco Gonzaga, future marquis of Mantua, although they did not marry until she was fifteen. Initially the marriage was extremely happy, quickly producing eight children. As a condottiere following the family business of mercenary war, Federico was often away, leaving Isabella both a great degree of personal freedom and many responsibilities of government on her husband's behalf. It was one of these occasions—the longest—that caused the dissolution of her relationship with Francesco.

In 1509, during the terrible events of the War of the League of Cambrai, Francesco was captured and held hostage in Venice for three years. Isabella functioned as regent and did brilliantly, keeping Mantua safe in very troubled times and proving herself a skilled and effective diplomat. Unfortunately for Isabella, Francesco heard from his entire court of her genius and success, implying that she was a far better ruler than he. His jealousy and humiliation effectively separated the couple until the marquis's death from syphilis in 1519. Thereafter, she functioned as regent for her young son Federico until he came of age in 1521.

Isabella was a great patron of all the arts. She constructed her *studioli* (there were two in succession within the ducal palace) to hold her collections and provide a quiet respite from the affairs of state and the court.[11] She was an obsessive collector of ancient objects, searching for only the best through agents throughout Italy. She commissioned works from contemporary artists as well, both to supplement her ancient objects and create a coherent environment of beauty and culture in her private apartments. She owned bronzes in the antique style by L'Antico (Jacopo Alari Bonacolsi) and paintings by Bellini, Mantegna, Giorgione, Perugino, and Raphael.[12] Her portrait was painted by Titian as well as drawn by Leonardo.[13] She commissioned a huge service of maiolica, all marked with her coat of arms, cipher, and motto (*nec spe nec metu*: with neither hope nor

11. Stephen Campbell, *The Cabinet of Eros: Renaissance Mythological Painting and the Studiolo of Isabella d'Este*. New Haven: Yale University Press, 2006.

12. Isabella's entire collection was inventoried after her death by the court notary Odoardo Stivini. For a comprehensive list of her remarkable collection see Odoardo Stivini, *Le Collezioni Gonzaga: L'inventario dei beni del 1540–1542*, ed. Daniela Ferrari. Milan: Silvana, 2003.

13. Despite years of intense pressure, Leonardo never painted Isabella, although the drawing of her in the Louvre appears to be a sketch for a complete portrait. See Francis Ames-Lewis, *Isabella and Leonardo: The Artistic Relationship between Isabella d'Este and Leonardo da Vinci, 1500–1506*. New Haven: Yale University Press, 2012.

fear).[14] Her jewels were spectacular and her costumes so famous that they inspired the court of France. She received the best editions of classical texts from Aldus Manutius in Venice and discussed them with the leading men of letters of her day, such as Baldassare Castiglione and Pietro Bembo, who compared her cultural and intellectual court to the splendors of the papacy and described her as the wisest among women. Her wide circle of correspondents resulted in a large surviving register of letters to the leading figures of Renaissance Italy.[15]

Isabella was in Rome when the city was sacked in 1527 by the uncontrollable Imperial army. She was lodged in the Colonna Palace and soon about two thousand terrified Romans sought her protection. Her reputation was such and her connections to the emperor close enough that she and her guests were left unmolested. Soon after, in 1530, she convinced Charles V to raise her son to the dignity of duke of Mantua. Returning to Mantua, Isabella tried to resume her previous life of patron and dowager marchioness. But her estrangement from her son drove her to move to the tiny territory of Solarola, which she ruled until her death in early 1539.

Federigo II and Giulio Romano

Perhaps surprisingly, it was not Isabella but her husband who invited the most important artist after Mantegna to work for an extended period in Mantua.[16] In 1524 Federico invited Giulio Romano (ca. 1499–1546) to the principality. Born Giulio Pippi in Rome (hence "Romano"), he was the most talented of the pupils from the workshop of Raphael. He had completed the work in the *Stanze* of Raphael (the Raphael Rooms) in the papal palace after the great artist's death in 1520. Giulio was also responsible for some wonderful additions to and decorations in the ducal palace in Mantua; but his greatest contribution to the civilization of the Mantuan Renaissance was the Palazzo del Te, constructed and painted for Isabella's son Federigo II (1500–40).[17]

Commissioned in 1524 but not completed until 1534, Palazzo del Te is hardly a palace in the traditional sense.[18] Rather it is a relatively small pavilion of one and a half stories erected on the site of the marquis's stables. Its deliberate position far from Castel San Giorgio and the court complex of the Palazzo Ducale was a physical indication of the

---

14. For Isabella as a collector of ceramics and their significance, see Lisa Boutin, "Isabella d'Este and the Gender Neutrality of Renaissance Ceramics," *Women's Studies*, 40 (2011), pp. 23–47.

15. Isabella d'Este, *Selected Letters*, ed. and tr. Deanna Shemek. Tempe: Arizona Center for Medieval and Renaissance Studies, 2017.

16. Francesca Mattei, ed., *Federico II Gonzaga e le arti*. Rome: Bulzoni Editore, 2016. Europa delle Corti studi 159.

17. Molly Bourne, *Francesco II Gonzaga: The Soldier-Prince as Patron*. Rome: Bulzoni, 2008.

18. Ugo Bazzotti, *Palazzo Te: Giulio Romano's Masterwork in Mantua*. London: Thames and Hudson, 2013.

estrangement between Isabella and her son. The cause of this rift was her uncompromising character in general and her disapproval in particular of Federigo's deep attachment to his mistress, Isabella Boschetti.

Isabella Boschetti was spectacularly beautiful, commonly called in fact the Beautiful Boschetti (*La Bella Boschetti*). She became the young Federigo's mistress while she was still in her teens, perhaps even before he succeeded as marquis in 1519. Although of very noble connections—her mother was Baldassare Castiglione's sister—there could be no question of a marriage between the lovers because of their difference in rank. Besides, Federigo had been betrothed since 1517 to Maria Paleologo, daughter of the ruler of the neighboring duchy of Monferrato. Despite the betrothal contract, however, Maria and her father, the duke, were so jealous of the bond between Isabella Boschetti and Federigo that they plotted to poison her. The conspiracy was discovered, and the pope was so appalled that he annulled the betrothal. Still, it was subsequently reinstated when it was clear that the Paleologo family was destined to die out in the male line. Whoever married Maria would thus succeed as ruler of Monferrato. In time, this dynastic union took place (1531), although not through Federigo marrying Maria but instead his marrying her younger sister, Margarita, as Maria had died young.

Palazzo del Te consequently represents Federigo Gonzaga's double life. It was the location of his illicit liaison of love and passion with Isabella Boschetti, while the formal ducal palace was the scene of his married and official life as the ruler of Mantua. Both attachments produced children. In fact, as soon as it was habitable, Isabella Boschetti moved into this pleasure palace, small enough to enjoy an almost bourgeois domesticity with Federigo yet splendid enough to satisfy the dynastic grandeur of the House of Gonzaga. With its gardens, pools, and loggias, Palazzo del Te was suited to every joy of life and a place of relaxation.

It celebrates not only the love between Federigo and Isabella in its decoration but also reflects the interests and patronage of the House of Gonzaga. For example, one of the rooms is a testament to Federigo's obsession with his horses, particularly his favorites. In this Room of the Horses, Giulio painted portraits of these wonderful animals, emerging outside the frames of the pictures and identified by their names below. The rest of the room carries chiaroscuro paintings of the labors of Hercules, responsibilities that Federigo largely avoided in his pavilion.

Amor and Psyche

In the astounding Room of Amor and Psyche Giulio preserves best both Federico's rather lubricious relationship with Isabella and the trendy Renaissance Neoplatonic ideal of love, although in a very physical way.[19] The tale of Amor and Psyche was one of

---

19. See Lucius Apuleius, *The Tale of Cupid and Psyche*, tr. Joel C. Relihan. Indianapolis: Hackett Publishing Company, 2009.

the most popular stories of the Renaissance. It is found in the ancient, second-century novel of *The Golden Ass* by Apuleius, which had only been fully discovered by Boccaccio in 1355 when he was hunting for classical manuscripts in the library of the abbey of Monte Casino. Giulio Romano had worked on this very beautiful and romantic story before, when he assisted Raphael and his workshop in decorating the Villa Farnesina (as it is now called) for the banker Agostino Chigi in Rome. But, his version in Palazzo del Te is considerably earthier.

The story tells of Psyche, a girl whose beauty was so great that it drove Venus to a fierce fit of jealous rage. To punish Psyche for her beauty, Venus sent her son Cupid ("Amor" in Latin) to cause her to fall in love with the ugliest man on earth. But, when Amor saw Psyche, he fell in love with her and became her lover instead. The difficulty was that a mortal cannot look upon a god and survive, so Amor insisted that they could only meet in the dark at night. When Psyche told her sisters of her new lover, they insisted he had to be a monster or he would let her see him. Together they contrived a plot to conceal a candle beneath Psyche's bed. When Amor had fallen asleep after love making, Psyche was to light it and look at his face. But, when she did so, a drop of wax fell onto his cheek, startling Amor awake. Horrified, they both knew this signaled Psyche's death.

Venus was naturally quite happy with this situation, but Amor asked Juno to intervene with Jupiter, who alone, as king of the gods, could save his beloved Psyche. Jupiter called a council of the gods to give him advice on this delicate question. Utterly charmed by Psyche, the council decided to make her a goddess so that she and Amor could marry and live happily ever after. This is the narrative described in the wonderful frescoes Giulio painted on the walls of the large room intended for feasts and entertainment.

There is a double allegory here. On one level the story of Amor and Psyche could be the story of Federigo and Isabella. On another level it is a Neoplatonic allegory of the ascension of the soul (*psyche* in Greek) to heaven through love (*amor* in Latin). And, it can be both simultaneously. Giulio, as we said, had painted the allegory by Apuleius before and in a similar kind of place: a pleasure villa where Chigi met with his serial mistresses, great Roman courtesans whom he also loved and one of whom he would eventually marry. Chigi's first mistress was the celebrated courtesan La Imperia (for whom the word "courtesan" was probably first used) and after her death Andreosia, his eventual wife. Adding to the theme of illicit love, a popular legend in Rome had it that the Villa Farnesina was constructed on the site of the villa occupied by Cleopatra after Marc Antony brought her to Rome.

Federigo, as a ruling prince, the son of the classically educated Isabella d'Este, and the center of a very sophisticated court, would certainly have known all of this gossip. And Giulio Romano would have consciously reinforced this knowledge, connecting Federico to other great unconventional loves and other great beauties celebrated in building and decoration. We must ask, then, whether the nude figure of Psyche portrayed in the scene of her wedding to Amor was a portrait of Isabella Boschetti? We will never know because there is no confirmed image of her. Not even the date of her death is known, because she likely died after Federigo, who died at age forty from syphilis inherited from his father.

Renaissance Court Culture

In so many ways, the Palazzo del Te is a microcosm of the highly cultivated court life of the Italian Renaissance principalities. The highest examples of painting and architecture effected by the most famous and able practitioners created a world of elegance and leisure, inspired by classical sources and personal taste. It was a world in which the profits from war and trade were translated into beauty and pleasure: the result was fame and grandeur, leaving a memory of rich accomplishment for future generations to enjoy and contemporaries to celebrate.

It was equally a culture of extravagant and self-indulgent individuality, with an element of barely disguised brutality and treachery. Isabella's husband, Francesco, was for some time the lover of her brother Alfonso's wife, Lucrezia Borgia, whose reputation had very much preceded her. Isabella was very cold and distant with her sister-in-law. Yet Isabella warmly—even ostentatiously—welcomed and befriended Cecilia Gallerani, the mistress of her sister Beatrice's husband, Lodovico *il Moro*, duke of Milan. We know her well—the cultivated and exquisitely beautiful woman portrayed in Leonardo da Vinci's *The Lady with the Ermine*. No wonder Isabella was desperate to have Leonardo finish her portrait!

The social, personal, and political complexities of Renaissance court life were almost always driven by personality, vanity, and ambition.[20] The court of Federigo was defined by his difficult relationship with his mother and his love for his mistress (whose first husband was, incidentally, brutally murdered under very suspicious circumstances). It was a universe of illusion and theatre, both in art and to a degree in life, where what was real depended on who and where you were at a given moment. It was self-referential and animated by those same elements that inspired Petrarch: love, the desire for fame, and the worship of antiquity—but in a far more intense way.

It would, of course, all come crashing down, just as the room around you appears to do when you stand in the last major *salone* of the Palazzo del Te: in the Room of the Giants, Giulio has painted a dystopia of struggle between Titans and Giants, with the walls collapsing, the floor buckling, and heavens falling. Although there would be some later moments of Gonzaga greatness, especially under Vincenzo II (d. 1612), the patron variously of Monteverdi, Galileo, and Rubens, the Room of the Giants was to become a predictive allegory of the fall of the House of Gonzaga. During the terrible events of the Thirty Years War, when forces beyond the control of these petty princes compromised

---

20. See Franco Cardini, "The Sacred Circle of Mantua," in Bertelli, 1986. pp. 77–125.

their thrones and independence, the huge art collections were scattered, the city looted, and the eclipse of the dynasty ensured.

What remains as points of access to the brilliant life of the Renaissance court of Mantua indicates just how sophisticated and cultivated these places were, and how great personalities, such as Isabella d'Este, could through patronage and force of will define an age, and do so with so much brilliance and depth that the glow remains even until today. But this was also the weakness of these petty principalities: their success depended altogether too much on the abilities and characters of their individual rulers. When the prince proved insufficient, disaster too often followed. *Sic transit gloria mundi.*

**Illus. 10.1 Domenico Morone (1442–1518), *The Hunting
of the Bonacolsi*, 1494. Palazzo Ducale, Mantova.**

Lodovico I Gonzaga (1267–1360), with the help of an army provided by the Ghibelline ruler of
Verona, Cangrande (Big Dog) della Scala, overthrew his brother-in-law Rinaldo (called Passerino) Bonacolsi of Mantua in August 1328 thus initiating the Gonzaga dynasty. He immediately
assumed the title of captain general and soon afterward was appointed as imperial vicar of the city
by the emperor. He welcomed Petrarch to Mantua in 1349 and lodged him in his palace, accompanying him on a pilgrimage to the putative tomb of the ancient poet Virgil. In a macabre act of
superstition, Lodovico had the body of Passerino Bonacolsi embalmed and put on display in the
palace where it resided until 1708. He did so in the belief that when the last of the Bonacolsi left
the palace the Gonzaga dynasty and the city would fall.

**Illus. 10.2 Pisanello (Antonio di Puccio Pisano, 1395–1455),
Detail of a Tournament Scene from *Scenes of War and
Chivalry*, ca. 1447. Palazzo Ducale, Mantua.**

Pisanello worked sporadically for the Gonzaga of Mantua between 1422 and 1447, as well as for other princes of Italy from Milan to Naples. In this fresco, which is unfinished and only recently recovered, he captures the chivalric culture of the Northern Italian courts, with scenes from the knights of Charlemagne and other tales of military virtue. His work for the Sforza, Este, and Gonzaga families reflected not only the shared chivalric culture of these condottiere dynasties but also their common use of artists who could capture the atmosphere of chivalric legends by covering palace walls with massed figures, often in exotic costume and dramatic interaction.

Illus. 10.3.a Andrea Mantegna (1431–1506), *The Court of Lodovico III Gonzaga, Marquis of Mantua,* **1465–1474. Castel San Giorgio, Mantua.**

Illus. 10.3.b Andrea Mantegna (1431–1506), *Meeting of Lodovico III Gonzaga, Marquis of Mantua, and His Son Cardinal Francesco Outside Rome,* **1465–74. Castel San Giorgio, Mantua.**

Mantegna painted the larger fresco on the north wall of the *Camera degli Sposi* (*Camera Picta,* the "Painted Room" as it was known at the time of Mantegna) in the tower of the Castel San Giorgio, Mantua, between 1465 and 1474. It is part of a narrative that places the family of the Gonzaga in both a dynastic and a domestic context. In this scene the marquis is shown with his family and courtiers. His wife, Barbara of Brandenburg, the daughter of the emperor, is surrounded by her children and one of the celebrated Gonzaga dwarves (who served as children's companions). The marquis's secretary is handing him a letter which notifies him that his son Francesco has been named a cardinal and hence will perhaps in the future become pope.

On the west wall Mantegna portrays Cardinal Francesco being honored by his father who visits him in Rome (shown imaginatively in the background). Also in the company are Emperor Frederick III of Habsburg and King Christian I of Denmark, placing the Gonzaga in exalted company. It has been suggested that the second and fourth figures on the right are portraits of Leon Battista Alberti (who designed Sant'Andrea in Mantua) and Mantegna himself.

Illus. 10.4.a Leonardo da Vinci,
Drawing of Isabella d'Este,
1499–1500. Louvre,
Paris.

Illus. 10.4.b Titian (Tiziano
Vecellio, ca. 1488–1576),
Portrait of Isabella D'Este, **1534.**
Kunsthistorisches Museum, Vienna.

Isabella was eager to have her portrait painted by Leonardo. She even asked Cecilia Gallerani to lend her own portrait by Leonardo (*Lady with an Ermine*) to verify his genius. Despite her importuning, Leonardo did not accept the commission, but after fleeing Milan in 1499 he stopped in Mantua en route to Venice. There he made a drawing from life of Isabella, the only drawing he ever colored. Nevertheless, no finished portrait was ever painted.

Later, in 1534, at the age of 60, Isabella commissioned a portrait by Titian. When it was delivered in 1536 Isabella was not satisfied. She sent it back to the artist and instructed him to make her look younger. The result is a wonderful portrait of a much younger woman: it is how Isabella would have liked to look in middle age rather than a true representation. In this exchange, her vanity and her manipulation of her memory and image for history are all at work.

Illus. 10.5 Niccolo da Urbino, *Maiolica Plate with Painted Scenes from Ovid: Phaedra and Hippolytus*, ca. 1524. Victoria and Albert Museum, London.

Isabella d'Este's humanist learning was prodigious. She was deeply familiar with the classics, creating in her *studiolo* and other personal places an environment that reflected her cultivated tastes and strong sense of her role as a powerful, learned woman in Renaissance society. She commissioned a maiolica service of exceptional quality, painted by some of the great masters of the art, such as Niccolo da Urbino. These tin-glazed, richly decorated earthenware plates were an extreme luxury, especially narrative or "*istoriato*" examples such as this *piatto da pompa* (ceremonial plate). Isabella is recorded as among the very few owners of these valuable objects who actually used them at her villa rather than merely displaying them on a credenza.

Because each was an individual work of commissioned art, Isabella could include elements that refer only to her and her carefully constructed image. The plate illustrated here contains the stories from Ovid but also in the center the Gonzaga arms and her personal *imprese*, or symbols, and motto. On the baluster at the right is inscribed "*nec spe, nec metu*," Latin for "with neither hope nor fear," her private motto. On the far left is the Roman numeral XXVII. This number, twenty-seven, in Italian is "*ventisette*," which sounds like "*vinti i sette*," meaning "I have conquered the seven (deadly sins)." Beneath the Gonzaga coat of arms is a musical notation. This is her celebrated "*tempi e pause,*" representing the quiet rest of contemplation and thought amidst the often demanding score of her life. These symbols also all appear in the decoration of her *studiolo*. The *tempi e pausi* caused a notable reaction when she had it embroidered into the dress she wore to the wedding of her brother, Alfonso, duke of Ferrara, and Lucrezia Borgia.

Isabella's taste, wealth, learning, and self-fashioning are all depicted on this superb *istoriato* maiolica, a medium that does not fade with time.

**Illus. 10.6 Giulio Romano, *Wedding Banquet of Amor
and Psyche*, 1532–35. Palazzo del Te, Mantova.**

The decorative program in the Hall of Amor and Psyche in Palazzo del Te, the pleasure palace Giulio Romano built and decorated for Federigo Gonzaga, duke of Mantua, is both a Neoplatonic allegory from the classical story from *The Golden Ass* of Apuleius (Lucius Apuleius Madaurensis, ca. 124–ca. 170 AD) and an allegory of the love between Federigo and his mistress, Isabella Boschetti, who was lodged in the building.

The scene of the wedding is simultaneously an exploration of the Renaissance imagination, with exotic animals such as elephants and camels, gods, satyrs, and humans engaged in daily activities. Federigo's role as captain general of the Florentine republic was demanding and his pleasures were consequently well-earned. The environment of a Renaissance feast is also shown, with a credenza on which valuable dinner services are artfully displayed, an illusionistic natural backdrop of an arbor, merging the bucolic outside with the festive inside of the palace. Finally, the wedding bed of Amor and Psyche is shown at the right, with the disturbed bedding sheltering a small dog, the symbol of faithfulness, in this case Federigo's fidelity to his mistress rather than his wife.

CHAPTER 11

FERRARA AND THE ESTE

Ferrara is another of those condottiere principalities whose princes used artistic patronage and reputation to compensate for the limitations of their patrimony.[1] Unlike other condottiere princes, however, the Este of Ferrara was an ancient and long-established dynasty, descendants of Germanic knights of the House of Welf, from which the papal faction of Guelf emerged. Ferrara itself was consequently usually a pro-papal state, and the Este ruled as vicars of the pope, even if they often played the pope against the emperor to maximize their advantage. They managed their game well in balancing the claims of emperor and pope, particularly when they expanded their dominion to include neighboring imperial cities, such as Modena and Reggio.

The Sordid Path to Legitimacy

The first Este to hold sway in Ferrara did so by acquiring the city as part of a dowry in 1146.[2] Then in 1208, Azzo d'Este was named podestà of Ferrara and consolidated his family's authority by declaring it hereditary. The biography and fate of Azzo and his son and grandson illustrate the complex, usually sordid, history of this one, very dysfunctional family. Azzo's son and heir, Rinaldo, was imprisoned by the Hohenstaufen emperor Frederick II in 1238, only to be poisoned together with his wife in 1251, leaving no legitimate sons.

However, he had managed to sire a bastard, Obizzo, with his laundress. Azzo recognized this natural grandson as his heir, because he was the only male available to continue the dynasty. To confirm Obizzo's status, Azzo asked the pope—who was Obizzo's wife's uncle—to make the boy legitimate. The pope did so in 1252, but only after Obizzo's mother—the laundress—had been drowned. Clearly, the family relationships in *Game of Thrones* have historical antecedents that even supersede fiction.

In 1264 Obizzo d'Este took control of Ferrara with the help of Venice and established a lordship for his family, an ambition reinforced by popular acclamation. The ambitious Obizzo then expanded his authority to the adjacent territories of Modena (1288) and Reggio (1289). The result was that by the end of the thirteenth century the Este were among the most powerful lords in north central Italy.

---

1. Alison Cole, "Varieties of Pleasure: Este Ferrara," in Cole, 2016. pp. 134–63.
2. Trevor Dean, *Land and Power in Late Medieval Ferrara: The Rule of the Este, 1350–1450*. Cambridge: Cambridge University Press, 2002; Luciano Chiappini, *Gli Estensi*. Varese, Italy: Dall'Oglio, 1967; Werner Gundersheimer, *Ferrara: The Style of a Renaissance Despotism*. Princeton: Princeton University Press, 1973.

Obizzo did not enjoy his powerful position for long, however, as he was murdered in 1293. The assassin was almost certainly his own son Azzo who preferred not to wait for natural causes to allow him to claim his father's title and possessions (we did suggest that the family was dysfunctional). Azzo was nevertheless challenged by his two brothers, resulting in the Este dominions being divided among the three of them. This exploit gained such notoriety that Dante incorporated it into the seventh circle of the *Inferno* (XII, 9), which is an appropriate place for such activity.

During the next centuries, alliances, warfare, and shifting loyalties between the pope and the emperor resulted in Ferrara not only sustaining its independence but also gaining a reputation for military skill and artistic patronage. For example, in 1385 Marquis Niccolo II commissioned the massive family castle—the Castello Estense—which to this day dominates the center of the city. His heir, Marquis Niccolo III (d. 1441), built a solid reputation as a condottiere, defending his city in the face of continual threats. His reign was long and his career distinguished. However, there was an issue that could cloud the succession, as his family life followed the Este tradition of sordid relationships.[3]

Niccolo was born illegitimate, but still inherited Ferrara at the age of ten in 1393. At the age of fifteen he was married to Gigliola, the young daughter of the ruler of neighboring Padua, Francesco da Carrara; sadly, she died of plague in 1416 without providing the needed legitimate heir. Consequently in 1418 he married again to the fourteen-year-old Laura, usually known as Parisina, daughter of the Romagnol condottiere Andrea Malatesta. Her family history was as bizarre as her husband's, as her mother had been murdered by her father just a few days after her birth.

Parisina did provide Niccolo with children almost immediately, but they all suffered unfortunate fates: their only son died soon after birth and their eldest daughter in her teens; the middle child, Ginevra, was murdered at twenty-one by her husband, the infamous Sigismondo Malatesta, a relation of her mother's. The young and beautiful Parisina sought love outside her husband's embrace. Niccolo had a natural son, Ugo, by one of his mistresses. In 1424 Parisina was permitted a visit to her father, but Niccolo insisted that Ugo accompany her as protection. The result was a consuming sexual affair between the stepmother and stepson.

Suspecting his wife of infidelity, Niccolo demanded that her maids spy upon her, with the result that the lovers were caught. Both were thrown into the Este castle dungeon, and in 1425 Niccolo had his wife and son Ugo beheaded because of their incestuous relationship.[4] His anger was such that he decreed that all women committing

---

3. Dennis Looney, "Ferrarese Studies: Tracking the Rise and Fall of an Urban Lordship in the Renaissance," in Dennis Looney and Deanna Shemek, eds. *Phaethon's Children: The Este Court and Its Culture in Early Modern Ferrara.* Medieval and Renaissance Texts and Studies. Tempe: Arizona Center for Medieval and Renaissance Studies, 2005. pp. 1–32.

4. *Diario Ferrarese dall'anno 1409 sino al 1502 di autori incerti,* ed. Giuseppe Pardi, in *Rerum Italicarum Scriptores,* 2nd ed., XXI:V, pt. 7 (Bologna, 1928), p. 17.

adultery were to be summarily executed, a law not only unenforceable but a threat to the demographics of his principality. The only positive consequence of this very sordid affair was great art: Byron and Gabriele d'Annunzio wrote dramatic poems and both Donizetti and Mascagni produced operas on the tragedy of Parisina.

Despite some younger, legitimate children by his third wife, Niccolo recognized the remarkable ability of Lionello, one of his eleven bastard children, so he determined that this highly educated and cultivated prince should succeed him. Fortunately, Lionello was extremely popular among the population of Ferrara and the pope had already legitimized him. (He shared the same mother as the unfortunate Ugo.) Thus, on the death of Niccolo III in 1441, Lionello d'Este (1407–50) became the marquis of Ferrara.

Lionello d'Este

Lionello was an ideal Renaissance prince, though one who was less interested in military affairs and politics than in cultural and educational policy.[5] Part of his obsession with culture derived from his education under one of the greatest of the humanist educators, Guarino of Verona. But, much derived from his recognition that this relatively small state of Ferrara, surrounded as it was by greater powers, needed more than military might to thrive: it needed a reputation and institutions that would attract useful men to the city and endow its citizens with richer opportunities.[6]

The first and most successful policy in support of learning was his re-founding of the University of Ferrara.[7] The school had existed since 1391 but had never been well endowed and had not achieved much of a reputation. There were few celebrated members of its bare-bones faculty and it had even ceased operating in times of crisis. So, in the second year of his reign, and through the encouragement of Guarino, Lionello re-founded the school, giving it sufficient income through a tax on butcher shops to employ excellent professors, including the brilliant Greek scholar and teacher Theodore Gaza. Ferrara almost immediately became an important place in the humanist scholarly geography. Students from across Italy and elsewhere in Europe traveled to the school. It was a diplomatic, cultural, and economic success.

The young marquis also wanted to honor his father, so he had Leon Battista Alberti come to Ferrara to advise on a competition for a statue of Niccolo III. Not only was the equestrian statue cast, but the 1451 original by Niccolo Baroncelli and Antonio di

---

5. See Alessandra Molfino and Mauro Natale, eds., *Le Muse e il Principe: Arte di Corte nel Rinscimento Padano*. Modena: Pannini, 1991. The sophistication of the Este court is richly illustrated in this huge exhibition catalogue.

6. Riccardo Bruscagli, "Ferrara: Arts and Ideologies in a Renaissance State," in Looney and Shemek, 2005. pp. 33–63.

7. Patrizia Castelli, ed., *In supreme dignitatis . . . : Per la storia dell'Universita di Ferrara 1391–1991.* Florence: Leo S. Olschki, 1995.

Cristofero was influenced by Alberti, the great Florentine theorist of art and architecture.[8] Sadly, what we see now raised on its pedestal in front of the Palazzo Municipale is a copy, as the original and its neighbor, the seated image of Lionello's brother and successor, Borso, were melted down by Napoleon's French army in 1796 for cannons. This clearly reflects the danger in working in bronze, as the same fate was shared by a great many other statues, including one of Pope Julius II by Michelangelo in Bologna.

While in Ferrara, Alberti was encouraged by Lionello to write his celebrated treatise on architecture (*Ten Books on the Art of Building*). It was intended to be dedicated to Lionello, but the marquis died before its completion, hence its dedication to the humanist pope Nicholas V.

Alberti was not the only great artist and theorist who made Ferrara a kind of Olympus in the mid-fifteenth century.[9] Other poets and humanists arrived as ornaments to the university and Lionello's court, as did the musicians who were particularly important to the Este. Lionello's *cappella dei cantori* was celebrated throughout Italy.[10] Artists came as well, especially those who would add to Ferrara's luster both in Italy and abroad and propagate the fame and reputation of Lionello.

Antonio Pisanello crafted medals of the marquis which to this day define how he is remembered. Piero della Francesco also came to Ferrara to work on a fresco cycle in the Este Castle, but sadly this is altogether lost. Jacopo Bellini came from Venice, and Mantegna from Mantua. And, as Lionello desired access to the other great tradition of Renaissance painting, the Netherlander Roger van der Weyden spent time in Ferrara where he would paint the splendid portrait of Lionello's son, Francesco, and popularize the use of oil paint.

Borso d'Este

Lionello died suddenly in 1450 at the age of 43. His successor was yet another illegitimate son of Niccolo III, Borso (r. 1450–71), born of the same mistress as Lionello. Borso from the beginning of his reign enjoyed the kind of support that usually only comes from legitimacy: the Holy Roman Emperor installed Borso as duke of Modena and Reggio, while Pope Paul II Barbo recognized him as marquis and later duke of Ferrara. Because Modena and Reggio were under the sovereignty of the Empire and Ferrara within the jurisdiction of the papacy, the Este had always to play a subtle game of managing both Guelf and Ghibelline expectations: in these maneuvers they were masters.

---

8. Charles M. Rosenberg, *The Este Monuments and Urban Development in Renaissance Ferrara.* Cambridge: Cambridge University Press, 1997.

9. Marianne Pade, Leene Waage Petersen, and Daniela Quarta, eds., *La corte di Ferrara e il suo mecenatismo, 1441–1598: Atti del convegno internazionale. Copenhagen, 21–23 maggio 1987.* Modena: Panini, 1990.

10. Lewis Lockwood, *Music in Renaissance Ferrara 1400–1505: The Creation of a Musical Center in the Fifteenth Century.* Oxford: Oxford University Press, 2009. pp. 30–91.

Borso's was a very different personality from that of Lionello. Poorly educated and not really interested in culture, he was nevertheless shrewd enough to see the glory that his brother's patronage had brought to Ferrara. Consequently, he worked to sustain that reputation.[11] The patronage of music and musicians continued.[12] And it was under his rule that a celebrated school of Ferrarese painting developed, with artists like Cosmè Tura, Ercole de'Roberti, and Francesco del Cossa achieving significant reputations.[13] These last two painters decorated rooms in Borso's summer palace of *La Schifanoia* (the name aptly means "without a care").[14] Their *Room of the Months*, with its narrative of Borso's activities, signs of the zodiac, and mythological and arcane figures constitutes one of the glories of Italian Renaissance decoration.[15] It is unfortunately not in the best of conditions, as the palace became a tobacco factory in the nineteenth century. The moist atmosphere and high temperatures required for the production of cigars and cigarettes were unfortunately not suitable for the preservation of frescoes.

Borso also appreciated small luxury objects, cabinet pieces, and fine books. The apogee of this patronage is one of the most sumptuously decorated manuscripts of the Italian Renaissance: the *Bible of Borso d'Este*. This manuscript of more than twelve hundred pages was decorated by many of the most talented painters of the Ferrarese school of the 1450s, including Taddeo Crivelli, Franco de Rossi, Giorgio D'Alemagna, Marco di Giovanni dell'Avogaro, and Girolamo da Cremona. Pisanello was obviously an inspiration, as was Mantegna and even Netherlandish style. The survival of this exquisite book is a tribute to Borso's taste and largesse—and his desire to compete with Mantua and Milan—despite his own lack of a humanist education.

It was one of Borso's courtiers who added the exceptional literary fame to his reign—a fame which would begin a tradition of epic poetry in Ferrara that would turn this northern town into one of the most important poetic centers not only of Italy but of all Europe for a century. Matteo Boiardo was an aristocrat possessed of a poetic genius. He served Borso well as a diplomat and as a regional governor, but it was his avocation that brought him and his prince the greatest renown. For his own and the court's amusement, Boiardo began to write a long epic based on the characters and exploits of

11. Charles M. Rosenberg, *Art in Ferrara during the Reign of Borso D'Este (1450–1471): A Study of Court Patronage.* Ann Arbor, MI: University Microfilms, 1974.

12. Lockwood, 2009. pp. 93–132.

13. Joseph Manca, *Cosme Tura: The Life and Art of a Painter in Estense Ferrara.* Oxford: Clarendon Press, 2000; and by the same author, *The Art of Ercole de' Roberti.* Cambridge: Cambridge University Press, 1992.

14. Paolo D'Ancona and Cesare Gnudi, *The Schifanoia Months at Ferrara.* Milan: Edizioni del Milione. 1954.

15. Vittorio Sgarbi, *Francesco Del Cossa.* Milan: Skira, 2007; Stephen J. Campbell, *Cosme Tura: Painting and Design in Renaissance Ferrara.* Boston: Isabella Stewart Gardner Museum, 2002.

Charlemagne and his knights, especially the heroic Orlando: *Orlando Innamorato*, or *Roland in Love*. The epic is hardly historical, but more concerned with themes of beauty, love, loyalty, and honor, themes close to the Este heart and illustrative of the culture of chivalry that arose from their service as condottieri.[16]

Ercole I d'Este

Borso died in 1471, having never married and having produced no legitimate heirs. But his death did not end Boiardo's court life. The new duke, Ercole I, was Borso's half-brother (born of Niccolo III and another mistress, Ricciarda da Saluzzo) and one of the most prolific and cultivated patrons of the Renaissance. In true Este fashion, Ercole managed to secure his inheritance only after beheading in 1476 two close relations, his nephew (Borso's illegitimate son, Niccolo) and his cousin, who attempted to seize the crown. But, once secure, Ercole embarked on a career of patronage that would make Ferrara one of the most famous cities in Europe for humanist learning and art.[17]

Ercole was a skilled diplomat, especially in securing advantageous marriages for himself and his children—a fortunate talent, given his general failure as a soldier. He himself married the daughter of the king of Naples while his son Alfonso was wed to the daughter of Pope Alexander VI, the infamous Lucrezia Borgia. His two remarkable, talented, and beautiful daughters were married to the future duke of Milan, Lodovico Sforza, *il Moro* (Beatrice), and the marquis of Mantua (Isabella, a princess we have already celebrated). He formed alliances and hired mercenaries to keep his state safe during the unstable period during the pontificate of Sixtus IV, who attempted to take control of Ferrara as a papal fief because the duke was illegitimate. He withstood the mainland ambitions of Venice and he successfully navigated the dangerous time after the French invasions of 1494.

One of his commissions stands out, however, as worthy of any great Renaissance prince: his expansion of his city through new fortifications and the construction of an entirely new town within them, known as the Herculean Addition (*Addizione Erculea*). The walls and new town were built between 1493 and 1505, although continued under Ercole's successors. These additions, which enlarged the city by two thirds, were given a powerful coherence by his architect Biagio Rossetti.[18] What is remarkable about the addition is that it is a fully planned district, in fact the first of its kind in Renaissance Italy. The straight grid-patterned streets reflect the clarity of the Renaissance mind and

---

16. *Dukes and Poets in Ferrara: A Study in the Poetry, Religion and Politics of the Fifteenth and Early Sixteenth Centuries* (Classic Reprint). London: Forgotten Books, 2017. The reprinting of this 1903 classic indicates that it continues to hold some significant value.

17. Werner L. Gundersheimer, "The Patronage of Ercole I d'Este," in *The Journal of Medieval and Renaissance Studies*, 6 (1976), pp. 1–18.

18. Bruno Zevi, *Biagio Rossetti: architetto ferrarese, il primo urbanista moderno europeo*. Turin: Einaudi, 1960.

the debt to ancient Roman town planning—a kind of urban humanism—paralleling the model of Augustus and his embellishment of Rome.[19]

The patronage of painting in Ferrara would have to await the next reign, when Ercole's equally cultivated son Alfonso I (r. 1505–34) became one of the most insightful patrons and collectors of his time.[20] He acquired works by Giovanni Bellini, Titian, and his court painter Dosso Dossi. His pictures and sculpture were displayed in one of Europe's most famous rooms, his *camerino*, known in English as the alabaster room. This was a *studiolo*, lined with white alabaster but capped with a gilded ceiling. Alfonso would retire here to contemplate his art and his policies for Ferrara.[21] Finally, like his father, he was a great lover of music, continuing the patronage of Netherlandish composers at his court, such as Josquin's successors, Antoine Brumel and Adrian Willaert.

Ercole II d'Este

Ercole II (r. 1534–59) attempted to sustain both the freedom of his territory and the tradition of lavish patronage. However, he fell into serious trouble with his sovereign overlord, the pope. In 1528 Ercole had married Renée de Valois, the daughter of King Louis XII of France. She brought with her a large French household and some dangerous ideas about religion. She had been converted to Calvinism, and John Calvin himself visited Ferrara in 1536.[22] The Calvinist poet Clement Marot was part of her household. Despite the duchess's protection, Marot was nevertheless charged with heresy by the Inquisition but managed to escape. She sheltered many other Protestants at her court and corresponded with their leaders, continually defying instructions to stop doing so by her husband. Renée's heresy was seriously undermining Ercole's control of his duchy of Ferrara, as he ruled it as vicar of the pope: to have a Calvinist wife with a household full of Protestant sympathizers endangered his throne.

Consequently, in 1534 Ercole began to move against the large French contingent at his court. He found them not only suspect in religion but profligate and arrogant. Many were sent back to France and Renée was ordered to have nothing more to do with

---

19. See Thomas Tuohy, *Herculean Ferrara: Ercole d'Este (1471–1505) and the Invention of a Ducal Capital*. Cambridge Studies in Italian History and Culture. Cambridge: Cambridge University Press, 1996. p. 195. The not-uncommon humanist parallel between Renaissance princes' building projects and the reign of Augustus was rehearsed for Ercole:

> Just as he found Rome in brick and left it in marble; so too will your Celsitude, by virtue of your Magnificence, be recognized by posterity with great glory. For you found a Ferrara of painted brick, and you will have left it . . . carved in adamantine marble . . . among the wonderful cities of the world.

Quoted in Gundersheimer, 1973. p. 265.

20. Vincenzo Farinella, *Alfonso I d'Este, le immagini e il potere*. Milan: Officina Libreria, 2014. pp. 1–28.

21. Farinella, 2014. pp. 78–212.

22. Anne Puaux, *La Huguenote: Renée de France*. Paris: Hermann, 1997.

Calvinists. She did not obey and was even briefly imprisoned by her husband. Unable to withstand the demands of the Roman Church, Ercole had his wife denounced before the Inquisition after she was discovered on several occasions taking the Calvinist form of the Eucharist and circulating Calvin's *Institutes of the Christian Religion* among her circle. Although he should have held her trial in Ferrara, which had its own office of the Inquisition, Ercole wisely chose to refer the matter to the Inquisition in his wife's native France, where she was tried for heresy and ultimately confessed in 1554. Initially she heroically refused to recant her Calvinism, despite the threat of losing all of her property. But, when her daughters were taken from her with the threat that she would never see them again unless she recanted, Renée at last relented. She refused, however, for the rest of her life to attend a Catholic Mass. After Ercole's death, Pope Pius IV insisted that her son, now Duke Alfonso II, banish his mother forever to France because of her Calvinism.

Tasso and the Chivalric Epic

Alfonso II (r. 1559–97) was the last Este duke of Ferrara. He, too, was a great patron of the arts. At his court, for example, was Giovanni Battista Guarini, the author of *Il Pastor Fido* (*The Faithful Shepherd*); and music excelled, including groups of female musicians, starting a rage for such groups across Italy. But it is with Alfonso's patronage of Torquato Tasso, the author of the pastoral *Aminta* (1573) and the epic poem *Jerusalem Delivered* (1581) that the Este reputation for patronage and culture reached a new level. Tasso was one of the most celebrated poets of the century. His *Jerusalem Delivered* is the story of the capture of Jerusalem in the First Crusade, with Godfrey of Bouillon as its ostensible hero, although the other characters, including the Muslim knights, are really more interesting. His model—again from classical antiquity—was Virgil, and his genius for poetry, romance, magic, and engrossing description made this long poem a still popular monument to the Este of Ferrara.[23]

Unfortunately, beginning in the 1570s, Tasso suffered from mental illness, manifested in an intense paranoia and an antisocial anger that he could not suppress. He was imprisoned in a madhouse in Ferrara from 1579 until 1586, and the following years until his death were increasingly tragic. Then in 1595 it seemed as though he was to be redeemed: Tasso was to emulate the example of Petrarch and be crowned poet laureate in Rome. His genius was at last to be recognized by the world. Sadly, Tasso died at 51, before the coronation could take place.

The Este appreciation for these chivalric romances, clad in the genre of Renaissance epic, very much reflected the culture of the condottiere principalities. These mercenary princes—and their nobles—fancied themselves as the continuators—if not the embodiment—of Charlemagne's knights, such as Roland, or Arthur's Knights of the Round Table. It is this element which contrasts so vividly with the mercantile, republican,

---

23. Angelo Solerti, *Vita Di Torquato Tasso*, 3 vols. Turin: Loescher, 1895.

bourgeois traditions of Florence. The principalities were in many ways artificial cultures in which feudal knighthood was celebrated in a place and time when there was no real feudal society. Instead, the mundane practices of trade and commerce produced the wealth needed to sustain these fantasies of knights, crusaders, griffins, magicians, Moors, and, of course, exquisite ladies who had strong characters of their own, able to fight and scheme, as well as love openly—concepts impossible for a Florentine woman to even imagine, and, as we have seen, dangerous for a woman even in Ferrara.[24]

Duke Alfonso had no legitimate children and Pope Clement VIII had declared that the rulers of all papal territories had to have been born legitimate. This was an old element of papal policy, but it was enforced rigorously in this case to ensure that Ferrara did not fall into the Habsburg sphere of influence. Consequently, although Alfonso willed Ferrara to his cousin Cesare, the succession was not recognized by the pope, as Cesare was also illegitimate. The emperor, however, did accept him as ruler of Modena and Reggio. The consequence was that Ferrara itself was incorporated into the States of the Church in 1598 by Pope Clement, although the Este continued to rule the other territories of their dominion as imperial vicars, with their new capital at Modena. Ferrara became an appendage of the Church, ruled directly by a papal governor: its age of glory ended with the expulsion of the Este in 1598.

---

24. Alessandro Marcigliano, *Chivalric Festivals at the Ferrarese Court of Alfonso II d'Este* (Stage and Screen Studies). New York and Bern: Peter Lang, 2003.

Illus. 11.1 Castello Estense, Ferrara.

The enormous Castello Estense was built to protect the Este lords of the city from their own subjects. After a riot against high taxes in 1385 threatened the dynasty, Marquis Niccolo II ordered the construction of the fortress, with towers and a moat. Throughout the Renaissance the castle was enlarged and redecorated, with its current appearance dating largely from the sixteenth century. The enormous castle was in fact a city within a city, with elegantly painted reception rooms, vast kitchens, a pharmacy (which traditionally produced poisons as well as medicines), and terrible dungeons, essentially unchanged and still redolent of the horrors they witnessed, such as the imprisonment of the young, incestuous royal lovers Parisina and Ugo before their beheading, and the fifty-three-year incarceration of Giulio d'Este, brother of Alfonso I, for conspiracy. When Giulio was finally pardoned when he was in his eighties, he walked across the drawbridge and through the city wearing the same clothes he had worn at the time of his arrest and acting with the elegant, polished court manners of a half-century before.

Illus. 11.2 Palazzo Municipale, Ferrara.

What is now the town hall of Ferrara was the original Este palace, constructed in 1245 and enlarged until the 1480s. Despite its tower and crenellations, it was considered not sufficiently secure to protect the Este, hence their commissioning of the Castello Estense. Its location is in the ancient heart of the city opposite the cathedral of St. George, one of whose Romanesque marble lions is visible at the bottom left.

On either side of the entry are bronze statues of two Este rulers. The equestrian figure of Marquis Niccolo III was created in 1451 by Florentine sculptors Antonio di Cristoforo and Niccolo Baroncelli (who was responsible for the horse) with the advice of the great Leon Battista Alberti. It stands on a symbolic Roman triumphal arch. On Niccolo's right is the seated figure of Duke Borso d'Este, dating originally from 1454. It shows the duke in the act of dispensing justice, as it was first placed before the Palazzo della Ragione (law courts) and only moved to the Palazzo Municipale in 1472, the year after his death. This proved providential because the courts were destroyed by bombing during the Second World War.

Sadly, both statues are modern copies. Napoleon, during his occupation of Ferrara in 1796 ordered both Renaissance works of art melted down for their bronze to cast cannons.

Illus. 11.3 Cosmè Tura and Francesco del Cossa, *Duke Borso d'Este Rewarding His Jester*, 1469–70. Palazzo Schifanoia, Ferrara.

Palazzo Schifanoia (literally meaning "Palace without Cares") was built in 1385 as a pleasure palace and banqueting house with expansive gardens. In 1469 Borso d'Este, who had been raised to the dignity of duke of Modena by the emperor, prepared for a similar elevation in Ferrara by the pope. He ordered the palace enlarged and a huge reception room decorated by the leading painters of the Ferrarese school: Cosmè Tura and Francesco del Cossa.

The program is the cycle of the year represented by the signs of the zodiac, pagan mythological allusions and scenes from the city and the court appropriate for those months. In this scene from the month of March, Duke Borso is rewarding his jester, Scoccola, surrounded by his courtiers. In other parts of this fresco, the annual Palio di San Giorgio, the foot race through the city is shown, as is the constellation of Taurus and the celebration of love, Venus and the three graces.

The intention of this complex iconography is to associate Borso's rule in Ferrara with the natural and astrological calendars. The influence of the stars and the seasons were believed to affect the lives of those on earth, and Duke Borso links them by governing in accordance with their patterns and precepts.

CHAPTER 12
URBINO AND THE MONTEFELTRO

The duchy of Urbino is in the middle of nowhere, a forty square mile tract of steep hillsides and forested gorges in the Apennines. It is not on the coast or on a major river or trade route. Its resources were and are minimal, and the harvests small and unreliable. In short, Urbino enjoyed none of the advantages of the other great states such as Florence or Mantua or Milan. So how can it be that the great art historian, Kenneth Clark, in his landmark television series and book, *Civilization*, could describe Urbino as perhaps the most civilized place that existed in Europe in the fifteenth century?

Like Mantua, Urbino's rulers were condottieri, mercenary captains who used their hardy subjects as soldiers to fight other peoples' wars.[1] The very inhospitable terrain of Urbino made the men tough, resilient, and able to withstand deprivation—perfect qualities for soldiers. The counts and dukes of Urbino were skilled commanders, especially one who established a reputation as a general, statesman, and humanist patron to such a degree that his duchy became that most civilized site, a place of exquisite beauty and learning and a kind of finishing school for the young men of the greatest families in Italy.[2] That man was Federigo da Montefeltro, duke of Urbino.[3]

Federigo da Montefeltro

Federigo was born illegitimate in 1422, the consequence of a liaison between his father, Guidantonio, lord of Urbino, and one of his wife's attendants.[4] There appeared to have been little animosity over Federigo's uncanonical entry into the world, however, as Guidantonio's wife interceded with her uncle, Pope Martin V, to legitimize Federigo in 1424. The boy also enjoyed an excellent humanist education in the classics and literature, despite serving as a hostage for his father when he was eleven. Indeed, those years were an essential part of his education as he was held in Venice and Mantua, two of Renaissance Italy's centers of learning and culture.[5]

There was no question but that Federigo would have to enter the family business of mercenary warfare, as it was the only truly profitable occupation possible for the young prince who was also a second, as well as a bastard, son. So, in 1435, a year after his first

---

1. For the history of the family, see Gino Franceschini, *I Montefeltro*. Milan: Dall'Oglio, 1970.

2. June Osborne, *Urbino: The Story of a Renaissance City*. Chicago: University of Chicago Press, 2003.

3. Old but still valuable is James Dennistoun, *Memoirs of the Dukes of Urbino, Illustrating the Arms, Arts and Literature of Italy, 1440–1630*, 3 vols. London: Bodley Head, 1909.

4. Benzoni, 1995; Bernd Roeck and Andreas Tönnesmann, *Federico da Montefeltro. Arte, stato e mestiere delle armi*, tr. S. Accornero. Torino: Einaudi, 2009.

5. Denis Mack Smith, *Federigo da Montefeltro*. Urbino, Italy: Quattroventi, 2005.

marriage at the age of fifteen, he was enrolled in the mercenary army of the celebrated condottiere Niccolo Piccinini: His career and training had begun in earnest. Then his prospects changed dramatically. In 1444 his legitimate older brother, Oddantonio, was assassinated in a court conspiracy. The degree to which Federigo was involved in the plot is unknown, but it was he who benefitted, as he was named ruler of his city in succession to his half-brother. Nevertheless, he still continued to lead his mercenary band, fighting for the Florentines for very high payments.

In 1450 Federigo shifted his allegiance to Milan and its new duke, Francesco Sforza. It was then that Federigo suffered a terrible wound while jousting in a tournament. He lost one eye and his face was permanently scarred. Remembering the fate of his brother, Federigo chose to further disfigure his face by having his physician remove part of the cartilage of his very prominent nose so that he had a wider field of vision with his one eye. He claimed it would help him see assassins. These wounds only briefly affected his ability to lead his army. He was soon fighting again—and again for very high fees—for Milan, Naples, Florence, and the papacy. He was remarkably fair and honorable for a condottiere, a class not particularly known for honesty or trustworthiness. In fact, he never betrayed a client, although he was free to switch sides when his contract with another was fulfilled. For example, he waged war both on behalf of and against Florence.

Here, though, there is more to be seen. Although Urbino was technically a Guelf state within the orbit of the States of the Church in the Marches of Italy, Federigo was sufficiently experienced and wise to know how dangerous the papacy could be. His mortal enemy was the ruler of Rimini, Sigismondo Malatesta, known as the "Wolf of Rimini." And this was an enmity shared by Pope Pius II, who warred with the Malatesta, ultimately leaving Sigismondo in control of little more than the city of Rimini itself. Federigo was totally aware that the same fate could happen to him, so he recognized that accommodation with the Church was good policy. Fortunately, Federigo and Pope Sixtus shared similar goals, cemented by family. So it was that Federigo was almost certainly in the pay of Pope Sixtus IV's nephew Girolamo Riario during the Pazzi Conspiracy against the Medici.[6]

There were also family connections at play in this alliance. Sixtus IV had his favorite papal nephew, Giovanni della Rovere, married to Federigo's daughter Giovanna. In 1474 Federigo was raised by papal grace to the dignity of duke of Urbino, the title his assassinated half-brother had carried. Urbino was now in the papal orbit secured through a dynastic marriage that benefitted both parties, and one which would have significant implications for the future. Federigo also made peace with Rimini after the death of Sigismondo by marrying another of his daughters to Roberto Malatesta, Sigismondo's illegitimate son, who had become lord of Rimini by poisoning his step-mother and two

---

6. The suggestion that Federico was deeply involved in the Pazzi Conspiracy is proposed in Marcello Simonetta, *The Montefeltro Conspiracy: A Renaissance Mystery Decoded*. New York: Doubleday, 2008.

half-brothers.[7] The times were dangerous, and the Malatesta were among the most murderous of the dynasties.

By 1475 Federigo was secure on this throne and in his title of duke of Urbino. Although still often away on campaign, he had the opportunity, the internal security, and the resources to engage in his obsessions with learning, art, architecture, and ideas. Federigo was in no way another thug of a mercenary leader: he was "the light of Italy," as described by his contemporaries. The scale of his patronage and the quality of the work he commissioned are truly astounding given that Urbino had few attractions other than an opportunity to make great art and participate in a splendid court. The focus of this patronage was the huge, magnificent ducal palace which Federigo ordered built beginning in 1466.[8]

The palace was designed by two great architects: the Dalmatian Luciano Laurana and the theorist and architect Francesco di Giorgio Martini.[9] Laurana had worked with Leon Battista Alberti in Mantua during the construction of Sant'Andrea, so he was familiar with Alberti's elegant classicism. However, Federigo's palace was not a church or a merchant's palace but the fortress of a condottiere as well as a pleasure dome. The result of the fusion of this classical vocabulary and castle design is what we still see today rising up the slopes of the Apennines, the wonderful building whose austere curtain walls, broken with balconies, windows, and towers, give way in the interior to one of Renaissance Italy's most sensuously elegant spaces.

From the wonderful, arcaded court of honor (*cortile d'onore*) to the dancing *putti* on fireplace mantles, overseen by the eagle of the Montefeltro, there is playfulness in the decoration of the huge rooms. The door frames, mostly inspired by classical motifs, are all different, and each celebrates the movement of Federigo and his court from one space into another. The doors themselves were richly inlaid with intarsia (inlaid wooden panels), providing trompe l'oeil images of ideal cities, classical gods, or sinuous arabesques. We know that much of the design for these intarsia panels was made by Luciano Laurana and that they were carved and effected by the Florentine sculptor Giuliano da Maiano.

Federigo's Studiolo

Of all of these spaces, however, it is Federigo's *studiolo* that stands out as one of the most exquisite and engaging rooms of the Renaissance.[10] As we saw with Isabella d'Este, a

7. For a discussion of the competition between the Montefeltro and the Malatesta, see Maria Grazia Pernis and Laurie Schneider Adams, *Federico da Montefeltro and Sigismondo Malatesta: The Eagle and the Elephant*. New York: Peter Lang, 1997.

8. Carlo Bo, *Il Palazzo Ducale di Urbino*. Novara, Italy: Istituto Geografico DeAgostini, 1982.

9. F. P. Fiore, ed., *Francesco di Giorgio alla corte di Federico da Montefeltro*, 2 vols. Florence: Olschki, 2004.

10. Olga Raggio and Antoine M. Wilmering, *Lo studiolo di Federico da Montefeltro*. Milan: 24 Ore Cultura, 2008. For a detailed discussion of Federico's *studiolo* from his palace in Gubbio, now in the Metropolitan Museum of Art (New York) and its restoration, see Olga Raggio, *Federico Da Montefeltro's Palace at Gubbio and Its Studiolo: Italian Renaissance Intarsia and the Conservation of the Gubbio Studiolo*, 2 vols. New Haven: Yale University Press, 2000.

studiolo is a small private study of a noble prince or prelate. It had to be small so that the owner could be alone with his or her thoughts, books, and inspiration and without requiring the help of servants. Federigo's *studiolo* tells us so much about the man and how he externalized and celebrated his intellectual and cultural interests through art. The room is completely faced—right to the cornice—with inlay, or intarsia. The panels on the wall are carefully crafted using perspective to make doors appear half open, revealing the contents of cabinets. These reflect the duke's multiple interests: there are scientific and musical instruments, his armor, books, and even a stylized view of the landscape of his duchy.

In his *studiolo* Federigo would read, write, or just think—probably standing up. There is little room for a chair, and it would have restricted his access to the inspiration all around him. The room would also be full of books: Federigo amassed the largest library in Italy after the collection in the Apostolic Vatican Palace. More than one thousand of the best manuscripts were bound in his distinctive red velvet, with the golden eagle of Urbino on the case. To create his library, he had a score of scribes copying the very best exemplars of classical authors, as well as some works of theology and philosophy.

His books also had to be beautiful. He acquired a great many of his manuscripts from that famous Florentine stationer and biographer Vespasiano da Bisticci (d. 1498).[11] Like Vespasiano, Federigo had only contempt for the new technology of printing. All of his books had to be original, handwritten in beautiful script and elegantly bound.[12] If you want the most famous example, look at the exquisite Urbino Bible now in the Vatican Library. It is a two-volume Bible, decorated in purple and gold, written on the finest vellum and illustrated with miniatures painted by the workshop of the Ghirlandaio in Florence. It is one of the most sumptuous books ever created and still a work of hypnotic beauty.

Federigo was an Aristotelian, as he was very pragmatic in his official life. He was also a devout Christian, so biblical and theological works appeared. But his greatest love was history. Federigo believed, like most educated Renaissance men inspired by humanism, that history provided the examples of the great deeds of the past to emulate and the sins and errors to avoid. He saw the rhetorical element in history as important to his diplomacy and to his clarity of thought.

His devotion to learning was manifested in the second part of the decoration in Federigo's *studiolo*. Above the intarsia panels were twenty-eight portraits of the duke's heroes. Some were ancient philosophers, like Plato and Aristotle; others were Biblical figures, like David and Solomon; and still others were learned contemporaries, like Cardinal Bessarion and Vittorino da Feltre. And, of course, there was Petrarch. The movement begun by the poet had traveled well beyond the fertile cultural fields of Venice, Tuscany, and Lombardy into these recesses of Italy. As a recorder of human emotions, Petrarch

---

11. Vespasiano da Bisticci, *The Vespasiano Memoirs: Lives of Illustrious Men of the XVth Century*, tr. W. George and E. Walters. Toronto: University of Toronto Press, 1997. pp. 102–5.
12. Marcello Simonetta, Jonathan J. G. Alexander, and Cecilia Martelli, *Federico da Montefeltro and His Library*. Vatican City: Biblioteca Apostolica Vaticana, 2007.

was celebrated everywhere; but in the palace of Urbino, his recognition of human agency and the magnetic power of fame was particularly powerful. It is not an accident that these visual inspirations were above Federigo while he worked in his *studiolo*, captured in the likenesses of those who inspired him, regardless of when they lived.

The artists who made the portraits for Federigo's studio were the court artists Justus van Ghent, a Fleming, and Pedro Berruguete, a Spaniard—Urbino was not sufficiently attractive to draw such luminaries as Leonardo or Michelangelo. Still, Piero della Francesca, that superb master of perspective, worked for Federigo and painted three of his most important pictures for him: the *Flagellation of Christ*; *The Montefeltro Altarpiece*; and that double portrait of Federigo and his duchess, Battista Sforza, niece of the duke of Milan.[13]

This double portrait, now in the Uffizi gallery in Florence, is undoubtedly the most famous of the Urbino masterpieces. It captures the duke and duchess in full profile against stylized backgrounds of the landscape of the Marches. While the choice of profile allowed Piero to omit the duke's terrible facial scar, it wasn't just adopted for the sake of flattery; rather, it followed the example of ancient Roman and Renaissance coins and medals, which always have the figure in full profile. On the reverse of the panels appear images of the triumphs of the duke and duchess. These are inspired by the *Trionfi* (*Triumphs*) of Petrarch, that series of poems in which virtue triumphs over adversity. Federigo looked for inspiration and validation and Italian writers in particular, like Petrarch, provided that impetus to aim ever higher.

Problems in Succession

All of Federigo's success was compromised, however, by his lack of a male heir. He had after the early death of his first wife married the lovely, highly educated and cultivated Battista Sforza when she was fourteen and he thirty-eight. She had been splendidly educated in Greek and Latin and was so precocious that she delivered her first public oration in Latin at four; and she was one of the few women to give a Latin oration in front of the pope—and not just any pope: Pius II, the humanist scholar Enea Silvio Piccolomini! Moreover, they had an extremely happy partnership, one in which the young woman acted as the duke's regent while he was on campaign; and he treated her with the greatest respect and love. Their devotion to one another was widely celebrated, with one poet describing them as having one soul in two bodies, and Federigo wrote that his wife was the comfort and strength of his private and public life. She accompanied him on state missions, as they did not want to be apart more than Federigo's job required.

Battista was constantly pregnant from the time of puberty, giving birth to seven children by the age of twenty-five. All were girls, except the last, finally a son and heir. The act of producing an heir cost her her life, as she died soon after from complications

---

13. Birgit Laskowski, *Piero della Francesca*. Cologne: Konemann, 1998. pp. 70–87.

from childbirth. Federigo died in 1482, a decade after his beloved duchess, in his sixtieth year. The light of Italy had gone out.

The son that Battista died to produce was Guidobaldo da Montefeltro.[14] In his youth, during his first decade when his father was alive, he showed great promise, remarkable intelligence, and sensitivity. He was given a good humanist education but was necessarily put to the practice of arms, as had his ancestors before him. He served as a captain in the service of the pope during the period of the French invasions of 1494, and subsequently accepted payment from Venice, also to protect the republic from the French. He did not, however, share his father's military genius or his energy; indeed, he was captured by opposing mercenaries in 1496 while fighting for Pope Alexander VI Borgia.

In 1489 he was married to Elisabetta Gonzaga, the sister of the marquis of Mantua.[15] By then Guidobaldo's illness had progressed, leaving him impotent; the marriage was likely never consummated, which made it canonically invalid. Nevertheless, Elisabetta never sought an annulment and supported her invalid husband during the difficult years after 1502. Despite Guidobaldo's having been in the service of the Borgia pope, Alexander VI's son Cesare occupied Urbino that year through treachery. It was, after all, a fief of the Church; but Cesare Borgia had sworn to respect the Montefeltro dynasty while campaigning to reassert the papacy's direct control of the semi-independent lordships that characterized the chaotic and largely ungovernable Papal States. The most likely reason for Cesare's treachery—beyond his psychotic personality—was that the obvious heir to Urbino after Guidobaldo's death was Francesco Maria della Rovere who was the nephew both of Duke Federigo and of Cardinal Giulio della Rovere, the Borgias's most hated enemy and the future Pope Julius II.

Guidobaldo was forced to flee Urbino in 1502. Once in control, Cesare set about to sell the treasures collected by Federigo, using the palace as a barracks for his soldiers and stable for his horses while his army looted the city. Fearing Cesare's wrath, the ducal couple fled to Venice to protect the Gonzaga, and it was there they received word in 1503 that Pope Alexander VI had died and that Cesare was dangerously ill as well. With the death of his holy father, Cesare's kingdom collapsed. His garrison was driven from Urbino and Guidobaldo and Elisabetta summoned home. To protect the succession, Guidobaldo formally adopted Francesco Maria della Rovere as his heir. Francesco Maria was powerfully supported in his ambitions when his uncle Cardinal della Rovere was elected pope as Julius II in 1503, giving Urbino unquestioned papal support.

---

14. The polymath from Urbino, Bernardino Baldi (1553–1617), wrote a history of Guidobaldo I and Urbino just decades after the duke's death: *Vita e fatti di Federigo di Montefeltro, Duca di Urbino: Istoria di Bernardino Baldi*, ed. G. Rosmini, 2 vols. Originally printed in 1824, it is now available in reprint (St. Albans, VT: Wentworth Publishing, 2016) and as a digital download.

15. Elisabetta was a close friend of Isabella d'Este and their surviving correspondence is voluminous. See Alessandro Luzio, *Mantova e Urbino: Isabella d'Este ed Elisabetta Gonzaga Nelle Relazioni Famigliari e Nelle Vicende Politiche; Narrazione Storica Documentata*. The Italian 1893 original is now available in reprint (London: Forgotten Books, 2018).

The court re-established in that year by Guidobaldo and Elisabetta lasted only five years, until the death of the sickly duke in 1508. But those years seemed a return to the glorious age of his father, although more in the vernacular culture of the sixteenth century than the Latin humanist environment of the fifteenth. Because of his deteriorating health, Guidobaldo was often in his bed, so much of the running of the duchy was left to his wife, Elisabetta. She was extremely intelligent, well educated, and cultivated, and exhibited a high moral tone that suffused the court, as perhaps is appropriate for a virgin duchess. The court, as it had from the time of Federigo, attracted young men from the greatest families in Italy, drawn there not only by the opportunity to study military matters in a city made famous by Federigo but also because of the elegant, refined atmosphere. Urbino was a kind of finishing school for the high Italian nobility.

This culture was described and codified by a member of that inner circle, a distant relative of Elisabetta from Mantua, Count Baldassare Castiglione. His great *The Book of the Courtier* (*Il Libro del Cortegiano*) reflected how Urbino managed to retain some of its cultural luster, even after the crises of the death of Federigo; the French invasions of 1494, 1498, and 1500; and the devastating policies of the Borgias. Urbino's reputation remained and was to a degree reinforced by the character of the duchess and the court over which she presided in the absence of her husband. Urbino continued as a cultural center that largely depended on the glorification of the person of the duchess, praised in verse by poets such as Pietro Bembo and Castiglione.[16] The palace might have been robbed of many of its treasures by Cesare Borgia but the atmosphere of cultivated elegance, knowledge, and beauty remained.

Baldassare Castiglione

The figure who immortalized the court of Urbino was that confidant of Duchess Elisabetta, Baldassare Castiglione (1478–1529).[17] Castiglione was born near Mantua in 1478, the son of a nobleman close to the ruling Gonzaga family. In 1494 he was sent to Milan for humanistic studies and for polish at the most brilliant court in Italy, the court of Duke Lodovico, *il Moro* and his duchess, Beatrice d'Este, the sister of Isabella, marchioness of Mantua. There he acquired a deep affection for classical studies and a broad cultural education. His education was interrupted by his father's death in 1499, which required him to return to Mantua to fulfill his responsibilities as a leading noble of the Gonzagas. He was a natural diplomat and an ornament to the court, attending on the marquis and representing Mantua abroad. On one of these missions, however, in Rome in 1504, he encountered Duke Guidobaldo of Urbino who was so impressed by

---

16. Stefania Signorini, *Poesia a corte: le rime per Elisabetta Gonzaga (Urbino, 1488–1526)*. Pisa: ETS, 2009.

17. Julia Cartwright Ady, ed., *Baldassare Castiglione, the Perfect Courtier: His Life and Letters, 1478–1529*, 2 vols. London: Forgotten Books, 2017 (reprint of the 1908 edition).

the young man that he asked his wife's brother, the marquis of Mantua, to release him so that he could serve the Montefeltro.

From 1504 until 1516 he resided at the court of Urbino. His duties as a diplomat were extended to include social responsibilities at court. He wrote—and acted—in court dramas; engaged in rich diplomatic and literary correspondence with the leading scholars and aristocrats of Italy and elsewhere in Europe; and he developed a deep but purely platonic love for the duchess Elisabetta, writing sonnets and letters that reflected their mutual intellectual admiration and affection. The death of Duke Guidobaldo changed nothing: he continued to serve the new ruler, Francesco Maria della Rovere, as both a diplomat and as a soldier. He participated in the Italian Wars and was appropriately acknowledged. He represented his prince at the court of his uncle, Pope Julius II, where he again became close to Raphael, who painted his portrait, one of the most evocative and celebrated portraits from Renaissance Italy, illustrating the long friendship and affection between them, a friendship begun in Urbino.

Castiglione still was the head of one of Mantua's most important noble families and his mother despaired of his ever marrying and having an heir. So, in 1516, Castiglione returned to Mantua where he married a very young girl from another leading aristocratic house and together they had a daughter, his only child. Sadly, the young countess Castiglione died in 1520, leaving the count emotionally shattered, especially since Castiglione was absent in Rome as an ambassador at the time. Rather than return to remarry and sustain his noble line, however, he stayed in Rome where in 1521 he was admitted to holy orders by Pope Leo X de'Medici.

Pope Leo used Castiglione's diplomatic skills as had the rulers of Urbino and Mantua. He was appointed in 1524 *papal nuncio* to Spain where he attended on Charles V. This proved disastrous to his reputation, because it was generally believed in Rome and even by Pope Clement VII that he had knowledge of the intention of the Imperial army to sack Rome in 1527 and did not convey this to the pope. The charge was absurd, but it drove Castiglione to write powerful letters justifying his actions. His letter to Pope Clement was sufficiently convincing that the pope apologized and approved Charles V's appointment of Castiglione as bishop of Avila. It was in Toledo, Spain, that Baldassare Castiglione died in 1529 of plague at the age of just fifty.

The Book of the Courtier

Castiglione had begun *The Book of the Courtier* (*Il Libro del Cortegiano*) while still at the court of Urbino in 1508 and spent the next twenty years polishing it, deciding to publish *The Courtier* in 1528 only after unauthorized copies had been circulating in Rome.[18] The

---

18. The best translation and discussion of *The Courtier* remains that of Charles Singleton, *The Book of the Courtier: The Singleton Translation: An Authoritative Text Criticism*. New York: W. W. Norton, 2002.

work is a dialogue, lasting over four intense evenings in Duchess Elisabetta's chambers. It begins as a game, presided over by the widowed relation by marriage to the duchess, the noblewoman Emilia Pia. The point of the game is to define the characteristics of the perfect courtier, three books of which are directed toward identifying the ideal gentleman and one the ideal court lady. However, it is so much more than a traditional Renaissance dialogue on a given theme, providing an opportunity for the interlocutors to show their rhetorical skill and learning, as well as revealing their characters.[19] Those involved in the debate are those same scions of celebrated families whom Castiglione knew at the court of Guidobaldo, that finishing school for Italian princes. The greatest names in the peninsula appear: Medici from Florence; Fregoso and Pallavicini from Genoa; della Rovere (the papal nephew and future duke); Gonzaga from Mantua (represented by a mutual cousin of Castiglione and the duchess); Pietro Bembo from Venice (who would become a cardinal and define the Italian vernacular); Count Lodovico da Canossa from Emilia-Romagna; and the brilliant playwright and humanist friend of Leo X, Cardinal Bernardo Dovizi da Bibbiena from Tuscany, whose niece was betrothed to Raphael (who painted the cardinal and decorated his bathroom). Although a cardinal of the Roman Church, Bibbiena was said to have more sympathy with pagan than Christian learning and displayed a very erotic frame of mind, as evidenced in his comedy *La Calandra*, which was in fact first performed at the court of Urbino.

There were other men in the duchess's rooms for those evenings as well, including professional wits and buffoons, but the two women are the figures unambiguously in charge. The role of the duchess is obvious and her naming her relation Emila Pia as mistress of ceremonies is instructive. Emilia was from near Modena and married to an illegitimate son of Duke Federigo da Montefeltro, Antonio, who had died in 1508, leaving her a widow. She remained at the court of Urbino, however, and was a very close confidante of the duchess Elisabetta and, like the duchess, was celebrated for her piety and goodness.

The Book of the Courtier is not a guide to manners and deportment: it is a collective vision of a once perfect world long past in Italy. It is defined, despite the light tone and frequent jokes, by an intense sense of melancholy, which is most clearly revealed in the prefaces. In part, this is nostalgia for the forever passed world of the Montefeltro; but equally, it surpasses this personal loss experienced by Castiglione and his fellows. The ideals of *The Courtier* are those of Duke Guidobaldo's Italy, governed by impotent rulers who could not sustain the civilization which their ancestors had created and which had led the world in all of the arts of human civilization.

Although specifically praised occasionally, Castiglione really saw Guidobaldo as the Fisher King, whose weakness in the face of brutality, represented by the Borgias and the French, was the cause of his nation's disasters and decline. Castiglione observes that

---

19. For the context and reception of *The Courtier*, see Peter Burke, *The Fortunes of the Courtier: The European Reception of Castiglione's* Cortegiano. University Park: Penn State Press, 1996.

certain shards had been collected against the ruin of their civilization: pieces of culture, manners, cultivated society. Nevertheless, Castiglione clearly thinks these to be insufficient, at least in the present circumstances, even though there is no other recourse, nothing more can be done. Hence, a strong impression of *après nous le deluge* pervades *The Courtier*, a feeling best illustrated by Castiglione's imaginary discussions with old men at the court who remember times past as better and whom Castiglione disingenuously implies were only expressing the wish to recapture their youth. For Castiglione, Urbino under the Montefeltro was a golden age, an ideal society which could not survive in an imperfect, fallen world, represented by the terrible events that followed the French invasions of 1494 and were exacerbated by the Italian Wars.

In this his Neoplatonism shines forth, a popularized notion of the philosophy which gives reality to perfect conceptions we can recognize only imperfectly on earth. In *The Courtier*, Urbino leaves the rugged soil of the Apennines and climbs higher, into the sphere of perfect forms, where it becomes the ideal court of which all other courts can be but pale reflections. The light of Italy was also the light of hope. Men like Federigo da Montefeltro were capable of defending Italy from the "barbarians" but his successors are not. After all, what do those noble men and women do in Urbino during the debates in *The Courtier*? They talk in a woman's boudoir. There is no action, only talk, and for that reason, the violence and faithlessness of the French, the Spanish, and the imperials will prevail; they can do what they want to Italy. A superior culture will not preserve Italians if it reduces the natural leaders of their society to mere courtiers and not men of action.

Think of the frame of *The Book of the Courtier*. The discussions last through the night, where the only illumination which can perhaps dispel the darkness comes from words. And the dialogues are presided over by two women—an inversion of the natural order to the Renaissance Italian male mind—with the legitimate duke lying impotent and immobilized in bed: this is a metaphor for Italy during the sixteenth century. The world is turned upside down, and there is no one capable of saving the civilization of Renaissance Italy and bringing back its light. It is a vision of great concern but not despair. Castiglione, humanist that he was, believes that the culture created during the Renaissance might be preserved and might again emerge when the heavy hand of the barbarians is removed. Here he is showing that the conversations during those evenings in the castle of Urbino hold some measure of hope, inasmuch as the learned and talented interlocutors in the dialogue might in fact be sustaining what matters in the face of barbarism: civilization.[20]

Again, the belief in the eternal qualities of ideal principles emerges from Castiglione's melancholic image of the current state of Italy; and there is still a kind of hope, although a rather feeble one. We saw that for Niccolò Machiavelli, the solution was to beat the barbarians at their own game through greater ruthlessness, faithlessness, and brutality,

---

20. Kenneth Bartlett, "Platonic Perfection amid Political Failure: The Text and Context of Castiglione's *Cortegiano*," in *Memini: Travaux et Documents*, 6 (2002), 170–202.

although only until the problem was solved and then civilization should be restored. Machiavelli saw men like Cesare Borgia as the solution rather than the problem, whereas Castiglione had seen the effects that such men had on Italian civilization when Cesare captured, looted, and terrorized Urbino in 1502–3. Desperate events, such as those precipitated by the French invasions and the Italian Wars, required dramatic responses; but what should those be? The urbane, cultivated, sensitive, and brilliant Castiglione sought hope through culture; Machiavelli, the pragmatist, through action. In so many ways it was Castiglione who had the right response. Italy did lose its independence for three centuries, largely ruled by foreign powers, but the cultural supremacy of the Renaissance endured in a great many ways, despite the concerted attempts to suppress its open, questioning nature through the imposition of a rigid ideology of obedience to the Church and the prince.

Urbino after Guidobaldo

When Guidobaldo died at age thirty-six in 1508, the duchy passed seamlessly to Francesco Maria della Rovere. Elisabetta served as regent for the young duke and Castiglione remained as well, sustaining that culture of refinement into the new dynasty. Unfortunately, papal dynastic politics were again to throw Urbino into crisis. After the death of Julius II in 1513, Leo X de'Medici was elected to the throne of St. Peter. He, too, was a highly cultivated and civilized man, as one would expect of the son of the Magnificent Lorenzo. But, he had to find a principality for his young nephew Lorenzo, the son of his deceased elder brother, Piero. In the only major war Leo X fought, the War of Urbino, the duchy was captured. Francesco Maria della Rovere was expelled and Lorenzo de'Medici made duke in his stead in 1516.[21] Lorenzo was, however, wounded in the capture of the city and had contracted syphilis years before. The result was that he died young in 1519, leaving as his greatest legacy his tomb by Michelangelo in San Lorenzo in Florence, and an infant daughter, Catherine, who would become queen of France. So, the duchy reverted to the della Rovere who ruled it until it was absorbed into the Papal States in 1626, with the extinction of the main line of the family.

The remarkable history of Urbino, completely inseparable from the dynasty of the Montefeltro during the Renaissance, was both fortunate and tragic. The brilliance and patronage of Federigo da Montefeltro raised the city to the height of Italian Renaissance culture, at least as practiced in a principality. But so much of the city's brilliance was dependent on this one man—the prince—and this is the danger of monarchy. Guidobaldo was unable to sustain his father's luster and protect Urbino from the Borgia because of his illness, which also ensured the end of the dynasty. As Urbino was a fief of the Church, papal policy was always a major factor in the success or failure of

---

21. William Roscoe, *The Life and Pontificate of Leo X*. London: Henry Bohn, 1846. Vol. 2, pp. 52–64.

principalities like Urbino. Indeed, Urbino illustrates just how unstable and dangerous this situation can be.

Kenneth Clark was right, then, in recognizing the amazing brief moment of cultural efflorescence in this tiny principality; and he, like so many others, saw that it was something of a miracle, the consequence of the concentrated genius and skill of Federigo da Montefeltro during his long and glorious reign. Federigo exemplified Petrarch's ideal of a self-fashioned, heroic individual, inspired by antiquity and capable of great things through the force of his will and the fruits of his studies. It is no accident, then, that a portrait of the poet graced the duke's *studiolo*, where he was most in touch with his own genius.

Illus. 12.1.a Piero della Francesca (1415–92), *Double Portrait of Battista Sforza and Federico da Montefeltro,* **ca. 1465. Uffizi, Florence.**

This celebrated diptych of Federigo and his beloved duchess, Battista Sforza, was painted between 1465 and 1471. The then fashionable full profile image reflects ancient coins and medals and connects the pair to ancient imperial portraits. It is also appropriate because Federigo had been terribly scarred in a tournament accident, losing his right eye and disfiguring his face and nose. The idealized landscape of Urbino lies behind them, illustrating the tranquility and prosperity he has brought to his realm. He is also depicted in court dress rather than armor on one side of the panel.

CLARVS INSIGNI VEHITVR TRIVMPHO ·
QVEM PAREM SVMMIS DVCIBVS PERHENNIS ·
FAMA VIRTVTVM CELEBRAT DECENTER ·
SCEPTRA TENENTEM

QVE MODVM REBVS TENVIT SECVNDIS ·
CONIVGIS MAGNI DECORATA RERVM ·
LAVDE GESTARVM VOLITAT PER ORA ·
CVNCTA VIRORVM ·

Illus. 12.1.b Reverse. *The Triumphs of Federico da Montefeltro*
***and Battista Sforza*, ca. 1472. Uffizi, Florence.**

The reverse is an illustration of the genre of *Trionfi* made popular by Petrarch. The triumphal chariot of Duchess Battista is populated by the feminine virtues, guided by an *amorino*, a young follower of Venus, and pulled by two unicorns, symbols of chastity and loyalty. Duke Federigo is shown in a triumphal chariot in full armor, crowned by Victory herself, and accompanied by the cardinal virtues of justice, temperance, fortitude, and prudence. The chariot is drawn by two war-horses but again guided by an *amorino*, linking his triumph to Battista's through love.

Illus. 12.2 Palazzo Ducale, Urbino.

Federigo da Montefeltro, duke of Urbino, began work on this huge condottiere fortress and palace around 1466, employing the Dalmatian architect and fortress builder, Luciano Laurana, probably with the assistance of the Sienese Francesco di Giorgio Martini, a follower of Leon Battista Alberti. It is a highly significant building because it represents the two elements of Federigo's personality. Although clearly a fortified stronghold of a prince, it is also opened by windows, balconies, and loggias. The decorative elements are splendid fifteenth-century Renaissance designs, and it enjoys a lightness that contrasts with its size and site, perched on a peak of the Apennines. It was in this palace, under Federigo's son Guidobaldo that Baldassare Castiglione (1478–1529) places, traditionally in the Hall of Vigils, the dialogues that constitute his *The Book of the Courtier.*

Illus. 12.3 *Studiolo* **of Federico da Montefeltro, 1473–76.**
Intarsia **(inlaid woodwork) by Giuliano (1432–90) and Benedetto**
(1442–97) da Maiano. Palazzo Ducale, Urbino.

Luciano Laurana or Francesco di Giorgio Martini likely designed the program for this intarsia decoration in Federigo's private study. (It is thought that the word *intarsia* is derived from the Latin word *interserere* which means "to insert.") The wooden panels are full of illusions, such as open cabinets; raised surfaces holding objects, like musical instruments; and even an open window, occupied by a charming squirrel.

The space between the wooden intarsia panels and the decorated ceiling above contained the images of twenty-eight celebrated men from Scripture, Antiquity, the Middle Ages, and Federigo's own time, ranging from Solomon through Euclid to Petrarch and Cardinal Bessarion. The originals were painted by his court artists, Joos van Wassenhove (Justus of Ghent) and the Spaniard Pedro Berruguete. Unfortunately, the portraits have since been dispersed.

When standing at his desk, working in his library of well over a thousand manuscripts Federigo could contemplate the greatness of these worthies as a context for his own ambition and responsibilities. He could also gain inspiration from the stylized landscape of his duchy and the various attributes of learning, wisdom, and military power that are illustrated in the illusionistic wooden inlay.

Illus. 12.4 Francesco di Giorgio Martini (?) or Sandro Botticelli (?), *Cristoforo Landino Dedicating His* **Disputationes camaldulenses Libri I-IV** *to Federigo da Montefeltro*, **1475. Apostolic Vatican Library, Urb. lat. 508, Rome.**

Federigo da Montefeltro was a significant patron of Renaissance culture. Cristoforo Landino (1424–98) is shown here on the right dedicating his *Camaldulensian Disputations* to the duke about 1470. The illustration is from the frontispiece of the book, now in the Vatican Library. It represents another example of the degree to which Federigo expected books to be luxury objects: the illustration is usually attributed to Botticelli (Alessandro di Mariano Filipepi, 1444–1512), although others suggest Francesco di Giorgio Martini (1439–1501). Landino was the tutor to Lorenzo de'Medici and a very important poet, philosopher, classicist, and professor of rhetoric and poetry in Florence as well as an active member of the so-called Platonic Academy that developed around Marsilio Ficino and the Medici.

Illus. 12.5 *Sala delle Veglie* (Room of the Vigils). Palazzo Ducale, Urbino.

Above is the *Sala delle Veglie*: that is, Room of the Vigils, or Room of the Late Night Duties. It was part of Duchess Elisabetta's private apartments in the ducal palace of Urbino, and the room where tradition places the discussions that Baldassare Castiglione fashioned into his *Il Libro del Cortegiano* (*The Book of the Courtier*).

These structured dialogues among cultivated men and women formed important elements of the evening entertainments in the courts of Renaissance Italy. The inclusion of women—often in leading roles, as in the case of *The Book of the Courtier*—constituted a marked divergence from parallel humanist discussions in the republic of Florence. No woman was ever present in the meetings of the informal Platonic Academy around Lorenzo de'Medici.

PART IV

The Renaissance at the Edges

While the Renaissance flourished in central and northwestern Italy, it arrived only late at the geographic extremes of the peninsula. Take, for example, the republic of Venice. This improbable city, founded after the collapse of the Roman Empire, had developed as a maritime empire with allegiance to the East, to Byzantium, to Constantinople. It adopted Renaissance principles much later than other centers such as Florence, that is, only after it had made the conscious decision to become Italian, redefining itself as a state on mainland Italy.

So it was that even though Petrarch spent some considerable time in Venice and ultimately deposited his library there, his gift had no immediate impact. It was not until 1525 that the poet's interest in language and self-knowledge found fulfillment in Venetian culture with the publication of Pietro Bembo's *Prose della volgar lingua*, a book that codified formal Italian based upon the writings of Petrarch and his fellow Tuscans Dante and Boccaccio.

At the far end of the peninsula, in Naples, the Renaissance could be said to have arrived only sporadically if at all. We've seen that King Robert of Naples recognized Petrarch and crowned him poet laureate in Rome. But even though the king and poet became personal friends, little of Petrarch's values followed his patron back to his kingdom. Rather than the profound legacy of Cicero, Ovid, Quintilian, and St. Augustine that Petrarch had practiced and advocated, the ancient Roman heritage as it manifested itself in Naples was that of the games, the amphitheaters, and the cruelty that had also been present in Roman society.

During his later visit to Naples (at that time ruled by the unfortunate Queen Joanna) Petrarch describes in his letters how he was absorbed into the royal entourage of beautifully dressed courtiers to participate in what he thought was a pageant. Instead, he found himself at one of the city's awful gladiatorial combats. When a handsome young man fell dead at his feet, Petrarch fled the kingdom, convinced he was in a barbarous place.

Petrarchism and the early examples of Renaissance culture obviously had not migrated to Naples from the north of Italy. Indeed, to a great degree it can be argued that the Renaissance ended geographically at Rome—with one exceptional moment in the Kingdom of Naples.

CHAPTER 13
VENICE IN THE RENAISSANCE

Venice was an anomaly in Italy with its history and traditions that looked more to the East and Byzantium than to the peninsula that lay behind the city on the lagoon. Nevertheless, during the Renaissance Venice began to re-evaluate its neglect of the Italian mainland. This shift was driven by the most practical of considerations—resulting from its need to feed its growing population as well as from its recognition that competition with neighboring Italian states would define its future and decide its role in the Mediterranean and in Europe.[1]

The Republic of Venice in the Middle Ages

The uninhabited marshland and lagoons near where the river Po meets the Adriatic are an improbable place to build a city, but they explain the foundation of Venice. The city had arisen in the sixth and seventh centuries as a refuge for the Roman inhabitants of the Lombard plain who were fleeing the incursions of barbarian tribes. Initially, the conditions of life were terrible. There was no fresh water, and the complex of small islands and sand bars made construction difficult, particularly since some of these sites were partly submerged during "high water" (*acqua alta*).

These challenges were overcome by the early inhabitants who built lasting structures on the larger islands, such as Torcello, later shifting by the ninth century to the area of the lagoon known as the Rialto. This Rialto (*rivus altus*, or deep stream) became the center of the city and the seat of government by the eleventh century. As its name indicates, water was deep enough to permit larger ships to navigate through the mosaic of shoals, islands, and sand bars that constituted the site. A bridge was later constructed over the Grand Canal to link the two parts of the city, and Venice as we know it was born.

Because the tough early inhabitants of the city had arrived in a territory claimed by no power, they were not subject to any prince or bishop. They developed their own system of government, a republic, in which the head, the duke—or doge in Venetian dialect— was elected as a kind of *primus inter pares*, a first among equals. The first doge was elected in 697, beginning the eleven-hundred-year republic—really an elective monarchy—that would characterize Venice and her empire. The community first thrived on fishing and local trade along the Adriatic, but the skill of Venetian sailors and shipbuilders permitted

---

1. There is a huge bibliography on Venice. See John Julius Norwich, *A History of Venice*. New York: Vintage Books, 1989; Thomas F. Madden, *Venice: A New History*. London: Penguin Books, 2013; Frederic C. Lane, *Venice: A Maritime Republic*. Baltimore: Johns Hopkins University Press, 1973.

the merchants of the city to capitalize on their connections to Constantinople and gain important concessions within the Byzantine Empire and its capital.

By the end of the tenth century, Venice had begun laying down the foundations of its maritime empire by colonizing the opposite shore of the Adriatic in Dalmatia, now mostly within Croatia, and the islands off its coast. This was the genesis of the *Stato da Mar*, or the territories of the republic of Venice reached by sea. It was not an attempt to build a true imperial state, rather a policy of fortifying and garrisoning defensible towns to protect the seaborne trade of the most serene republic of Venice. There was little movement inland, and the Venetian presence in these garrison cities was often only superficial; but it was sufficient to cement the territory to Venice, the dominant city (*città dominante*) until the end of the republic.[2]

The Crusades

Venice is also known as *La Serenissima*—meaning "the most serene." But the origins of its great wealth were hardly tranquil or peaceful. The true making of the city was the calling of the Crusades, the first being launched in 1095 by Pope Urban II. Although the Crusades were ostensibly mounted to recapture the Holy Land from Muslim control, they were also an opportunity for Europeans to seek land, wealth, glory, and adventure on foreign soil. The crusading knights and their hundreds of retainers and attendants, horses, and equipment needed passage to the Holy Land. Once they were there, they required logistical support. With its knowledge of the Mediterranean, its position on the Adriatic coast, its experience as a trading power, and its fleet of large galleys, Venice was the supplier of choice.

So it was that for the next two hundred years the city's merchants and sailors ferried the crusaders across, charging considerable fees for the service. When the galleys returned, they were weighted not with men and armor and horses but with luxury goods like spices and silks to be traded back in Europe. The value of this trade to the Venetians became blatantly clear in the Fourth Crusade.[3] Instead of taking the army directly to the Holy Land, the aged, blind Doge Enrico Dandolo proposed a deviation. He convinced the troops to voyage first to the Dalmatian city of Zara (now Zadar), one of the garrison towns of the republic that had recently rebelled against its Venetian masters. After restoring the city to Venetian control, he then urged the army to attack Constantinople rather than fight Muslims in the Holy Land. The Byzantine Greeks, he pointed out, were

---

2. Don Alfonso della Cueve, "The Dominions of the Venetian Republic: A Report by the Spanish Ambassador, c.1618," in David Chambers and Brian Pullan, eds., *Venice: A Documentary History.* Toronto: University of Toronto Press, 2004. pp. 31–35.

3. Donald E. Queller and Thomas F. Madden, *The Fourth Crusade: The Conquest of Constantinople.* Philadelphia: University of Pennsylvania Press, 1999; for an eyewitness account of the Fourth Crusade, see Robert of Clari, *The Conquest of Constantinople,* tr. Edgar Holmes McNeal. New York: Columbia University Press, 2005.

schismatic Christians following the Great Eastern Schism of 1054, which divided Christendom into two sects, one Orthodox and one Latin. They were by extension, he argued, equally as dangerous as the Muslims to Christian unity on earth.

The Fourth Crusade of 1204 breached the walls of Constantinople, capturing the city and initiating the Latin Empire. There was some talk of the aged Doge Dandolo being named emperor, but he declined the honor, and the title fell to a pious and gallant crusader Baldwin of Flanders. Still, as a reward for their support, the Venetians were granted extensive trading concessions within the city. They were also given a substantial portion of Byzantine territory in the form of islands and places on the Greek mainland convenient for protecting Venice's long-distance trade.

But Venice had rivals in this commerce from two great maritime powers in their own right: Pisa and Genoa. The Genoese ended the competition from Pisa by thoroughly defeating its fleet at Meloria in 1284, a disaster from which Pisa never recovered. Similarly, soon after, the struggle with Venice for Mediterranean supremacy saw Genoa triumphant: in 1298 at Curzola (modern Korčula) off the Dalmatian coast a Genoese armada decisively defeated the Venetians.[4] Venetian losses were considerable, and it took some time for the *Serenissima* to recover. The defeat was reversed only in 1380 when the Venetians triumphed conclusively over the Genoese in the War of Chioggia.[5] Genoa never regained its earlier power because of internal instability and factionalism, especially between the nobles and plebeians. The result was that Venice found itself the greatest naval power in the Mediterranean and one of the richest and most powerful states in Europe.

Stability and Harmony

The city had obvious advantages over the rest of the Italian peninsula. First, it had no landed territory just outside its borders. The result was that Venice never had to struggle with the Guelf–Ghibelline division that caused such devastation in city-states such as Florence. Also, there was none of that tension to contend with between feudal landed magnates and wealthy urban merchants.

Equally significant, Venice didn't suffer from the unstable influence of the papacy in Italian affairs—the pope was essentially irrelevant, at least initially. Rather, the Venetian Church saw itself as subject more to the Patriarch of Aquileia-Grado. And in keeping with the Byzantine tradition, the Venetian state exercised authority over the power and property of the Church. Most tourists to Venice think that the glorious basilica on the Piazza San Marco in the heart of the city was the cathedral—the seat of religious authority.

4. Steven A. Epstein, *Genoa and the Genoese, 958–1528*. Chapel Hill: University of North Carolina Press, 1996. pp. 169, 183.
5. Epstein, 1996. pp. 239–40; Gary Wills, *Venice: Lion City: The Religion of Empire*. New York: Washington Square Press, 2001. pp. 55–56; Madden, 2013. pp. 219–32.

But that wasn't the case. Rather, San Marco was the private chapel of the doges, linked directly to the doges' residence in the Palazzo Ducale. The Venetians ensured that the actual cathedral (San Pietro di Castello) was a modest structure in the Castello district, located far away from the center of political life.

Similarly, there were not the kinds of class and occupational struggles we saw in Florence. There was no equivalent of the *ciompi*, for example, because the skilled manual workers in Venice tended to be very well paid and protected. The largest production center was the Arsenal, where the Venetian galleys and their fittings were built. Initially founded in 1104, by 1320 this maritime factory was a huge industrial site, comprising 110 acres in the heart of the city. At the height of the republic there were about sixteen thousand men at work in the Arsenal whose skills and coordination were such that they could build a fully equipped war galley in just one day. Henry Ford would have been just as impressed as was Henri III of France when he witnessed the feat during his visit to Venice in 1574.[6]

Because the city lived by the sea, the workers, or *arsenalotti*, were greatly privileged and respected: there was no sense of their being menials. In fact, they were honored, permitted to indicate their occupation by wearing small red caps, and allowed to participate in festivals and civic occasions as important contributors to the republic's wealth and power.[7]

The other great industry was glassmaking—a production for which Venice is still justly famed. Even today the label "Murano glass" is a draw for collectors, and most tourists to the city will find themselves returning home with at least one colorful glass object as a souvenir. Venice likely acquired its celebrated skill in glassmaking and decorating from the Middle East. But, the development of this industry into a virtual monopoly on expensive glass objects and mirrors was because of Venetian genius and organization alone. This manifested itself from earliest days when in 1295 all of the glass factories were required to leave the city proper and relocate to the island of Murano in the lagoon. The difficulty was that the heat from the furnaces had caused too many fires and endangered the entire city, which was still partly built of wood. In some ways, however, gathering all the glassmakers together was a benefit, as it encouraged cooperation and both the raw materials and the finished products could be transported more efficiently.

Venice's control over decorative glass throughout Europe endured for centuries, and this required a highly capable, protected, and engaged workforce. Here, too, the artisans were advantaged and well-compensated. So privileged were the leading glassmakers that they could marry their daughters into the patriciate without any loss of status to the noble family of the groom. Furthermore, if a glass artisan committed a crime—even on

---

6. Frederic C. Lane, *Venetian Ships and Shipbuilders of the Renaissance*. Baltimore: Johns Hopkins University Press, 1992. See p. 144 for Henri III of France's visit to the arsenal.

7. Robert C. Davis, *Shipbuilders of the Venetian Arsenal: Workers and Workplace in the Preindustrial City*. Baltimore: Johns Hopkins University Press, 2007.

occasion a major crime such as murder—he would be pardoned because his skills were needed to sustain Venetian markets and dominance. On the other hand, any artisan who thought to take the secrets of his craft abroad became an enemy of the state. Those of his family still in Venice were punished, and a team of state assassins was sent in search of him. The Venetians took competition seriously.

The government of Venice was also remarkably stable, particularly after the *Serrata*—the closing of the Great Council in 1297. This Great Council was comprised of several hundred wealthy merchants, the commercial nobility who had in the past been elected to conduct affairs of state. Under Doge Pietro Gradenigo (r. 1289–1311) the members decided that it was in the best interests of the republic to enforce continuity. Thus, in a classic case of pulling the ladder up behind them, the patricians who were on the council passed a law that said only members of those families who had been part of the council during the preceding years would be allowed to serve. All other citizens were essentially locked out of political office.[8]

Consequently, the *Serrata* transformed the Venetian mercantile elite into a closed caste of patricians who enjoyed a monopoly on access to political office. It meant that no other families, regardless of how wealthy or distinguished, should have this privilege in the future. (Of course, the Venetians being an eminently practical people, a few select families *were* allowed to buy their way into the council on those occasions when the republic desperately needed their money.) Venice was now a republic in which the state vested all political power in the hands of a hereditary noble caste, a caste that was kept pure by official censors who inscribed the names of newborn patricians into a Golden Book kept in the ducal palace.[9]

Despite the *Serrata*, there were two failed attempts to overthrow the state. The first was to have important consequences for Venice. On June 15, 1310, a group of disaffected young patricians led by Bajamonte Tiepolo decided to call for the resignation of Doge Pietro Gradenigo and the Great Council. Not particularly well-organized and unaware that their plot had been betrayed at the last moment, the rebels rode noisily toward the Piazza San Marco and right into the path of forces loyal to the doge.[10] The popular support that they had counted on never materialized. Indeed, one elderly Venetian lady was so annoyed by the commotion that she threw her kitchen mortar out the window,

---

8. There were compensations, however. Some old, quite wealthy but not yet politically active families were designated as *cittadini originari* (original citizens), constituting between five and eight percent of the population. They formed the highly professional civil service, and the important position of chancellor was reserved for a member of this class. They were inscribed in a silver book and usually felt fortunate, as they were paid and given respect without the expense and responsibilities that attended patrician status. Furthermore, they could achieve high positions in the many important *scuole* (confraternities) that offered public recognition and social contacts across class divisions.

9. Lane, 1973. p. 114; Norwich, 1989. pp. 184–85.

10. Madden, 2013. pp. 186–87; Norwich, 1989. pp. 192–99; Lane, 1973. pp. 115–17.

dispatching Tiepolo's standard-bearer with a direct hit to the head. The renegades dispersed, and Tiepolo, after a brief manhunt, was captured and exiled.

Five years later, the dreaded Council of Ten was formed to prevent conspiracies and uncover plots against the state before they could be carried out. In this the Council was totally successful. Only one other plot came to wide public attention in the eleven-hundred-year reign of the republic, and that was the quixotic attempt of Doge Marin Falier in 1355 to establish a monarchy. His scheme was betrayed, and he was arrested. No exile for him. Rather, he was ceremoniously beheaded on the exact same spot where he had been crowned just one year previously.[11]

The Arrival of the Renaissance in Venice

While the political situation within Venice remained remarkably stable and envied by all—even by Florentines and northerner Europeans—uncertainties in the world outside drove the republic to expand onto the mainland. The first such event was the War of Chioggia with Genoa in 1380. Venice won the conflict, but the war left the political and economic elite of the city uneasy. The population of the city had grown to the point that substantial imports of food were required. This was not only expensive but also threatened the security of the city should any hostile power block the fleets of grain ships.

Added to the fear of siege and possible famine was the Turkish threat to the maritime empire. The whole last half of the fourteenth century had been enormously challenging for Venice as powerful enemies continued to wrest parts of Venetian territory away from the republic. Fearing an assault on the city itself, the Venetians realized that a buffer territory behind the city on the mainland would be a kind of *cordon sanitaire*, increasing the protection offered by its watery terrain.

Of additional concern was the infrastructure necessary for getting Venetian goods to market. Venetian control of the luxury trade with the East continued to produce great profits, but opposition to Venetian rule was increasing. This was particularly clear with a revolt on the strategic island of Crete in the 1360s that took years to quell. To sustain their fortunes, the merchant nobles realized that control of the overland trade routes into northern Europe would help build a retail network for the spices and silks that Venice imported and at the same time protect Venetian merchants from blockades or extortion.[12]

With all these forces in play, Venice made the collective decision to become an Italian state. Although Venice had controlled pockets of its northern frontier around Treviso and Friuli, as well as the Dalmatian coast, for many years, the new thrust onto the mainland to the south and west was as swift as it was ambitious. In a short period of time after 1404, major territories were conquered, including cities that had long threatened

---

11. Norwich, 1989. pp. 223–29; Madden, 2013. pp. 204–10.
12. Michael Mallett and John Hale, *The Military Organization of a Renaissance State: Venice c. 1400–1617*. Cambridge: Cambridge University Press, 1984. pp. 8–19.

the landward side of the republic and whose ambitions had challenged Venetian territorial integrity. By 1405 Venice had annexed Verona, Vicenza, and Padua. By 1410 territory in Dalmatia had been reacquired through a cash payment to the king of Hungary. It took several decades more for official sanction, but finally the sovereignty and territorial integrity of the mainland or *Terraferma* Empire of Venice was recognized by the four other major Italian states. At the 1454 Peace of Lodi, Milan, Florence, the papacy, and Naples affirmed Venetian rule in northern Italy as far as the river Adda. Venice was now very much on solid ground.

It was the absorption of these sophisticated, ancient, and once powerful northern Italian states into the Venetian polity that brought the Renaissance into Venice in a rapid and dramatic way. Cities with ancient Roman memories, such as Verona, were now inspirations to Venetian humanists and artists. The celebrated University of Padua provided the intellectual foundation for a new orientation toward Western, Latin scholarship, as well as the finest law and medical schools in Europe.

Previously, Venetian artists had looked more toward Eastern, Byzantine models, or the International Gothic style of painting. Now they had direct access to some of the most inspirational Renaissance works. Giotto's Arena (Scrovegni) chapel fresco cycle in Padua was now in Venetian territory. Altichiero's fresco in the Oratory of St. George from the 1370s in that same city carries a portrait of Petrarch—a symbol as well as a model. Andrea Mantegna would paint his wonderful cycle in the church of the Eremetani in Padua. And other leading lights of the Renaissance, such as Donatello, would leave masterpieces in the city, both inside the basilica of St. Anthony and outside where his monumental equestrian bronze of the mercenary captain Gattamelata (The Honeyed Cat) is still to be seen.

It was in this context that the Bellini family of painters succeeded in domesticating the Renaissance style in Venice. Jacopo Bellini quite probably studied in Florence, and he did become Mantegna's father-in-law. But it was his sons, Gentile and Giovanni, who developed into the most influential painters in this new style in Venice, creating emotionally moving religious pictures, formal portraits, and dynamic narratives of Venetian events in the ducal palace.[13] Sadly, these last works were mostly lost to a fire in 1574. But there was a distinction in their approach—one that reflected the dancing light on the waters of the lagoon. For unlike the Florentines who were obsessed with composition (*disegno*), the Venetians were consumed by color as the defining element of a painting— *colore*. This privileging of *colore* over *disegno* was passed down to such great Venetian artists as Giorgione and Titian, both of whom trained in the workshop of Giovanni Bellini.[14]

---

13. Patricia Fortini Brown, *Art and Life in Renaissance Venice*. New York: Abrams, 1997. pp. 54–56.
14. Peter Humfrey, "Introduction," in Peter Humfrey, ed., *The Cambridge Companion to Giovanni Bellini*. Cambridge: Cambridge University Press, 2003. pp. 1–12; Paul Hills, "Bellini's Colour," in Humfrey, 2003. pp. 182–94.

By the end of the fifteenth century, then, Venice had grown into one of the largest cities in Europe, with the most formidable fleet of more than three thousand ships and a wealth that was beyond imagination. It remained a conservative society and one whose institutions and culture changed only slowly, despite the impact of the new *Terraferma* cities and the Renaissance culture they contained. It had also grown overly confident, indeed arrogant, in its dealings with other Italian and European states. It was this territorial ambition in Italy and lack of sensitivity to the traditions of old and proud cities now under its control that would lead to one of the republic's greatest existential crises.[15]

In fact, the myth of Venice as the model of a perfect, balanced constitution, with a stable government and highly regulated social structure, was exactly that: a myth. Certainly, there were only two significant attempts to overthrow the republic. But, behind this façade of stability and balance was a more complex story in the Renaissance. The constitution praised by Florentine humanists such as Poggio Bracciolini was in reality an aristocratic gerontocracy which habitually used the offices of the state for its own benefit, often at the expense of opponents and less privileged citizens, not to speak of those non-Venetians who lived under the harsh control of the lion of St. Mark. This more complex reality can best be illustrated in the career of Venice's longest serving doge, Francesco Foscari (1373–1457).

The Reign of Doge Francesco Foscari

Francesco Foscari (r. 1423–57) enjoyed the longest reign in the eleven-hundred-year history of the republic, although perhaps "enjoyed" is not quite the right word. He presided over both the widest expansion of Venetian power on the mainland and over the most humiliating moment in its eastern maritime frontier: the capture of Constantinople by the Turks in 1453. His family was distinguished, and he had won much praise as an administrator in the most powerful offices of the state, including the Council of Ten. But he also had a reputation for arrogance, bellicosity, and a restless ambition. Consequently, when his predecessor, the old Doge Tommaso Mocenigo, lay dying in 1423, he made a forceful, almost desperate plea to elect *anyone* as doge but Francesco Foscari.[16]

There were two factions struggling for power and influence, one led by the Loredan family, the other by the Foscari. Foscari won, elected doge at the remarkably young age of 50. That hardly seems young to us now, but Venice was very much a gerontocracy, so to give a patrician the highest office in the republic at such a relatively young age was revolutionary in itself, especially as the election was for life. It also might well have proven to be a serious error.

---

15. Mallett and Hale, 1984. pp. 200–2.

16. Mocenigo's words were recorded as: "Francesco Foscari . . . a vainglorious braggart, vapid and light-headed, snatching at everything and achieving little. If he becomes Doge you will find yourselves constantly at war. . . . Where you are now masters, you will become slaves." Quoted in Norwich, 1989. pp. 198–99.

Foscari was chosen as doge because he wanted to continue the wars on the Italian mainland that had resulted in Venice expanding into northern Italy, building a *Terraferma* state that could withstand any challenge. This had been the policy of his predecessor as well, but Mocenigo was more circumspect: he knew that Venice needed a period of peace to consolidate its new territory and recover its financial stability. He also knew that the threat of a belligerent and expansionary Venice would drive the powerful states on its borders to attempt to contain the immensely rich, ambitious republic.

Added to this, Foscari's election had earned him the hatred of the Loredan family and their allies.[17] The other contender in the election of 1423 was a celebrated hero of earlier naval campaigns, Pietro Loredan, who had won continual victories against Venice's enemies both in Italy and on the Mediterranean, such as his triumph at Gallipoli in 1416. In fact, the tensions between the doge and the Loredan would follow Foscari throughout his career, destroy his family, and result in his being prematurely removed from office.

Doge Tommaso Mocenigo had been right in his assessment of Foscari. Not content with the territories already under Venetian control on the Italian mainland, Foscari engaged in a series of very expensive wars, fought by mercenary armies, to enlarge the Venetian *Terraferma*. His argument was that Venice should not wait until the aggressive, expansionist Visconti of Milan should attack them. Rather, he felt that Venice should take the initiative with a pre-emptive campaign. The war lasted from 1426–28 and resulted in a Venetian victory, inasmuch as the republic took possession of Bergamo and later Brescia in Lombardy, greatly extending the influence of Venice on the mainland. But it also brought Venetian power close to Milan itself, virtually guaranteeing there would be a return to hostilities.[18]

In 1431 war broke out again but with little success on any side, although a later struggle with Bologna gave Venice more land to the south, which eventually included the city of Ravenna very near the Adriatic coast. In fact, Venice was at war almost constantly until the general exhaustion of the major states and need for peace by the new rulers of Florence (Cosimo de'Medici) and Milan (Francesco Sforza—who once fought as a condottiere for Venice) resulted in the 1454 Peace of Lodi, which brought at last forty years of tranquility to the peninsula.

While Foscari was promoting his war policy, he was also behaving increasingly independently, which made his ambitions suspect. Did he intend to turn the ducal office into one of real—rather than ceremonial—power, as Marin Falier had attempted to do

---

17. The contemporary Venetian diarist Marin Sanuto remarked that Ca' Loredan (the House of Loredan) never forgot or forgave a wrong. Quoted in Robert Finlay, *Politics in Renaissance Venice*. New Brunswick: Rutgers University Press, 1980. p. 81.

18. Foscari's interest in mainland expansion dated from almost the beginning of the century; in 1421 he was significantly one of the first appointments to the *Savi super terris de novo acquisitis* (the five officers responsible for newly acquired territory, largely in the *Terraferma*); Mallett and Hale, 1984. pp. 159–61.

in 1355, during the struggle with Genoa, another time of dangerous warfare? To indicate where power resided, the Council of Ten in 1432 moved against Foscari's mercenary captain, Francesco Bussone, known as Carmagnola. Carmagnola had fought for the Milanese but felt underappreciated so he migrated to the service of Venice to campaign against his former employers. Despite some important victories, Carmagnola seemed unwilling to pursue them with aggressive tactics, even though Foscari and the Venetians had made him rich offers of land to rule after a complete victory.

The reality, however, was that this mercenary captain was doing what all condottieri did: draw out the fighting to maximize his fees and not risk his own capital—his army—in a major battle. And, there was constant interaction with the Milanese, driving the Venetians to question his real loyalty. Finally, in March of 1432 Carmagnola was invited to Venice to discuss the progress of the campaign. Once in the ducal palace, however, he was arrested, charged with treason, tortured, quickly tried, and summarily beheaded. This rather faithless act was directed, obviously, against Carmagnola; but it also was a clear and powerful warning to Doge Foscari to temper his ambitions.[19]

Weakened by the loss of his friend and general Carmagnola, Foscari himself was then attacked by his enemies. As doge, he was difficult to bring down; but as a father whose two marriages had produced only one living son, he was vulnerable. The truth was that Doge Foscari loved his son, Jacopo, deeply. The vendetta waged by the Loredan was escalated when the war hero and Foscari's rival in the 1423 ducal election, Pietro Loredan, was murdered in 1439. Much of Venice and all of the Loredan faction believed that Jacopo Foscari was behind the assassination though his enemies had insufficient evidence. Then, suspected of collusion with foreign powers—including Milan—and bribery, Jacopo was charged with treason and corruption in 1445. He was found guilty and exiled, much to the grief of Doge Foscari.[20]

Another murder followed when one of the judges who ruled against Jacopo was found dead. Jacopo was again suspected; indeed, the Council of Ten was convinced of his guilt. Two further treason and corruption charges followed in 1450 and 1456, during which Jacopo was brought back to Venice and put to torture because some evidence emerged that he might have sold Venetian secrets to the Milanese. Finally, he was exiled in perpetuity to Crete where he was driven mad by the long vendetta against him and his separation from his family. He died alone in exile at the beginning of 1457.

It is worth noting that the head of the Council of Ten in the proceedings against Jacopo Foscari was Francesco Loredan, the nephew of Pietro, the hero defeated by Doge Foscari in the election of 1423 and later murdered. The traditional belief that the persecution of Jacopo was the revenge of the Loredan has made for some great Romantic works of art. The story was turned into a play by Lord Byron, an early opera by Giuseppe

Verdi, and a famous painting by Francesco Hayek. Unlike so many others, this conspiracy theory might even have some truth to it.

Not content to torture the aging doge through the constant persecution of his only son, the Council of Ten moved at last against Doge Francesco Foscari himself. On hearing of Jacopo's death, Doge Foscari had withdrawn in depression and exhaustion from the execution of his office, and some months later was forced to abdicate, only to die the following week.[21] There is little doubt but that Foscari's enemies intended to bring him down and humiliate him, even after the death of his son. Doge Foscari had offered on two earlier occasions to abdicate but this was refused by his enemies: it was more effective to persecute him in office. Only after the death of his son in exile was he removed from office; but even then the justification was his inability to fulfill his duties because of his age. This was the final vengeful act: he was not to be permitted to die as doge of Venice.

Prophecy Fulfilled

There is, of course, more to this story. Foscari's long reign was an anomaly and brought deep divisions in the Venetian ruling class to the surface, something the Loredan capitalized on effectively.[22] The aggressive, expansionist policies of the Venetians on the Italian mainland alienated their neighbors as well as committed the republic to constant and not always successful warfare. The cost was enormous and, as Doge Mocenigo had prophesied, the wealth of both the state and its leading citizens decreased. Also, this policy was to the benefit of those families, like the Foscari, whose wealth came mostly from estates and mercantile activity on the Italian mainland, whereas older families, more likely partisans of the Loredan, were still connected to the traditional maritime trade in the eastern Mediterranean.

Foscari's obsession with the expansion of Venice onto the mainland was seen to further his own interests; and his son's indictment for treason and bribery for the benefit of Milan heightened the tensions between those patricians who wanted the wealth and might of the republic used to protect the eastern dominions of the *Stato da Mar* and what remained of the Byzantine Empire. The effect of Foscari's policies was thrown into high relief when the Turks captured Constantinople in 1453. The ancient Christian Byzantine Empire, once the source of Venetian sovereignty, was now in the hands of the Muslim Turks. Foscari was identified as part of the cause of this disaster to the West and to Venetian trade and influence in particular.

---

21. Decisions of the Council of Ten, "The Deposition of Francesco Foscari, 1457," in Chambers and Pullan, 2010. pp. 71–72.
22. For a description of the divisions between old (long) and new (short) patrician families, see the description from the diary of Marin Sanudo in Chambers and Pullan, 2010. pp. 72–73.

Finally, it is reasonable to ask to what extent a doge of Venice could actually influence policy? The traditional perspective was that he was only a figurehead, the symbol of the republic, possessed of little power and carefully controlled by other offices and councils.[23] But Foscari was clearly the impetus behind the Venetian expansionist policy. Part of his power came from his long reign and his knowledge of how the complex Venetian institutions worked and his ability to construct patronage networks. There was clearly, however, some residue of authority in the office that permitted him to direct or at least influence policy; hence, the myth of Venice must be reconsidered to some degree. That said, he was not permitted to resign until the very end of his long reign; and he could do nothing to protect his son from persecution by his enemies, indicating how little real, discretionary power his ducal crown bestowed.

And, to what extent should we accept the evidence brought against his son? The very fact that there were so many prosecutions over such a long period of time and that two murders were attributed to him, one of which he very well seemed to be party to, shows that the processes against Jacopo Foscari were not all the work of factional and personal enmity. Jacopo lacked judgment and probably did become involved in activities he should not have touched as the only son of the doge. Nevertheless, the evidence was such that although he might have been tortured and exiled, he was not executed, a penalty that the Council of Ten would not have hesitated to employ under defensible circumstances, regardless of Jacopo's exalted rank.

Taken together, therefore, the long reign of Francesco Foscari indicates that Venice in the Renaissance was a far more complex place than the "myth" presumes. Indeed, the tragedy of Doge Foscari and his son makes for not only wonderful theatre and music but also an illustration of the unique culture of *La Serenissima* and the shadowy operations of its institutions. It highlights the tensions caused by the republic's expansion onto the Italian mainland and the consequent neglect of its ancient ties to Constantinople and the eastern Mediterranean.

Italian Renaissance culture, artistic style, and humanist learning might have made significant progress into the unique world of Venice by 1457. But its older Eastern traditions continued. It would take the crisis of Agnadello to relax the embrace of the past and accept the new humanist style as represented by Andrea Palladio.

---

23. Mallett and Hale, 1984. pp. 160–64.

Illus. 13.1 Domenico Tintoretto (Domenico Robusti, known as Tintoretto, 1560–1635), *The Capture of Constantinople During the Fourth Crusade*, 1598–1605. Palazzo Ducale, Venice.

The Byzantine Empire, with its capital of Constantinople, had grown weaker as a consequence of the Ottoman conquest of Anatolia; dynastic tensions among the Greeks; and the ambitions of the Venetians, especially in their competition with the Genoese. This made Constantinople a convenient and attractive target for the Europeans of the Fourth Crusade. The crusaders under Baldwin of Flanders and the Venetians under Doge Enrico Dandolo finally captured the city in April of 1204, beginning the Latin Empire of Constantinople. Dandolo died in Venice but in a highly symbolic move was then buried in Hagia Sofia in Constantinople.

The scene here by Tintoretto that hangs in the Room of the Great Council in the ducal palace in Venice shows the very elderly Dandolo in the center of the battle, together with Roman clergy. The terrible looting of the city provided a number of important Venetian treasures, such as the bronze Quadriga from the Hippodrome then placed on the façade of St. Mark's basilica. Today visitors see only replicas: the originals of these magnificent equine statues are now preserved indoors.

Illus. 13.2 A nineteenth-century engraving of a Venetian galley fighting a Genoese fleet at the battle of Curzola in 1298. The Granger Archive, Brooklyn, NY.

It was with galleys such as these that Venice established and defended its maritime empire. These large ships were floating fortresses, carrying soldiers who fought pitched battles on water. The moment illustrated here in this nineteenth-century engraving is the engagement of a Venetian and Genoese galley at Curzola (now Korčula in Croatia) in 1298. The two maritime republics were at war from 1294–99, and this battle saw the lowest point in Venetian fortunes, as the republic's fleet was entirely destroyed. Besides the Venetian admiral Andrea Dandolo, perhaps also captured at sea was Marco Polo (1254–1324), who is sometimes said to have been a native of Curzola, although this is unlikely. It is also possible that Marco Polo was captured as early as 1296 near the coast of Turkey.

Nevertheless, the incontrovertible fact is that Marco Polo did spend some months in captivity, and it was during his imprisonment in Genoa while sharing a cell with the popular writer Rustichello da Pisa that Marco Polo dictated the story of his adventures at the court of the Great Khan. This book, *Il Milion*, became one of the iconic stories of Venetian trade, the silk road, and the contact between East and West.

Illus. 13.3 *La Veccia (The Old Woman)*: **A Nineteenth-Century Commemoration of Giustina Rossi Throwing Her Mortar during the Conspiracy of Bajamonte Tiepolo, June 15, 1310.**

This nineteenth-century plaque on the site of the house of Giustina (or Lucia) Rossi celebrates her as *La Veccia (The Old Woman)* who threw her stone mortar at the noisy conspirators. The tradition, which seems to have some element of truth, is that she struck Tiepolo's standard-bearer, knocking him off his horse, and thus permitting the forces loyal to the doge and Great Council to disperse the rebels.

Bajamonte Tiepolo and his noble co-conspirators were exiled and their palaces razed. On the land where Tiepolo's house had stood there was erected a Column of Shame on which was written in Italian: *On this site was the house of Bajamonte [Tiepolo] for whose criminal treason this column has been placed to warn others and record these words for all time.*

The column was broken by one of Tiepolo's followers, resulting in his being blinded as a punishment; but it was reset behind the church of Sant'Agostino where it remained until a descendant of another of the conspirators purchased it at the end of the eighteenth century and placed instead a marker on the site.

Illus. 13.4 *Bocca del Leone* **(Mouth of the Lion). Palazzo Ducale, Venice.**

The Conspiracy of Bajamonte Tiepolo resulted in the establishment of the feared Council of Ten (*Concilio dei dieci*) and the erection of "Lions' Mouths" (*Bocche del leone*) throughout the city. These were erected for citizens to post denunciations of individuals they suspected of crimes against the republic. Although called secret, the denunciations were only investigated if they were signed and also contained the names of witnesses. The penalties for denunciations that were found to be vexatious were severe.

The *bocche* served, then, more as a deterrent and warning. The *bocca* that was most feared was the one in the ducal palace. Only senior members of the republic would have had access to it. In recognition of its significance, all three of the Heads of the Council of Ten (*capi dei dieci*) had to be present to turn their keys simultaneously to open the box.

**Illus. 13.5 Francesco Hayez (1791–1881), *The Death
of Doge Marin Faliero*, 1867. Brera, Milan.**

This romantic historical portrayal of the moment before the execution of Doge Marin Falier in
1355 is by the popular nineteenth-century Italian nationalist painter Francesco Hayez. Despite its
narrative drama and correct allusions to certain historical elements of that unfortunate event, it is
still anachronistic. The doge was beheaded at the very place where he had been crowned, at the top
of the stairs leading into the Palazzo Ducale. However, the image refers more to the Renaissance
staircase than to the original of 1355, which was farther down the interior courtyard. To record its
site, the Venetians, always intent on recognizing sacred space, marked the location of those Medieval stairs in the pavement of the courtyard of the ducal palace, a mark that is still visible to this day.

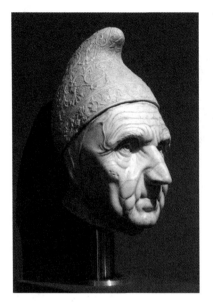

Illus. 13.6.a Bartolomeo Bon, Portrait bust of Doge Francesco Foscari, ca. 1442. Palazzo Ducale, Sala Erizzo, Venice.

This splendid bust of Doge Francesco Foscari was sculpted by Bartolommeo Bon (1400–67), one of the greatest Venetian sculptors of the fifteenth century. The bust reflects Bartolommeo's skill at modeling and his ability to capture detail to reflect the aged doge's strength of character, some of which Bartolommeo must have recognized while also constructing the elegant *Porta della carta* for the doge.

Born in Ticino (now in Switzerland), Bon trained under his father, Giovanni, with whom he worked on the splendid Ca' d'Oro (1424–30) for the immensely rich Venetian patrician Marin Contarini. The name of the palace reflects the signature technique of the Bon family: the use of gold leaf applied to Gothic tracery.

The Ca'Contarini (Ca' d'Oro) is now in the Giorgio Franchetti Museum (Galleria Giorgio Franchetti alla Ca' d'Oro). Even with the loss of its gilding in the gothic quatrefoil tracery of the loggias and windows, and although much damage was done to the gothic integrity of the interior and court-yard when it was the home of the great ballerina Marie Taglioni, it remains one of the grandest palaces of the Grand Canal.

Illus. 13.6.b Giovanni and Bartolommeo Bon, Grand Canal Façade of the Ca' d'Oro (1424–30).

CHAPTER 14
VENICE IN THE AGE OF PALLADIO

Those who had opposed Francesco Foscari's policy of aggressive expansion onto the Italian mainland were proved right in their fears: acquiring this territory came at a considerable price. The *Terraferma* cities had previously been within the sphere of influence of Milan and the papacy, and by challenging that traditional suzerainty Venice generated great anger and hostility. The tension came to a head in the militant opposition of Pope Julius II.

Doge Leonardo Loredan

The doge at the time of this great threat to Venice was Leonardo Loredan (r. 1501–21). Loredan was, of course, a member of that same clan that had destroyed the family and later career of Francesco Foscari. Consequently, there is somewhat less sympathy for his own humiliation, suffered at the hands of Venice's enemies, in circumstances that almost led to the extinction of the republic.[1] Before his election at the age of sixty-five he was seen as a pious man of good will, if some arrogance; but faced with the crisis of war, he was seen as offering little leadership, a coward, and one who put his family before the needs of the state by initially refusing to send his sons to war. Indeed, his son Lorenzo was accused of abusing power and taking advantage of his father's office, while the doge "put his head between his legs."[2]

Loredan had been elected in 1501, the year in which Cesare Borgia, son of Pope Alexander VI, was created duke of Romagna after his capture of cities in the Marche, such as Pesaro and Rimini, all extremely close to Venetian mainland territory. The very next year Cesare took Urbino. Louis XII of France had conquered Milan in 1499, driving Lodovico Sforza, *il Moro*, into exile. For Venice, these circumstances were both welcome and a threat: welcome because Lodovico had been hostile to Venetian expansion into Lombardy and now he was gone; a threat because the much more powerful king of France might make the same claims to all of Lombardy and because Cesare Borgia's violent and restless ambition was pressing hard against the Adriatic and northeastern provinces of the Venetian *Terraferma*.

The death of Pope Alexander and the grave illness of Cesare in the summer of 1503 saw his principality dissolve, particularly after the Borgia's archenemy, Julius II, was elected pope. Having seen the consequences of their weakness, some of the cities taken

---

1. See "Leonardo Loredan's Want of Leadership in the War Crisis, 1509," in Chambers and Pullan, 2004. p. 75.
2. Finlay, 1980. pp. 119–24.

by Cesare, particularly Rimini and Faenza, offered to recognize the sovereignty of the Venetian republic in return for protection. And Venice, seeing an opportunity to gain important strategic territory at little cost, agreed. Prior to becoming pope, Julius II had been extremely solicitous toward Venice. After all, they shared a common enemy in the form of the Borgias. Unfortunately, the Venetians took this earlier friendship as an indication that the Church under Julius would not object to their expansion of the republic. They were very wrong.

In fact, once he came to power, Julius demanded that the Venetians abandon those territories traditionally subject to the Holy See. Although Venice offered to recognize the Church's abstract sovereignty over cities in the papal ambit and even pay tribute to Rome, Venetians adamantly refused to withdraw from their territories. The pope would do little for some time because he was occupied in Rome with some costly building projects including the planning of his tomb under the hand of Michelangelo, the rebuilding of the basilica of St. Peter, and then the construction of the expanded apostolic palace. Subsequently, Julius also became embroiled in the recapture of the important and strategic city of Bologna. This was an equally costly enterprise, as was the huge bronze statue of the pope made by Michelangelo for the facade of Bologna's basilica of San Petronio in celebration of the fall of the city. Julius's ego was legendary.

The League of Cambrai

If he was to move against the Venetians, Julius, then, needed allies who would not only do the fighting for him but also pay the costs of battle. Unfortunately, his first choice, the Emperor Maximilian, proved a weak campaigner. In 1507 Maximilian set out for Rome, eager to receive a traditional imperial coronation at the hands of the pope. But to get there, he had to pass through hostile Venetian mainland territory. Instead of winning passage, Maximilian was decisively defeated and never reached the holy city, having to content himself with a lesser ceremony at Trent. The sting lingered. So, he was glad in late 1508 to join a huge international alliance assembled by Julius consisting of France, the Empire, Spain, and the Church. The principal parties signed their pact at a meeting in the French town of Cambrai and thus became popularly known as the League of Cambrai.

The League wanted nothing less than the obliteration of Venetian authority on the Italian mainland.[3] According to their pact, all the parties were to receive appropriate parts of the Venetian *Terraferma*: the Emperor Maximilian would occupy Friuli, the Istrian peninsula, and receive the cities of Verona, Padua, and Vicenza; Ferdinand the Catholic, as king of Spain and Naples, could expand up the Adriatic coast from the south as far as the Cape of Otranto; France, already in possession of Milan, would expand its control in Lombardy to include Brescia, Bergamo, and Cremona; the Church would

---

3. For the League of Cambrai, see Mallett and Shaw, 2012. pp. 88–95.

take the Adriatic cities of Ravenna and Rimini. Venice was to be completely dismembered, reduced only to the city itself and those *Stato da Mar* outposts it could protect by sea.

But it was important not to move against Venice without obvious cause. Julius's opportunity came when Venice appointed the bishop of Vicenza against his wishes. He immediately imposed an interdict on all Venetian territory. Julius declared the League a "Holy League"—a coalition of Christian nations at war with a heretical, schismatic, dangerous power. Territories that had been subject to Venice were declared freed from their obedience, and Julius also ordered that Venetian property should be confiscated.

It was Louis XII of France who made the first military move, entering Venetian territory early in 1509. For this encounter Venice had engaged the same condottieri who had previously defeated Maximilian; but these Orsini cousins could not now agree on strategy. This divided their armies, with one part avoiding battle, the other confronting the French. The result was the disastrous Venetian defeat at Agnadello in the territory of Cremona in May of 1509.

The destruction of the mercenary army fighting for the republic and the collapse of resistance cost Venice almost all of its mainland territory, at least temporarily. The French took the Lombard cities; Maximilian acquired Verona, Vicenza, and Padua; the pope reclaimed cities in the Romagna and along the Adriatic coast. Ferrara had joined the League and occupied the Polesine in the Po delta and the city of Rovigo. Venice itself was threatened, as it was left defenseless after the defeated mercenary armies melted away.

But once again, Venice was saved by its strategic location on water-logged swampland. The League's artillery was useless in an attack as it didn't have the range to reach across the lagoon, and so they were forced to retreat. Soon after, the occupying imperial forces in the Veneto proved so unpopular that Padua revolted and was reacquired by Venice in 1509, followed by other nearby cities. In a case of déjà vu, Venetian mercenaries defeated the armies of Maximilian and managed to drive the imperials out of more mainland territory.

In fact, although the League was initially successful, friction between Julius and Louis caused it to collapse completely by 1510. In an extraordinary about-face, Julius then allied himself with Venice against France. The Venetian–Papal alliance eventually expanded into the Holy League, which drove the French from Italy in 1512.[4]

You might think that would have been the end of it, but disagreements about the division of the spoils led Venice to abandon the alliance with the pope in favor of one with France. Under the leadership of Francis I, who had succeeded Louis to the throne, the French and Venetians would, through victory at Marignano in 1515, regain the territory they had lost. The treaties of Noyon and Brussels, which ended the war the next year, would essentially return the map of Italy to the status quo of 1508. So much turmoil, so

---

4. Mallett and Shaw, 2012. pp. 96–111.

many lives lost, to achieve absolutely nothing! Venice and the *Terraferma* were saved, but the republic was hardly the confident, powerful state it had been before Agnadello.

Winds of Change

The depredations of war and defeat on the battlefield caused something of an existential crisis in the republic. These disasters, moreover, were exacerbated by a long-term decline in Venice's other source of wealth and power: trade with the East. The fall of Constantinople to the Turks in 1453 had begun a cascade of victories by the Ottomans at sea and on land. It appeared that the lucrative eastern luxury trade was mortally wounded by the expansion of Turkish power. If that had been the only threat, Venice might have found a mechanism to mitigate the losses. However, an ever more pernicious set of circumstance started to devour Venetian wealth and self-confidence.

In 1497–98, the Portuguese sea captain Vasco da Gama made the first successful voyage around the coast of Africa to the ports of India. The repercussions of this achievement were monumental. No longer was the Mediterranean the psychological and actual *Media Terra*—the center of the earth; and no longer was it the sole route to access the spices and silks in such demand in Europe. It didn't take merchants long to adapt, and the impact on prices was dramatic. As early as 1505, spices could be bought in Lisbon for twenty percent less than in Venice. The longer journey somewhat reduced their potency, but the lower price more than compensated for this disadvantage.[5] In 1509, the year of Agnadello, Venice made common cause with the Ottomans, the sultan of Gujarat, and Arab Mameluks to stop the Portuguese control over this trade around Africa, but the Portuguese defeated the Muslim fleet that had been assembled with Venetian help in the Arabian Sea off the coast of India. This was, in fact, the nail in the Venetian spice monopoly's coffin.

The insightful members of the mercantile nobility of the republic were immediately aware of what was happening, and they were consequently in a state of panic. Obviously Venice needed to diversify its economy, and the only way it could do so was through headlong expansion onto the mainland. In this instance, perhaps, Francesco Foscari was being proven right after all, even if for the wrong reasons. To survive and thrive, Venice was compelled to change its outlook, seeking ways to capitalize on the opportunities offered by *Terraferma* lands to compensate for the decline of income from its trade at sea in the *Stato da Mar*.

In this endeavor, however, Venice enjoyed a tremendous advantage over the rest of Europe. The Lutheran revolt of 1517 and Luther's excommunication in 1521 were utterly cataclysmic, causing enormous political and military instability on the continent.

---

5. For the decline in prices and market share of spices imported by Venetian merchants, see H. Van Der Wee, *The Growth of the Antwerp Market and the European Economy*. Dordrecht: Springer, 1963. pp. 127, 130.

But for Venice this was an opportunity rather than a setback. As a trading nation in the Mediterranean, Venice had long pursued a tradition of freedom and latitude for hetero-dox religious belief, the city being a refuge for Eastern Orthodox Christians, Jews, and even Muslims. Provided these groups did not proselytize or disrupt the social order, they had been left unmolested. With Luther's revolt there was now an opportunity to assert a similar measure of independence by protecting Protestants as well. The Fondaco dei Tedeschi, the German warehouse and hospice in the city, had many Protestant residents, and in keeping with Venetian traditions of tolerance, they were deliberately left undisturbed.

This hallmark of tolerance was extended on the mainland to the University of Padua, which had reopened in 1517 after the war. Under Venetian control, the university was guaranteed a degree of freedom to teach and learn that was astonishing in a world of closing minds and imposed conformity.[6] As a result, Padua became perhaps the greatest university in Europe for law and medicine and a leading school for arts and humanistic studies. Its most celebrated professors were Andreas Vesalius, whose 1543 *De Fabrica Humani Corporis* set the standard for anatomy, and Girolamo Fracastoro, a physician whose theory of disease and its spread was central to medical thought until the nine-teenth century.

Padua served as a barometer for the recovery of Venice after Agnadello and its escape from the heavy hand of papal authority. By 1528 most of the operations of the university, including the curriculum, came under the control of a committee (*Tre Rifor-matori*) of the Venetian senate. As a guild of students rather than masters, it was the students—the entire student body, including even Lutherans—who determined who would be the rector. In 1547 a committee of three Venetian lay patricians constituted the republic's control over heresy (*Tre savi sopra l'eresia*), and the Inquisition in Venice became an instrument of the state, not the Church.[7]

These were signals that Venice was not a harsh imperial authority but a protector and a benign master against the dangerous currents of European affairs. The War of the League of Cambrai had taught another lesson as well. Venice could not treat the once proud and independent cities of the mainland in the same way it had managed the sub-ject cities of the Dalmatian coast or Aegean. There would have to be more integration of these territories with the society, structure, and culture of Venice as the *città dominante*

---

6. The university's motto illustrates this tolerance: *universa universis Patavina libertas*. It increas-ingly became subject to the Venetian Senate rather than to the archbishop of Padua, especially after 1528. This liberal scholastic environment attracted students of many nationalities and reli-gious beliefs: "the exchange of scholars, students, books and ideas with all countries of Europe was lively and continuous, receiving vital nourishment from the liberty of thought which the pro-tective wing of the Lion of St. Mark sheltered"; Biagio Brugi, *Gli Scolari dello studio di Padova nel cinquecento*. Padua: Drucker, 1905. p. 8.
7. See the ducal decree "The Appointment of Three Noblemen to Attend the Inquisition, 1547," in Chambers and Pullan, 2004. p. 229.

in an Italian state—and it would be more effectively achieved through soft rather than hard power.

A New Kind of Education

In the days when Venice looked to the East, young patricians who were groomed for service to the republic had received only the most basic formal education. Instead, their training consisted of considerable time spent at sea and in the *Stato da Mar*, gaining practical experience in the subject cities along the Dalmatian coast. With the turn westward and to the *Terraferma*, the skills acquired through such experience were no longer useful. In this new world of the sixteenth century, residence at the University of Padua, elegant social polish, equestrian skills, and experience in the managing of estates became the desirable accomplishments.

This was in part was the consequence of the loss of Venice's virtual monopoly in the luxury trade with the East. But it was also the case that the rise of the Turks magnified the dangers of pursuing a career at sea. Thus, almost for the first time since the foundation of Venice, huge fortunes were pulled from trade and invested in land. True, the ground rents earned from landed estates did not generate the enormous profits of the luxury trade. But they were stable and secure, and, perhaps more important, they didn't require risking one's life at sea on a galley. The territories on the mainland offered substantial opportunities for Venice as a whole. Nobles were now encouraged to live in the *Terraferma*, thereby helping integrate it into the Venetian orbit through contact, administration, and intermarriage.[8] And, consequently, there arose a new model for aristocratic living more in keeping with the practices of the French and Spanish who were now in control of most of the peninsula.

Expanding onto the mainland through aristocratic colonization solved another pressing problem: how to feed the huge city. Venice had reached a population of at least 130,000 by 1540. As long as the regular grain ships could reach the lagoon safely, this concern was minor. However, the attacks of Muslim pirates were increasing, with many of these corsairs acting as agents of the Ottomans and operating from bases in the Adriatic and North Africa. There was, then, a real threat to the food supply of the now enormous city of Venice. Thus, buying and efficiently cultivating large estates on the mainland provided another secure source of food, making the Venetian movement into Italy even more imperative.

By the 1540s, then, there was a market for a new kind of house for the cultivated Venetian owners of these *Terraferma* estates. The need was great, but the requirements were complex. The villa had to be at once a pleasure palace, elegant and comfortable, but

---

8. For aspects of this interpenetration of Venetian and local *Terraferma* cultures, see James Grubb, *Provincial Families in the Renaissance: Private and Public Life in the Veneto*. Baltimore: Johns Hopkins University Press, 1996.

it also had to be the center of a working farm, easily accessible by road or water and able to house agricultural equipment and store grain if necessary.[9] And it had to be cheap to construct. It was psychologically difficult enough for the Venetian patriciate to take money from trade to invest in land, so at least initially costs should be kept to a minimum both to preserve capital and reduce risk.

It was a challenging program for any architect. Fortunately, however, one emerged who responded to these needs perfectly. In so doing, he created not only a style that defined the lifestyle of the Venetian villa that characterized the last two centuries of the republic, but also an architectural vocabulary that extends to this very day. That architect was Andrea Palladio.[10]

Andrea Palladio

Andrea Palladio was not only a genius at building and architectural theory: he became a symbol of a new age, the age of Venice in the decades after Agnadello, when a new image of the *Serenissima* was being created, one linked to Italy and the *Terraferma* and one in communion with the humanist culture of the Renaissance. Strangely, we know little about the man Palladio. He was born Andrea di Pietro della Gondola in 1507, in Padua in the *Terraferma*, the son of a miller. Put to work in a mason's workshop, he clearly had a tense relationship with his first master in Padua as he ran away in 1523, only to be returned by force from Vicenza for breach of his apprentice's contract. However, the following year he matriculated in the guild of stonecutters and bricklayers in Vicenza, entering the workshop of the celebrated Podemuro.

The next years are largely undocumented, although Palladio himself records that he studied the art of architecture and building as well as honing his skills as a mason. He also became sufficiently secure to enter into a marriage contract in 1534 with a carpenter's daughter, a marriage that was to produce four sons and a daughter, a family to whom he was deeply devoted. He has been described as courtly and genial, even to the point of working beside his builders to ensure quality and encourage dedication. Not deeply educated, he was, rather, a man of observation, experience, and wide reading, with an open mind and an agile intellect, able to convert abstract models into coherent and effective buildings. These are the marks of true genius.

Palladio began to accept commissions from the local nobility, one of whom was Count Giangiorgio Trissino. Trissino was a rich and immensely cultivated man of letters,

---

9. For a discussion of this transformation of the *Terraferma*, see Denis Cosgrove, *The Palladian Landscape: Geographical Change and Its Cultural Representations in Sixteenth-Century Italy*. University Park: Pennsylvania State University Press, 1993.

10. There is a rich bibliography on Palladio. See Paolo Marton, Manfred Wundrum, and Thomas Pape, *Palladio: The Complete Buildings*. Cologne and London: Taschen, 2008; Lionello Puppi, *Palladio*. Milan: Electa, 1973; Robert Tavernor, *Palladio and Palladianism*. London: Thames and Hudson, 1991; James S. Ackerman, *Palladio*. London: Penguin, 1991.

a poet, playwright, and humanist scholar. As such, he could read Latin, as well as Greek. He constructed plays based on ancient models, and his epic poem—*Italy Liberated from the Goths*—closely followed the examples of Virgil and other Roman poets. Unfortunately, his rather slavish classicism meant his literary productions were stilted and derivative. Many of his contemporary poets are still read; Trissino is not.

Nevertheless, his enchantment with all things classical also included a particular obsession with ancient Roman models of building. He became enchanted with the idea of recovering the built glory of ancient Rome based on Vitruvius's *Ten Books on Architecture*. Although Vitruvius had been superficially known in the Middle Ages, it was not until Poggio Bracciolini discovered a complete manuscript in 1414 that the text became celebrated as the essential ancient guide to building. A printed version of the book had appeared in 1486, significantly in Verona, now part of the Venetian *Terraferma*. By 1520 there were Italian translations, making the contents available to practitioners like Palladio.

It appears that Trissino and the stonemason Andrea di Pietro della Gondola met when work was underway on the count's Villa Cricoli in 1538–39. So impressed was Trissino with the skill and intelligence of his mason that he arranged for him to study classical architecture actively, supporting and accompanying him on his first visits to Rome in 1541 to investigate ancient buildings. It was Trissino who gave him his nickname of "Palladio" in 1545, both the name of a liberating angel in the count's epic poem and an allusion to Pallas Athena, the Greek goddess of civilization and of the arts and crafts, as well as of wisdom.[11]

Villeggiatura Veneziana

As early as 1540 Palladio was beginning to assert his unique, heavily classical style. About 1542, he completed his first independent commission for a villa in the *Terraferma*, the Villa Godi at Lonedo di Lugo near Vicenza. Palladio was obviously proud of this very early work as he included it in his *Four Books on Architecture* (first printed in 1570), his own response to Vitruvius. In a caption for its illustration he wrote:

> *The following building owned by Signor Girolamo de'Godi is in Lonedo di Lugo in the region of Vicenza. It is on a hill with a wonderful view, with a river flowing past which is used by fishermen.*[12]

This rather bucolic description does not reflect the rather massive façade of the villa, which is reminiscent of Trissino's Villa Cricoli. Palladio was still clearly influenced by the traditional fortified villas of rural northern Italy. But there is at the same time a symmetry and harmony that already reflect the style that would ultimately make

---

11. For Trissino, see Tavernor, 1991. pp. 16–24.
12. Marton, Wundrum, and Pape, 2008. p. 10.

Palladio's buildings synonymous with the *villeggiatura veneziana*: the civilized lifestyle of the Venetian villa.

Palladio proved to be a genius at constructing elegant yet functional buildings anchoring working estates while still profoundly allusive to the architecture of ancient Rome. These country houses were often decorated inside with Arcadian landscapes and trompe l'oeil frescoes to delight the eye and succeeded in changing the nature of Venetian culture by adding an element of a rustic life to a highly sophisticated and hierarchical urban culture. It was almost as if the calm civilization, elegant proportions, and symmetry of Palladio provided the cure for the post-traumatic stress caused by war, defeat, religious revolution, economic decline, and discord. The myth of Venice was reinterpreted as the bringing of justice and peace to the *Terraferma*, reflecting the ideal republic of *La Serenissima*.[13]

Trissino's death in 1550 actually expanded Palladio's influence, as he was given commissions by the most powerful of the noble families in Venice to build their country houses in his style of overt and elegant classicism underpinned by functionality and convenience. Some, like his justly famous Villa Rotonda (1552), illustrate his ability to site a house perfectly. For this timeless structure he created not one but four pedimented entries—one on each side—to take advantage of the commanding views of the surrounding countryside. Inspired by the Pantheon in Rome, this villa has in its turn inspired countless imitations, most famously Thomas Jefferson's Monticello.

Later, two Barbaro brothers patronized Palladio, again sending him to Rome to study classical architecture on site.[14] The results of this collaboration were two: one was Palladio's book of 1554, *The Antiquities of Rome* (*L'Antichità di Roma*); the other was the exquisite Villa Barbaro at Maser (ca. 1560–70), which achieved the ultimate integration of an elegant country house and a working estate building. Paolo Veronese was engaged to fresco the interior, creating one of the Veneto's most iconic structures.[15]

Public Architecture

Besides villas, Palladio was experimenting with a new classical vocabulary for public, official structures on the mainland. As early as 1546 he proved his talent in designing an exterior loggia for the law courts in Vicenza: the *Palazzo della Ragione*.[16] By encasing a

---

13. In his *The Four Books on Architecture* (1570), Palladio wrote about the interior decoration of one of his first villas: "[Villa Godi] has been adorned with paintings of a beautiful invention by Messer Gualtiera Padovano, by Messer Battista del Moro Veronese, and by Messer Battista Venetiano." Andrea Palladio, *The Four Books on Architecture,* tr. Robert Tavernor and Richard Schofield. Cambridge, MA: MIT Press, 1997. p. 143.

14. For Palladio's relations with the cultural and intellectual environment of the Barbaro family and with Jacopo Contarini, see Manfredo Tafuri, *Venice and the Renaissance*, tr. Jessica Levine. Cambridge, MA, and London: MIT Press, 1989. pp. 122–38.

15. Marton, Wundrum, and Pape, 2008. pp. 118–33.

16. Marton, Wundrum, and Pape, 2008. pp. 64–73.

fifteenth-century structure with open arcades, adorned with the signature Palladian windows, Palladio was introducing a new aesthetic to public buildings. This contribution was later reinforced in the Loggia del Capitaniato[17] for the city hall of Vicenza. But it was his last work, the *Teatro Olimpico* or Olympic Theatre in Vicenza, which has cemented his genius.[18]

This classically inspired space for public performances was commissioned by the learned *Accademia Olimpica* for productions of plays and recitations in the classical tradition. The Academy was a largely aristocratic gathering of scholars and dilettantes, all devoted to humanism. They saw Palladio himself as a member—quite a rise for the son of a Paduan miller once apprenticed to a stonecutter! But his membership was well deserved given the extraordinary theatre he designed. The theatre's trompe l'oeil stage reveals a streetscape that allows for the classical unities of ancient drama to operate while simultaneously offering perfect acoustics.

What's more, the *Teatro Olimpico* was an exemplary exercise in cost control. In fact, another signature of Palladio's work—a feature that possibly appealed more to his patrons than even the classical elegance of his buildings—was his insistence on economical building techniques. To entice individual members to pay for the structure, Palladio designed a row of life-sized statues above the stage, and individual members were encouraged to pay for their likenesses to preside forever in the theatre. But rather than producing these statues in marble, as might have been expected, Palladio used plaster—a much more economical medium. Similarly, much of the theatre is painted to look like stone when in actual fact it is merely wood. Modern architects indeed have much to learn from this master!

As in any Renaissance city, the Church was a major patron of architects, and Palladio provided some of Venice's most beautiful churches. San Francesco della Vigna,[19] for example, displays a double order of columns to represent the dynamic dialogue of the human and divine. His façade of San Giorgio Maggiore on an island in the Basin of St. Mark, opposite the Piazzetta of San Marco, shows the power of symmetry in providing a human scale to a huge building, with few openings in the façade.[20] His *Redentore* (Redeemer)[21] is a perfect building in its proportions, symmetry, and classical inspiration. And there are others, like his work for the *Scuola della carità* (the Confraternity of Charity, now the *Accademia* Art Museum), which blends old and new structures and provides an almost theatrical sense of power and place, but on a human scale.[22]

Palladio's fame and reputation as an architect became much more broadly recognized after the printing in 1570 of his *The Four Books on Architecture* (*I quattro libri*

17. Marton, Wundrum, and Pape, 2008. pp. 216–22.
18. Marton, Wundrum, and Pape, 2008. pp. 226–33.
19. Marton, Wundrum, and Pape, 2008. pp. 210–11.
20. Marton, Wundrum, and Pape, 2008. pp. 148–55.
21. Marton, Wundrum, and Pape, 2008. pp. 156–63.
22. Marton, Wundrum, and Pape, 2008. pp. 146–47.

dell'architettura), a title obviously indebted to Vitruvius. This treatise, printed in Venice, would become enormously influential, not only for its application of the classical vocabulary of building but also for its rehearsal of the achievements of Palladio himself. The descriptions of the buildings he designed reflect a rich legacy in which his genius can be seen developing and adapting to the needs of his patrons and the sites and functions of the structures. Discussions of materials, proportions, and variety are revealed in this great book as elements of the ingenuity and creativity of an artist in brick and stone.

A Renaissance Architect

The Barbaro's patronage resulted in Palladio being named the *Proto della Serenissima* (honored citizen architect of the republic) following the death of Jacopo Sansovino in 1570. This position was recognition not only for the impressive list of villas in the *Terraferma* that he had produced for the Venetian patriciate but also for Palladio's urban public buildings, palaces, and churches. It was evident that Palladio could bring his genius to any project and the result would connect the city and territory of Venice with the authority and visual perfection of the ancient world. What is more, his buildings were not merely exceptional to behold: they actually worked! And so in 1574 he received what would be his most political commission: the reconstruction of the state rooms of the ducal palace in Venice after the devastating fire of that same year.[23]

Despite another fire a few years later, much of Palladio's program for these rooms remains for us to visit today. They are a mixture of traditional Venetian hypnotic magnificence, designed to make all visitors feel insignificant in the face of the wealth and power of the republic, and his genius for spaces that function beautifully. In this commission, Palladio has become part of the image of Venice itself, but of the new Venice after Agnadello and the re-conquest of the *Terraferma*, that is, an Italian Venice with mythological links not only to Byzantium and the East but to ancient Rome and the West.

In short, Palladio was not only one of the Renaissance's most influential geniuses but one who came to define a new age in the republic of Venice. The new reality after the 1540s, when Venice finally emerged from the trauma of the War of the League of Cambrai and the subsequent Italian wars, was symbolized in bricks and mortar. The policy of Francesco Foscari of privileging expansion onto the mainland was the cause of the rise of Vitruvian classicism, and Palladio became its architect. The villas, palaces, and churches he designed, using the vocabulary of Vitruvius and the models of ancient Rome, brought Venice into Italy and made connections where there had been few—if any—real antecedents.[24]

Venice was not a Roman foundation; the history of the city until the fifteenth century is really one of consort with the trade and traditions of the East. Palladio, therefore,

---

23. Ackerman, 1991. pp. 34–35.
24. Tavernor, 1991. pp. 11–15.

defined a new myth of Venice, one which connected the most serene republic with the virtuous Roman Republic and cemented those *Terraferma* cities with deep Roman roots, such as Verona and Padua (the birthplace of the historian Livy, as well as Palladio himself). Palladio changed not only the appearance of Venice but reimagined its myth. Petrarch would not have recognized two centuries later the Venice he had so often visited and respected so greatly, but it is certain that he would have approved, because the ancient world of Rome was transplanted there through the buildings of Palladio.

Illus. 14.1.a Giovanni Bellini (ca. 1430–1516), *Portrait of Doge Leonardo Loredan,* **1501. National Gallery, London.**

The splendid portrait to the left illustrates the depth to which Renaissance style had entered Venice by the beginning of the sixteenth century. Giovanni Bellini's father, Jacopo, had spent time in Florence in the 1420s and had observed the latest techniques practiced by Masolino, Masaccio, and Donatello. Both Giovanni and his brother, Gentile, were trained in their father's Venetian workshop, where these new influences were further elaborated by Netherlandish elements, including the use of oil paint: the Loredan portrait is, in fact, oil on wooden panel.

This image of Doge Loredan is certainly a state portrait, completed at the beginning of his reign. He wears the regalia of a Venetian doge, particularly the horned crown, or *corno,* set on a linen cap. Bellini has caught the intelligence and steadfast gaze of this man, the doge who had to deal with the critical events of the War of the League of Cambrai, the defeat at Agnadello, and the consequent evaporation of the Venetian *Terraferma* empire.

Despite the crushing defeat at Agnadello, the Venetian artistic propaganda machine subsequently responded by redefining the humiliation of the *Serenissima* as a victory. The image on the left by Palma il Giovane (1544–1628), painted in the chamber of the Senate (*Senato*) in the ducal palace in 1590, seems to portray Doge Loredan crowned with victory, while the personified Venice, armed and encouraging her attendant attacking lion, engages the enemies of the republic. It would be interesting to hear the response of Loredan's colleagues had the picture been placed in 1509 rather than 1590.

Illus. 14.1.b Palma il Giovane (Jacopo Negretti (ca. 1548–1628), *Allegory of the Victory Over the League of Cambrai* **(detail), 1590–95. Palazzo Ducale, Sala del Senato, Venice.**

Illus. 14.2 Antonio Canal (1697–1768, known as Canaletto), *The Piazza San Marco, Venice*, 1720. Metropolitan Museum of Art, New York.

This eighteenth-century view of the Piazza San Marco illustrates better than a modern photograph the political center of the Venetian republic. The wings of the two procuracies (*procuratie*)—the old on the left and the new on the right—held the offices of the Procurators of St. Mark, financial officials of the state responsible for the treasury of St. Mark, as well as other duties. Besides the doge, these were the only officials chosen for life. Even today the doors leading to their offices are visible, particularly in the old procuracy. The *procuratie vecchie* dating from the sixteenth century, replaced a building destroyed by fire; the *procuratie nuove* were begun by Vincenzo Scamozzi in 1586.

At the end of the piazza is the basilica of St. Mark, the private chapel of the doge, reflecting the Byzantine interpenetration of Church and state. The bell tower (*campanile*) dominates the square. Just behind it on the right rises the ducal palace, while approximately opposite it on the left is the clock tower designed by Mauro Coducci (1499) to complete the end of the *procuratie vecchie*.

Illus. 14.3.a Andrea Palladio (1508–80), Villa Godi. Lonedo di Lugo near Vicenza.

Illus. 14.3.b Giovanni Battista Zelotti, Villa Godi. Interior Fresco.

Villa Godi at Lonedo di Lugo near Vicenza was Palladio's first major villa commission (ca. 1542). It still retains robust references to the fortified country house and of the Villa Cricoli of his patron, Count Gian Giorgio Trissino. But it is the message of the interior decoration, dating a decade later, that reinforces the recovery of Venice and its emerging culture of cultivated authority. The bucolic landscapes of Battista del Moro and the frescoes of Giovanni Battista Zelotti and Gualtiero Padovano created an idealized, perpetual Arcadian golden age where peace and justice rule, populated by cultivated and beautiful patrician men and women in the company of deities and muses. The destruction and despair occasioned by Agnadello are far distant from this happy place set in the verdant landscape of the *Terraferma*, protected by Venice and the lion of St. Mark.

Illus. 14.4 Andrea Palladio, Villa Barbaro, ca. 1554–60. Maser, Veneto.

Villa Barbaro at Maser in the province of Treviso was designed by Andrea Palladio between 1554 and 1560 for the brothers Daniele and Marcantonio Barbaro, with the building likely finished by 1558. The residential central block of the villa containing its reception rooms was modeled on ancient Roman temples, with columns supporting an impressive pediment. The open loggias on either side incorporate the agricultural spaces needed for a working farm but made a harmonious part of the façade through perfect proportions and the insertion of classically inspired sculptures at the far ends. Paired sundials complete the perfect, functional symmetry of the building. The villa illustrates profoundly how Palladio captured the need for the Venetian republic to integrate the *Terraferma* into a common culture defined by the *Serenissima*, one in which the rural realities of an agricultural estate could merge with the classical, humanist ideals of the educated patrician elite.

CHAPTER 15
THE KINGDOM OF NAPLES

Few narratives of Renaissance Italy devote much space to the Kingdom of Naples, known as *Il Regno*, "The Kingdom," as it was the only such monarchy on the peninsula.[1] The truth is, the Renaissance was received there only cursorily and sporadically and never set down deep roots. In many ways this was because the state of *Il Regno* changed with inconvenient regularity: for example, the island of Sicily was sometimes integrated into Naples and then sometimes ruled independently, occasionally by different, even hostile, dynasties. Naples was also fundamentally different in social and economic structure from the states to the north. Much of this difference resulted from the complex history of southern Italy, but some also was the consequence of the policies and practices of the monarchs who ruled this often ungovernable region.

The disjunction between the traditions and institutions of the South and those in the North made humanism a foreign and even inappropriate ideology for the various elites of the *Regno*. The conditions that gave rise to the culture of humanism in a city such as Florence were either absent or vestigial in a city like Naples. The latter was a huge metropolis—perhaps the second largest on the continent—but one completely dependent on the royal court. In some ways, then, there are similarities with the monarchical regimes of the northern principalities, such as Milan. But these similarities are superficial, as there were no other major urban centers in the region that might have sparked the kinds of competition that led to dynamic innovation and experimentation elsewhere.

Nevertheless, there were moments of significant interest in Renaissance culture and ideas, particularly during the reigns of Robert the Wise (r. 1309–43), that friend of Petrarch and Boccaccio,[2] and Alfonso I of Aragon, the Magnanimous (r. 1442–58). So, it is reasonable to investigate, if only briefly, the unique experience of Naples (and occasionally Sicily) during the period of the Renaissance.

---

1. As a consequence, there is not a rich bibliography in English on late Medieval and Renaissance Naples. See Benedetto Croce, *History of the Kingdom of Naples*, tr. F. Frenaye. Chicago: University of Chicago Press, 1970; Jerry Bentley, *Politics and Culture in Renaissance Naples*. Princeton: Princeton University Press, 1987; David Abulafia, "The South," in John Najemy, ed., *Italy in the Age of the Renaissance, 1300–1550*. Oxford: Oxford University Press, 2004. pp. 208–25; Alan Ryder, *The Kingdom of Naples Under Alfonso the Magnanimous*. Oxford: Oxford University Press, 1976; Eleni Sakellariou, *Southern Italy in the Late Middle Ages: Demographic, Institutional and Economic Change in the Kingdom of Naples, c.1440–c.1530*. Leiden: Brill, 2011; Ronald G. Musto, ed., *Medieval Naples: A Documentary History, 400–1400*. New York: Italica Press, 2013; Caroline Bruzelius and William Tronzo, *Medieval Naples: An Architectural & Urban History, 400–1400*. New York: Italica Press, 2011.

2. Romolo Caggese, *Roberto d'Angiò e I Suoi Tempi*. Florence: Bemporad, 1922. 2 vols.

A Tortured History

Southern Italy had played host to a series of invaders before falling to the dynasty of the Angevins, that is, the House of Anjou, the cadet branch of the French royal house, in 1266. From the eighth century BC, the Greeks, Romans, Arabs, Normans, and Germans in succession had taken possession and to a degree colonized the kingdom and Sicily, and all the invaders left their mark. In some ways this rich tapestry should have provided some energy to particular elements of Renaissance thought. For example, the study of Greek, a language still alive in some southern towns, might have been a natural fit. But in reality, the complexity of this region's history created an environment not altogether receptive to any new cultural models.

With the arrival of the Germans came the existential battle between the papacy and the imperial House of Hohenstaufen—the old conflict between Guelfs and Ghibellines. When Charles, count of Anjou and younger brother of King St. Louis IX of France, defeated the Hohenstaufen forces in Italy, he naturally expected a reward, so Pope Clement IV in 1266 offered him the crown of Naples which at that time included Sicily. Charles of Anjou was a seasoned crusader like his brother Louis. He also had broad ambitions in the Mediterranean and was not lacking in ability. So, the gift was appropriate. However, his understanding of his new subjects left much to be desired. And his high-handed manner together with the high taxes he imposed did not make him any more appealing.

This was particularly true in Sicily, an island with very deeply entrenched social customs and practices, most of which the French officials of Charles ignored or reviled. Furthermore, the ancient magnate families of the island were used to operating as laws unto themselves in the political and economic affairs of the island. They held an almost proprietary control of high Church offices and disliked the intervention of the crown in areas they thought theirs alone. All of this resentment came together in the revolt of the Sicilian Vespers, 1282.[3]

The cause of the violence was rehearsed by the Florentine humanist chancellor Leonardo Bruni. He wrote that on Easter Monday, at the beginning of the liturgical hour of vespers, French soldiers were sent to search those entering Palermo, the Sicilian capital, for weapons or contraband. There had been a violent scene just outside the city walls at the church of Santo Spirito, caused by the aggressive attention of a Frenchman toward a young married Sicilian woman. Her husband had killed the soldier in fury and a general melee occurred. This was exacerbated by the extremely intrusive searching of the bodies of the women, an offense against traditional morality and the modesty of Sicilian women.

---

3. Steven Runciman, *The Sicilian Vespers: A History of the Mediterranean World in the Later Thirteenth Century*. Cambridge: Cambridge University Press, 2012.

Enraged, the Sicilians turned en masse against the French force, killing them all, and then mobs roamed Palermo slaughtering any French man or woman they encountered. Even the monasteries and convents were invaded in search of French monks and nuns. Those suspected of being French were required to repeat difficult words in Sicilian dialect, and if they were unable to do so, they were killed on the spot. About three thousand men, women, and children were slaughtered that night, as riders crossed the island stirring up other communities against the hated French king in Naples. Mobs killed entire garrisons, while others set fire to Charles's fleet in the harbor of Messina. French control of Sicily dissolved.

The nobility and other important men of the island gathered to form a new government. They petitioned the pope to make Sicily a free commune, although subject to the papacy. However, Pope Martin IV was himself French and he still needed the alliance with the Angevins to block any attempt by the imperial party to recover their authority. So he not only rejected the Sicilians' request but also demanded that they return to complete obedience to Charles as king of Sicily and Naples. Meanwhile Charles was outfitting a new fleet and marshaling an army to return.

There was an alternative for the Sicilians. The last legitimate descendent of the emperor Frederick II of Hohenstaufen was Constance, married to King Peter of Aragon. Realizing that they would need a protector if the French were to be excluded from the island, the Sicilians offered the crown to Peter. Fortunately, Peter had built a powerful fleet to fight the pirates of North Africa who were endangering the important Mediterranean commerce of Barcelona. So he sailed from Tunis to Trapani, landed an army, and marched to Palermo. Once there he swore to uphold the traditions of the island and not oppress his subjects as the French had. Peter was crowned in the cathedral of Palermo in September of 1282, an act that began the Spanish regime in the south of Italy and separated Sicily from Naples, where Charles still ruled.

The Angevins in Naples

Charles of Anjou would rule in Naples until his death in 1285. This French connection would make Naples an integral part of the culture of Italy, and Naples remained a major player in the game of Guelf politics on the peninsula. We have already seen how these Neapolitan princes became involved in Florentine affairs, especially under Charles's grandson Robert of Calabria, also known as Robert the Wise of Naples. (This was that duke of Calabria who entertained an offer for the position of protector of Florence as leader of the Guelf party and papal vicar of Tuscany and the Romagna.)

Robert (r. 1309–43) deserved his epithet "the Wise." He was a cultivated and discerning leader and patron. It was he, after all, in his role as papal senator of Rome, who examined Petrarch in 1341 for his suitability to be crowned as poet laureate. Petrarch became a personal friend of the king, whom he called "a second Solomon," and they delighted in one another's company. Robert even lent Petrarch his own royal mantle to wear at the laureate coronation. Together they made a pilgrimage to Virgil's tomb as a symbolic gesture of their shared love of ancient Rome. So although his time in Naples might not have been the most inspiring because of his horror at the gladiatorial combats common among the city's youth, Petrarch always maintained warm relations with Robert. He dedicated his epic poem *Africa* to the king, and it was Robert who was Petrarch's hope for the unity of Italy.

King Robert was himself a lover of books, and he is described by Petrarch as always having them by his side, resulting in a significant—and therefore costly—library. He was also a patron of building, commissioning even before his succession the town of Città Ducale (his title then was duke of Calabria). He built the harbor at Salerno to stimulate commerce, and he ordered the massive Castel Sant'Elmo overlooking the Bay of Naples to be enlarged and strengthened to protect his capital from assaults by sea.

It was Robert and his queen, Sancha of Majorca, who commissioned the church and convent of Santa Chiara in about 1310 (completed by 1338). It consequently became the burial site of the royal family and many of the most powerful nobles of his court. Robert himself is interred here in a still-spectacular tomb commissioned by his granddaughter Queen Joanna.[4]

Unfortunately, the loss of Sicily had been something of an economic and political disaster for the Angevins. Sicily, with its rich agricultural lands, had provided much wealth to Naples, wealth that was now lost to the opposing House of Aragon. To compensate for what was becoming a serious financial deficit, Robert turned to Florentine bankers to provide loans. In return, Florentines were given licenses to manage the Neapolitan grain trade, with much of the cheap grain going to Florence itself. The significant wealth earned by the Florentines motivated them to build elegant palaces and decorate churches in the new style that was capturing Tuscany.

It was as a representative of the great Bardi family bank that Giovanni Boccaccio's father came—together with his family—to live in Naples between 1327 and 1341. The young Boccaccio[5] studied law at the University of Naples, an institution which Robert had richly endowed and staffed with notable scholars who taught classical letters as well as law. Robert had realized the opportunity Naples offered in sustaining Greek studies, as many native speakers remained in his kingdom, and, consequently, he patronized Greek scholarship long before it became fashionable in Florence.

---

4. Caroline Bruzelius, *The Stones of Naples: Church Building in Angevin Italy, 1266–1343*. New Haven: Yale University Press, 2004. p. 150.

5. Boccaccio's time in Naples is not only recorded in stories in *The Decameron* but also in his *Filocolo* and *Fiammetta*, where he praises his muse and mistress, Fiammetta. The real Fiammetta was Maria d'Aquino, the illegitimate daughter of Robert the Wise. She was sadly beheaded in 1382 as a result of her earlier involvement in a conspiracy against Queen Joanna I. See Gur Zak, "Boccaccio's Fiammetta and the Consolation of Literature," *MLN*, 131 (2016), pp. 1–19.

A connection through Boccaccio and the Bardi bank also brought the painter Giotto to Naples in 1328. Having just completed the Bardi Chapel in Santa Croce, Giotto was invited to Naples on the advice of Giovanni Boccaccio to decorate the city and be another ornament to the Angevin court. This explains the appearance of St. Louis of Toulouse, the saintly brother of Robert, in Giotto's frescoes in the Bardi Chapel in Florence.[6]

Despite these deep economic and superficial but important cultural links, the commerce between Florence and Naples was centered on the court and was often highly personal in nature. Naples became a more beautiful and cosmopolitan city under Robert, but the institutions of the Angevin state did not change. Everything depended on the king and his court in the capital, with little interest outside that rarified circle in experimenting with new elements of culture or applying the lessons of antiquity to the conduct of the present.

The Exception to the Rule

Given the remarkable character, ability, and connections of Robert of Naples, why didn't Petrarch's ideas put down roots in Naples? And given his role in fixing Petrarch's message in Florence, why did Boccaccio not do the same in Naples? The brilliance of King Robert and his court concealed the reality of the kingdom. In fact, many of his close associates illustrate exactly why the early humanism of Petrarch could not gain traction in the Angevin capital. Culture is like Velcro®: it needs two sides to adhere. The influence of Petrarch might have been present, but the environment in which it needed to develop was altogether absent.

There was an important—if second tier—university in Naples, one with a distinguished faculty of law, again patronized by King Robert.[7] Subjects of the kingdom were encouraged to attend the Neapolitan *studio*, but the number of students who traveled abroad to more prestigious schools remained high. This is likely the recognition that work could be more easily found in the North; there was little need for lawyers in the *Regno* outside of Naples. The kingdom had few important urban centers and was predominantly an agricultural state. Furthermore, its trade was in commodities. The class of educated, urban, secular guildsmen or merchants was small and mostly foreign dominated. Thus, the class that succeeded in institutionalizing humanism in Florence was in Naples insignificant, weak, and disinterested.

---

6. Giotto remained in Robert's service for five years (1328–33), honored and praised by the king who granted him the title of royal *familiaris*, that is, an official member of his personal household. Remnants of his work remain in the royal foundation of Santa Chiara. See Anne Derbes and Mark Sandona, eds., *The Cambridge Companion to Giotto*. Cambridge: Cambridge University Press, 2004. p. 6. See also pp. 131, 143, 193–94.

7. Paul Grendler, *The Universities of the Italian Renaissance*. Baltimore: Johns Hopkins University Press, 2002. pp. 41–45.

The Neapolitan nobility was also a very different group from the magnates of northern Italy. The feudal traditions imposed by the Normans made the great barons above the law. They owned vast *latifundi* (huge private estates) and obeyed the royal edicts when it suited them and ignored them when it didn't. The great families also controlled the high ecclesiastical offices, uniting enormous political, economic, and even spiritual power in a way quite absent from elsewhere in Italy. Some of the great families kept palaces in Naples in order to have access to the king and the court; but their attitudes were rural and feudal.[8]

Moreover, the Angevins of Naples and the Aragonese in Sicily were foreign dynasties. They were never fully embraced as Neapolitan. Rather, they were seen as kings imposed upon a people with an ancient culture and different principles of power and government. There was resentment of foreign rulers among the people and the supercilious foreign officials they employed to enforce their will. What is more, the rural subjects (and even some of those who lived in the city) had closer ties to the old noble clans who promised them protection from both banditry and taxation.

Naples was seen as divorced from the rest of the *Regno*, an urban, foreign-dominated metropolis dependent economically on the labor of rural communities with whom they could not even communicate because their dialects of Italian were so different. Most of the population, the vast majority, probably more than ninety percent, was illiterate, living in rural poverty and hardly open to new genres of literature or the recovery of antiquity. The landlords claimed to speak for these native southerners, protecting them against the culture and oppression of the Neapolitan elite. This was not an environment conducive to the spread of Petrarch's concepts of individual human dignity, the validity of this life, and the value of classical letters and elegant speech.

This situation was complicated by the division of Sicily from Naples. Many of the powerful feudal clans had estates on both sides of the Straits of Messina, which divided their attention and even their loyalty. These families were skilled in playing all forces against each another, relying when necessary on the private armies of their peasants. They could impose oaths of loyalty on their tenants; they were the judges in most disputes; and they could tax them, even as the Aragonese monarchs were abandoning some of their traditional rights to the nobility to ensure their acquiescence. Moreover, these great feudal baronial families had no tradition of patronage or learning.[9] They were a hunting, hawking warrior nobility, often rusticated on their vast estates, often in rebellion against or at least hostile to the crown and the court and not open to new ideas.

Members of the peasant class—essentially impoverished sharecroppers—were completely dependent on the feudal landlords for almost every necessity of life, including justice—such as it was—and protection. They sought solace in the Church, which

8. See Croce, 1970. pp. 58–75.

9. Bentley, 1987. p. 9; M. Finley, Denis Mack-Smith, and Christopher Duggan. *A History of Sicily.* New York: Viking Penguin, 1987. pp. 79–81.

was itself dominated by the feudal nobility, and whose vast estates were run like any of the other *latifundi* in the South. In fact, the Church was an extension of these families, with major clerics appointed from within their ranks and seen as great feudal lords in their own right, the owners of huge rural properties. The monasteries and convents were either the dumping ground for the surplus children of great families or a place for religious zealots to practice a form of devotion that did not allow for much learning.

Urban life, which we have seen as central to the development of the Renaissance, was in *Il Regno* vestigial and dependent on agriculture, not trade and commerce. Towns were not like the towns of Tuscany, centers of entrepreneurial ambition and open to the ideas flowing from larger cities like Florence. Rather, the Kingdom of Naples had few significant towns, and only a tiny educated professional class. Law was occasionally important as a discipline but was taught in the traditional Medieval manner until the years of Alfonso in the fifteenth century.

The Church played a critically important role, not only because of the wealth and land it controlled and the influence it held over the population, but also because of the curious role of the papacy in Neapolitan political and dynastic life. The Angevins, and before them, the Normans, had come to the South as papal representatives. There they were charged with specific responsibilities: the destruction of the imperial Ghibelline power of the Hohenstaufen in the former and the conversion or elimination of Greek Orthodox and Muslim communities in the latter case. Naples was technically a fief of the papacy, and popes claimed the right to decide disputed successions and install monarchs acceptable to papal power and ambitions. This added another level of instability to the South, one which would have dangerous consequences in our period.

These circumstances in many ways made King Robert's reign even more remarkable, indicating how some elements of change and Renaissance culture might be imported into the South through the court. Unfortunately, Robert's successors did not build on his legacy. In fact, the narrative of the dynastic crises of the Neapolitan Angevins during the later fourteenth and fifteenth centuries reads like an improbable tale of incompetence, violence, invasion, war, and division.

The Unfortunate Tale of Joanna I

The story of Naples following the death of Robert the Wise is complicated to a degree that defies credibility. The plot twists constitute a roller coaster ride through history and illustrate why the flirtation with humanism and Renaissance ideas in Naples wasn't consummated under the House of Anjou. The story of Robert's successor, his granddaughter Joanna I (r. 1343–82), will suffice as exemplar of this tumultuous period. Her intricate narrative helps explain the repeated foreign interventions in the affairs of the Italian South, the role of the papacy in the story of Naples, and the circumstances that led to the acquisition of Avignon by the Holy See, a significant factor in the longevity of the Avignonese papacy during the Great Schism.

Joanna's life is really the stuff of romantic historical fiction or opera rather than the narrative of an anointed monarch.[10] Early in his reign, Robert the Wise had recognized that not having a legitimate male heir in a family with several competing claims to the throne would cause difficulty for his dynasty. His son, Charles of Calabria, died young in 1328. So, to pre-empt any possibility of civil war or further foreign intervention, Robert had married Charles's five-year-old daughter, Joanna, to her six-year-old cousin, Andrew, who was the son of King Charles of the Hungarian branch of the Angevins.

Robert, however, had no intention of giving his grandson-in-law any authority, so in Robert's will naming Joanna as queen, Andrew was excluded from any right to succeed. Furthermore, Robert also tried to exclude the papacy from any role in the royal succession by establishing a regency council during her minority, rather than, as would have been expected, relying on a papal legate. In 1344, having reached her majority, Joanna was crowned by Pope Clement VI himself. But in keeping with the terms of Robert's will, Andrew was not afforded the dignity of a coronation, although he was given the courtesy title of "king."

For Andrew the situation was humiliating. So, he began stirring up opposition to Robert's will, asking for the intervention of his royal Hungarian parents and the pope. Clement took this opportunity to assert the papacy's traditional role of feudal authority over Naples and its monarchs. The pope had already outmaneuvered the regency council established by Robert the Wise, sending a legate, Cardinal de Chatelus, to act as regent in the last months of Joanna's minority. Seeing yet another chance to exert more control over Naples, Clement responded positively to the demands of Queen Elizabeth of Hungary and her son Andrew that he be granted a coronation, much against the wishes of Joanna and her court. The pope tried to soften his intervention by claiming that it was only Joanna's anointing that would be blessed by divine will—but Andrew would still be crowned king.

Recognizing the opprobrium that his promised coronation and royal pretensions raised at court, Andrew feared a conspiracy against his life. So his mother presented him with a magic ring that would offer protection against assassination. (You were warned that this was the stuff of opera.) Sadly for Andrew, the ring proved to be a dud. During the summer heat of 1344, Joanna was struck with a debilitating illness. Andrew took the opportunity to pardon a family of brutal nobles who had been found guilty of many terrible crimes and to restore their property to them, all in an attempt to build a faction of his own. But the estates of that family had already been given to loyal courtiers of Joanna,

---

10. Nancy Goldstone, *The Lady Queen: The Notorious Reign of Joanna I, Queen of Naples, Jerusalem, and Sicily*. London: Walker Books, 2009. An 1824 biography of Joanna is also available in modern reprint: Frances Moore, *Historical Life of Joanna of Sicily, Queen of Naples and Countess of Provence, with Correlative Details of the Literature and Manners of Italy and Provence in the Thirteenth and Fourteenth Centuries* (Classic Reprint). 2 vols. London: Forgotten Books, 2017.

and they were aggrieved at the risk of losing them. Exasperated by Andrew's actions, these nobles plotted his demise.

The time came in September of 1345. One night, after Andrew had gone hunting, he returned late, only to find himself barred from his room. He was set upon by a group of thugs who strangled him, tied a cord around his testicles, and threw him from a window. Most of Europe believed that Joanna was involved in the plot, though there is little evidence of her collusion. Regardless, she gave birth to Andrew's posthumous son in December, believing thereby that the succession was secure.

It was not to be that easy. Joanna made a political error when she subsequently decided to marry her cousin Louis of Taranto, rather than Andrew's younger Hungarian brother as the royal Hungarian Angevins demanded. It is probable that Joanna wanted the protection offered by Louis's military power and his experience in Neapolitan court intrigue. They married quickly, not even waiting for the necessary papal dispensation required by their consanguinity. The union was extremely unpopular, as the king of Hungary now openly accused Joanna of the murder of Andrew and Joanna's subjects were beginning to share that belief.

Disaster struck when Andrew's older brother, King Louis of Hungary, led an army to conquer Naples, claim it as part of his patrimony, and expel Joanna and her new husband, Louis of Taranto.[11] In January 1348, as King Louis's army reached Naples, Joanna fled, followed the next day by Louis of Taranto. At the same time Joanna left behind her young son by Andrew, and when the Hungarians captured Naples, the boy was taken to a castle in Hungary where he soon died.

Joanna had taken refuge in another of her realms, the county of Provence, where the papacy was residing in Avignon. She sought an audience with the pope with the intention of having her latest marriage recognized, despite the close affinity between her and Louis of Taranto. At the same time, she requested papal absolution from any role in Andrew's murder. Clement VI demurred, instead calling for an investigation into Andrew's death. The commission eventually found in Joanna's favor, the deciding factor probably being Joanna's willingness to sell Avignon to the pope. As well as rendering Joanna guiltless in Andrew's murder, this historically significant transaction gave the Church ownership of the city and surrounding territory and reinforced the legitimacy of the Avignonese papacy.

At this point another intervention occurred—the Black Death. As the plague ravaged the city of Naples, Louis of Hungary and his army withdrew to healthier places in the kingdom. Although the population had initially welcomed the Hungarians, their brutality—including the execution of a number of leading nobles and even Joanna's elderly nurse and her family—made the return of Joanna and her husband to Naples now

---

11. Andreas Kiesewetter, "Luigi d'Angiò," in *Dizionario Biografico degli Italiani*. Vol. 66. Rome: Istituto della Enciclopedia Italiana, 2006.

palatable. Louis of Taranto proved to be an effective military commander and defeated the Hungarians, driving them from the *Regno*. He proved equally skilled in political intrigue to the point that in 1352 he was recognized by the pope as a legitimate and joint ruler. Of course this action also benefitted the pope as it clearly made the recognition of papal jurisdiction an important part of Louis's right to rule.

The issue of the succession again became critical with the death of Louis of Taranto in 1362. Joanna and Louis had had two children, both girls, but both had died as infants. Because Joanna was still of childbearing age, she made a third marriage just six months after Louis's death. Her new husband was James, king of Majorca, although only in title not in fact. He was a decade younger than Joanna, so there was hope of an heir, but the match was disastrous from the beginning.

James was in effect mad, driven to this unfortunate state by his uncle, the king of Castile, who had held him prisoner in an iron cage for fourteen years. Unstable and consequently incapable of becoming co-ruler with Joanna, he left Naples in anger and disappointment, determined to reclaim his own kingdom of Majorca. He failed and was imprisoned again, was briefly ransomed by Joanna, attempted further conquests, again failed, and finally died in Castile in 1375 of poison. Needless to say, Joanna had no more children.

This did not mean that Joanna was finished with marriage. In 1375, the year of James's death, she entered into a union with a German prince, Otto of Brunswick, who was from the beginning deemed only a royal consort, not king, with no right to rule. Nevertheless, this marriage and the papal approval it carried greatly angered Joanna's cousin Charles of Durazzo, who had hoped to succeed her. Charles then made common cause with King Louis of Hungary and threatened war. At this point another geopolitical event undermined Joanna: the Great Western Schism.

The papacy had returned to Rome from Avignon in 1377, but that pope, Gregory XI, died in 1378. The result was a schism that divided Europe between two popes: one in Rome and another in Avignon. As the countess of Provence and out of fear of the ambitions of the Roman pope, Urban VI, who had been archbishop of Bari in her territories, Joanna recognized the Avignonese papacy to the point of protecting and harboring the French claimant as he fled to Avignon. Thus, the Roman pope declared Joanna deposed as a heretic—among other things—and awarded the kingdom to her angry, disappointed cousin Charles of Durazzo. Joanna responded by adopting as her heir another French cousin, Louis of Anjou. But this Louis could do little, and Charles and a Hungarian army invaded the *Regno*, capturing Naples and Queen Joanna in the summer of 1381.

Intending to assure his inheritance of Naples, Louis of Anjou assembled an army in Avignon, intent on rescuing the queen. However, by the time he had passed through Turin and Milan, it was too late. Joanna had been transferred to a fortress in the remote interior where she died in July of 1382. As might be expected, Charles of Durazzo claimed that she had died of natural causes; on the other hand, contemporary accounts assert she was murdered, some saying she was strangled with a silken cord while at prayer, others that she was smothered with pillows.

Charles had Joanna's body put on display in Naples as public proof of her death and hence the legitimacy of his own rule. Because she had been excommunicated by the pope, the queen couldn't be buried in consecrated ground. Instead, she was dumped unceremoniously into a well on the grounds of the church of Santa Chiara. Such a different memorial from the splendid monument she had raised in that very church to her grandfather Robert the Wise!

It is difficult to credit this unfortunate tale of the Queen of Naples as history: Hollywood itself would find her story too unbelievable a script. But it is worth reciting if only to provide an example of the political intrigue that characterized the rule of Naples for the next century as competing factions fought for the succession. In truth, the situation was no more stable through the ensuing reigns of Charles of Durazzo (r. 1382–86), Ladislaus (r. 1399–1414), Joanna II (r. 1414–35), and René of Anjou (r. 1435–42). All ruled through times of manipulation, maneuvering, murder, and mayhem.

It was only with the arrival of the House of Aragon that some of these problems were addressed by another unique monarch, one who was in many ways a Renaissance prince of outstanding quality and ability: Alfonso the Magnanimous.

Illus. 15.1.a Andrea del Castagno, Giovanni Boccaccio, ca. 1450. Uffizi, Florence.

This portrait of Boccaccio by Andrea del Castagno was painted about seventy-five years after the poet's death. It is one in a series of portraits depicting famous men and women for the Villa Carducci at Legnaia, now a suburb of Florence. Boccaccio's years in Naples provided much material for his work and much inspiration. Favored at court, he found his first enduring poetic muse and perfect love in the form of Robert the Wise's illegitimate daughter Maria d'Aquino. She is idealized as the heroine Fiammetta who appears in Boccaccio's *Il Filocolo*, the first example of an Italian vernacular novel in prose, which he penned while in Naples (ca. 1338). Unfortunately, the beautiful Fiammetta was beheaded by Charles of Anjou in 1382 when she became embroiled in a conspiracy against Andrew of Hungary, one of the many plots that characterized Neapolitan politics after the death of King Robert.

The story of Boccaccio and his muse Fiammetta had lasting fame as seen by the nineteenth century (1879) Pre-Raphaelite portrayal of "Fiammetta Singing" by Marie Spartali Stillman. The scene comes from another of Boccaccio's works inspired by his Fiammetta, *The Elegy of Madonna Fiammetta*. This 1343–44 work represents a confessional narrative of the love between a Florentine merchant (Boccaccio?) and Fiammetta and is often claimed as the first psychological novel in Europe.

Illus. 15.1.b Marie Spartali Stillman (1844–1927), *Fiammetta Singing*, 1879. Private collection.

Robert the Wise commissioned the church of Santa Chiara in 1310. It appropriately holds his tomb, erected by his granddaughter, Queen Joanna I. The epitaph engraved beneath the image of him seated upon a throne that is set at the top of his monument truly describes this most remarkable man: *Cernite Robertum regem virtute refertum*: "Look upon King Robert replete with virtue." Robert's fame long outlived him as seen in his portrait in the *Anjou Bible* (ca. 1340).

Illus. 15.2.a Tomb of King Robert the Wise of Anjou. Church of Santa Chiara, Naples.

Illus. 15.2.b Portrait of King Robert of Naples (ca. 1340) from the *Anjou Bible*. Maurits Sabbe Library, Leuven.

Illus. 15.3 Joanna I of Naples (1326–82) in an illustration from Boccaccio's
De Mulieribus Claris **(***On Famous Women***). Cognac, fifteenth–sixteenth**
century. Bibliothèque Nationale de France, Paris, cote François 599. 93v.

Despite his murder of his cousin Joanna I of Naples, Charles of Durazzo did not enjoy his Neapolitan kingdom for long. Early in 1385 Pope Urban VI in Rome thought Charles duplicitous and believed he was dealing treacherously with the competing pope in Avignon. A cardinal verified this fear—under torture—so Urban excommunicated Charles and put the *Regno* under an interdict, all while a French and Italian army descended on Naples. In that same year, King Louis of Hungary died, so an ambitious Charles went to Hungary to claim that throne as well. Although initially successful, he was murdered in February of 1386.

Illus. 15.4 Mato Celestin Medović (1857–1920), *The Coronation of King Ladislas*, early twentieth century. Croatian Institute for History, Zagreb.

This turn of the twentieth century painting by the Croatian artist Mato Celestin Medović captures the coronation of Ladislaus in 1403, well after he began his reign in Naples. Young King Ladislaus (r. 1399–1414) did not have papal support, as Urban VI had urged the great feudal barons of the kingdom to revolt, which they were more than happy to do, and recognize instead Louis of Anjou as the legitimate king. In 1389, however, the subsequent Roman pontiff admitted Ladislaus as king of Naples, resulting in a war with the count of Anjou that lasted almost a decade.

Likely on the instructions of the Avignon pope, the archbishop of Arles administered poison to Ladislaus, which he survived but from which he suffered a partial loss of speech and a much-weakened body. Despite this, Ladislaus was able to dislodge Louis of Anjou from Naples and make war against those barons who had supported the pope and the French. He also attempted to claim the crown of Hungary, investing himself with titles in Hungarian territory, but to little effect. Then, in 1406, he was deposed as king of Naples by the pope.

In retaliation, Ladislaus then invaded the States of the Church, capturing Rome in the spring of 1407. Moving his army north into the Romagna, he threatened Florence and the rest of Tuscany. He was so successful in defending his gains that Florence and Siena needed to ensure active papal support to weaken him. As a result, Cosimo de'Medici strongly promoted Cardinal Baldassare Cossa, who was elected one of three popes in 1410. As Anti-pope John XXIII, Cossa, who was a Neapolitan from the island of Procida, declared a crusade against Ladislaus, thus forcing a compromise.

Ladislaus yielded some of his conquests in central Italy and in 1412 John XXIII signed a peace recognizing him as king of Naples and promising a large financial restitution. Ladislaus was hardly finished with his ambitions in Tuscany, however, as his military success forced Florence to recognize him as ruler of those places in the Papal States he had captured.

By the summer of 1414 Ladislaus was able to return to Naples. He had, however, become increasingly unwell, a condition that led to his death in August. He had no legitimate children, despite three marriages. Thus, he was succeeded as the last member of the Neapolitan Angevins of the senior line by Joanna II, his sister.

Illus. 15.5 Image of Joanna II of Naples (and her consort James of Bourbon), early fifteenth century. Chartres Cathedral, Vendome Chapel, France.

Joanna II (r. 1414–35) was forty-one when she became queen, and her character was defined mostly by lust and bad judgment. These two factors conspired to result not only in the extinction of the senior Angevin dynasty but also in a threat to the integrity of the Italian state system that would occasion the French invasion of 1494, the beginning of the catastrophe that eventually extinguished the Italian Renaissance.

Joanna had first been married to Duke William of Austria, although this union of five years' duration produced no children. Perhaps as consolation she took as her lover her Grand Chamberlain, Pandolfello Alopo, a manipulative and self-serving courtier. In 1415 she married again, this time to a French noble, James of Bourbon. James was to receive a courtesy title, but he would have no right to rule; however, when he arrived in Naples the honor was withheld, an insult the haughty James blamed on the machinations of Alopo, whom he consequently arranged to have murdered. The ambitious consort then demanded to be named king and even imprisoned Joanna so that she would not be able to interfere with his assumption of royal power and dignity.

This high-handed treatment of the regnant queen galvanized the court nobility who demanded Joanna be freed. It also occasioned a popular revolt by her subjects in the city against James, who was forced to abandon his title and use Neapolitans as officials and not the Frenchmen who had accompanied him to Italy. This humiliation of her husband provided an opportunity for Joanna to choose another lover, this time a noble of the powerful Caracciolo clan, another ambitious courtier who would become the real power in the realm and the cause of some of her most foolish decisions. Nevertheless, she was in a position to celebrate her coronation as queen in October of 1419.

Illus. 15.6 Nicholas Froment, *René of Anjou, King of Naples*, 1474. Louvre, Paris.

René of Anjou (1409–80) was unable to enter Naples immediately after the death of Joanna II in 1435, so his wife Isobel, duchess of Lorraine, ruled on his behalf. Finally, in 1438, René sailed to Naples to take up residence in his kingdom. However, his position in Naples was relatively weak because he was seen as just another foreign ruler with few close ties to the *Regno* beyond his nomination as king by Joanna. He was also quite poor, with few resources of his own, having had to mortgage his property to pay a ransom for his relief after being captured earlier in his life and held by the duke of Burgundy.

Added to these impediments was that fact that Alfonso of Aragon and Sicily had never accepted Joanna II's changing of her will in favor of the cadet branch of the House of Anjou. Her first will adopting Alfonso as her heir seemed the just and appropriate succession because it would have again united Sicily with Naples. Consequently, Alfonso began a war to seize the territory he believed was rightfully his. René of Anjou was forced to flee and never returned, although he always claimed the title of king of Naples. However, the reality was that after 1442 the Angevin dynasty of Naples was defunct, supplanted by the House of Aragon.

CHAPTER 16
THE RE-EMERGENCE OF RENAISSANCE CULTURE IN NAPLES

The dynastic and political chaos of the reigns following the age of King Robert the Wise left little if any opportunity for humanism to become established in Naples. Everything in the *Regno* had always depended on the court as the source of patronage and learning. Even the university flourished only to the degree that it was patronized by the king or queen currently in power.

The Florentine and other Italian merchants who established companies in Naples and lived among the Neapolitans occasionally brought with them ideas that had developed elsewhere, ideas informed by Italian humanist practice and knowledge. However, the ideas were usually person specific and dependent on the individuals who cultivated them. Except for those remarkable years of King Robert's reign, there was little institutionalization of humanism or northern Italian cultural practice before the mid-fifteenth century.

Even the abundance of classical ruins within Naples itself seems not to have functioned as a stimulus to humanism or even to have generated much curiosity. Greek was spoken in some isolated communities of the *Regno*, but there was little attempt to build on this tradition to access the ancient world of classical letters; and their Orthodox liturgy and traditions isolated these Greek speakers even more. Similarly, the vernacular spoken in the *Regno* was a language far removed from the literary Tuscan of Dante, Petrarch, and Boccaccio. Even the rarified language of the court was *napolitano misto*, a somewhat artificial dialect of Italian that did produce some literature but nothing that could easily migrate to other centers. Latin remained the language of learning, and it is perhaps for this reason that when humanism did emerge again in Naples, philology became a primary interest.

The situation changed with the arrival of Alfonso of Aragon (r. 1442–58) in Naples: his personal engagement in humanism, intellectual pursuits, and the patronage of scholars and artists were exemplary and appropriately celebrated in his title, "The Magnanimous." The foundations he laid permitted a Renaissance humanist culture to flourish, but again, one that was dependent on his person as the king and to a lesser extent his court.

The Ascension of Alfonso the Magnanimous

As was traditional in Neapolitan dynastic politics, Alfonso's assumption of the crown of Naples did not come easily.[1] His claim was based on the will of another unfortunate

---

1. The best study of Alfonso remains Alan Ryder, *Alfonso the Magnanimous: King of Aragon, Naples, and Sicily 1396–1458*. Oxford: Clarendon Press, 1990.

Queen Joanna, this one Joanna II (r. 1414–35).[2] Joanna II had made the mistake of refusing Pope Martin V when he asked for her support—both military and financial—as he struggled to re-establish the papacy in Rome. In angry retaliation, Martin declared that she was a vassal in revolt against her liege lord and summoned Louis III of Anjou for help.

Louis III had some prior claim to Naples through his own father. Consequently, he eagerly acceded to Martin's request and by 1420 had invaded Joanna's kingdom, his eyes on the crown. Belatedly recognizing the dangers of dividing the *Regno* through invasion, Martin V tried to mediate between Joanna and Louis. But Joanna, spurred on by her disreputable and meddling lover, Sergianni Caracciolo, refused any compromise. Instead, she offered the succession of the crown of Naples to King Alfonso of Aragon—who also happened to be ruler of the island of Sicily—in return for his driving out Louis and the French. In this he succeeded, entering Naples as a victor in the summer of 1421.[3]

Alfonso rightly expected to be welcomed as a hero by Joanna and Caracciolo. However, the pair refused either to cooperate with him or to let him exercise any authority, a right he felt he had won through force of arms. Believing Caracciolo to be behind Joanna's opposition and not willing to alienate the people of Naples who saw her as their legitimate queen, he ordered Caracciolo imprisoned and Joanna put under house arrest in the Castello Capuano. It was not long before they were able to negotiate their release, upon which Joanna and Caracciolo fled Naples together.

These two now hated Alfonso sufficiently that they met with their former enemy, Louis III of Anjou, and worked out a complete reversal of policy. Joanna abrogated her adoption of Alfonso as heir and in his place named Louis. Alfonso, for his part, refused to accept her change of mind and disregarded her decision. Confident in the rectitude of his position as future ruler of Naples, he went back to Aragon to tend to the affairs of his own kingdom, allowing Joanna and her lover to return to Naples in 1424.

Louis III of Anjou patiently awaited Joanna's death but, to his misfortune, he predeceased her in 1434. In order to maintain the Angevin succession, Joanna then named Louis's brother, René of Anjou, as her successor, a role he assumed on entering Naples in 1438. However, her first will adopting Alfonso as her heir was still seen as valid in Palermo. It was considered the just and appropriate succession because it would have again united Sicily with Naples. Needless to say, Alfonso himself was of the same opinion.

In 1441 Alfonso besieged Naples for six months, eventually capturing and sacking the royal capital, although he stopped the rape, looting, and violence after just four hours so as not to seem like a vicious conqueror. René was forced to flee and never returned. He claimed the title of king of Naples for the remainder of his days, but the reality was that the Angevin dynasty was finished. It had been replaced by the House of Aragon

---

2. Alan Ryder, "Giovanna II d'Angiò," in *Dizionario Biografico degli Italiani*. Vol. 55. Rome: Istituto della Enciclopedia Italiana, 2001.
3. Bentley, 1987. p. 9.

under King Alfonso who once more united Sicily and Naples. He would rule from 1442 to 1458 as Alfonso the Magnanimous, one of Naples's and Sicily's great kings and the patron and connoisseur of learning who came closest to adding Naples to the cultural geography of the Italian Renaissance.

Humanist Luminaries at Alfonso's Court

Even before he captured the crown of Naples, Alfonso had a reputation as a scholar, bringing with him from Aragon and Palermo a substantial library and the desire to converse with learned men.[4] After 1442 this library was held in Naples's ancient Castello Nuovo, an imposing Medieval fortress that had been first erected in 1279 and served as the seat of the Neapolitan crown. There is no doubt but that Alfonso, like the condottiere princes in the North, also saw patronage of scholarship and culture as a means of celebrating his rule and dynasty. Such patronage was compensation for the reality of having had to take his kingdom by force of arms, dislodging the last of the Angevins, notwithstanding Joanna II's second will.

Riputazione—one's good repute—was an important element in the noble complexion of a Renaissance prince, and Alfonso assiduously aspired to that status. Consequently, Alfonso extended invitations to a great many celebrated humanists, some of whom refused, like Leonardo Bruni, and others of whom accepted. He also repatriated southern scholars who had moved north, men such as Antonio Beccadelli (1394–1471) who had been born in Palermo, hence his academic nickname of "Panormita" (from the ancient Greek name for Palermo).[5]

Panormita was a fascinating member of the Italian humanist community. He studied law at Bologna and taught at Pavia in the 1430s. He became a court poet to the last Visconti duke of Milan, Filippo Maria, and was seen as such an ornament to letters that he was crowned laureate by the Holy Roman Emperor at Parma in Lombardy, thus achieving the same status as Petrarch. Panormita was repatriated to his native Palermo by Alfonso as king of Sicily and was given the responsibility of overseeing the royal library. Further elevated to the senior administration of the court, he also served as a diplomat.

Following Alfonso to Naples, Panormita wrote a book in praise of his patron, adding to his master's reputation, as was his duty. His *De Dictis et factis Alfonsi* (*The Words and Deeds of Alfonso*) was an anthology of anecdotes and a collection of his patron's sayings, observations, and actions.[6] It put Alfonso in the same category as the ancients and that fundamental text read by humanist educators, Valerius Maximus's *Facta et dicta memorabilia* (ca. 30 BC, *Memorable Deeds and Words*). Alfonso clearly appreciated both

---

4. Vespasiano da Bisticci respectfully and affectionately describes Alfonso in the lives he wrote of his famous clients of his stationer's busines; da Bisticci, 1963. pp. 59–83.
5. For Beccadelli's career and writings, see Bentley, 1987. pp. 84–100, 135–37, 160–68 et passim.
6. Bentley, 1987. pp. 224–27.

the flattering connection of his reign to the examples of the ancients and the work's considerable popularity because he gave Panormita a significant bonus on top of his already comfortable salary. Alfonso knew good press when he saw it!

A notable characteristic of Alfonso's court was the evening literary discussions, readings of plays, and learned conversations that followed dinner. These informal dialogues seem after about 1447 to have been shaped by Panormita into a kind of humanist academy. Members of the court with literary interests or pretensions or those who aspired to capture the attention of the king participated in these meetings presided over by the celebrated Sicilian. As a result, he became more than just a court poet, counsellor, and ornament: he was the literary arbiter of the court and one whose opinion and recognition mattered. Thereby, the kind of competition which we have seen as so important to the development of the Renaissance north of the *Regno* was transported in a highly concentrated form to Naples, building a context for cultural excellence.

One of the most prominent humanists from the North to enter Alfonso's orbit was Lorenzo Valla (1407–57). Lorenzo's was a prickly personality.[7] He was a Roman and belonged to that small group of highly verbal, educated families that served the Holy See in many secular capacities, including as secretaries, lawyers, and notaries. He was a stupendously able scholar, having studied with Leonardo Bruni in Florence before assuming a position as professor of law at Pavia at a very young age. On the other hand, his singular capacity for making enemies saw him driven from that position quickly, as his students ran him out of town for exposing the mistakes, misreadings, and stylistic inelegance of their most esteemed professor, the fourteenth-century lawyer Bartolus of Sassoferrato, one of the stars of the Pavian legal galaxy. Would that students were always so devoted to their teachers!

Having met Panormita in 1428, Valla accepted an invitation to Naples, where he established his astounding reputation as a philologist; stylist; humanist author; and edgy publicist for his master, Alfonso.[8] Some of the most influential works of the Italian Renaissance outside of Florence were consequently produced in Naples by Valla: *On Free Will, On the Profession of the Religious*; and his *Annotations on the New Testament*[9] (in effect a new translation of parts of the Vulgate) supported a revolutionary approach to God and man's place in the universe. His *De Voluptate* (*On Pleasure*) became a popular book to both quote and refute. As for his philological works, his *Elegance of the Latin Language* (*Elegantiae linguae latinae*) became one of the most popular books ever written on Latin style, based on golden-age authors and full of close readings to help others polish their Latin prose.

---

7. Girolamo Mancini, *Vita Di Lorenzo Valla*. Florence: Sansoni, 1891. It is now available in a modern reprint through Forgotten Books, 2018.
8. For Valla, see Bentley, 1987. pp. 108–22 et passim.
9. Bentley, 1987. pp. 237–38, 294–95.

However, the most revolutionary of Valla's texts was the cataclysmic *On the False Donation of Constantine*.[10] The document on which his text was based purportedly recorded the Emperor Constantine transferring control over the western part of the Roman Empire to the papacy in the fourth century. Using philological and historical tools, Valla proved that the celebrated donation was an eighth-century forgery and, consequently, that papal claims to be emperor as well as pope were bogus. Valla's text was purposely composed to destroy the papacy's claim to feudal suzerainty over Naples and written to support Alfonso's struggles with the pope. In recognition of both his talent and his useful service, Alfonso appointed Valla royal secretary. The humanist remained close to Alfonso, although his difficult personality caused some tensions at court.

The difficulty was that nothing escaped Valla's search for philological truth, not even fundamental texts of religion such as the Apostles' Creed. When he proved definitively that the Creed had been written centuries after the Apostles had lived, he was summoned by the tribunal of the Inquisition for heretical thinking. The inquisitors were incensed by what they perceived as his vanity in his uncompromising scholarship. It didn't help Valla's case that he had also demonstrated that other traditional religious texts were equally suspect in their sources or were outright fakes.

It took the personal intervention of Alfonso to extricate Valla from this process, but he was nevertheless forced to retract his claims. That hardly stopped him from continuing to attack his colleagues and friends, including Panormita. In 1444 Valla was invited to Rome but was compelled to run from the city by the anger of his enemies and those who believed him to be a heretic. Only by getting as far away as Barcelona could he feel safe. Once there, he recognized that his best option was to return to Naples and Alfonso's protection.

There was, then, a narcissistic quality to Valla and a sense of absolute certainty in his ideas and readings. Any doubt or question raised about his work provoked a vicious response, and so it was that his genius was truly compromised by his vanity. The inquisitors were not altogether mistaken. Yet despite his provocative attacks on traditional sacred texts, Valla eventually returned to his native Rome to assume a position under the humanist pope Nicholas V, becoming, somewhat ironically, an apostolic secretary in the curia. Like Alfonso, Nicholas was willing to overlook Valla's personal faults and see only his brilliance.

One scholar who was a particular target of Valla's verbal barbs was Bartolomeo Facio (ca. 1410–57)—often known by his Latinized name of Bartholomaus Facius. He is most remembered today for his bitter quarrels with Valla—it is unfortunate that Facio was on the receiving end of the invectives of one of Renaissance Italy's most able masters of insults.

---

10. Lorenzo Valla, *The Profession of the Religious and Selections from The Falsely-Believed and Forged Donation of Constantine*, tr. and ed., Olga Zorzi Pugliese. Toronto: CRRS, 1998.

Originally from Genoa, Facio reached Naples as a result of the friendship he had established with Panormita. Facio had studied Greek in Florence but worked as an educator and diplomat in Genoa, Lucca, and Venice, where he was tutor to the son of Doge Francesco Foscari.[11] Facio met Panormita in Venice and rekindled their friendship when he undertook a diplomatic mission to Naples in 1444. Invited to stay, Facio became an intimate of the court and a favorite of Alfonso, producing among a great many works and translations the flattering opus *De Rebus gestis ab Alphonso primo neapolitanorum rege* (*The Deeds Accomplished by Alfonso I, King of Naples*).[12] This served both to praise the king and establish a lucrative position at court where Facio was named official court historian in 1446.[13]

Another great humanist, Giannozzo Manetti (1396–1459), joined the galaxy of Alfonso's court at about this time. One usually associates Manetti with Florentine humanism. He was, after all, a Florentine from a good patrician family and held significant offices under the republic. He matriculated in the Cambio (the Guild of the Bankers and Moneychangers) and looked forward to a rewarding and civilized life as a scholar and merchant in his native city.[14]

In 1443, Manetti was sent on a diplomatic mission to Naples where his learning and personality drew him into the orbit of King Alfonso. The four visits he made to Naples and his growing familiarity with the king led to rumors of his betraying the interests of Florence to the Neapolitans. Although these charges were unfounded, a faction of his enemies worked with Cosimo de'Medici to have Manetti indicted for treason. The humanist fled first to Rome, where he secured a position in the papal chancery, and then moved onward to Naples.

Alfonso served as a generous patron from the outset, giving Manetti a rich sinecure whose only responsibilities consisted of writing and translating. Manetti produced Latin versions of Aristotle and even worked on a new translation of the Bible; this was, after all, the circle of Lorenzo Valla and his *Annotationes*, or *Annotations on the New Testament*. Manetti's most famous work, *On the Dignity and Excellence of Man*, resulted from long evening discussions with Alfonso and other learned members of the court. It is, then, significant that a work so associated with the Florentine humanist perspective should have been written in Alfonso's Naples.

---

11. For Valla, see Celenza, 2018. pp. 157–227; Thomas Izbicki, "Lorenzo Valla: The Scholarship in English through 1992," in J. W. O'Malley, Thomas M. Izbicki, and Gerald Christianson, eds., *Humanity and Divinity in Renaissance and Reformation: Essays in Honor of Charles Trinkaus.* Leiden: Brill, 1993. pp. 287–301; Maristella de Panizza Lorch, "Lorenzo Valla," in Rabil, 1988. pp. 332–49; Bentley, 1987. pp. 100–8 et passim; Trinkaus, 1970. pp. 103–70.

12. Trinkaus, 1970. pp. 104–5, 228–32.

13. Facio wrote more than encomia of Alfonso, however. See Trinkaus, 1970. pp. 200–29, "Bartolommeo Facio and Fra Antonio da Bargo on Human Misery."

14. Vespasiano wrote Manetti's biography: see da Bisticci, 1963. pp. 372–95; Bentley, 1987. pp. 122–27.

Despite Manetti's horror at Alfonso's actions in war—an attitude that is reminiscent of Petrarch's at the court of Robert the Wise—the Florentine developed a deep and legitimate respect for the king. He recognized his talents and even acknowledged the fame that his military activities had brought him. Consequently, near the end of his life, Manetti began a flattering work based on Plutarch that extolled the parallel lives of Alexander the Great and Alfonso the Magnanimous. Sadly, Manetti developed a serious illness and died before he could complete this encomium.

Ferdinando I (Ferrante of Naples)

Alfonso was succeeded by his natural son, Ferdinando I (r. 1458–94), usually called Ferrante. As he was illegitimate, his position was initially insecure, but he was eventually recognized as king by Pope Pius II Piccolomini. But it was not his problematic birth that defined Ferrante's reign.

Cruel, rapacious, and unsavory, he was challenged on several occasions by very serious baronial revolts; an invasion by Jean of Anjou, son of King René, to regain his father's kingdom; and by incursions of the Ottomans, including the Turkish capture and occupation of Otranto. Ferrante waged war against Lorenzo de'Medici in the War of the Pazzi Conspiracy and he murdered many of his own nobles, despite his having guaranteed them pardon. His cruelty was universally feared, and best illustrated by his having the corpses of many of his enemies preserved, dressed in their own clothes, and seated around a macabre dining table, an installation Ferrante delighted in displaying to visitors.[15]

Ferrante did, however, maintain the traditions of that other dinner table—that of his father with its learned discussions after supper. Panormita continued to lead this informal academy until he died in 1471. His role was then taken by his friend and protégé Giovanni Pontano (1429–1503).[16] Pontano had been born in Umbria, where he received his humanist training, but arrived penniless in Naples in his early twenties in search of patronage after having first met Alfonso in Tuscany. His talents had soon caught the attention of Panormita, who used his influence to secure Pontano a position in the royal chancery.

Not lacking in confidence, Pontano soon gave his name to what had been Panormita's humanist club, rebranding it the *Accademia Pontaniana*.[17] It became a more structured society of learned men and attracted even young, fashionable nobles who sought both a social entrée into the royal circle and a veneer of educated polish. He also became a leading member of the royal household and tutor to Alfonso's nephew.

---

15. Burckhardt, 1958. pp. 52–53.
16. Bentley, 1987. pp. 127–37, 176–94.
17. Bentley, 1987. pp. 93–95.

Pontano's exceptional abilities in many areas resulted in important diplomatic as well as educational appointments. He counselled his king during his wars and wrote important political treatises praising monarchy and the need for obedience.[18] This royalist ideology distanced him from the Florentine humanist tradition, but it also embedded him more deeply into the royal family's trust.

Pontano is remembered today mostly for his Neo-Latin poetry; his political writings praising monarchical rule; and his translations, including a Latin version of Ptolemy's *Tetrabiblos*. He was an indefatigable scholar and a talented royal servant. Like Panormita, Pontano benefitted greatly from royal generosity. He was granted estates, a patent of nobility, and rich monetary rewards. His elegant house in Naples was the center of humanist activity and the *Accademia* usually met there. And, in what is probably the greatest tribute to his career, the *Accademia Pontaniana* continued after his death in 1503 without a change in name.

Ferrante would never be the accomplished patron his father had been, despite the survival of the *Accademia Pontaniana* and Ferrante's support of Pontano. The young king anticipated the cataclysmic events in Italy attendant upon the French invasion of 1494, but Ferrante had the good fortune to die in that year, leaving the crown to his son, King Alfonso II. So, it was Alfonso II who abandoned Naples when Charles VIII and the French entered the city in triumph in 1495. It was reported that Pontano delivered the formal welcome to Charles. If this was indeed true, it was a craven act of betrayal on the part of an elderly scholar desperate to keep his job under a new regime. Regardless, Pontano did retire from public life after 1495 and devoted his last years to writing, composing a great many new dialogues, philosophical and ethical treatises, and revisions of some older work.

Neapolitan Humanism

What is most unusual and compelling about the humanists at the Aragonese courts of Alfonso and his son Ferrante is their mixture of theory and practice. All of them, with the exception of Manetti, held positions in the chancery, the court, or the royal diplomatic service. They were more like Leonardo Bruni, that humanist chancellor of the Florentine republic, than not. They were given rich rewards, as Alfonso in particular was extremely generous with his scholars at court. And they reciprocated by writing in favor of monarchy, obedience, and duty, sometimes openly flattering the king, but sometimes showing him the moral and ethical path for his reign.

Although the titles of some of their works may seem to modern readers somewhat sycophantic, being dependent on the king's largesse did not turn these talented men into mere courtiers: they maintained a good degree of integrity. Alfonso was said to have

---

18. Cappelli, 1993.

enjoyed setting his scholars against one another during those after-dinner discussions in which he reveled. He believed that through debate—even the heated arguments and invective for which Valla was known—clarity of speech and mind would result.

It is obvious, then, that the court of Naples in the second half of the fifteenth century developed a unique form of civic humanism, different from that of Bruni, but valid nevertheless as an alternate model of humanist engagement with the state and with power. Unlike Florence, Naples remained a Latin culture. The vernacular *napolitano misto* never acquired the literary caché of Tuscan, in part because Naples did not produce a Petrarch or Boccaccio, despite those luminaries having been resident in the city. In this Naples was more like papal Rome or even ducal Milan.

The chaotic years after the death of Alfonso's son, Ferrante of Naples, in 1494, and the intervention of Charles VIII of France in that year, followed by the rapid succession of three Aragonese kings between 1494 and 1501, meant that maintaining any kind of court patronage was impossible. The duel between the French and the Spanish over Naples resulted in the *Regno* becoming almost a colonial appendage of the Spanish crown, thus ensuring that the brilliant court of Alfonso could never be recovered.

Naples fell into an intellectual lethargy from which it did not emerge for centuries. The Spanish viceroys brought with them not only their own culture and language but also the Spanish Inquisition and the enforcement of the expulsion of Jews and Muslims, as Naples had now to accede to Spanish law. The most telling and tragic manifestation of this was the suppression of the *Accademia Pontaniana* in 1542 on suspicion of spreading heretical ideas.[19]

Humanism in Naples, then, was a series of brief eruptions, completely dependent on the personal interests and aspirations of certain kings like Robert the Wise and Alfonso the Magnanimous. Still, those reigns and that of Alfonso's son Ferrante defined a unique moment of monarchical political thought and brilliant philological scholarship that enriched the entire experience of the Renaissance in Italy.

---

19. Bentley, 1987. pp. 284–87.

Illus. 16.1 Juan de Juanes, *Alfonso of Aragon, The Magnanimous*, 1557. Zaragoza Museum, Zaragoza.

This portrait of Alfonso in armor symbolizes his role as a soldier and king. The conquest of the kingdom of Naples in 1442 made Alfonso one of the most powerful rulers in all of Europe, as he had dominion over Aragon and Catalonia in Spain, together with Naples, Sicily, and Sardinia in Italy. He was a gifted military commander—and innovator, especially in the early use of siege artillery.

The Dalmatian sculptor and builder Luciano Laurana—who was also responsible for the castle of Federigo da Montefeltro in Urbino—designed this triumphal arch as a monumental entrance to the Castel Nuovo, the fortress palace of the kings of Naples. This huge marble gate, inserted between Medieval cylindrical towers, consists of not one but two superimposed triumphal arches and took fifteen years to construct. The scene in the detail commemorates Alfonso of Aragon's entry to Naples, Italy, on January 26, 1443. It is clearly based on friezes of ancient Roman triumphal arches, columns, and altars. Alfonso's arch is the first example of the revival of the Roman triumphal arch in Renaissance Europe. Through these references Alfonso is not only celebrating his conquest of Naples but also linking his patronage and rule to ancient Roman emperors in a classically humanist manner.

Illus. 16.2a Triumphal Arch. Castel Nuovo, Naples.

Illus. 16.2b Detail, Triumphal Arch. Castel Nuovo, Naples.

PART V

———

Rome in the Renaissance

When the papacy abandoned Rome in the fourteenth century, the pope was fleeing a city in desperate decline. Instead of lawlessness and poverty and ruin, he found in Avignon a peaceful and orderly domain where it was possible to live a life of luxurious indulgence. Yet Rome had always been an idea as much as a place. So, despite its melancholy ruins it was still seen as the heart of a great empire as well as the true center of a universal, or catholic, Church to which all those faithful Christians in the West belonged. Rome was still the *caput mundi*, the head of the world, at least metaphorically.[1]

When Petrarch came to Avignon as a young man, he was appalled by what he saw as the moral depravity of the papal court and the undue influence of the French crown on the pope.[2] In his collection of letters published as *Liber Sine Nomine* (*Book*

---

1. Following his coronation as poet laureate in Rome in April of 1341, Petrarch crystallized both the wonder and melancholy of the ruins of the ancient city, having toured the ancient sites with Fra Giovanni Colonna. Surveying the largely abandoned Imperial city from the Baths of Diocletian, he recorded his emotions and observations in his *Epistolae Familiares*, VI, 2. See E. H. Wilkins, "On Petrarch's Ep. VI, 2" in *Speculum*, 38 (1963), pp. 620–22.

2. Petrarch's letter on the Avignonese Papacy merits quotation at length:

Now I am living in France, in the Babylon of the West. The sun in its travels sees nothing more hideous than this place on the shores of the wild Rhone, which suggests the hellish streams of Cocytus and Acheron. Here reign the successors of the poor fishermen of Galilee; they have strangely forgotten their origin. I am astounded, as I recall their predecessors, to see these men loaded with gold and clad in purple, boasting of the spoils of princes and nations; to see luxurious palaces and heights crowned with fortifications, instead of a boat turned downward for shelter.

We no longer find the simple nets which were once used to gain a frugal sustenance from the lake of Galilee, and with which, having labored all night and caught nothing, they took, at daybreak, a multitude of fishes, in the name of Jesus. One is stupefied nowadays to hear the lying tongues, and to see worthless parchments turned by a leaden seal into nets which are used, in Christ's name, but by the arts of Belial, to catch hordes of unwary Christians. These fish, too, are dressed and laid on the burning coals of anxiety before they fill the insatiable maw of their captors.

Without a Name), he likened the Avignon residency to the Babylonian Captivity—that period six centuries before Christ when Jews were captive to Nebuchadnezzar, the king of Babylon.[3] This association of the exile of the papacy to Avignon with the slavery of the Israelites struck a chord. Petrarch's invocation of the Babylonian Captivity acknowledged a crisis of biblical proportions for those Christians sincerely worried about their souls, and for those princes concerned with their inheritance.

Rome has always reflected the ambitions of its rulers, and this observation is never truer than in the 170 years following the return of Martin V to Rome in 1420. Much has always depended on the personalities and interests of individual popes; but much also depended on the larger political, religious, and economic factors that influenced their policies. Humanism was brought from elsewhere in Italy not only by popes but also by the cultivated and learned curialists and clerics who populated their courts and administrations.

Some successors to Peter were themselves celebrated humanists, such as Nicholas V, Pius II, and Leo X. On the other hand, others, like Paul II and Paul IV, had no interest whatsoever in the humanist tradition. Nevertheless, humanism, especially the use of elegant Latin style and knowledge of Greek, became institutionalized in Rome simply because it had become the expected means of discourse and educated frame of reference throughout the peninsula. The Roman Curia was also a good place for men with scholarly ambitions to find employment. The tradition, then, that Petrarch established in Avignon continued throughout the Renaissance in Rome.

Instead of holy solitude we find a criminal host and crowds of the most infamous satellites; instead of soberness, licentious banquets; instead of pious pilgrimages, preternatural and foul sloth; instead of the bare feet of the apostles, the snowy coursers of brigands fly past us, the horses decked in gold and fed on gold, soon to be shod with gold, if the Lord does not check this slavish luxury. In short, we seem to be among the kings of the Persians or Parthians, before whom we must fall down and worship, and who cannot be approached except presents be offered. O ye unkempt and emaciated old men, is it for this you labored? Is it for this that you have sown the field of the Lord and watered it with your holy blood? But let us leave the subject. I have been so depressed and overcome that the heaviness of my soul has passed into bodily affliction, so that I am really ill and can only give voice to sighs and groans.

Quoted in James Harvey Robinson, ed., *Readings in European History*. Boston: Ginn and Company, 1904. p. 502.

3. Petrarch, 1973. pp. 62, 67. "Babylon [Avignon], foulest of cities . . . the opposite of the mistress of virtues [Rome] . . . the enemy of the good, the dwelling place and refuge of evil, seated on the savage banks of the Rhone, famous—or rather infamous—whore with whom kings of the earth have committed fornication."

CHAPTER 17

THE REDEMPTION OF ROME

The story of Rome during the Renaissance begins with disorder and decline but then changes to celebration and expansion. The Rome of the Middle Ages might well have been the See of the Vicar of Christ, the successor to St. Peter and the center of the religious world, but it was also an often impenetrable city of dark, narrow alleys, aristocratic violence, family feuds, and urban insecurity.[4] It was an ecclesiastical administrative center, attracting powerful and wealthy clerics to serve the court of the pope or represent their secular monarchs or interests.

A Lopsided Economy

Rome was a city of consumption: it produced virtually nothing. There was a small textile and tanning trade, and the local feudatories used it as a market town for their grain and cattle. Luxury objects were crafted to adorn prelates and nobles, as well as provide the altar furniture for its many churches; but this was a limited economy in a city with a huge service class, providing for the daily comfort of the rich and powerful.[5]

The real economy of the city, at least in terms of cash flow, came from the payment of taxes from across Christendom to the Church, including the often substantial fees required to secure benefices, annulments, or other decisions in the papal courts. Added to this was the money left by pilgrims who came in the tens of thousands (and more than a hundred thousand in Jubilee years) to the shrines of the two apostolic martyrs, Peter and Paul, the patriarchal basilicas and other holy places. They also spent money on accommodation and food, depending on their class and wealth, and they often made special provisions for masses or other rites as a surety for a hopeful return home or some other immediate concern.[6]

There was also significant wealth available to the pope, not as bishop of Rome but as the secular ruler of a large Italian principality in the center of Italy. Harsh taxes on the agricultural lands and towns outside the walls of Rome provided a substantial income, and one which was elastic, as those taxes could be raised. The effect of this was often a seething hatred of the city by the rest of the Papal States. This anger would be felt in tax wars, peasant disturbances, and adherence to powerful rural noble clans who often had

---

4. See Richard Krautheimer, *Rome, Profile of a City, 312–1308*. Princeton: Princeton University Press, 1980.
5. Charles Stinger, *The Renaissance in Rome*. Bloomington: Indiana University Press, 1998. pp. 14–31.
6. Stinger, 1998. pp. 31–59.

disputes with the papacy, leading to further urban instability and dangerous patches of road leading into the city.

By the very early sixteenth century, the pope realized that a great deal of ready cash could be squeezed through the selling of offices and high ecclesiastical positions, even cardinals' hats. Although simony—the selling of Church offices, a practice strictly forbidden in canon law and in doctrine—caused many to demure or even complain about the practice, it was simply too lucrative to stop. Indeed, more and more sinecures in the papal court and elsewhere in the Church were created just to reap the income available from their sale. To be sure, there were a great many inappropriate men advanced by this method; but it can also be argued that it permitted ambitious laymen willing to invest in an office to enter the Church's service through the only means open to them.[7]

A Distorted Population

Rome was a city of foreigners, with only a small percentage of the population actually born there. The various communities of foreign-born inhabitants organized themselves into groups for protection, mutual support, and employment. In time, these structures would add to the rich tapestry of Roman life through the institution of national confraternities and churches which served both those already in residence and the newcomers who arrived in significant numbers. These organizations provided everything from hiring halls to funeral rites, from dowries to accommodation. As a result, Rome was divided into districts reflecting the origin, occupations, and needs of the many foreigners. The Lombards tended to be builders and masons, the Germans bakers, the Florentines bankers, the Genoese boatmen, and the English sellers of rosaries.

It was also a city of men. Many of the new arrivals came as pilgrims, traveling long distances from everywhere in Europe, seldom coming as families, as the roads were too difficult and dangerous for women and children. Once they reached Rome, they found support in their national communities and stayed, finding life in the city more rewarding than in their rural villages or crowded towns elsewhere in Italy or across the Alps. Similarly, as the city was the headquarters of the Catholic Church, the many clerics who sought advancement or service in the Curia, the pope's court, or the administration of the Church were adult males. In theory and by law they were celibate, but in reality they were often susceptible to the weaknesses of the flesh.

As a consequence of this curious demography, a huge and complex service industry developed, providing servants to ensure that a comfortable life could be lived, often in the language and culture of the employer's native land. Prostitution flourished, with women coming into the city to work this trade at every social level. There were the grand courtesans who numbered cardinals, bishops, or nobles among their clients, and street

---

7. Peter Partner, *Renaissance Rome 1500–1559: A Portrait of a Society.* Berkeley and Los Angeles: University of California Press, 1979. pp. 47–74, 113–32; Stinger, 1998. pp. 126–27.

prostitutes who picked up whatever trade came their way. Once these women reached an age when their market value declined, they could be transformed into laundresses, because men did not do laundry.

It became something of a commonplace to consider washerwomen ex-prostitutes, even if their early lives admitted to no such work. And, because Spanish prostitutes had a particular cachet, especially under the Borgia popes but not exclusively, many ambitious women of the night adopted Spanish-sounding names, such as La Spagnola or Spagnoletta, making any determination of their national origin or subsequent profession impossible. Courtesans occasionally assumed names from classical antiquity or names with aristocratic connotation, trying to move up-market among the educated curialists or gentlemen of the city. Regardless of their names or hopes, this large group of women constituted a significant proportion of the secular female population of the city.[8]

The Urban Landscape

Rome was a unique urban environment. The ancient city at the height of the empire had a population of more than one million, protected by the immense circuit of walls constructed by the emperor Aurelian in the third century. But by the 1420s the population had fallen to about twenty thousand living in the large bend in the Tiber River opposite the basilica of St. Peter, an area known as the inhabited part of the city, the *Abitata*. This was an area rich in Roman ruins and even some still-functioning structures, such as the Pantheon. It was crowded, with winding footpaths leading to churches and around the vestiges of the Imperial city.[9] Servicing the city was consequently difficult, inhibiting a more complex economy; and the entire densely populated area was subject to recurring visitations of pandemics and flooding of the Tiber.

There was no fresh water available, as the barbarians had broken the Roman aqueducts by the sixth century. Although the rich could purchase clean water from water sellers who carried it in from the springs that surrounded the city or from private wells, most of the population relied on the Tiber for drinking water and transportation. The result was cholera, dysentery, and high prices for food. In the summer the marshes around Rome gave rise to malaria, which would remain a problem until the twentieth century. Moreover, the regular influx of pilgrims carried disease as well as wealth into the city. The consequence was an insalubrious, indeed dangerous, place to live. The death rate was always far greater than the birthrate because of disease and the skewed demography of the population. Without the regular infusion of newcomers, Rome would have not been able to sustain anything like urban life.

---

8. Stinger, 1998. pp. 75–112.
9. For a description of ruins, churches, and the city as it appeared about 1140, as well as the Medieval legends attached to them, see Eileen Gardiner and Francis Morgan Nichols, eds and tr, *The Marvels of Rome: Mirabilia Urbis Romae*. New York: Italica Press, 2008.

In 1300 Pope Boniface VIII proclaimed the first Jubilee. It offered a plenary indulgence to all pilgrims who visited the patriarchal basilicas and the tombs of Peter and Paul and who felt sincerely contrite for their sins. Initially, there was to be a Jubilee only every fifty years but the consequent generation of enormous amounts of cash and the popularity of the event soon resulted in a Jubilee celebrated every twenty-five years, with extraordinary Jubilees available for particular moments, whether theological or economic.[10]

What the Jubilees did reveal, however, was the lack of sufficient infrastructure in the city, with no roads providing easy access to the required holy sites and with only a single bridge over the Tiber leading to St. Peter's. This was the ancient Pons Aelius, built by Hadrian to connect his tomb to the city. Later (410 AD) this huge sepulcher became part of the defense network of the city. Then in 590 it became known as Castel Sant'Angelo, named for the angel sheathing his sword that appeared to a papal procession led by Pope Gregory I in hopes of ending a terrible plague. The bridge then also became the Ponte Sant'Angelo. Since all of the routes through the *Abitata* toward St. Peter's required pilgrims to converge on this one crossing, there were several disasters in which crowding resulted in pilgrims being trampled or drowned. Investment in infrastructure was desperately required, but little was done: the building, decoration, or expansion of churches seemed always to take precedence.[11]

Private investment in Rome was also limited because of the clerical nature of civic authority; although the city was in theory a free commune, it fell largely under papal or at least ecclesiastical influence. Canon law stated that any cleric with real property in Rome could not pass it on to his heirs: instead it was to revert to the Church and for obvious reasons. It was widely known and accepted that clerics used Church funds for palaces, villas, and estates as it was considered a reasonable claim that a high cleric could make upon the Church. However, the property was for the use of that one prelate and hence for his lifetime only. An unintended consequence for Rome of this practice was that even the highest princes of the Church—cardinals and very senior members of the Curia—did not invest in building. They rented palaces and other properties but did not spend significant amounts to improve them. Thus, the appearance of Rome was shabby compared to that of other Italian cities, with little private interest in improving the urban landscape. Certainly, there were wonderful churches, but the routes to them were strewn with rubble and lined with buildings that were badly constructed and unimposing.

Similarly, the secular nobility was not inclined to indulge in artistic or architectural patronage: their concern was defense. During the Middle Ages, the great feudal clans, such as the Colonna, Orsini, Savelli, Frangipani, and Caetani, divided the city

---

10. Arsenio Frugoni, *Il Giubileo di Bonifacio VIII*, ed. Amedeo De Vincentiis. Rome and Bari: Editori Laterza, 1999.

11. James S. Ackerman, "The Planning of Renaissance Rome," in P. A. Ramsey, ed. *Rome in the Renaissance: The City and the Myth*. Binghamton, NY: Medieval and Renaissance Texts and Studies, 1982. pp. 4–10.

into spheres of influence, dominated by tall defensive towers, some of which survive at least vestigially, like the Torre dei Conti, Torre delle Milizie, Torre Millina, and Torre Sanguigna. These symbols of noble power and privilege reflected the reality that the civic government of Rome was often inconsequential during much of the Middle Ages and even into the Renaissance. Indeed, the attempt by powerful popes, such as Julius II at the beginning of the sixteenth century, to control the great Roman feudatories constitutes a history of the city and the countryside around it in itself.

However, during most of the fourteenth century any kind of consistent and effective control of the Roman factions was abandoned because of the power vacuum that resulted from the residence of the papacy in Avignon, followed by a lengthy period of schism in which there were two and eventually three competing successors to the chair of St. Peter.

The Babylonian Captivity

The origins of the removal of the papacy from Rome are in the struggle between the secular and clerical claims of universal dominion; that is, the Guelf–Ghibelline division that we have seen often driving Italian policy during the Middle Ages and even later. In 1302 Pope Boniface VIII issued a polarizing bull, *Unam Sanctam*, declaring that all Christians—and by extension all humanity—fell under the jurisdiction of the papacy.

There had been tensions already with the French crown, which was intent on building a centralized dynastic monarchy with control over all persons and jurisdictions within the kingdom, not just the fractious provincial feudatories but also the Church. King Philip IV the Fair of France objected to the papal claims of *Unam Sanctam*. In retaliation, Boniface excommunicated both the king and the nation, placing France under an interdict and threatening to declare Philip deposed and French clergy no longer in communion with Rome. In 1303 a small army led by anti-papal Roman nobles and the French agent Guillaume de Nogaret invaded the fortified papal palace at Agnani and abused the person of the pope. Sciarra Colonna actually slapped the aged pope, a blow, it is said, that caused him such humiliation that he died soon after.

The conclave that followed elected a pope who tried to solve the crisis with France but who died only months after he had assumed the throne of St. Peter. The election that followed proved to be rancorous and hopelessly divided, lasting almost a year. But ultimately in 1305 the archbishop of Bordeaux, Bertrand de Got, a Frenchman, was elected as Clement V.[12]

Clement was a councilor of King Philip and sympathized with his position. He also was a foreigner and saw that the papacy had become mired in the Roman urban political

---

12. For the papacy in Avignon, see Guillaume Mollat, *The Popes at Avignon, 1305–1378*, tr. Janet Love. London: Thomas Nelson, 1963; Edwin Mullins, *The Popes of Avignon: A Century in Exile*. New York: BlueBridge Books, 2011.

instability that characterized the city, with a weak secular government but powerful noble clans who controlled their neighborhoods through violence and intimidation. This indeed had been part of the tragedy of Pope Boniface: he came from one of those clans, the Caetani, and was thus seen as an enemy by other noble factions, such as the Colonna, the family that struck the pope that infamous blow at Agnani.

Consequently, Clement was in no mood to move to Rome. The city was riven by instability and factional urban warfare and was slipping increasingly into chaos. He was not, as was commonly believed, a creature of the French king; but he equally did not want to be the prisoner of warring Roman noble clans. As a result, he first established his court in Poitiers and then in 1309 moved to Avignon, in the papal enclave of the Comtat Venaissin, which had been subject to the papacy since the 1270s. The Holy See was to remain there until 1377; and during the Great Western Schism, the Comtat Venaissin became again one of the seats of the divided papacy until 1417.

The popes at Avignon were committed centralizers and used the new statecraft of secular rulers, such as the kings of France, to build relatively efficient and effective central offices of the Church. The effect of these policies on the city of Rome was disastrous. With the single greatest generator of income now gone, the economy and population of the city contracted. The huge service industry no longer had great clerics to serve; the luxury trade of goldsmiths and robe makers moved elsewhere; and the constant flow of cash to rebuild or redecorate churches and palaces was reduced. Many churches deteriorated, to the point that even the pope's residence, the Lateran Palace attached to the cathedral of St. John Lateran, began to decay.

And, with the only force able to restrain them gone, the noble clans of Rome became even more lawless and violent, making economic activity of any kind difficult and even life itself precarious. Pilgrims did continue to come, although in smaller numbers, and many of them stayed, as they had always done. But, the possibilities of employment and community had declined to the point that Rome was hardly what it had been before 1305. Its population fell to as low as fifteen or twenty thousand inhabitants, with serious unemployment and uncertain income. In such an environment, the great noble families could easily recruit thugs and so were not as reliant on bringing peasants into the city from their rural estates to fashion their private armies.

Cola di Rienzo

It was in this environment that Cola di Rienzo emerged. This remarkable man has been the subject of works by Byron and Wagner, an icon of the Risorgimento, and a hero to a great many generations of young Italians. But, in some ways the story is even more incredible than the imagination could create.[13]

---

13. There is a contemporary biography of Cola: John Wright, tr. *The Life of Cola Di Rienzo*. Toronto: Pontifical Institute of Mediaeval Studies, 1975; see also Ronald G. Musto, *Apocalypse in Rome: Cola di Rienzo and the Politics of the New Age*. Berkeley and Los Angeles: University of California Press, 2002.

Cola (an abbreviation for Nicola, or Niccolò) was born about 1313 to a washer-woman and a poor tavern owner: his later claims to have been the natural son of the Holy Roman Emperor were pure narcissistic fantasy. Despite his humble origins, he was given a good education in the classics and trained as a notary. As such, he was sent on an administrative mission from Rome to the pope in Avignon in 1343. There he delivered such a brilliant Latin oration, full of classical allusions and stirred by his hatred of the noble clans of the city, that the pope employed him as one of his representatives. The Church shared the young Roman's contempt for the brawling nobles, although Cola's anger was more immediate, as his brother had been murdered during a skirmish between the Colonna and the Orsini. At that moment he had sworn revenge.

Returning to Rome, Cola laid plans to restore the grandeur of the Roman Empire and make Rome again the *caput mundi*, or head of the world. He acquired a large follow-ing, including the papal vicar of Rome, who saw the young man's ambition to free the city from aristocratic violence as useful to the Church. So, in May of 1347 Cola and the papal vicar summoned the people of Rome to the ancient Capitoline Hill and declared a set of laws to restore order and control the nobles. The huge crowd gave him the author-ity to act, seconded by the papal vicar, so Cola was proclaimed the tribune of peace, freedom, and justice and liberator of the Sacred Roman Republic.

Order was indeed restored. Miscreant noble thugs were severely punished to the point that the leaders of the noble clans left Rome for their feudal holdings in the coun-tryside. Consequently, security returned to the streets in the city and to the roads leading to Rome and economic activity began to recover. The Church saw Cola as a powerful and useful ally, and even Petrarch became a profound admirer, calling Cola the new Bru-tus, writing one of his most moving poems, "Gentle Spirit" (*Spirito gentil*), in his honor.[14]

Putting his dream of restoring Rome's greatness and the Roman Empire into action, Cola called for an assembly representing the various states of Italy to come to the city to discuss an Italian federation guided by Rome. Some states, like Naples, seemed agree-able; others less so. In particular, the Holy Roman Emperor was angered by Cola's appar-ent assumption of Imperial dignity. At the same time, the pope was becoming alienated by Cola's independent actions and vanity. His increasingly bizarre affectations also began to disturb the people of Rome who were not impressed by his splendid costumes, pro-cessions, feasts, and extravagant court: they realized they were paying for these things from ever-higher taxes.

Seeing an opportunity, the Colonna assembled an army of nobles and their retain-ers to recapture the city. But several Italian states had sent troops to defend Rome, and this "Italian" army defeated the nobles, killing their leader, Stefano Colonna. Despite

---

14. For the relationship between Petrarch and Cola, see Mario Cosenza and Ronald Musto, eds. *Petrarch, The Revolution of Cola di Rienzo.* New York: Italica Press, 1996. For *Spirito gentil*, see Cosenza and Musto, 1996. p. 33; Unn Falkeid, *The Avignon Papacy Contested: An Intellectual History from Dante to Catherine of Siena.* Cambridge, MA: Harvard University Press, 2017. pp. 95–120.

this victory and the opportunity it promised in fulfilling his dream of a resurgent Rome, Cola did nothing to follow up on his success. Rather, he spent his resources on elaborate rituals and entertainments. His claims and his vainglory finally lost any sympathy once felt by the papacy, so Cola was excommunicated and branded a heretic. In December of 1347 he fled Rome.

First hiding in a remote monastery and then seeking the support of the emperor in Prague, Cola was eventually turned over to the pope for punishment. He was sentenced to death, but before his execution, the pope died. His successor wanted to restore peace to Rome and weaken the feudal nobles who had made the city even more chaotic through their violence. So, he rescinded the order for execution and instead returned Cola to tumultuous acclaim in 1354 accompanied by a papal army commanded by a cardinal and furnished with the papal title of senator of Rome.

This second chance was quickly dissipated, however, through incompetent military activity, taxation, and arbitrary action. Finally, a mob moved on the Capitol to confront the tribune. Always a physical coward, Cola changed his clothes and tried to hide but the furious Romans recognized him, and in a frenzy of violence they literally tore him to pieces. By the nineteenth century his reputation had been rehabilitated to the point that the spot where he died was marked by a bronze statue.

Although it was initially hoped that Cola could have been the instrument to permit the return of the papacy to the city after its pacification and release from the violent feuds of the baronial families, the adventure of Cola actually delayed any plan to reunite the bishop of Rome with his flock. The city reverted to its instability and grew even more derelict. It would require the intervention of a saint to undo Cola's quixotic dreams and connect the divine authority of the pope with the secular needs of government, thus ensuring the return of the papacy to Rome.

The End of the Babylonian Captivity

By the 1370s there was increasing pressure for the pope to quit Avignon for Rome, but the Curia was naturally reluctant to vacate the magnificent *palais des papes* and trade the comforts and elegance of the court at Avignon for the squalor and menace of Rome. Nevertheless, events like the War of the Eight Saints with Florence (1375–78) and allegations such as Petrarch's indictment of the papal court for scandal, libertinism, and secular ambition gave urgency to the cause. So it was that a young girl with mystical visions acted on her powerful mission to convince the pope that he was the successor to St. Peter and his see was Rome. Saint Catherine of Siena, together with the lesser known Bridget of Sweden, preached before the pope and his Curia about the necessity of repatriating the Holy See.[15] In 1377 she prevailed, and Pope Gregory XI decided to return.[16]

---

15. Falkeid, 2017. pp. 121–72.
16. Paul Thibault, *Pope Gregory XI: The Failure of Tradition*. Lanham, MD: University Press of America, 1986.

The city he found was a dark, dystopian vision of the *caput mundi*. Many of the churches were in ruins; the Apostolic Lateran Palace was uninhabitable; the roads were often impassible; and the population had declined to about seventeen thousand souls without regular employment or security. The challenge of rebuilding not only the physical infrastructure of the city but also the offices of the Church and government and controlling the Roman nobles would be enormous in the best of times but the economic foundations of the city had been sapped, and the French cardinals and senior members of the Curia had no desire to even begin these tasks. Rather they were determined to remain in Avignon and saw the return to Rome as a threat to their power base and legitimacy. But to confound all of the hopes there might have been for a resurgent papacy in Rome, Gregory inopportunely died in 1378. There had been no time for him to begin the huge work of rebuilding the city and restoring the tarnished image of the Holy See.

The conclave that met to choose Gregory's successor was dominated by a plurality of French cardinals, none of whom had any significant connection to Rome, or, for that matter, to Italy. The people of Rome, having been offered some hope of redemption through employment, patronage, and largesse, feared that the cardinals would choose one of their own who would immediately give up on Rome and return to Avignon where all was quiet, orderly, comfortable, and familiar. So the Romans rioted around the conclave, demanding an Italian be chosen to ensure that the papacy would remain in the Holy City.[17]

Fearing the mob, the cardinals did indeed elect an Italian, the elderly archbishop of Bari, who took the name of Urban VI. The Roman people were delirious with joy, believing that the papacy would stay in Rome, and that the economic, security, and demographic problems would be soon behind them. The French cardinals, however, soon regretted their choice. Although a learned and seemingly reasonable cardinal, Urban was a rather high-handed and judgmental pope. In particular, he tried to reform the Sacred College by insisting the French cardinals live modestly and not in the luxurious and rather secular manner they had acquired in Avignon. Within months, the French cardinals revolted, slipping away from Rome to a papal fortress where they stated that Urban's election had not been through the Holy Spirit but through coercion. He was declared deposed, and a new conclave chose a French pope who naturally returned to Avignon.

The difficulty was that Urban refused to resign, deeming this new conclave schismatic and excommunicating the rebellious cardinals, who had also returned to Avignon. The Avignonese pope then excommunicated Urban and his supporters. The consequence was two popes, one in Rome and one in Avignon, both of whom established parallel offices of the Church. With this began the Great Western Schism, a schism that would not be resolved until thirty-five years later with the Council of Constance (1414–18).

---

17. Joelle Rollo-Koster, "Civil Violence and the Initiation of the Schism," in Joelle Rollo-Koster and Thomas M. Izbicki, eds., *A Companion to the Great Western Schism (1378–1417)*. Leiden: Brill, 2009. pp. 9–66.

The Great Western Schism

For all of Christendom it was a scandal: the situation was absurd with two popes excommunicating each other and denouncing each other as the "Anti-Christ." States lined up behind one pope or another from political rather than theological considerations. Whole populations questioned whether the pope they were instructed to recognize was the true successor to St. Peter or the Anti-Christ. With the official diplomatic, fiscal, and legal structures of the universal Church divided, Rome once again suffered: the anticipated renewal of revenue, prestige, power, and influence was sapped by Avignon, yielding insufficient wealth to rebuild the derelict, shabby, and underpopulated city. In an attempt to heal the Schism, both colleges of cardinals met at Pisa in 1409, declaring the competing pontiffs guilty of heresy and thus deposed. Although they elected a new pope to rule a united Church, the two pontiffs refused their judgment. This resulted in the even more bizarre situation of not just two but now three popes claiming universal authority.[18] The vacuum in Church leadership and the questions among the faithful as to the very role of the bishop of Rome were cataclysmic. In particular, the Holy Roman Emperor, Sigismund, was alarmed by divisions in the Church in Bohemia between its largely German leadership and its Czech congregation of the faithful.

The radical Jan Hus had galvanized the Czech people to reject many traditional Catholic doctrines, such as clerical celibacy. He demanded strict reforms such as the Church divesting itself of property and preaching from a vernacular Bible. If this revolt continued to build, Sigismund feared the separation of Bohemia from the Imperial crown. So, he arranged to call a Council of the Church to end the Schism and deal with Hus. It was not unprecedented for an emperor to call a Church Council. After all, the great Councils of the early Church, like Nicea (325 AD), had been summoned by Constantine. But in an effort to reinforce the validity of this gathering, Sigismund also manipulated one of the popes to support his call.

The Council met from 1414 to 1418 at Constance in what is now Switzerland. Hus was duly tried and burned, despite his carrying an Imperial safe conduct.[19] The high clerics and learned or powerful laymen then addressed themselves to the matter of the Schism. All three popes were eventually declared deposed and hence anti-popes. This time, the depositions were sustained. And finally, in 1417 a new, singular pontiff was chosen: Oddone Colonna, from one of the great baronial families of Rome. This new pope took the name of Martin V.[20]

---

18. Nelson H. Minnich, *Councils of the Catholic Reformation: Pisa I (1409) to Trent (1545–63)*. London: Routledge, 2008. pp. 18–21.

19. Thomas A. Fudge, *The Trial of Jan Hus: Medieval Heresy and Criminal Procedure*. Oxford: Oxford University Press, 2013. pp. 116–347.

20. Philip H. Stump, "The Council of Constance (1414–18) and the End of the Schism," in Fudge, 2013. pp. 395–442.

Although he was anxious to start the rebuilding of the united papacy in Rome, Martin recognized that the disorder in the city would delay his return. He was also required by the Council to sign an undertaking that acknowledged the authority of Councils of the Church over the pope himself. The agreement bound him to hold regular Councils and have his actions subject to oversight. The intent was to make the pope the chief executive officer of the corporate Church and subject him to performance reviews, so that if he was found wanting, he would be eligible for removal.[21] Martin hardly liked this Conciliarism, as it was called, but he had no choice. It was left to his successors, especially Pius II and Sixtus IV, to abrogate this decree of the Council of Constance and restore the absolute and irrevocable authority of the bishop of Rome.

---

21. Phillip H. Stump, *The Reforms of the Council of Constance (1414–1418)*. Leiden: Brill, 1994. For three contemporary theological positions on papal authority and Conciliarism, see J. H. Burns and Thomas Izbicki, eds., *Conciliarism and Papalism*. Cambridge: Cambridge University Press, 1998.

Illus. 17.1 The Papal Palace, Avignon.

This enormous Gothic palace in the present South of France was the seat of the papacy during its residence in Avignon from 1309–77; a total of seven popes ruled the universal Church from this papal enclave. Two more popes lived here during the Great Western Schism (1378–1417), but they are recorded as anti-popes: that is, they are not recognized as true successors to St. Peter.

Although begun by the first pope in Avignon, Clement V (1305–14), it was really his successors, John XXII (1316–34) and Benedict XII (1334–42), who largely built this elegant complex. Later known as the Old and New Palaces, it held sumptuous decorations, now mostly lost, and contained a great library, chapel, dining hall, and throne room. At the height of papal occupancy, the palace accommodated as many as fifteen hundred clerical residents and lay workers.

The Pre-Raphaelite British painting on the left captures the moment when the notary Cola di Rienzo swore to avenge his brother who had been killed by the incessant violence in Rome between noble families. Although highly romanticized in this image, the event illustrates the lawlessness and anarchy of Rome at the turn of the fourteenth century.

Illus. 17.2.a William Holman Hunt (1827–1910), *Rienzi* **[sic]** *Vowing to Obtain Justice for the Death of his Young Brother, Slain in a Skirmish Between the Colonna and the Orsini Factions,* **1848–49. Private collection.**

While history tends to focus on Cola di Renzo's hatred of the great feudal clans, this diminishes his sincere desire to recover the grandeur and order of the Roman Empire, an ambition that made him a hero to Petrarch and many others. His desire to unite the Italian peninsula under the authority of Rome, as well as his ultimate rejection of the claims of both emperor and pope, later raised him in the nineteenth century to the status of a prophet of Italian unification. Similarly, Cola's assumption of the role of tribune of the people cemented him in the pantheon of Italians who favored popular sovereignty during the *Risorgimento* (the nationalist Italian movement of unification in the nineteenth century).

Illus. 17.2.b Girolamo Massini (1840–85), *Cola di Rienzo, Tribune of the Roman People* **(d. 1354). Rome.**

The mythology surrounding Rienzo has been preserved in the bronze sculpture by Girolamo Massini. It rests on a plinth composed by Francesco Azzurri (1827–1901) from remnants of ancient Roman buildings and placed next to Michelangelo's Capitoline *cordonata*. Erected in 1887 during the bitter period of tension between the papacy and the Italian monarchy after the capture of Rome in 1870, it was both a symbol of liberty and of the belief that Rome was the permanent and necessary capital of a secular, united Italian state.

Illus. 17.3 Giorgio Vasari, *Return of Pope Gregory XI to Rome from Avignon in 1377*. Apostolic Vatican Palace, Sala Regia, Rome.

This fresco is in the Sala Regia, an anteroom of the Sistine Chapel constructed by Antonio da Sangallo for Pope Paul III and completed in 1573. The image shows Pope Gregory XI, led by the Roman apostolic martyrs Peter and Paul, processing in front of the façade of old St. Peter's basilica and the Apostolic Vatican Palace. The pope and his entourage are guided by St. Catherine of Siena toward the Goddess Roma, the personification of the ancient city, accompanied by the personified Tiber at her feet. This highly symbolic fresco reveals the importance of the reconnection of the pope with his apostolic See of Rome, offering an unbroken link with the ancient empire and confirming the pope's succession to St. Peter.

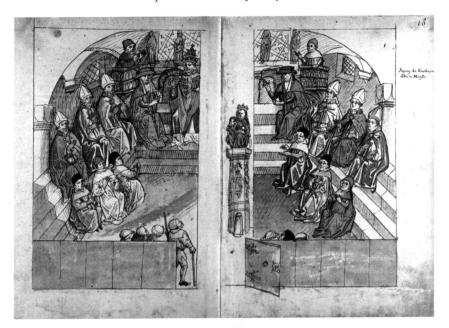

Illus. 17.4 Ulrich von Richental, *The Council of Constance 1414–1418*. Manuscript illustrations from 1460–ca. 1465), *The Chronicle of the Council of Constance*. Rosgartenmuseum, Konstanz.

These pages are from an illustrated manuscript of *The Chronicle of the Council of Constance* by Ulrich von Richental (d. 1438). They represent the dialogue of theologians, bishops, cardinals, and scholars in the cathedral of Constance presided over by the Anti-Pope John XXIII (Baldassare Cossa). The Council was called in 1414 to heal the Great Western Schism (1378–1417), which had at that point divided the Church among three competing pontiffs.

The moral decline of the office is clearly illustrated by the career of Cossa (d. 1419). From the island of Procida in the Bay of Naples, he had been a bandit along with other members of his family before entering the Church. He gained the support of Cosimo de'Medici, who saw him as a useful instrument for protecting the Medici bank and Florentine interests in general. As John XXIII, Cossa was forced to resign by the Council. But his fortunes were not completely crushed as he spent his few remaining years in Florence where Cosimo commissioned for him a magnificent tomb by Donatello and Michelozzo still visible in the baptistery of Florence.

Thus, the years between the return to Rome of a united papacy under Martin V Colonna in 1420 and the death of Julius II in 1513 mark the attempts of popes to escape from the restrictions of Conciliarism imposed on Martin V at Constance. The bull *Frequens* (1417) required regular and frequent Councils to be called to address Church problems collectively and redress the idea of papal theocratic absolute monarchy. This was a limitation of power that no Renaissance pope wished to obey. Once back in Rome and unchallenged, the papacy again assumed the authority of both Constantine and St. Peter.

CHAPTER 18
THE RESTORATION OF ROME

When Martin returned to Rome in September of 1420 he found a city so derelict that his first business was to re-establish the revenue-producing offices of the Church. To do this he had to unite the competing jurisdictions caused by the Schism so that some rebuilding could begin.[1] Even the question of his residence had to be postponed: the Lateran Palace was in such disrepair that it was not habitable, so Martin lived in his family's Colonna Palace or in the better maintained Vatican palace adjoining St. Peter's. Nevertheless, the return of a united papacy was a powerful tonic for the enervated city. Cardinals renovated palaces for their households, and princes sent influential representatives to extract favors from the re-energized Church. Pilgrims returned and left even more money in the hands of both the Church and the service industries that cared for them, from innkeepers, tavern keepers, and prostitutes to national confraternities or hospices.

The result was an immediate improvement in the economic health of the city, with a great many laborers employed in the building trades and new households of servants. The luxury market benefitted from commissions from individual prelates, churches, ambassadors, and wealthy Romans who felt that they could again engage in conspicuous consumption. With the support of his feudal Colonna clan, Martin also managed to impose some order on the territory around the city and on the turbulent barons within Rome.[2]

Among this swarm of strangers who arrived in Rome from elsewhere in Italy was a throng of humanists.[3] The explosion of interest in classical culture and correct golden-age Latin style, already established in Florence and elsewhere on the peninsula, soon became a necessary element at the papal court.[4] Likewise, Renaissance painting at last came to Rome. Giotto had actually painted in the city under Boniface VIII, but the subsequent events of the Babylonian Captivity and Schism had robbed the city of the resources needed for competitive patronage on the level of Florence with its indigenous workshop tradition. Under Martin V in 1425 the most inventive of the Florentine school, Masaccio, arrived with his older collaborator, Masolino, to fresco the Castiglione Chapel of St. Catherine in the basilica of San Clemente. This wonderful work presaged the coming of the artistic Renaissance to Rome and constituted the most important

---

1. Stinger, 1998. p. 99.
2. Stinger, 1998. p. 96.
3. Paolo Brezzi and Maristella Lorch, eds., *Umanesimo a Roma nel Quattrocento*. New York and Rome: Columbia University and L'Istituto di studi romani, 1984.
4. See John F. D'Amico, *Renaissance Humanism in Papal Rome*. Baltimore: Johns Hopkins University Press, 1983.

commission of Martin's reign. Other artists were invited as well: Pisanello painted in the cathedral of St. John Lateran (works now sadly lost), and Gentile da Fabriano was at work in Rome when he died in 1427.[5]

Even the baronial families took advantage of the presence of these foreign artists, with Cardinal Giordano Orsini engaging Masolino and the then-youthful Paolo Uccello to create inspiring images of famous men (also lost) in his fortress–palace on the eponymous Monte Giordano.[6] A familiar of Florentine humanists, such as Poggio and Bruni, and a friend of Lorenzo Valla, Cardinal Orsini also acquired a huge library of manuscripts. In addition, he commissioned a theatre for his palace, perhaps the first permanent structure for plays in the city since antiquity. But, while the Renaissance did come to Rome during the pontificate of Martin, the tribulations of his successor meant that those early seeds never had an opportunity to germinate.

From Eugene IV to Paul II

The popes that followed Martin had their own problems resulting from the Schism and the Council of Constance.[7] For example, Martin's immediate successor, Eugene IV (r. 1431–47), faced a renewed threat of schism because of his hostility to the requirement that all popes hold regular Councils: he refused to submit to such a performance review by the body of the faithful, resulting in an anti-pope elected to challenge him.

Eugene was forced to spend some considerable time in Florence because of the continuing violence and instability of Rome.[8] While there he also presided over the end to another schism—this one the Great Eastern Schism that had occurred in 1054 between Latin and Orthodox Christianity. By the late 1430s the fate of the Byzantine Empire appeared so perilous that without help from the West, it was expected to fall to the Ottoman Turks. In an attempt to gain support, the Byzantine emperor; the patriarch; twelve metropolitans (bishops); and a large retinue of courtiers, scholars, and theologians traveled to Italy to settle that dispute, which was now almost four centuries old. In 1439, under Brunelleschi's recently completed dome of Florence's cathedral, this Schism was declared healed. The optimism would not last, however: Constantinople was captured by the Turks just fourteen years later.[9]

While in Florence Eugene saw the full flowering of the cultural and scholarly Renaissance. Greek scholars had brought with them ancient texts of philosophy, as well as theology; and Platonism was given that intellectual imprimatur that would lead to

---

5. For an excellent survey of art and patronage in Rome in the fifteenth century, see Maria Grazia Bernardini and Marco Bussagli, eds., *Il '400 a Roma: La Rinascita delle arti da Donatello a Perugino.* Geneva–Milan: Skira, 2008.
6. Helmut Wohl, "Martin V and the Revival of the Arts in Rome," in Ramsey, 1982. pp. 171–83.
7. Nelson H. Minnich, *The Renaissance Papacy 1406–1565.* Harlow, UK: Longmans, 2011.
8. da Bisticci, 1997. pp. 17–31.
9. Joseph Gill, *The Council of Florence.* Cambridge: Cambridge University Press, 2011.

the so-called Platonic Academy. Not only books but also great artworks stimulated his ambitions. In particular, Ghiberti's doors to the baptistery in Florence drove Eugene to commission Ghiberti's student Filarete (whose real name was Antonio di Averlino, ca. 1400–65) to create bronze doors for St. Peter's basilica. Visitors to St. Peter's can to this day see these doors celebrating Eugene's role at the Council of Florence and his divine mission as the successor to St. Peter, from whom he is seen receiving the keys to heaven and earth. So, despite a troubled pontificate, Eugene IV did move Rome further along on the road to the new culture of Renaissance Italy.[10]

Nicholas V

It was Eugene IV's successor, Nicholas V (r. 1447–55), who most dramatically brought the Florentine Renaissance to Rome. Nicholas, as Tommaso Parentucelli, had lived in Florence for some time and was a friend of Cosimo de'Medici and his humanist circle. When he became pope in 1447 he declared that he had three ambitions: to be a good pope, to restore the ancient grandeur of Rome, and to restore learning. There is no doubt but that he was a good pope, to the point that Anti-Pope Felix V, who had challenged Eugene, resigned in Nicholas's favor.[11]

Nicholas's avowed intention to restore the glory of the ancient city was in reality a huge undertaking.[12] To ensure that the best minds would be applied to the challenge he engaged, among others, the Florentine theorist and polymath Leon Battista Alberti[13] to develop a comprehensive urban plan equal to both the memory of the ancient Empire and its role as capital of Western Christendom. Nicholas also knew that the city could never grow substantially in size unless it had greater access to clean water, so he commissioned the reconstruction of the ancient Aqua Virgo aqueduct that had been built by Marcus Agrippa to supply the first public baths in Rome. The end of this water course was to be a great fountain: it was the original Trevi Fountain.

Alberti was also given the delicate and difficult job of producing an engineering report on the state of the basilica of St. Peter. He warned the pope that the building was in serious danger of collapse as the apse had already detached from the rest of the basilica, which itself was held together mostly by its roof trusses. Nevertheless, the prospect of either pulling down or fundamentally rebuilding the holiest site in Western

10. Giorgio Vasari, "Life of Filarete," in Vasari, 1996. I, pp. 389–92.

11. da Bisticci, 1997. pp. 31–59; Christine Smith and Joseph F. O'Connor, *Building the Kingdom: Giannozzo Manetti on the Material and Spiritual Edifice.* Arizona Studies in the Middle Ages and the Renaissance, Vol. 20. Turnhout, Belgium: Brepols, 2006. This book contains Gianozzo Manetti's contemporary biography of Nicholas V (*De Gestis Nicolai Quinti Summi Pontificis*).

12. Charles Burroughs, "A Planned Myth and a Myth of Planning: Nicholas V and Rome," in Ramsey, 1982. pp. 197–207.

13. Carroll William Westfall, *In This Most Perfect Paradise: Alberti, Nicholas V, and the Invention of Conscious Urban Planning in Rome, 1447–55.* University Park: Pennsylvania State University Press, 1974.

Christendom—after all, the basilica had been constructed by Constantine over the tomb of the apostle Peter—proved simply too radical. So, Nicholas compromised by merely repairing the apse. A new church would have to wait.

In recognition of St. Peter's significance, Nicholas also made the momentous decision to move the center of the Church to the Vatican Hill and Apostolic Palace. Up to this point, the heart of the Roman Church had been the Lateran, Rome's cathedral, where popes had ruled from the early fourth century. Once Nicholas had formalized the move, he commissioned the building of a new private papal chapel, the Cappella Niccolina.

Finally, to fulfill his promise to restore learning, Nicholas founded the Vatican Library, endowing it with a small room and a few significant theological tomes. Not satisfied by the books that were available, the pope commissioned large numbers of copies of Greek and Latin manuscripts to provide humanist depth to the holdings. More Greek manuscripts were copied in the eight years of his pontificate than had been in the previous eight centuries. Consequently, when Nicholas died he was truly mourned. He had installed Renaissance culture in Rome and raised the moral and cultural reputation of the pontificate from the depths to which it had fallen during the Babylonian Captivity and Schism and which it had continued to suffer under the beleaguered Eugene IV.[14]

The successors to St. Peter who followed Nicholas were a mixed lot who did little for Rome. Calixtus III Borgia's (r. 1455–58) only significant contribution was to appoint the humanist and grammarian Niccolo Perotti[15] as his secretary—he had previously served in the same capacity to Cardinal Bessarion, the Byzantine scholar and bibliophile—beginning a career that would see him help renew the Vatican Library under Sixtus IV and introduce new standards of Latinity in Rome. Calixtus is perhaps better known, however, for making his young nephew, Roderigo, a cardinal, a promotion that would later lead to his election as Alexander VI, the infamous Borgia pope.

Pius II Piccolomini (r. 1458–64) was a fine scholar, historian, diplomat, writer of poetry and fiction, and lover of art and architecture whose elevation resulted in a great many humanists traveling to Rome for employment.[16] However, Pius spent his declining energies (he suffered terribly from gout) on turning his hometown of Pienza (originally Corsignano near Siena) into the humanist ideal city rather than focusing on rebuilding Rome. He did, though, commission the construction of the benediction loggia for the basilica of St. Peter, a structure prominent in all early images of the church until it was sacrificed in the seventeenth century for the new façade by Carlo Maderno. His one

---

14. Anthony Grafton, ed., *Rome Reborn: The Vatican Library and Renaissance Culture.* New Haven: Yale University Press, 1993.

15. For Perotti (who was named Archbishop of Siponto in 1458), see da Bisticci, 1997. pp. 181–84.

16. Emily O'Brien, *The "Commentaries" of Pope Pius II (1458–1464) and the Crisis of the Fifteenth-Century Papacy.* Toronto: University of Toronto Press, 2015.

obsessive policy was spent attempting to assemble a crusade to recapture Constantinople from the Turks.[17]

The next in papal succession was Paul II Barbo (r. 1464–71), who proved to be both a contributor and a danger to the development of Rome as a Renaissance capital. He did build his splendid, enormous palace near the Capitoline, now known as the Palazzo Venezia (1455), where he lived even after his election to the papacy.[18] Vain and acquisitive, he kept the goldsmiths and jewelers busy with his constant demand for the expensive bright shiny things that he so loved. On the other hand, he was hostile to Renaissance humanism[19] and to learning in general, believing humanists to be pagans or even atheists. He dismissed many of the scholars who had been hired by Pius II and Nicholas V, an act that ensured that his reputation would always be tarnished by the eloquent testimonies of those professional writers who found themselves summarily thrown out of work. It appears that about 1470, at the end of his life, he took some interest in the restoration of St. Peter's basilica, engaging Lorenzo de'Medici's favorite architect, Giuliano da Sangallo, to address the decaying structure of the apse on the Constantinian church, continuing work begun by Nicholas V and Alberti.

In contrast, the pope who succeeded Paul II to the apostolic see was one who was powerfully dedicated to both the city and humanism. Sixtus IV della Rovere (r. 1471–84) may have been one of the church's most controversial popes, an ineffectual politician and shameless benefactor of his family, but his patronage of building, culture, learning, and urban planning would make him one of the most admired of all the bishops of Renaissance Rome.

The Rule of Sixtus IV

Francesco della Rovere, the future Sixtus IV, was not born to be a pope. His family, from near Savona in the republic of Genoa, was modest in wealth and achievement. Furthermore, he chose the Franciscan Order when he entered the Church, an order known more for asceticism than Curial ambition. But, when he began his formal theological studies at the University of Pavia, his keen intellect shone, resulting in a professorship at several universities, including the celebrated University of Padua. His reputation for piety, scholarship, intelligence, and integrity resulted in his election in 1464 as general of the Franciscan Order, a position that led to his appointment to the College of Cardinals in 1467. It was his learning and his apparent lack of political ambition that led to his unexpected election as pope in the conclave of 1471.

---

17. Cecilia M. Ady, *Pius II: Æneas Silvius Piccolomini, The Humanist Pope*. London: Methuen, 1913. There is a modern reprint by Forgotten Books, 2016.

18. Anthony F. D'Elia, *A Sudden Terror: The Plot to Murder the Pope in Renaissance Rome*. Cambridge, MA: Harvard University Press, 2011.

19. A. J. Dunstan, "Paul II and the Humanists," *The Journal of Religious History*, 7 (1972–73), pp. 287–306.

It is said that the papacy ennobles some men and reveals the weakness of others. In the case of Sixtus IV, both observations were true. His sanctity led him to undertake a number of failed initiatives in foreign policy: a futile crusade against the Turks, an abortive attempt to unite the Russian Orthodox Church with Rome, an unfulfilled ambition to bring the French Church firmly under direct papal rule, and a craven acquiescence to the excesses of the Spanish Inquisition. He did manage to declare the papacy free of the conciliar oversight that Martin had been forced to accept.[20] But overall his political performance was ineffectual.

That said, Sixtus did sustain a serious concern for the welfare of his subjects in Rome and the Papal States. He strove to control the price of grain and to limit the almost unchecked power of the great Roman feudal clans, but his excessive generosity to the insatiable demands of his large assortment of nephews reduced his resources for these policies. It did not stop him, however, from finding the money to embark on the most ambitious rebuilding of Rome since antiquity.

Rebuilding Rome

At the end of the third century, Rome had been a great metropolis that ruled the world, with public buildings, temples, and fora that were a wonder to all observers. The city had enjoyed a population well in excess of one million, serviced by eleven aqueducts and protected by vast walls built by the emperor Aurelian between 271 and 275 AD. But by the time Sixtus rose to the papacy, the population had declined to under thirty thousand inhabitants who lived huddled in the bend of the Tiber, with the rest of the great Imperial city otherwise largely abandoned. The Aurelian walls remained the essential defense of the city, enclosing large neglected spaces, filled with the decaying monuments of its ancient glory. The Ponte Sant'Angelo, built originally by the Emperor Hadrian to connect with his tomb, was the single bridge left spanning the Tiber. It was the only way that pilgrims to St. Peter's could reach the basilica from the *Abitata*, or inhabited part of the city.[21]

Rome, despite the grand churches and waves of pilgrims, must have seemed a melancholy and ruinous place. Indeed, Sixtus realized that the city he ruled as the successor both to St. Peter and to Constantine was an unacceptable jumble of poorly constructed

---

20. Conciliarism had been constantly eroded since Constance, even by Pius II who underwent a conversion from ideological conciliarism to papal theocratic monarchy after his election. His bull of 1460, *Execrabilis*, forbade on pain of excommunication any appeal of papal acts to a Council. But it was Sixtus IV who finally shut down the conciliarist movement, and hence has been described as the first Renaissance "pope-king" (*papa-re*). See Marco Pellegrini, "A Turning Point in the History of the Factional System in the Sacred College: The Power of Pope and Cardinals in the Age of Alexander VI," in Gianvittorio Signorotto and Maria Visceglia, eds., *Court and Politics in Papal Rome, 1492–1700*. Cambridge: Cambridge University Press, 2002. pp. 13–15, 17.

21. See James McGregor, *Rome from the Ground Up*. Cambridge, MA: Belknap Press of Harvard University Press, 2005. pp. 61–106.

houses, muddy streets, ancient ruins, and rubble. He was determined to arrest that decline so that his papacy would be praised for the restoration of Rome as *caput mundi*, the head of the world.[22]

As we have seen, one reason why Rome was in such a sorry state of jerry-built structures, unpaved streets, and narrow, rubble-strewn lanes was the curiosity of canon law that on the deaths of ecclesiastics and Curial officials in Rome, their real property was confiscated by the Church.

Because their properties could not be passed down to members of their families, there was little incentive for the ecclesiastics to build grandly. Sixtus recognized this drawback and changed the law, allowing curialists and clergy in Rome to leave their property to their heirs. Thus, they were encouraged to put down roots in their neighborhoods and to construct splendid structures that announced the wealth and position of their families to the world. Of course, that meant the skimming of even more funds from Church coffers. But what did that matter when it assured the return of grandeur to Rome?[23]

Sixtus's own family illustrated the wisdom of this innovation, as the pope's nephew, Raffaele Riario, commissioned the construction of the huge and imposing Cancelleria as his own palace, inscribing for all posterity his offices and dignities on the façade where they can still be read. There is a story that the funding for the palace came from Raffaele winning a fortune (fourteen thousand ducats!) at dice from the son of Cardinal Cybo. Although his son may have been a brutish dullard and hopeless at games, Cybo himself was a prominent ecclesiastic who would eventually succeed Raffaele's uncle as Innocent VIII.[24] Knowing that he would likely be required to give at least some of his winnings back, Raffaele immediately secured the funds by purchasing the lot and building materials needed for constructing the Cancelleria. Even if the story is spurious, it illustrates well both the moral decay and the material grandeur that would characterize the pontificate of Sixtus IV.

Secular Nepotism

The nephews whom Sixtus advanced in secular power were also a mixed lot. His nephew Giovanni della Rovere was married to a daughter of the great Federigo da Montefeltro, the duke of Urbino, and was given the city and territory of Senigallia to rule. Most of

---

22. Jill Blondin, "Power Made Visible: Pope Sixtus IV as 'Urbis Restaurator' in Quattrocento Rome," *The Catholic Historical Review*, 91 (2005), pp. 1–25; Paolo Brezzi, "La Funzione di Roma nell'Italia della seconda metà del Quattrocento," in Massimo Miglio, Francesca Niutta, Diego Quaglioni, and Concetta Ranieri, eds., *Un Pontificato e una Città: Sisto IV (1471–1484)*. Rome: Istituto Storico Italiano per il Medio Evo, 1986. pp. 1–18.

23. Stinger, 1998. p. 30. See also Partner, 1979. pp. 17, 163.

24. Paolo Portoghesi, *Rome of the Renaissance*, tr. Pearl Sanders. London: Phaidon, 1972. pp. 41–43.

his life he himself served as a condottiere captain, but the son he sired by Giovanna da Montefeltro went on to become the first della Rovere duke of Urbino.

But it was another of the pope's nephews, Girolamo Riario, who benefitted the most from his uncle's nepotism, usually at the expense of other families' property. Girolamo was appointed captain general of the Church, in effect commander in chief of the papal armed forces. Then in 1473 Sixtus arranged a marriage between Girolamo and Caterina, the illegitimate daughter of the duke of Milan, Galeazzo Maria Sforza. To provide him with independent authority, the pope gave Girolamo the rule of Imola, which brought him—and the papacy—into conflict with Lorenzo de'Medici of Florence, a tension that resulted in the 1478 Pazzi Conspiracy, the murder of Giuliano de'Medici, and the war of the Pazzi Conspiracy.[25]

Girolamo and Pope Sixtus hated Lorenzo because of his refusal to extend the funds needed to secure Imola, recognizing the threat to Florentine interests that a Riario's control of that strategic town would provoke. Added to this, there were rumors that if the plot had succeeded, Girolamo was toying with the idea of becoming ruler of Florence as well. Happily, Lorenzo lived, but the instability caused by the pope's nepotism and Girolamo's ambition hardly ceased.

Forlì was a substantial town in the Romagna within the States of the Church but ruled from the thirteenth century by the staunchly Ghibelline Ordelaffi family. In 1480, the year the War of the Pazzi Conspiracy ended, Sixtus had the Ordelaffi expelled and made Girolamo the count of Forlì in addition to being ruler of Imola. Girolamo fortified the city by rebuilding the imposing fortress of Ravaldino and improved it by pulling down less attractive structures to construct others he thought more elegant. Despite his growing collection of territories, Girolamo mostly lived in Rome close to his uncle, whose enemies inevitably became his own. In particular, Sixtus coveted some of the property of the great Colonna family, a greedy ambition which drove the noble clan into opposition to the pope and his family.

Sixtus IV was, then, a destabilizing figure in Italian affairs, driven by an obsessive nepotism and a complete lack of respect for the lives or property of those opposed to his family strategy. In some ways Sixtus was a precursor to the moral decline of the papacy and the nepotism and ambition of the Borgia Pope Alexander VI (r. 1492–1503) who also used his papal authority and his family in an attempt to turn the Romagna into a Borgia duchy. In fact, it can be argued that Sixtus's pontificate began the practice of treating the States of the Church as just another Italian principality ruled, at least temporarily, by the dynasty of the pope.

Add to this the persistent rumors of Sixtus's active homosexual life (which included the naming of cardinals for their beauty) in contravention of his vows of celibacy, and the dubious moral environment of Rome in the last quarter of the fifteenth century emerges.

---

25. For the Pazzi Conspiracy, see pp. 62 et sqq. above.

These charges come from a firsthand chronicler with the closest connections to Roman humanist society and the papal curia—Stefano Infessura (d. 1500). His *Diarium urbis Romae* (*Diario della Città di Roma; Diary of the City of Rome*) is admittedly written from the perspective of a partisan of the Colonna family, the pope's enemies. Still, enough of the other elements of his inside "gossip" can be substantiated, so we need to take his evidence seriously.[26]

Aggrandizing the Church

Sixtus might have suffered from a great many moral failings, and he substantially increased the level of instability in the years prior to the French invasion of Italy, but he was also one of the greatest and most ambitious popes for the city of Rome. What he accomplished in the thirteen years of his papacy was astounding, changing the face of the city and adding to its level of culture.

In particular, when Sixtus came to the throne there was much hope for a revitalization of the intellectual and cultural environment of the city—a hope that he more than fulfilled. For example, he founded the Sistine Choir. More important, he not only re-founded the Apostolic Vatican Library, but he also expanded its holdings and gave it larger and better accommodations in the Vatican palace. He opened it to all scholars and engaged a humanist as librarian, Bartolommeo Sacchi, known as Platina, whose *Lives of the Popes* attests to his abilities and gift for flattery. Sixtus surrounded himself with men of letters and lived up to his reputation as a scholar, established when he was a university professor before his elevation to papal office.[27]

Sixtus also addressed the large number of ancient sculptures being unearthed in the city—in part as a consequence of the building boom he had started—by establishing what would become the Capitoline Museum, the first public museum since antiquity, through his donation of several ancient statues. One of these was the iconic Capitoline *She Wolf*, now a symbol of Rome.[28] In fact, it was probably Sixtus IV who commissioned the figures of the twins Romulus and Remus, perhaps cast by Antonio del Pollaiuolo, to be added to the sculpture.

But it was as a city planner that Sixtus IV is most celebrated in Rome. In order to assist pilgrims in their route to St. Peter's and to reduce the pressure on the Ponte Sant'Angelo, Sixtus ordered the construction of the first bridge over the Tiber since antiquity, a bridge aptly named for himself—the Ponte Sisto. Although it was built on the foundations of the ancient Pons Aurelius, the bridge was specifically designed as

---

26. Infessura was a civic official in Rome and hence hostile to the encroachments of the papacy on the administration of the city. His diary is available in Italian: *Diario della Città di Roma di Stefano Infessura*, ed. Oreste Tommasini. Rome: Forzani e tipografi del senato, 1890.
27. See Egmont Lee, *Sixtus IV and Men of Letters*. Rome: Edizioni di Storia e Letteratura, 1978.
28. Stinger, 1998. pp. 255–56.

a preparation for the Jubilee of 1475. It proved its value immediately, as the pope also cleared a street from the bridge into the Campo de'Fiori.[29]

Similarly, to provide a direct route through the densely settled area in the bend in the Tiber, Sixtus paved and straightened a road that became the Via Recta, that is, "the straight street," now the Via dei Coronari, named for the rosary sellers who once lined it. Pilgrims also benefitted from his reconstruction of the hospice near St. Peter's, the Ospedale di Santo Spirito in Sassia, which was originally founded in 728, but which had been damaged in a fire in 1470. This large hospice to care for ill or exhausted pilgrims still exists as a testament to Sixtus IV.[30]

To modern observers, however, Sixtus's most celebrated commission was a huge new papal chapel, which he instructed his architect, Baccio Pontelli, to design in the same proportions as the Temple of Solomon in Jerusalem, as described in the Book of Kings. This Sistine Chapel was built between 1477 and 1480 and became not only the chapel for the pope's liturgical function as the successor to St. Peter but also the site where all popes were subsequently elected.

The decoration on the walls commissioned by Sixtus was to be by the finest painters of his time. As Rome had not yet developed a celebrated school of painting, Sixtus imported fresco masters from Tuscany and Umbria: Perugino, Luca Signorelli, Cosimo Rosselli, Botticelli, and Ghirlandaio.[31] Indeed, it was in the securing of these artists that Sixtus made personal peace with Lorenzo de'Medici after the War of the Pazzi Conspiracy. Sixtus needed the painters—as well as Florentine support in his campaign to drive the Turks from Otranto—more than he desired to sustain his and his nephew's resentment against the Medici.

Born from a family from Liguria, Sixtus did not enjoy deep Roman roots, so he needed a church to serve as the burial chapel for his family. His choice was significant: Santa Maria del Popolo in the eponymous piazza just inside the Flaminian Gate. The original church had first been built in 1099 on the site of the tombs of the family of Nero. Sixtus commissioned Andrea Bregno to add a Renaissance façade and rebuild the church in 1472, not long after becoming pope. We know the date because of two inscriptions promising plenary indulgences to worshippers who attend mass at appropriate times. The della Rovere chapels, built and decorated by several branches of the family, remain with their splendid Renaissance tombs and paintings by Pinturicchio, among others.

Of course all of these activities cost a great deal of money. Consequently, Sixtus was driven to hugely increase taxation in Rome and the Papal States, something which hardly endeared him to his already burdened subjects, and quite in opposition to his

---

29. Stinger, 1998. p. 32.
30. For a comprehensive study of the Ospedale, see *L'Antico ospedale di Santo Spirito dall'istituzione papale alla sanità del terzo millennio. Atti del Convegno internazionale di studi*. Rome: Il Veltro Editrice, 2001.
31. John Shearman, "The Chapel of Sixtus IV," in Massimo Giacommetti, ed., *The Sistine Chapel: Michelangelo Rediscovered*. London: Muller, Blond and White, 1986. pp. 22–91.

early desire to be a benevolent pontiff to his subjects. Still finding his income insufficient, he fell back on the papal tradition of simony, selling Church offices to the highest bidder, a practice that further reduced the moral authority of the papacy and was a source of scandal to many of the faithful.[32]

Finally, although he did so much for Rome through his generous and informed patronage, the city was made even more unsafe for those living or visiting it because of Sixtus's provocation of the Colonna family and the outbreak of almost a feudal war between the Orsini and Colonna. His nephew Girolamo Riario tortured and murdered Lorenzo Colonna, a papal protonotary, simply because the pope wanted some Colonna estates. But this iniquity brought the Holy See into the traditional enmity between the two great Roman houses. It is hardly surprising, therefore, that Sixtus was unable to stop the violence or enforce peace between them.[33]

A Violent Accession

Just as so much of Sixtus's life was characterized by his relations with his nephew, Girolamo, so were the events surrounding his death. When the pope died in August of 1484, rioting broke out in Rome fanned in part by his heavy taxation but also stirred by the Colonna and other enemies of the della Rovere/Riario clan. A violent mob broke into the Orsini palace where Girolamo lived with his wife, Caterina Sforza, who was at the time about to give birth.[34]

Girolamo had forbidden Caterina from becoming involved in politics, but she was astute and fearless. Despite her pregnant state, she left the palace as it was being looted and gathered some retainers and rode to the Castel Sant'Angelo. There she commanded that the fortress be turned over to her as she was acting in her husband's name. Simultaneously she demanded that the soldiers in the garrison obey her orders and that the cannons of the Castello be directed toward the Apostolic Palace. Her intention was to pressure the Sacred College through force to elect a new pope who would be allied to the Riario and keep them in their positions. At the same time, Girolamo was entering Rome with an army.[35]

---

32. Stinger, 1998. p. 127; Marco Pellegrini, "A Turning-Point in the History of the Factional System in the Sacred College: The Power of the Pope and Cardinals in the Age of Alexander VI," in Signorotto and Visceglia, 2002. pp. 17–18.

33. Paolo Cherubini, "Tra Violenza e Crimine di Stato: La Morte di Lorenzo Oddone Colonna," in Miglio et al., 1986. pp. 355–80.

34. The life of Caterina Sforza has become material for both scholarly and general interest books. See Ernst Breisach, *Caterina Sforza: A Renaissance Virago*. Chicago: University of Chicago Press, 1967; Elizabeth Lev, *The Tigress of Forlì: Renaissance Italy's Most Courageous and Notorious Countess, Caterina Riario Sforza de' Medici*. Boston: Houghton, Mifflin, Harcourt (Mariner Books), 2012.

35. Shaw, 1993. p. 55.

While this was happening, unruly mobs were looting the palaces of unpopular rich and powerful citizens and intimidating the others. The cardinals who were arriving in Rome for the conclave were too afraid to meet. Indeed, they refused to attend Sixtus's funeral mass in the Sistine Chapel because it was in range of the artillery in Castel Sant'Angelo that Caterina had demanded be trained on the papal palace. Rome was being reduced to mayhem, so the cardinals requested that Caterina abandon Castel Sant'Angelo, which she refused to do, saying it was under her husband's command and only a new pope could take away the authority that Sixtus had granted his nephew.

Caterina refused all compromise and offers, so the cardinals approached Girolamo and offered to absolutely confirm him in the positions granted by Pope Sixtus: lord of Imola and Forlì and captain general of the Church. Furthermore, they would compensate him for the looting and damage to his palace. Seeing that the cardinals were beginning to gather a military force as well, Girolamo realized that his best course was to agree. Caterina argued against the deal, but Girolamo prevailed. Finally, over two months after the death of Sixtus IV, Caterina handed control of Castel Sant'Angelo to the cardinals and left Rome. The conclave to elect Sixtus IV's successor could begin.

**Illus. 18.1 Fra Angelico, *St. Lawrence Receiving Deacon's Orders*,
1447–51. Apostolic Vatican Palace, Cappella Niccolina, Rome.**

Pope Nicholas V Parentucelli (r. 1447–55) was a wonderful and knowledgeable patron of learning and building to the point of proclaiming that the redevelopment of Rome was one of his ambitions as pope. For example, he commissioned Fra Angelico, whom he had met in Florence in the circle of his friend Cosimo de'Medici, to fresco his new chapel in the Vatican Palace. This small space, with images from the lives and miracles of Rome's two protomartyrs, St. Stephen and St. Lawrence, remains one of the most exquisite early Renaissance monuments in Rome to this day.

This image from the chapel is a portrait of Nicholas in the role of third-century Pope Sixtus II. He is portrayed at the moment of St. Lawrence's investiture as deacon responsible for the protection of the riches of the Church and distribution of alms to the poor. Yet, the ceremony takes place in what is clearly a Renaissance classical basilica. This program reinforces the continuous authority of the papacy while at the same time celebrating St. Lawrence's sacrifice and martyrdom in protecting the treasure of the church.

Illus. 18.2 Palazzo Venezia, 1455. Rome.

This vast palace, largely constructed from finished stones looted from the nearby Roman forum, was traditionally in part attributed to Leon Battista Alberti. Venetian Cardinal Pietro Barbo, later Pope Paul II (r. 1464–71), ordered the building of a palace that would match his love of grandeur and display. It is in effect the first large Renaissance private palace in the city, with elements of classical decoration but still surmounted by a tower, the symbol of power. In order to build this huge structure, the ancient church of San Marco (named for St. Mark, Venice's patron saint) had to be incorporated into the palace. Originally founded in the fourth century, the church contains splendid ninth-century mosaics, which fortunately were preserved. However, the ceiling was replaced with a new one (still intact) displaying the arms of Paul II. Finally, a new façade was added, with an open loggia in the latest Renaissance style, the material for which was looted from the nearby Theatre of Marcellus.

Later, Palazzo Venezia served as the residence of the ambassador to the Holy See from the republic of Venice. After Venice's absorption by Austria following the Napoleonic Wars, it was also inhabited by the Austrian legation. It was taken by the Italian state as enemy property during the First World War, and then in the 1920s it served as the office of Fascist dictator Benito Mussolini. It is now a museum.

Illus. 18.3 Melozzo da Forlì (1438–94), *Pope Sixtus IV*
Appoints Bartolommeo Sacchi (Platina) Prefect of the Vatican
***Library*, 1477. Apostolic Vatican Library, Rome.**

Although Sixtus IV was a wonderful patron for Rome, as shown in this depiction of his appointment of Platina (kneeling) as prefect for his re-founded Vatican Library, he was also guilty of the most flagrant nepotism. He proved to be exceptionally good at advancing the interests of his family, a policy that brought disgrace and war to the Church. Sixtus had fifteen nephews, all of whom benefitted from their proximity to the Holy See. Three were raised to the Sacred College as cardinals, and one of these, Giuliano della Rovere, would be elected as Pope Julius II in 1503. Others were granted lucrative offices in the Church. Pietro Riario, for example, the son of Sixtus's sister, became Archbishop of Florence in 1473 and prospered enough thereby to become the richest man in Rome. Illustrated from the left are the papal nephews Giovanni della Rovere, Girolamo Riario, Giuliano della Rovere (the future Julius II), and Raffaele Riario.

Illus. 18.4 Bertoldo di Giovanni, *Medal Celebrating the Survival of Lorenzo de'Medici during the Pazzi Conspiracy,* with Lorenzo's portrait and a narrative of the events in the cathedral, 1478.

It was Sixtus IV's ambition to create a Riario state in Italy that caused the most deplorable events of his pontificate to develop. The pope identified his nephew, Girolamo Riario, as the one who would establish the Riario among the princes of Italy. Girolamo was married to Caterina Sforza, the natural daughter of Galeazzo Maria, duke of Milan, and this marriage was part of a complex arrangement between the duke of Milan and the pope over the town of Imola near the Tuscan border.

Traditionally Imola formed part of the territories of the Church but was usually governed by various condottiere families. In 1470 Imola had been entrusted to the Sforza, but Lorenzo de'Medici coveted it because it could be used to protect the trade route between Florence and Venice. The Milanese had initially agreed to sell Imola to Florence for one hundred thousand florins. However, Duke Galeazzo Maria changed his mind and in 1473 sold it instead to the papacy for far less, as it formed part of the dowry of Caterina Sforza. Lorenzo was now faced with an ambitious, restless neighbor occupying a fortress town very close to Florentine territory. Pope Sixtus then gave the town to Girolamo Riario.

As papal bankers, the Medici were required by the pope to finance this sale—that is, to participate in their own humiliation and insecurity. Lorenzo didn't just refuse to oblige the pope: he went even further by instructing the other Florentine bankers not to cooperate in the financing. The Pazzi, however, held an old grudge against the Medici and wanted the papal accounts, so they not only lent Sixtus the money but informed him of the Medici warnings not to do so. Girolamo Riario was incensed to the point that he, together with the Pazzi family and the archbishop of Pisa, plotted the assassination of Lorenzo and Giuliano de'Medici to take place at Easter 1478.

As we know, the conspiracy failed, although Giuliano was killed. The violent aftermath of the assassination saw the killing of the archbishop and several members of the Pazzi family and their co-conspirators in Florence. Sixtus declared war on Lorenzo and the Medici; and Florence only escaped death and destruction from the armies of the king of Naples and the pope by Lorenzo's personal diplomacy in 1480. Sixtus was forced to make peace with the Medici and Florence when the Turks captured the town and Cape of Otranto in 1480. Italian unity in the face of the Ottoman threat was more important than Sixtus's nepotism and hostility to Lorenzo.

It is impossible to know the degree to which the pope was personally involved in the Pazzi Conspiracy. He was certainly aware of it and did offer absolution in advance to his nephew, should it be needed. That said, it is unlikely that he condoned murder, especially in front of the high altar of the cathedral of Florence at Easter at the profoundly significant moment of the Elevation of the Host. Still, his guilt by association and the subsequent War of the Pazzi Conspiracy (1478–80) have seriously tarnished Sixtus's reputation and illustrated the negative aspects of his nepotism on both Italy and the Church as, too, did the striking of this commemorative medal. The medal shows Lorenzo de'Medici, the attack in the cathedral, and the phrase *salus publica* or "public salvation."

CHAPTER 19
JULIUS II

Giuliano della Rovere—who eventually assumed the pontifical name of Julius II— could be said to have been the defining pope of the High Italian Renaissance. Referred to by his contemporaries as the Warrior Pope or the Formidable Pope (*papa terribile*) he twice personally led his troops into battle. But, he will also forever be associated with the audacious demolition and rebuilding of St. Peter's basilica, the commission of the new wings of the Apostolic Palace, as well as with his tumultuous relationship with Michelangelo that saw, among other remarkable commissions, the painting of the Sistine Chapel ceiling.[1]

The Path to the Papacy

Giuliano's path to the papacy was not direct. He did, it is true, enjoy a very fortunate genealogy, as he was the son of Pope Sixtus IV's brother, Raffaele della Rovere. His influential uncle supported Giuliano's studies under the Franciscans, and then, just months after Sixtus was elected pope, he made Giuliano a cardinal. However, Giuliano was not the only papal nephew benefitting from such patronage. Pietro (or Piero) Riario, the son of Sixtus's sister, Bianca, was elevated at the same time. Pietro seemed to be the favorite, having lived in the future pope's household from an early age as a result of the premature death of his father.

In a mark of great esteem, Pietro was appointed a papal protonotary and also granted some of the most lucrative sees in the Roman Church, including the Latin patriarchate of Constantinople, the archbishopric of Seville, and, in 1473, that of Florence. Nevertheless, although he was quite cultivated personally as a humanist, Pietro was far more famous for his luxurious living and his feasts, arrogance, and ambition. He also saw his cousin Giuliano as a competitor for their uncle's favor. But his self-indulgent career ended abruptly when he died in 1475 at the age of twenty-nine. The evidence suggests that his death was probably from natural causes, but that didn't stop the general belief in Rome that he had been poisoned.

Giuliano immediately assumed Pietro's worldly goods and attracted some of his cousin's clients. He was also raised to the important See of Avignon, soon followed by other lucrative preferments. In 1474 his uncle assigned him to the very difficult military and diplomatic role of restoring peace and papal influence in the Romagna. Violence and instability called for a firm hand in ending the factional divisions in some significant

---

1. For a complete biography of Julius, see Shaw, 1993.

towns. However, the inexperienced Giuliano showed that he lacked the confidence and ability needed to accomplish his mandate. For example, he lost control of his soldiers when they viciously sacked Spoleto, and he proved unable to restrict the influence of Niccolo Vitelli, the powerful condottiere lord of Città di Castello whose ambitions were proving corrosive to Sixtus's authority in the Papal States. It required Federigo da Montefeltro, duke of Urbino, to use his reputation to broker a negotiated settlement, one which permitted Vitelli to leave his city with honor and with compensation. Many in Rome, particularly the powerful Orsini faction, doubted Giuliano's ability in military and diplomatic matters.

This reputation of being out of his depth was reinforced when Sixtus made Giuliano archbishop of Avignon and gave him the challenging task of keeping the papal territory around Avignon out of the hands of the king of France. At the same time he was made cardinal legate to the French king, Louis XI, charged with derailing French claims to Naples and Milan. Although Giuliano was not a total failure in these ambitions, he was generally seen as ineffectual. Thus, many in the Sacred College—and even his uncle, the pope—shifted their allegiance increasingly to Girolamo Riario, who was seen as more adept.

Tension consequently grew among the members of the della Rovere–Riario clan to the point that Giuliano was implicated in a conspiracy to kill Girolamo, an accusation that Sixtus appeared to credit. Add to this the appointment of Girolamo's son, Raffaele, to the College of Cardinals in 1477, and it was clear that Giuliano's prospects had greatly dimmed. But nothing is ever certain in papal politics. The tide turned in 1478 when the Riario faction was implicated in the failed Pazzi Conspiracy, and they lost influence dramatically with Sixtus's death in 1484. In the conclave called to choose the next pope, Giuliano della Rovere, together with Cardinal Rodrigo Borgia, the future Alexander VI, conspired to elect another Ligurian, Cardinal Cybo, who took the title of Innocent VIII. The Riario were effectively cut out of power.[2]

Initially Giuliano had the support of the new pope, who was in need of both quick loans and advice. And the assassination of Girolamo Riario in 1488 had at last removed a bitter enemy. Consequently, between 1488 and 1492, Giuliano seemed to be in a strong position for continued preferment and high office. However, the death of Innocent VIII shattered all of Giuliano's ambitions and made his prospects under the next pope hopeless and his fate uncertain.

The difficulty was that although Giuliano della Rovere and Roderigo Borgia had been allies in the conclave that elected Innocent, the death of that pope in 1492 dissolved their mutually beneficial relationship. It was a moment of high, if macabre, drama. At the very deathbed of the pope, the two cardinals fell into a heated, vituperative argument over the distribution of the late pope's property. When Roderigo was then elevated

2. For the conflicting accounts of the details of the conclave see Shaw, 1993. pp. 55–57.

to the chair of St. Peter—more correctly, after he had *bought* the papacy[3]—his hostility to Giuliano became pathological. Any hope Giuliano had for high office and recognition was shattered, and Borgia ruthlessness put his very life in danger.[4]

Alexander VI and the Borgia Papacy

It was not only the competing greed of the two cardinals that drove them into mutual hatred: there was also a profound policy divergence regarding the succession in Naples and the role the Holy See should play.[5] The usual narrative is that the Borgia pope ordered the murder of Giuliano in 1493, but the cardinal managed to escape his would-be assassins. He fled to his see at Ostia, which, as a seaport, gave him quick access to ships. Alexander then summoned the cardinal to Rome, but Giuliano refused to go for fear of his life. Instead, he very prudently sailed to France, seeking safety at the court of Charles VIII where he was known and where he could offer useful advice regarding Charles's planned invasion of Italy. He also—together with Ascanio Sforza and others—implored the king to depose Alexander VI for his crimes and character.[6]

When Charles crossed the Alps to claim the crown of Naples in 1494, Giuliano accompanied him, hoping that the invasion would result in Alexander's deposition.[7] Later, when that was evidently not going to happen, he stayed with the French and became a trusted advisor to the new king Louis XII on his accession in 1498. Alexander was now in a difficult position regarding Cardinal della Rovere: the pope needed a good working relationship with King Louis and that meant reconciling with Giuliano, which Alexander cynically managed in 1498. Giuliano, however, knowing the Borgia's proclivity to assassination, never returned to Rome while Alexander was alive.

For Giuliano's security this was a wise policy, particularly near the end of the Borgia papacy. Rumors abounded around the murder of opponents or clerics who were simply too rich to be tolerated by Alexander and his son Cesare. Machiavelli repeats the famous description of Cesare's slaughter of his condottiere generals, including two members of the Orsini family, who Cesare thought were conspiring against him. They were all ruthlessly executed at Senigallia in 1502 after having been invited to a feast ostensibly to reconcile their differences. In 1503 all of Rome believed that old Cardinal Orsini had been poisoned by Alexander, despite the pope's claims of innocence. The death of the vastly

3. See Francesco Guicciardini's discussion of the character of Alexander VI and his election: Francesco Guicciardini, *The History of Italy*, tr. Sidney Alexander. New York: Macmillan, 1969. pp. 9–10.
4. Guicciardini, 1969. pp. 79, 81–82.
5. For Alexander VI, Cesare, and Lucrezia Borgia, see Michael Mallett, *The Borgias: The Rise and Fall of the Most Infamous Family in History.* Chicago: Academy Chicago Publishers, 2005.
6. Guicciardini, 1969. p. 69.
7. Guicciardini, 1969. p. 46.

wealthy Venetian Cardinal Michiel was also believed to be the result of the administration of the famous Borgia poison, known as *La Cantarella.*

Even Pope Alexander's own death and his son Cesare's almost fatal illness at the same time were attributed to their attempt to poison Cardinal Adriano Castellesi da Corneto. According to the rumor, the Borgias wanted to dispose of Cardinal Castellesi, even though Adriano had been close to Alexander and had paid handsomely for his elevation to the Sacred College. The perfect opportunity arose when the cardinal invited the Borgias to dinner at his palace. Cesare sent some excellent wine ahead, wine that was heavily laced with *La Cantarella.* The servant who received the wine was told that it was under no circumstances to be consumed until the dinner attended by Pope Alexander and Cardinal Castellesi. At that point, Cesare's steward was intended to serve it to the cardinal. The servant who accepted the wine, however, misunderstood and thought that this was the best wine and was to be reserved for the pope and Cesare alone; so, it was served to them. The pope died soon after while Cesare, who was younger and stronger, survived—but barely.

Although this version of events was highly improbable, it illustrated the popular distrust of the Borgia pope and his son, to the point that the rumor is still accepted by some historians. Francesco Guicciardini, after all, describes it as fact.[8] The most likely cause, however, of Pope Alexander's death in 1503 and Cesare's serious illness was malaria, or "the Roman fever," as it was often described.[9] (It was not until Mussolini drained the swamps around the Tiber in the 1930s that the scourge of malaria was lifted from the city.) Nevertheless, the story helps support the wisdom of Giuliano's decision to stay away from Rome as long as Alexander lived.

All such rumors reinforced both contemporary and subsequent views of the Borgias as wicked and murderous tyrants. Indeed, much of the received opinion on the pontificate of Alexander VI Borgia has focused on his character, his family, and the politics of the Church and the peninsula during that turbulent period. Recently, however, there has been a reassessment of his patronage of art and building. The significant commissions, such as Pinturicchio's decoration of the Borgia apartments in the Apostolic Palace, Bramante's Tempietto on the Gianicolo, and the work on Castel Sant'Angelo were always recognized; but, it appears that the Borgias had an even more significant influence on Rome in the decades around the turn of the sixteenth century. Naturally, much of this material was designed for the aggrandizement of the pope and his family. Nevertheless, Alexander and his court did employ very skilled practitioners of the

---

8. The story of the pope's and Cesare's accidental poisoning is told in detail by Guicciardini, 1969. pp. 165–66.

9. Shaw, 1993. pp. 117–18. It is significant, however, that Alexander's master of ceremonies, Johannes Burchard, describes having seen the pope's corpse on two occasions and both descriptions match the discolorations and other features often associated with poison. See Johannes Burchard, *At the Court of the Borgia,* tr. Geoffrey Parker. London: The Folio Society, 1963. p. 225.

minor and decorative arts to create an atmosphere of luxury and taste that characterized his reign.[10]

The death of the Borgia pope in August of 1503 drew Cardinal Giuliano della Rovere immediately to Rome, arriving in the city in September of that year. Cesare was still extremely ill and hence had limited ability to influence the conclave. That meant there was a good chance that Giuliano would be chosen the next pope, an event that would be devastating to the Borgias but celebrated by their many enemies. Still, being a man not known for taking chances in a volatile situation, Giuliano entered Rome with a large armed guard. He feared an assassination attempt ordered by Cesare, who he believed would do anything—even from his deathbed—to ensure that Giuliano not be elected.

But Giuliano's time had not yet come. In the conclave, a compromise candidate emerged, Cardinal Piccolomini, the nephew of Pius II, who took the name Pius III in honor of his uncle. Pius III was hardly a compelling selection. Although a competent scholar and an experienced prelate, he was not very distinguished, except for the fact that he was one with whom both factions could live for a time. After all, he had been consecrated by Giuliano della Rovere while also confirming Cesare Borgia in his office as papal commander in chief. Thus, the conclave seemed to welcome a breathing space after Alexander's particularly fractious regime. There was clearly a desire to pause and see whether the Borgia or the della Rovere faction would coalesce with the greater support.

What no one imagined, however, was that the pontificate of Pius III would be as short as it was: the new pope died just twenty-six days after his election. He was sixty-eight and had long been in frail health, seriously afflicted by gout; but again the rumors of poison were universal. In this improbable version of events, however, neither Borgia nor della Rovere were suspected: the suspect was Pandolfo Petrucci, the tyrant of Pius's native Siena, a ruthless man who had killed before and who feared a Sienese pope opposed to his continued rule as *signore* of a traditionally republican city. Nevertheless, the reality was that Pius was old for the times, ill, and indeed elected just for these reasons: the opposing factions in the conclave needed a brief hiatus to see what would develop. Once again, Giuliano's path to the pontificate had been fortuitously cleared by an unexpected death.

The conclave that followed was the shortest in memory. Giuliano della Rovere, Cardinal of San Pietro in Vincoli, was elected and took the name Julius II. It was a title that by legend he chose to signal a parallel to Julius Caesar, in the same way the Borgia pope had honored Alexander the Great. It's also worth pointing out that *Julius* is merely a variant of the Italian name *Giuliano*. The new pope was not about to inhibit his own personality in service to the Holy See.

---

10. Felipe V. Garin-Llombart, "Alessandro VI a Roma: Cultura e Committenza Artistica," in *I Borgia. Catalogo mostra Palazzo Ruspoli Fondazione Memmo Roma 3 ottobre 2002–23 febbraio 2003*. Milan: Electa, 2002. pp. 119–77. This catalogue of the extensive exhibition in the Fondazione Memmo examined the Borgias and their times through art and material culture.

Pope Julius II

Julius confronted a number of problems immediately upon his election. The ambitions of the Borgias had exhausted papal resources—there was no money left in the papal treasury. The subject territories in the States of the Church were unstable, and allegiance to his papacy was fragile. And the Venetian republic was taking advantage of the situation by expanding southward into the Romagna and the Marche, claiming control over cities and territories like Faenza and Rimini that had traditionally been within the orbit of the Holy See.

Newly invigorated by his ascension, Julius took immediate control. To raise money he took the time-honored expediencies of putting off repaying papal debts and simultaneously selling offices within the Curia for considerable sums. He decapitated the threat from the Borgias by in effect making Cesare a prisoner. To show his resolve and stamina—and perhaps erase his earlier reputation as an unskilled military leader—Julius personally led his army against Bologna in 1506, using both spiritual and military weapons to restore papal authority over this extremely important strategic city. The image of the *papa terribile* was being established!

His distrust and indeed dislike of the great Roman dynasties was balanced by a rather astute marriage policy for his family. Marriage alliances were potent weapons in the papal arsenal, even among popes like Julius who were not addicted to nepotism.[11] The alliances he made were forged to bring the fractious baronial clans into the orbit of the papacy and link the pope's family to the stability of Rome. So it was that Julius married his natural daughter, Felice, into one of those great feudal clans, the Orsini. Furthermore, he arranged matches between his nephew and a Colonna and between his niece and another Orsini. His nephew, Francesco Maria della Rovere, he supported as duke of Urbino to replace the extinct Montefeltro dynasty. But that succession had been previously arranged by Duke Guidobaldo da Montefeltro; and, perhaps as a consequence, Francesco Maria's allegiance was more to Urbino than to his uncle and the Church.

The Rebuilding of St. Peter's

Julius had both a restless and imperious character. He did not like to be challenged and had very clear ideas about how his office as Christ's vicar on earth should be recognized. One of his missions was to leave Rome more beautiful and powerful than he found it. As Augustus had found a city of brick and left a city of marble, Julius wanted later generations to associate the rebirth of papal Rome with his pontificate.

He had always recognized the power of a great building to embellish a ruler's reputation. While cardinal archbishop of Avignon, he had rebuilt the archbishop's palace in a manner both to his taste and to his sense of grandeur: to this day his arms are visible

---

11. Stinger, 1998. pp. 104–6.

on the façade of his former residence. What is more, he enjoyed the company of architects, having become an intimate of the Sangallo family well before his elevation. It is in this context that he resolved to undertake the greatest work a pope could envisage: the rebuilding of the basilica of St. Peter.

The original basilica, the church that had been commissioned by Constantine and stood over the tomb of the apostle Peter, was the holiest site in Western Christendom. As early as the 1450s, there had been plans to restore or reconstruct a building that Leon Battista Alberta had described in a report as being held together mostly by its roof beams. Nevertheless, it required the confidence and ambition of Julius II to initiate the reconstruction.[12]

Despite his earlier association with Giuliano da Sangallo, Julius chose the design prepared by the elderly (b. 1444) Donato Bramante from Urbino. The contract was fixed in 1503, and construction began in April of 1506. The church would take 120 years to finish, for rather than totally demolishing the original structure from the outset to make way for the new basilica, the various architects who managed the project in succession all kept at least part of the church functioning throughout the long process of reconstruction. Thus, a steady flow of pilgrims was always guaranteed—and the money they brought with them funded much of the rebuilding. To make access easier for pilgrims, Julius constructed an efficient, straight street that led from Sixtus IV's bridge across the Tiber, Ponte Sisto, toward St. Peter's, a major artery that he planned to furnish with important new buildings. This eponymous street, the Via Giulia, running parallel with the Tiber for much of its course, is still used as a relatively quick route across the city.[13]

At the time of Julius's death all that had been completed of the new St. Peter's was the setting of the huge piers required to support the dome, but that established the center of the church for all time. To secure his place in history, Julius had medals struck in 1506 that illustrated Bramante's design: one set of which was to be placed beneath the foundations of the great piers to acknowledge forever who had commanded the basilica to be built.

In fact, one of the driving considerations for Julius's rebuilding of St. Peter's was to create an appropriate site for his own tomb. In 1505 Michelangelo was summoned from Florence to create the massive monument. Not by any means afflicted with modesty, Julius was adamant that the monument equal in size and grandeur the fourth-century BC eponymous Mausoleum of Mausolus, Satrap of Caria, in Helicarnassus, one of the wonders of the ancient world. And, wonderful it was to be: it was to stand three stories high, with forty-seven life-sized figures displayed around the monument.[14]

---

12. Christof Thoenes, "Renaissance St. Peter's," in William Tronzo, ed., *St. Peter's in the Vatican*. Cambridge: Cambridge University Press, 2005. pp. 64–92; R. A. Scotti, *Basilica: The Splendor and the Scandal: Building St. Peter's*. New York: Viking-Penguin, 2006. pp. 3–101.
13. McGregor, 2005. pp. 211–16.
14. See Christoph Luitpold Frommel, ed. *Michelangelo's Tomb for Julius II: Genesis and Genius*. Los Angeles: The J. Paul Getty Museum, 2016.

Transforming the Vatican Palace

In addition to the ambitious plans for St. Peter's, Julius charged Bramante with designing a vast new papal palace which would link the Medieval Vatican Palace to the Belvedere built by Innocent VIII on the summit of the Vatican Hill.[15] The distance and the steep grade of the hill made the entire plan suspect. The task seemed daunting, if not impossible. But Bramante developed an ingenious structure of stepped terraces linked by stairs and ramps. Although only the eastern side of the two wings was finished by the architect's death, his plan was largely borne out, creating the largest palace in Europe.

In the courtyard of Innocent's villa, Julius indulged his own interest in ancient marbles by establishing a sculpture court. He saw this as an illustration of the reconciliation between the old, pagan culture of Rome with the new Christian dispensation, of which he believed himself to be the head. It was there that Julius placed the most important discovery yet of the Renaissance: the *Laocoön*, representing a scene from the first book of the *Aeneid* in which the Trojan priest and his two sons are killed by serpents after he tried to warn his fellow citizens against accepting the Trojan Horse from the Greeks.[16]

Humanists had known about this sculptural group through the testimony of Pliny (Gaius Plinius Secundus, the Elder, 23–79 AD) in his *Natural History* (*Historia Naturalis*, XXXVI, 37). Pliny had written rapturously about the work when he first saw it in the palace of the emperor Titus. Long thought to have been lost, when it was unearthed in February 1506 in a vineyard on the Esquiline, Julius was overcome. He coveted the statue so fiercely that he gave the owner of the vineyard a position in the Curia and assigned him a lucrative income from certain tolls assessed at the gate of San Giovanni. In return, Julius acquired the *Laocoön* for the Vatican collection in perpetuity. It was a wise choice. Together with the *Apollo Belvedere*, discovered in Grottaferrata in 1489, the *Laocoön* remains among the most important ancient sculptures in the papal collection. Julius would have well understood the crowds of modern tourists who daily throng to the Belvedere courtyard and struggle to secure an unimpeded view of these works.

Besides his interests in architecture and sculpture, Julius was also passionate about painting. But, he had only very reluctantly moved into the boldly decorated papal apartments in the old Vatican Palace. The rooms painted by Pinturicchio for Alexander VI held far too many Borgia memories for Julius to feel comfortable: bulls (the Borgia symbol) and family portraits of the pope, his daughter Lucrezia and his mistress Vanozza Catanei, abounded. While Julius most certainly appreciated the technique of Pinturicchio's work, the images were an odious reminder of a pope and a family who had tried to murder him and who had forced his exile to France. Given his character and ego, it is testimony to Julius's appreciation of fine art that he refrained from whitewashing the entire space and starting again.

---

15. Carlo Pietrangeli, ed., *Il Palazzo Apostolico Vaticano*. Florence: Nardini Editore, 1992.
16. Stinger, 1998. pp. 77, 271.

Instead, in 1508 Julius commissioned Raphael, a distant relation of Bramante's from Urbino, to decorate what were to be the new apartments of the popes, immediately above those of Alexander. These four spectacular rooms (*stanze* in Italian) were not completed until after Julius's (1513) and Raphael's deaths (1520). But, by that time their program had been firmly established. The images were, like those Pinturicchio had painted, potent examples of propaganda, but this time they were not in the service of just a single papal family: rather, they were propaganda celebrating the Roman Church ascendant on earth.[17]

That same year, Julius entrusted an even more ambitious and significant project to Michelangelo. Even though the artist was not an expert in fresco technique and saw himself more as a sculptor than a painter, Julius commissioned him to paint the vault of his uncle's Sistine Chapel. The painter began the enormous task a few months after signing the contract in March of 1508, completing the ceiling in under four short years.[18] Even Raphael, an experienced fresco artist, was overwhelmed by its composition, color, and dynamic figures. In fact, in tribute to Michelangelo's obvious genius, Raphael added a portrait of his rival to the *School of Athens*, a portrayal of the great classical philosophers like Euclid and Aristotle. This quintessentially humanist work, often acknowledged as Raphael's masterpiece, was in the *Stanza della Segnatura*—Julius's private study. Julius was pleased.

With the Sistine commission complete, Michelangelo returned to work on the tomb, although there were disputes as to where it should be placed and, hence, as to its size and design. To ensure that the work would be finished, Julius left a substantial sum in his will for its completion and ordered it be set in the Sistine Chapel. But this was never done. A wall tomb was eventually constructed from the few figures Michelangelo had completed, of which the *Moses* is the most renowned. The monument was installed in the pope's former titular church, San Pietro in Vincoli, where it remains, although even then not quite in the form Michelangelo had devised. So much for Julius's vainglory!

The Warrior Pope

In the midst of his extravagant patronage of building and art, Julius returned to his hostility toward Venice. The republic had annexed substantial papal territory and claimed traditional papal cities as part of its *Terraferma* territory. Julius's first attempt at an alliance with the Holy Roman Empire against Venice resulted in the complete rout of the Imperial forces in 1508. So, in the following year, Julius cobbled together a larger alliance, the League of Cambrai, which also included France and Ferdinand of Aragon (and Naples).

---

17. Christiane L. Joost-Gaugier, *Raphael's Stanza della Segnatura: Meaning and Invention*. Cambridge: Cambridge University Press, 2002; Louisa Beccherucci, "Rapahel and Painting," in Mario Salmi, ed., *The Complete Works of Raphael*. New York: Raynal-William Morrow, 1969. pp. 79–173.
18. Giacommetti, 1986. pp. 92–175, 218–59.

Differences between the condottieri fighting for Venice resulted in the complete defeat of Venice at Agnadello in 1509, after which the Venetian *Terraferma* state disintegrated, with important cities and territories occupied by the victors.[19]

Yet, Julius saw the danger of a complete collapse of Venice as he knew the French were ambitious for even more Italian territory. Although forced to accept the punitive peace demanded by the pope, Venice then became his ally. Nevertheless, this didn't stop the French. They continued their advance and recaptured Bologna and occupied much of the Romagna by March 1511. Determined to overcome his losses, Julius formed the Holy League to "drive the barbarians out of Italy," despite the obvious fact that his major allies *were* barbarians—including the Holy Roman Emperor, Ferdinand of Aragon and Naples, and Henry VIII of England. The war raged, and the very divergent ambitions of the allies ironically drove Venice back into the arms of France. Yet the French soon suffered severe losses, not only in Italy but also in northern France, which Henry VIII had invaded.

The one element for which there was general agreement among the allies had to do with Florence rather than Venice. All agreed it was important to suppress the reconstituted Florentine republic and facilitate the return of the Medici by force of arms. Julius was keen on punishing the government of Soderini for agreeing to hold a stillborn Council of the Church in Pisa with the intent of deposing him, or at least putting him on trial. So in 1512 a Spanish army defeated the Florentines, despite Machiavelli's investment in and hopes for the citizen militia he had formed. Cardinal Giulio de'Medici, the son born posthumously to Lorenzo *il Magnifico's* murdered brother Giuliano, was returned to the Palazzo Medici with papal approval.

The rest of the Holy League began to dissolve. Henry of England made peace with the French and the Spanish forces could not repeat their decisive victories, relying instead on skirmishing, in an inconclusive campaign that continued to devour vast sums of money for little gain. Julius became more interested in securing a favorable peace than in continuing the war.

It was in this environment that Julius II took ill in the winter of 1513. He knew he was dying, so he called the Sacred College to his deathbed and admonished them to choose the next pope carefully. And, the wound still raw, he vindictively made them swear to disallow any cardinal from voting who had participated in the Council of Pisa called to question the validity of his pontificate.[20] On February 20, 1513, Julius died. There was much irony in the timing of his death. His one great overarching foreign policy had been that of sustaining the territorial integrity and ecclesiastical independence of the Holy See. In that ambition he had been only partly successful, and then at an enormous cost to the Church and to an independent Italian state system, and now he was dead in the midst of the unraveling of the Holy League. The *papa terribile* was terrifying no more.

---

19. Shaw, 1993. pp. 209–78.
20. Shaw, 1993. p. 312.

Viewed from a modern lens, the failure of his political ambitions seems irrelevant. Julius's legacy has been far greater than that of the papal control of defiant territories. Through his patronage and commissioning of some of the greatest artwork and building projects in the history of Europe he did much to establish the Renaissance in our consciousness. The new St. Peter's, the wings of the Apostolic Vatican Palace, the sculpture court of the Belvedere, the *Stanze* of Raphael, the vault of the Sistine Chapel—all these have a longevity, resonance, and glory well beyond that of transitory political domination.

**Illus. 19.1 Raphael, *Julius II from The Room of Heliodorus* (*Stanza
di Eliodoro*), detail, 1511–12. Apostolic Vatican Palace, Rome.**

While the four rooms (*stanze*) of Raphael represent one of the most significant achievements in Renaissance painting, we also need to acknowledge that they were powerful instruments of propaganda promoting the ascendency of the pope and Church under Julius II della Rovere.

The *Room of Heliodorus* takes its theme from the apocryphal *Book of Maccabees*, which recounts Heliodorus's expulsion from the Temple when he attempted to steal its treasure. In this fresco, Pope Julius appears in person to reinforce the message of divine retribution against those who would steal the treasure, or territory, of the Holy See. The fresco therefore represents not only a celebration of the union of human and divine power and wisdom but also the divine mission of the Church and the authority of the papacy, which included papal control over the States of the Church, a policy rigorously pursued by Julius.

Julius II, as in this image, is usually depicted with a beard, the first pope since antiquity to appear unshaven. However, the fact is that the pope only wore his beard for nine months, beginning in June 1511, as a sign of mourning at the loss of the city of Bologna from the Papal States, shaving it off nine months later when the tide turned in March 1512. Yet his facial hair was captured here for eternity as well as in Raphael's depiction of him in the role of Pope Gregory IX in the *Stanza della Segnatura* and in his famous panel portrait.

CHAPTER 20
THE MEDICI POPES

While the Medici had achieved power in Florence and renown in Italy, they had not yet achieved the papacy. Under Julius II, the young Cardinal de'Medici proved useful in deflecting a schismatic Council that had been called for Pisa in Florentine territory. As a reward for the Medici and a punishment for the citizenry of Florence, Julius provided an army to return the Medici to power. In 1512 the cardinal entered Florence as head of the Medici family, restoring the rule that had been taken from his brother in 1494. Although that was a great victory for Giovanni, it was soon superseded: Cardinal de'Medici heard in March of 1513 that he had been elected to the papacy. Rome had chosen its first Medici pope.[1]

The Pontificate of Leo X

Giovanni de'Medici was the second son of Lorenzo *il Magnifico*.[2] He had been elevated to the Sacred College when only thirteen years of age by Innocent VIII, whose son, Franceschetto, was married to Giovanni's sister Maddalena. Because of his youth, the boy was declared cardinal deacon of Santa Maria in Domnica *in pectore*, which meant that he was a cardinal "in the pope's breast"; that is, not yet an active member of the college.

While still in his teens Giovanni received significant benefices. Given his rank and position, he might have succumbed to the life of an indolent playboy. But, in a sign of his serious nature, he pursued his education under the humanist tutors engaged by his father such as Angelo Poliziano, while later at the University of Pisa he studied canon law and theology, disciplines appropriate to his future clerical career. By 1491, he had reached the age when he could assume an active role in the College of Cardinals. Traveling to Rome in 1492, he was able to vote in the conclave that elected Alexander VI Borgia.

Giovanni had been part of the faction that tried to block Alexander's election, so he thought it wise to return home to Florence. But the Florence he found had changed dramatically from the city he had known under his father. His older brother Piero was now the head of the family and alienating the Medici faction ever more each day, and Girolamo Savonarola was rising in influence. The events of the autumn of 1494 following the French invasion and Piero's capitulation to the French resulted in not only his brother but also Giovanni being forced to flee, both with prices on their heads. Because Rome was still too volatile and because he feared the Borgias, Giovanni spent the next

---

1. Herbert M. Vaughan, *The Medici Popes (Leo X. and Clement VII)*. London: Methuen, 1908 (reprinted by Andesite Press, 2015).
2. Roscoe, 1846.

years traveling widely throughout Europe, returning to Rome only in 1500, where he was tolerated by Pope Alexander and Cesare Borgia. Prudently, however, he stayed out of political intrigues and devoted himself to his beloved humanist scholarship.

The death of Alexander and ultimate election of Julius II were a relief, as both the new pope and the young cardinal had been known to be opposed to the Borgias. Moreover, in that same year Giovanni's brother Piero had died, drowning while fleeing with the French army after the defeat at Garigliano. Consequently, many *Palleschi* (Medici supporters) recognized him as the new head of the family, despite his clerical position and residence in Rome.

Julius II shrewdly used Giovanni as a legate to Bologna during the years when the Council of Pisa was threatening the pope and the papacy was hostile to the French. When open warfare broke out, Giovanni, in command of papal troops, was captured by the French. Despite this embarrassment, the rapidly changing landscape of the War of the League of Cambrai saw the Medici returned to Florence in 1512, after the papal troops, with Giovanni in charge, captured his native city and expelled Soderini. The Medici made a triumphal entry into the city as the *Palleschi* tried to turn the clock back to 1492.[3]

The death of Julius II in January 1513 required Giovanni to return to Rome for the conclave. The election in March of 1513 was unusually quick with Giovanni winning a majority of votes on March 9, despite his not having been ordained a priest and despite his remarkably young age of thirty-seven. The first obstacle was easily dealt with: within ten days Giovanni had been invested with priest's orders and crowned as Pope Leo X. The era of the Medici popes had begun.

A Humanist's Papacy

Whether it is true or not that Cardinal de'Medici skipped out of the conclave of 1513 saying "Now that God has given us the papacy, let us enjoy it!" the character of Leo's pontificate certainly involved a good measure of delight. The tone of his reign was set with the procession of his *Possesso*, in which the pope traveled from the Vatican to the basilica of St. John Lateran; that is, from his election as the successor to St. Peter to his installation as bishop of Rome. This parade was one of characteristic magnificence, for magnificence in ritual was one of his signature elements, as was befitting to his declared desire to found a Leonine Age of Gold.[4] His day was described as a civilized mixture of responsibility and indulgence. It began by hearing mass and holding audiences, receiving information on matters of Church and state, giving instructions, and meeting with his household officials. But then there was time for pursuits like riding and hunting (despite the prohibition on blood sports for priests) and games like chess. Evenings consisted of

---

3. Guicciardini, 1969. pp. 261–67.
4. Signorotto and Visceglia, 2002. pp. 43–46.

elaborate feasts, entertainments, and recitations. There was always time, as well, for listening to music, for which Leo had a great appreciation: he himself was an accomplished singer.[5] There is no doubt but that Leo enjoyed his papacy.

He was even more serious about art. Leo began his reign by confirming Raphael's contract under Julius II to paint the *Stanze* in the Apostolic Palace. In return, the artist flattered his new patron in the *Stanza di Eliodoro*, portraying the pope as his namesake, Leo the Great, who famously dissuaded Attila the Hun from attacking Rome. Leo soon extended Raphael's employment by commissioning the painting of the loggias in the palace and the design of a series of tapestries to be hung in the Sistine Chapel. Finally, to ensure preservation of the best examples of Roman sculpture and decorative arts, Leo charged Raphael in 1515 with the responsibility of evaluating all future classical discoveries made in the city and its environs. It is as a consequence of this wise appointment that the splendid ancient marbles depicting the Tiber and the Nile entered the Belvedere courtyard.

Leo was equally concerned with learning.[6] Having enjoyed a superb classical education himself, he avowed at the beginning of his pontificate to bring the best scholars to Rome, employ them in the Church, and honor them as ornaments to the city. He purchased books throughout his pontificate, enlarging the Vatican collection significantly. Poets, masters of elegant Latin prose such as Pietro Bembo (who became his Latin secretary), playwrights, and scholars were his companions and friends. Leo also invited celebrated Greeks, such as Janus Lascaris, to Rome and established the Greek College to teach that language.[7] The university thrived during his reign. He dedicated specific revenues like the tax on wine to fund the *studio*. Professors' salaries were effectively doubled from their level under Sixtus IV, and their number reached the highest concentration of talent of any school in Italy by 1514–15.

There were eighty-seven teachers of theology, civil and canon law, philosophy, medicine, ethics, logic, astronomy, astrology, mathematics, Greek, and even botany—the first such appointment in Italy. Leo's own particular interests—Greek and rhetoric—benefitted particularly. Some famous scholars were added to the roster of professors, including Agostino Nifo in philosophy and Fra Luca Pacioli, the most celebrated mathematician of the Renaissance, whose book *De Divina proportione* (printed in 1509) was illustrated by his friend Leonardo da Vinci.

Leo loved gardens and animals, so he combined the two into an extensive menagerie constructed in the Vatican Gardens. In this private zoo were monkeys; leopards; a cheetah; a great many rare birds; and his beloved elephant, Hanno, who had been a gift

---

5. Anthony M. Cummings, *The Lion's Ear: Pope Leo X, the Renaissance Papacy, and Music*. Ann Arbor: University of Michigan Press, 2012.

6. D'Amico, 1983. pp. 41–45.

7. Stinger, 1998. p. 287.

from the king of Portugal.[8] They first met when Hanno entered Rome with a massive silver howdah set on his back. To greet the pope, the great creature knelt and trumpeted his obedience. Leo had a preserve created specifically for Hanno who became one of the sights of Rome, with the public invited to see him on Sundays. Hanno was often part of the papal cortege, and artists of the quality of Raphael depicted him at the pope's request. When the beloved creature passed away, Leo was sincerely distraught, keeping vigil with his dying pet until the end.

In a more typical ambition, Leo also had an obsession with rebuilding the city of Rome. Of most concern was the reconstruction of St. Peter's that had begun under his predecessor, Julius II. On the death of Bramante in 1514, Leo appointed Raphael chief architect. Originally, Leo had hoped that Giulio da Sangallo would replace Bramante, perhaps because of the wonderful work the architect had done in Florence and because of Giulio's relationship with the pope's father, Lorenzo de'Medici. But Sangallo was too old for a responsibility that required a great deal of energy and commitment, so he declined. To compensate for Raphael's lack of experience in the construction of any building, let alone one the size and complexity of the basilica of St. Peter, Leo provided him with the practical assistance of that monk-architect Fra Giacondo.

Also like his immediate predecessors, Leo saw the need for more straight roads and easier access both for servicing parts of the city and for pilgrims to reach St. Peter's. Consequently, he built a street paralleling the Tiber over the remains of an ancient Roman thoroughfare.[9] The street ran from the Piazza del Popolo to near his family palace, Palazzo Madama, an edifice completed in 1505 and his home and that of his cousin Giulio, before they became Leo X and Clement VII, respectively. It formed one of the three streets of the Trident (*Tridente*), to this day existing as the Via del Corso, Via Babuino, and Via di Ripetta.

In his self-appointed role as advocate for the poorer citizens of Rome, Leo also briefly engaged Leonardo da Vinci to drain the Pontine Marshes, known for their unhealthy miasma, if not the terrible incidence of malaria in the city during the summer.[10] He tried to control the price of food and other basic commodities required by the poor. He was active in the endowment of hospitals and other public charities from his own resources. Crippled soldiers, poor scholars, distressed convents, orphanages, and other social agencies benefitted from a largesse amounting to as much as six thousand gold florins annually. Leo, despite his reputation for luxury and indulgence, was manifestly also a sincerely dutiful pastor to his flock.

---

8. Silvio A. Bedini, *The Pope's Elephant*. London: Penguin Books, 2000.
9. It was then appropriately named the Via Leonina but is now the Via Ripetta. McGregor, 2005. p. 266.
10. Stinger, 1998. pp. 18–19.

The War of Urbino

Leo did not like war, as it was expensive; but he was absolute in his commitment to his family and his desire to restore the Medici to the front ranks of Italian princely dynasties. This was no better illustrated than in the history of his young nephew Lorenzo de'Medici (1492–1519), the son of Piero the Unfortunate. Lorenzo had briefly represented the family's newly recovered hegemony in Florence but the possibility of creating a Medici duchy out of the Papal States, perhaps by uniting Ferrara and Urbino, was too attractive a prospect to the dynastically inclined Leo. In 1516 he named his nephew duke of Urbino, deposing the previous duke, Francesco Maria della Rovere (the nephew both of Julius II and of the last of the Montefeltro dynasty, Guidobaldo). Francesco Maria was not willing to acquiesce and was determined to recover his duchy. Taking advantage of the ending of the War of the League of Cambrai, Francesco Maria managed briefly to re-enter Urbino by engaging an experienced mercenary army and defeating the papal troops in January of 1517.[11]

The people of Urbino welcomed him warmly. The pope responded, however, by both excommunicating Duke Francesco Maria and paying for a huge condottiere army under his nephew to recapture the city. In the ensuing battle, Lorenzo was badly wounded and felt unable to continue, so he returned to Florence where he was nominally governor of the city.

In his place, Leo appointed Cardinal Dovizi da Bibbiena (1470–1520). The cardinal was an odd choice for a papal military commander. He was a celebrated wit, scholar, and humanist; a famous playwright (*La Calandra*, 1513);[12] and the subject of a splendid portrait by Raphael, who also decorated his bathroom. His main qualification was that he was a loyal friend of Leo's from his earliest days when his family served the Medici household in Florence. Not surprisingly, Bibbiena proved unable to lead an army and suffered a sound defeat at the hands of the della Rovere duke.

Despite his victories, Francesco Maria was unable to pay his soldiers. Recognizing that Leo was in financial difficulty as well, Francesco Maria successfully sued for peace. His excommunication was lifted, but he was required to leave the palace built by his great uncle Federigo da Montefeltro, for Mantua, taking with him his military hardware and the wonderful library collected by Duke Federigo.

The cost of this short war (February to September 1517) was enormously disproportionate to its length. Ironically, however, although Lorenzo was restored as duke, he never had the chance to rule. His wound refused to heal and the syphilis and tuberculosis that wasted his body ultimately led to his early death in May of 1519. Arrogant, rash, and unpopular, Lorenzo did, however, leave two lasting memories: his baby daughter, Caterina, who would later become queen of France, and his tomb in San Lorenzo,

---

11. Mallett and Shaw, 2012. pp. 134–36; Stinger, 1998. pp. 105–6.
12. D'Amico, 1983. p. 19.

Florence, by Michelangelo. Urbino reverted to papal rule under Leo, but with the pope's death in 1521 Urbino was recovered by Francesco Maria della Rovere. Five years of turmoil and enormous expense only to return to the status quo![13]

The Conspiracy of the Cardinals

The months of the War of Urbino also saw a conspiracy against Leo, the Conspiracy of the Five Cardinals.[14] The most prominent of these, Cardinal Alfonso Petrucci, was accused of masterminding a plot to poison the pope. Indeed, Petrucci, who was in his mid-twenties, had a strong motive: He was the son of Pandolfo Petrucci, the lord of Siena, Florence's traditional enemy, which Leo had had brought under the protection of the Holy See after deposing the Petrucci family. Alfonso and his brother had been expelled from Siena and lost the basis of their wealth, making it difficult for Alfonso to sustain the dignity of his rank in Rome, despite his previous support of Leo in the Curia.

The other conspirators had somewhat less clear motives for sedition. One cardinal, the elderly Raffaele Riario, was simultaneously the nephew by blood or marriage of Sixtus IV, Girolamo Riario, and Archbishop Salviati of Pisa—all three having been accomplices in the Pazzi Conspiracy against Leo's father, Lorenzo the Magnificent. Two others were the wealthy Cardinal Sauli of Genoa and Cardinal Francesco Soderini, the brother of the former Florentine Gonfaloniere for Life in the republic suppressed in 1512. The last was Cardinal Adriano Castellesi da Corneto, bishop of Bath and Wells in England and that kingdom's protector at the papal court.

It is easy to see that Leo X would have some hatred for or jealously of all these men or would be willing to act for others who did. The desire to rid himself of Petrucci the Sienese was obvious, as was Petrucci's fury at his own family's exile and loss of wealth and power at the hands of Leo. Cardinal Riario was a legacy of the conspiracy of the Pazzi, and Leo clearly harbored a lingering enmity to all of those involved in the plot. Soderini was the brother and, to a degree, protector of the head of the republic that had expelled the Medici from Florence in 1494. Castellesi and Sauli were immensely rich and Leo was in need of cash.

Money, in fact, had a great deal to do with the harsh punishment of the conspirators, who were found guilty on what seemed to be hearsay or evidence obtained through torture. In the end only Petrucci and lower-ranked individuals were executed, the cardinal by strangling and the others by being drawn and quartered and their body parts set on Ponte Sant'Angelo. Riario was forced to pay an immense fine of 150,000 ducats and surrender his palace, which became, as a result, the papal chancery, or *cancelleria*. He was

---

13. Christopher Hibbert, *The House of Medici: Its Rise and Fall.* New York: William Morrow, 1975. pp. 220, 223–24, 235–36.
14. The conspiracy is described in detail by Guicciardini, 1969. pp. 294–97. See also Fabrizio Winspeare, *La Congiura dei Cardinali Contro Leo X.* Florence: Olschki, 1957.

then ordered to Naples. Sauli paid a fine of 25,000 ducats and lost almost all of his rich benefices. Castellesi and Soderini fled Rome, with Castellesi deprived of his cardinal's rank and his Church accommodations.

This was a very strange affair, with many contemporary observers believing that it had been stage-managed so that Leo could gain personal revenge on Petrucci, Riario, and Soderini. The humbling of Sauli and Castellesi not only enriched Leo's pockets but was, in the case of the latter, a favor to Thomas Wolsey of England, whom Leo had raised to the Sacred College in 1515. The details of the plot made little sense, with a doctor supposedly suborned to administer the poison. But because most of the documentation of the trial is lost, we will never know exactly what happened. What is certain, however, is that it casts Leo's pontificate and personality in a darkly ruthless light.

After the conspiracy, in July of 1517, Leo named thirty-one new members of the Sacred College: the largest single elevation ever up to that time. Some of these new princes of the Church were worthy candidates (Cardinals Cajetan, Canisius, and Adrian of Utrecht[15]); others, rumor suggested, purchased their red hats, a practice perfected earlier by Julius II when he needed money—and Leo needed money because of the debts of the war of Urbino.[16] He also undid the policy of his predecessor by naming several members of great Roman families to the College.[17] Julius had tried to control families like the Orsini and Colonna, but perhaps Leo felt that they could be useful and that the old policy no longer was necessary as the large number of new cardinals had diluted the influence of them all.

Leo X's Legacy

As for foreign policy outside Italy, Leo was not as engaged as he should have been. The capture of Belgrade (1521) by the Turks and the real threat to Europe by the Ottomans should have galvanized him to work harder to create a Christian alliance to protect central Europe. He did call for a crusade and elaborated some plans for both a defense of the continent and an assault on Constantinople, and he did give money to the Hungarian king; but he was not truly active in trying to use his office to settle the differences between the Habsburgs and Valois in the name of Christian unity. In fact, rather than assuming the role himself, Leo allowed Thomas Wolsey to be the mediator between the northern powers.[18]

Given the rivalries among the Christian powers, it is unlikely that any concerted crusade against the Turks could have been realistically launched. However, Leo's use of the money that had been raised for the crusade was somewhat self-serving. He, of course, would not live to see the consequences: the 1526 battle of Mohacs (in which the

---

15. Adrian would be elected pope as Adrian VI in succession to Leo in 1522. See below.
16. It was believed in Rome that the minimum contribution to the papacy was 25,000 ducats for a cardinal's hat. See Signorotto and Visceglia, 2002. pp. 18–19.
17. Guicciardini, 1969. pp. 297–98.
18. Guicciardini, 1969. pp. 300–2.

king of Hungary and the Christian forces were annihilated) and the 1529 siege of Vienna by Suleiman the Magnificent.

It was also under Leo X that the Lutheran Reformation began. Initially, Leo paid little attention to Luther after the monk's 1517 rejection of indulgences. Leo thought of this more as another competition between religious orders, the Augustinians against the Dominicans, than an attack on the Church as a whole. When Leo's nuncio failed to bring Luther back into obedience to the Church, Leo branded forty-one of Luther's theological positions as heretical, and Luther himself was excommunicated in January of 1521.

Leo seemed unable to halt the spread of Lutheranism in Germany and Scandinavia. Most of this resulted from the pope's focusing on Italian politics in those difficult years of the Italian Wars. Furthermore, Leo's cultural and intellectual conditioning was peculiarly Italian and humanist; the pope and his advisors could not really grasp what Luther was doing. To them, the Church was the continuation of the classical tradition of ancient Greek and Roman culture, a culture they so greatly admired and which formed the platform of their worldview. Luther rejected Rome, humanism, the role of tradition, and the ritual of the Church; that is, things Leo saw as essential in Christian life.[19]

Whatever his thinking, Leo clearly hoped that the newly crowned and extremely pious young emperor Charles V would handle the problem of Lutheranism, but Charles was facing a great many other serious threats in his vast empire and in the Mediterranean. In the end Luther proved impossible to silence, and Leo's pontificate is remembered as much for the dissolution of the singular Catholic Church as for anything else.

Leo was not a man of action and decisive policy like Julius II. He was by nature irenic and an aesthete, a scholar and a musician at a moment in history when a powerful, engaged, decisive pope was required. His obsession with his family and with Florence diluted his overall strategy and compromised his resources, as did his extravagant personal life. Altogether, Leo was a pope made for another time, a quiet, peaceful, and expansive time, but his pontificate lacked the luxury of choosing its context. When he died unexpectedly in December of 1521, he was only forty-five years of age. There were, naturally, rumors of poisoning, but this was probably not the case: he had been beset by illness for some time.[20] Many sincerely mourned his loss, especially the papal bankers who were ruined because of his huge unpaid debts and the humanists who had enjoyed his company and benefitted from his patronage. Many of those who had been less distressed equally came to mourn his loss, for although the reign of this first Medici pope was troubled, it was nothing compared to the tribulations of the second.

---

19. Stinger, 1998. pp. 336–37.
20. Leo died at his hunting lodge of Magliana. His chamberlain, Bernabò Malaspina, was imprisoned and questioned about what he had brought the pope to eat and drink before his death. Malaspina was released, however, on the orders of Cardinal Giuliano de'Medici who either refused to credit such suspicions or because the rumor circulated that Malaspina had acted at the instigation of the king of France, a monarch the Church did not want to offend. See Guicciardini, 1969. pp. 327–28.

A Brief and Unhappy Pontificate

To say that Pope Adrian VI was a compromise candidate is an understatement. At the conclave called rapidly to elect a successor to Leo X, it appeared that his cousin Giulio de'Medici had every advantage. But, as the saying goes, if you enter the conclave a pope, you come out a cardinal. The political divisions in Europe between the Habsburgs and Valois were mirrored in the deliberations of the conclave, as neither the French nor the Imperial cardinals cared to support one another's candidate. But, the situation in Europe was becoming even more fraught. Luther's revolt had spread and threatened to divide the Church forever, and the Turks continued their relentless progress. There had to be a pope, so a compromise was sought.

Adrian of Utrecht (b. 1459) came from a remarkably humble background, the son of a carpenter. But his intelligence and hard work saw him rise rapidly into official ranks. He had been a pupil at the school of the Brethren of the Common Life where he acquired an excellent command of Latin and was a star student. Hence, when he was seventeen he was awarded a scholarship to study theology and canon law at the University of Louvain. His career there was impressive. He was already teaching by the time he was ordained in 1490, which was the year before he successfully defended his doctorate in theology. By 1493 he had been promoted to the position of rector of Louvain.

Adrian's success attracted the attention of Margaret of Austria who was at the time the governor of the Netherlands. She appointed him a counselor in 1506, a position in which he caught the eye of the emperor who named Adrian as tutor to his young nephew Charles of Ghent, the future Charles V. This developed into a full-time position at Charles's court in 1512. Appointed a diplomat and emissary to Spain, Adrian was elevated to bishop of Tortosa in 1516 and inquisitor general of Aragon. The following year, after the Conspiracy of the Five Cardinals, he was one of the thirty-one new cardinals named by Leo X. This new honor encouraged Charles to appoint him first as co-regent and then, in 1520, as sole regent of Spain.

In the conclave called to elect Leo X's successor, there was no doubt of Adrian's intelligence and skill. On the other hand, he had never even been to Rome, and many regarded him as a mere creature of the Habsburgs. Consequently, it was a great surprise when he was chosen pope in 1522. Adrian's forceful statement that he would rule for the good of the Church and not for any single nation seems to have been believed. It certainly mollified the French cardinals. So, he set out for the Holy City, arriving for his coronation in August of 1522, the last pope not to change his birth name on his elevation.

From the outset, however, it was clear to Adrian that he did not enjoy universal popularity. In part, the portents were badly received in the superstitious city: plague had broken out on his arrival and the island of Rhodes, defended by the Knights Hospitallers of St. John of Jerusalem, had fallen to the Turks. Because he had never been to Rome and thus lacked even the pretense of *Romanità*,[21] when he arrived in the city in August of 1522 he was called a barbarian. There was general fear in the Curia and the city at large that the complex networks of clerical patronage would be disrupted. And that fear proved right: Adrian was destined to be the most unpopular pope of modern times.[22]

Certainly, the challenges Adrian faced were overwhelming: the Protestant Revolt, which was spreading and putting down roots in Germany; the Turkish threat, which increased exponentially with the capture of Rhodes from the Knights Hospitaller of St. John of Jerusalem; and the failure to secure a peace in Europe that could permit concentrated action against either danger. He had few friends in the Curia. And, he truly believed that corruption and wealth in Rome was one of the causes of the Reformation.

So it was that Adrian set out to cleanse the Church. He rescinded the change in canon law enacted by Sixtus IV that permitted clerics to leave real property owned in Rome to their families. Adrian demanded that it be returned to the Church. Consequently, building and renovation in the city largely ceased and unemployment rose.[23] He shut off the Cortile del Belvedere, ending work on Bramante's new wings of the Apostolic Palace, and closing access to the sculpture garden of the Belvedere.[24] He attempted to impose canonical living on the College of Cardinals, starving them of financial advantages, reducing their income, and forcing economies in their households. Again, unemployment rose. Moreover, these reforms together with the reduction of the papal *familia* meant that a great many humanists, previously employed in these households, lost their ability to secure an income in Rome. Some left for better opportunities; others stayed to wait out Adrian's pontificate.

Adrian was equally unbending and self-righteous in doctrinal matters. He refused any discussion with the Lutherans on dogma or papal authority, demanding instead that Luther be handed over and tried for heresy. The sophisticated cardinals in the Curia despised and obstructed him to the point that he relied on only a few loyal curialists, isolating himself even more. He cared nothing about classical letters and humanism, causing the cultivated members of the Curia to endorse the initial description of him as a barbarian. The Roman nobility avoided him, and the princes of Italy thought him a foolish, incompetent prig. His parsimonious personality hugely affected the papal household which had greatly expanded under Leo X. Those who lost their jobs added to the chorus of disdain, especially as many of them were professional rhetoricians and poets, able to skewer the hated pope with both wit and calumny. The many musicians who had worked for Leo left the papal court, as Adrian cared nothing for music. Rome became a boring, poor, angry, and divided city, with terrible unemployment and an atmosphere of decline.[25]

---

21. Roman-ness (Latin *Romanitas*) meant being imbued with the culture of both ancient and contemporary Rome.
22. Guicciardini, 1969. pp. 328–36.
23. Partner, 1979. pp. 58, 163.
24. Stinger, 1998. p. 272.
25. D'Amico, 1983. pp. 11, 86, 111.

Despite his sanctimonious, uncompromising character, Adrian had a very thin skin. When anonymous citizens started to post witty but savage commentary about him on the statue of Pasquino, he ordered the sculpture thrown into the Tiber. Wisely, a cardinal he respected told Adrian that if Pasquino went into the Tiber he would soon follow: consequently, Pasquino remains where it has stood since 1500, serving to this day as the voice of the Roman people, who paper it with satiric verses (pasquinades) commenting on current events.

Isolated, bewildered, angry, and uncertain of his role as supreme pontiff, Adrian died in September 1523, slightly more than a year after his coronation. Although there were rumors of poison, as there would be for such a hated pope, his death was likely natural. On hearing that he had died, the people of Rome broke out in spontaneous celebrations and went to the house of his doctor, carrying the man on their shoulders in triumph around the city.[26] Adrian's legacy was such that there was no other non-Italian pope until John Paul II, four centuries later. Ironically, his only positive memory in Rome is the splendid tomb by Baldassare Peruzzi in the church of Santa Maria dell'Anima, the German church in the city. Of course Adrian would probably have vetoed its construction as far too grand and expensive.

Clement VII

Giulio de'Medici was born to Fioretta Gorini, a mistress of Giuliano de'Medici, the brother of Lorenzo de'Medici, a month after Giuliano's murder during the Pazzi Conspiracy of 1478. Lorenzo took responsibility for the boy and gave him an excellent humanist education. He even argued somewhat successfully for the boy's legitimacy by saying (however improbably) that Giuliano and his mistress had been betrothed and secretly married. If this were to be believed, canon law deemed Giulio's a legitimate birth.

Giulio's career took flight with his cousin's election as Pope Leo X in 1513. A few months after his elevation to the Holy See, Leo appointed Giulio Archbishop of Florence, cementing the family's recovery of the city after 1512. Then, soon after, in September 1513, Giulio was named a cardinal—all this despite the fact that Giulio would not take holy orders to become a priest until 1517.

Giulio's family connections led to even more rich benefices. In particular, the Conspiracy of the Cardinals resulted in his cousin granting him the palace of the Cancelleria and with it the titular church of San Lorenzo in Damaso, which had been incorporated into the vast palace by Raffaele Riario. Giulio was very close to his cousin the pope, and served as a close advisor. His reputation was that of a very learned, clever, and insightful prince, devoted to his cousin and to the success of the Church and the Medici family. Leo X's early death was a shock to Giulio, even though he was seen as *papabile*, one suitable

---

26. The Roman mob also carved on the doctor's door: *Liberator patriae. SPQR* (The Liberator of the nation. The Senate and People of Rome). See Guicciardini, 1969. p. 335 and note.

for election in the conclave of 1521–22. But his time had not yet come. Giulio gave Adrian VI his support and became a trusted counselor to the neophyte pope on his entry into Rome. Fortunately, Adrian's unpopularity did not infect Cardinal Giulio de'Medici. Consequently, when Adrian died just a year after his coronation, Giulio was chosen pope in the long, divided conclave of November 1523, taking the name of Clement VII.[27]

In other times, Clement, like his cousin, would have been celebrated as a truly exceptional pontiff, inasmuch as his experience and learning; his careful, deliberative personality; his cultivated patronage; and his knowledge of peninsular Italian politics were exemplary. His election engendered the greatest hope among humanists and artists, especially given the arid period of patronage that characterized the Rome of Adrian VI.[28] Sadly, these qualities were exactly what the Church did *not* need in the incendiary world of the 1520s.[29] Luther's revolt had spread widely and his excommunication from the Roman Confession seemed to embolden him and add to his popular appeal. The ambitions of the emperor in Italy and the duel between Francis I and Charles made a concentrated counteroffensive in Germany difficult. The Church, and Clement in particular, found themselves caught between the French and the Imperials, as both powers would be needed if there were ever to be a crusade to stop the advance of the Turks.

The concern for the independence of the Church's patrimony in Italy and Clement's own dynastic obsession with Medici control of Florence; its position in Tuscany; and, indeed, any reconfigured state system that might emerge from some kind of Habsburg–Valois détente, made a coherent papal policy challenging. But Clement made the entire situation worse by his constant realigning of the Church, shifting its support from the French to the Empire and back again to the French. He seemed a ditherer, unable to make a decision, while in reality he was playing a weak hand and trying to factor in far too many variables to sustain any clear policy.[30] The consequence of this was a series of disasters for the Church, Rome, Clement personally, and the Medici family.

---

27. Guicciardini, 1969. pp. 336–38.

28. The humanist papal secretary Pietro Bembo ecstatically wrote that "Clement will be the greatest and wisest pope whom the Church has seen for centuries," and Michelangelo exalted that "there will be a lot of art to be made." Quoted in Kenneth Gouwens, "Clement and Calamity: The Case for Re-evaluation," in Sheryl Reiss and Kenneth Gouwens, eds., *The Pontificate of Clement VII: History, Politics, Culture.* London and New York: Routledge, 2005. p. 3.

29. T. Price Zimmerman, "Guicciardini, Giovio and the Character of Clement VII," in Reiss and Gouwens, 2005. pp. 19–28. Zimmerman argues that the negative assessment of Clement's character resulted from two sources close to his pontificate, Paolo Giovio and Guicciardini. The one was alienated by his belief that the pope failed to sufficiently reward his loyalty; the other to shift the blame from himself to his master for choosing disastrous policies. See Charles Stinger, "The Place of Clement VII and Clementine Rome in Renaissance History," in Reiss and Gouwens, 2005. pp. 165–88.

30. Guicciardini describes Clement as having many excellent qualities and wide experience but possessing "a timidity of spirit . . . a certain innate irresolution and perplexity so that he remained almost always in suspension and ambiguous." Guicciardini, 1969. p. 363.

The cataclysm of Clement's reign was brought about by the pope joining the League of Cognac, which allied the Church, Milan, Venice, and France against Charles V. Clement had become seriously concerned by the rapid increase in Charles V's power in Italy after his victory at Pavia in 1525. The pope, then, hoped to balance that influence through the League. The consequences were hardly what the pope intended. The Imperial army recaptured Milan in 1526, and the League forces were dealt a crippling blow when Clement's cousin, Giovanni delle Bande Nere de'Medici, head of a celebrated condottiere army, was killed at the end of November, leaving the rest of Italy open to the Imperials.

The Imperial army was comprised of battle-hardened Spanish veterans and German Lutheran landsknechts—arguably the most feared and violent soldiers in all Europe. It was said that even the devil himself was so petrified by these landsknechts that he would not allow them into hell. The men were also unpaid and restless to the point of mutiny. Their commander was a French traitor, Charles, duc de Bourbon, who had gone over to the Habsburgs after quarrelling with Louise of Savoy, Francis I's mother and regent during his captivity in Madrid. By May 5, 1527, the Imperial force had reached the walls of Rome, most probably intent on extorting tribute. But, the next day dawned with dense fog, and the army spontaneously assaulted the walls. Trying to reassert control, Bourbon joined them in scaling the ramparts, but he was killed, leaving the brutal army leaderless. There was little defense for Rome, as Clement had not prepared for a siege.[31]

The Sack of Rome, 1527

As the Imperial army streamed into the city and across the bridges, Romans panicked, and many tried to flee. Nobles attempted to protect their property by quickly fortifying their palaces, but only the Palazzo Colonna, occupied by Isabella d'Este, was secure. This had nothing to do with her ability to block the invaders but with the fact that her son, Ferrante Gonzaga, was a general in the Imperial army, and she herself had a warm relationship with the emperor, so she was consequently granted safe conduct. She shared this by opening the huge palace to more than two thousand Roman nobles, clerics, and common citizens whose lives were likely spared through her protection.

Meanwhile Clement, together with those of his Curia who could join him, fled along the *passetto*, the walkway connecting the Apostolic Palace and Castel Sant'Angelo. He was able to escape only because his Swiss guards held back the invaders long enough

---

31. For a contemporary account, see Luigi Guicciardini, *The Sack of Rome*, ed. and tr. James McGregor. New York: Italica Press, 2008. Luigi was the elder brother of Francesco Guicciardini and a close friend of Niccolò Machiavelli. See also Judith Hook, *The Sack of Rome*. London: Palgrave Macmillan, 2004. For the effect of the sack on artistic patronage and a reappraisal of Clement's role as patron, see André Chastel, *The Sack of Rome, 1527*, tr. Beth Archer. Princeton: Princeton University Press, 1983. For the humanist response and commemoration of the sack, see Kenneth Gouwens, *Remembering the Renaissance: Humanist Narratives of the Sack of Rome*. Leiden: Brill, 1998.

for the papal party to flee the palace. This heroism cost every one of the guards their lives, and to commemorate this sacrifice new Swiss Guards are to this day sworn into papal service on the anniversary of May 6.

Barricaded in Castel Sant'Angelo, Clement could only watch as the city was sacked, looted, and burned, and sacrilegious theatrics taunted him and Catholicism. Parodies of the mass and conclaves were performed, asses were dressed in episcopal vestments, a cardinal was paraded in a sarcophagus in a mock funeral, common soldiers wore papal robes, and scurrilous verses and recitations abounded among the better educated.[32]

The savagery was indescribable. Whole convents of nuns were sold or served as prizes in gambling, turned over to soldiers who raped them until they died. Cardinals, bishops, nobles, wealthy citizens—even artists—were suspended from the roof beams of their houses until they divulged where their treasures were hidden. Papal tombs were pried open and the bodies thrown into the street, while rings, gemmed miters, or gloves were taken, and the sepulchral vestments burned to extract the gold or silver threads. Altar furniture and reliquaries were melted down, antiquities smashed, defaced, or stolen. No one and nothing escaped.

The name of Martin Luther was carved with a pike on the wall of the Stanza della Segnatura. German soldiers billeted in the Villa of Agostino Chigi (now the Farnesina) defaced frescoes with graffiti—some scrawls visible to this day—that included such taunting observations as the Germans were laughing because they had the pope on the run. Great libraries, including that of the university, were burned for warmth, as were archives, documents, and private accounts. The Vatican Library was only inadvertently protected because the Imperial commander used the space for his headquarters. Similarly, the Sistine Chapel was spared only because it was there that Charles of Bourbon's body lay in state before burial.

Those Romans who tried to flee with some property were attacked on the roads outside the city by bands of armed peasants who robbed them and then murdered them out of both greed and hatred for a city whose ruler had squeezed from them every possible cent. Some of these peasant gangs were organized from the estates in the Campagna of the Colonna princes who hated Clement; others were led by the Orsini abbot of Farfa. When winter arrived, furniture, doors, shutters, and eventually roof beams were burned for warmth. Plague returned and the starving inhabitants succumbed in great numbers because of poor health and nutrition. The population of the city fell by more than two thirds. Just one Spanish contingent of sappers who had been assigned to bury the dead claimed to have dug ten thousand graves and thrown another two thousand bodies into the Tiber during the ten months of the city's occupation. Yet there was nothing Clement could do.[33]

---

32. Mallett and Shaw, 2012. pp. 160–64.
33. Partner, 1979. pp. 30–31; Stinger, 1998. pp. 320–24.

**Illus. 20.1 Raphael, *Pope Leo X de'Medici with his Cousins,*
Cardinal Giulio de'Medici (Future Pope Clement VII), and
Cardinal Luigi de'Rossi, 1518–19. Uffizi, Florence.**

This wonderful portrait of the humanist Pope Leo X (Giovanni de'Medici, 1513–21) captures not only his likeness but his love of luxury and his exquisite taste. Also shown are his two cousins. On Leo's right is Giulio de'Medici, the son of the Giuliano murdered in 1478 during the Pazzi Conspiracy, and now a cardinal destined to become the second Medici Pope. To Leo's left is depicted Cardinal Luigi de'Rossi, son of Maria de'Medici, and a close companion of the pope's since childhood.

Leo's *famiglia*—his personal household as pope—was the largest yet seen in Rome, consisting of more than seven hundred men. This vast array of personal servants, grooms, stable masters, musicians, cooks, letter-writers and sealers, gardeners, animal-keepers and jesters—even an astrologer—stretched the papal finances enormously. Also, these prized appointments, at least in the upper ranks, caused some local discontent, as Leo preferred Tuscans and other northern Italians—that is, men from anywhere but Rome. Moreover, his closest advisers were relatives and friends from earlier days, such as Bernardo Dovizi da Bibbiena, whose brother had been an important official in his father's household in Florence, and his secretary, Pietro Bembo, a Venetian, both of whom were named cardinals.

Some of this propensity for surrounding himself with Roman outsiders resulted from the opposition that the older cardinals had expressed to his elevation in 1513. There was to blame, as well, his unfamiliarity with Rome and his lack of deep roots in the papal city, despite his mother having been an Orsini. But mostly it was a result of his highly refined, exquisite taste: his proclivity was to favor the styles and sophistication of the northern half of the peninsula.

Illus. 20.2.a Raphael and Workshop, *The Coronation of Charlemagne*, 1516–17. Apostolic Vatican Palace, Room of the Fire in the Borgo (*Stanza dell'Incendio di Borgo*), Rome.

Illus. 20.2.b Workshop of Raphael, *The Donation of Constantine*, 1520–24. Apostolic Vatican Palace, *Sala di Costantino*, Rome.

This anachronistic fresco of Pope Leo X de'Medici's namesake, Pope Leo III (795–816), crowning the Frankish king Charlemagne (Charles the Great) in Old St. Peter's on Christmas Day 800 actually portrays Leo X putting a crown on the head of the contemporary Holy Roman Emperor Charles V of Habsburg. The symbolism is significant at a time when papal authority was being challenged, as it implies that the power of the emperor is subject to the pope and reinforces the myth of the Donation of Constantine. Although the document on which the Donation was built was proved to have been a forgery some sixty years earlier by Lorenzo Valla, it still appears as a propaganda tool both here and again in the *Stanza di Costantino* (to the right).

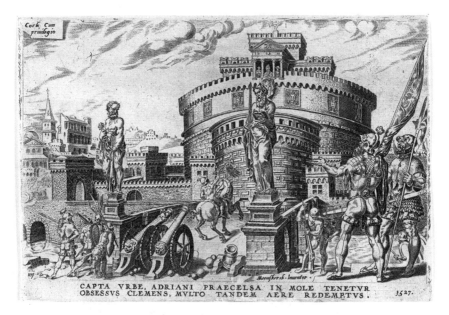

CAPTA VRBE, ADRIANI PRAECELSA IN MOLE TENETVR
OBSESSVS CLEMENS, MVLTO TANDEM AERE REDEMPTVS.   1527.

Illus. 20.3 Maarten van Heemskerck, *Siege of Castel Sant'Angelo*.
Engraved by Hieronymus Cock, 1555–56. Rijksmuseum, Amsterdam.

This etching, after a design by Martin Van Heemskerck, is part of a series illustrating the victories of Emperor Charles V. It shows a central episode from the Sack of Rome in 1527 when mutinous Imperial troops plundered the city. The image depicts not only the hapless Clement VII who has taken refuge in the Castel Sant'Angelo but also the contemporary appearance of the Ponte Sant'Angelo, the Apostolic Palace, and old St. Peter's with the new church rising above the façade.

When the unruly Imperial army under Charles, duc de Bourbon, streamed into Rome in May of 1527, Pope Clement VII de'Medici ran for safety along the *passetto*, the elevated passage between the Apostolic Palace and the fortress of Castel Sant'Angelo, thereby likely saving his life at the expense of his dignity. It is ironic that Clement VII was actually a serious proponent of Church reform and wished to address some of the problems identified by Luther and others. He supported reform groups within the Church, spent liberally restoring or decorating churches, and enriched the Apostolic Library. Moreover, his manner of life was somewhat more subdued than that of his Medici predecessor, Leo X.

Although this engraving was included in an illustrated book of 1555–56 celebrating Charles V, the emperor did not order the sack. Indeed, he was somewhat embarrassed by the assault of Protestant Germans on the center of the Church that he sincerely believed he had God's mission to preserve.

Illus. 20.4 Pasquino, The Talking Statue (*Statua Parlante*). Piazza Pasquino, Rome.

Pasquino was a severely damaged ancient marble that once formed part of a sculptural group of Menelaus with Patroclus. It was found in about 1500 during the construction of Palazzo Carafa, near the bottom of the Piazza Navona, a site now occupied by the eighteenth-century Palazzo Braschi. Cardinal Carafa inadvertently began the "speaking statue" tradition by installing Pasquino near his palace and declaring it the focus of a rather pompous exchange of Neo-Latin poetry. In Cardinal Carafa's time, Pasquino was even dressed in a Roman toga.

However, the common people of Rome had no interest in such pomposity. So, they began writing their own poems in local dialect (pasquinades), poems that satirized the papacy, the clergy, and anyone else who incurred their wrath. Nearby lived a tailor named Pasquino who was known for his witty gossip, so the tailor and the statue became blurred, hence its name. Pasquino was not a lone voice, however. He enjoyed a straight man named Marforio, a large statue of a river god that once formed part of a fountain in the forum. Mistaken for Mars during the Middle Ages, the statue received his name from *Mars in foro*, that is, Mars in the forum. The dialogue between the two took on a powerful critique of the Church in particular until Marforio was moved into the Capitoline Museum where it remains today.

There are four other "talking statues": Il Babuino (the baboon, set up in the sixteenth century and who has given his name to the Via Babuino); Il Facchino, the porter, actually a water seller, forming a small mid-sixteenth-century fountain now on the Via Lata; Abbate Luigi, an ancient Roman orator set beside Sant'Andrea delle Valle, called Luigi because of his resemblance to the church's Renaissance sacristan; and Madama Lucrezia, at a corner of the Palazzo Venezia, the only female talking statue, named either for a mistress of the king of Naples or a celebrated courtesan, both of whom heard political secrets from powerful men during pillow talk. Together, these six talking statues were known as "The Conference of Wits" (*congresso degli arguti*). Pasquino speaks powerfully to this day, with Il Babuino and Abbate Luigi still occasionally adding commentary.

CHAPTER 21

ROME AND THE COUNTER-REFORMATION

From the moment the Imperial army had entered Rome, the papacy was effectively under the control of Emperor Charles V. The pious but pragmatic emperor was embarrassed that an army which was in theory subject to his rule had destroyed the city and humiliated the papacy. But he also knew that meant he could impose his will on Clement and that France was at a serious disadvantage. In June of 1527 Clement capitulated to Charles V, agreeing to pay a huge ransom and ceding a number of important towns to the Empire. After six months of torment, the pope was able to escape Rome, dressed ignominiously like a gardener. He fled to the papal fortress town of Orvieto and did not return to the ruined Holy City until October of 1528.[1]

Eventually a treaty was negotiated that returned much of the Papal States's territory to the Church. Florence was to be returned to Medici rule by a Spanish army, including soldiers who had just recently so barbarously sacked Rome. (For the Medici popes, dynasty mattered as much as policy and duty to the Church.) Most significantly, in return Charles was promised an Imperial coronation.

Clement met with Charles in Bologna and crowned him in the basilica of San Petronio in February of 1530. His capitulation to the Habsburgs was necessary but humiliating and corrosive for the Church. In particular, Clement was unable to grant Henry VIII of England his desire to divorce Katherine of Aragon so that he could marry Anne Boleyn. The stumbling block was that Katherine of Aragon was Charles V's aunt. Any attempt to have her marriage to Henry declared invalid and his cousin, Mary Tudor, consequently deemed illegitimate was not going to succeed. Clement tried his usual route of temporizing, but it failed completely: The Act in Restraint of Appeals of 1533 effectively separated the English Church from the Roman Confession. Catholicism had lost another nation to the reformers.

In the fall of 1534, Clement set out to officiate at the marriage of Henry, the son of Francis I of France, and Catherine de'Medici, the daughter of that Lorenzo, duke of Urbino, on whom Leo X had wasted so much papal treasure and credit in advancing. The pope took ill on the journey, barely managing to return to Rome where he died in September of that year. His long reign of ten years had proven to be one of the most dramatic of all of the successors to St. Peter. His body and that of his cousin Leo X were eventually translated to the Dominican church of Santa Maria Sopra Minerva where their monuments still stand in the choir, united by family and profession, and to a great degree by destiny.

---

1. Anne Reynolds, "The Papal Court in Exile: Clement VII in Orvieto, 1527–28," in Reiss and Gouwens, 2005. pp. 143–64.

Paul III

Alessandro Farnese was born into a middle-rank noble family in Lazio in 1468, although his mother was a Caetani, a member of a powerful and ancient Roman clan, indeed the family of Pope Boniface VIII.[2] Trained in classical studies in Rome in the humanist circle of Pomponio Leto and at the University of Pisa, young Alessandro developed a friendship with the Medici in Florence, particularly Giovanni, who would become Pope Leo X. However, it was not this connection that would facilitate his rapid and early rise into the highest echelons of the Roman Church.[3]

In 1491 the intelligent and cultivated young cleric entered the Roman Curia as an apostolic notary, only to be raised by Pope Alexander VI Borgia in 1493 to the Sacred College of Cardinals. Despite his abilities—and he was precocious—a primary reason for his astonishing rise depended on his young sister, Giulia, who had become the mistress of the pope:[4] it was she who intervened on her brother's behalf and secured his promotion.[5] As a result of this uncanonical elevation, Farnese was insulted with various nicknames, such as "the petticoat cardinal" and "the Borgia-in-law"—and these are among the least offensive; Giulia was called "the bride of Christ." These typically Roman, suggestive epithets did not, however, reveal the complete rationale for Alexander's elevation of Alessandro: the Farnese estates around Lake Bolsena were large and the family influential. Thus, the Farnese could be of significant strategic value in controlling the Orsini, whose power base lay just to the south.[6]

Nevertheless, lust was clearly part of the Farnese character. Despite his subsequent clerical vows, Alessandro's mistress gave him five children,[7] all of whom would later be legitimized (1505) and advanced in the Church or as rulers of principalities that were dependent on the Holy See. However, at some point after becoming bishop of Parma in 1509 Alessandro abandoned his dissolute life and devoted himself to the reform of the Church and his interests in culture. A pattern of patronage began about 1513 when he began discussing plans with Antonio da Sangallo, who was then working on the rebuilding of St. Peter's basilica, for a grand palace in Rome. It was to be on a site Alessandro had acquired close to the Tiber near the new Via Giulia. By 1515 construction had begun

---

2. Helge Gamrath, "The History of a Success in the Italian Renaissance: The Farnese Family, c. 1400–1600," *Analecta Romana Instituti Danici*, 24 (1997), pp. 93–111.

3. Helge Gamrath, *Farnese: Pomp, Power, and Politics in Renaissance Italy*. Rome: L'Erma Di Bretschneider, 2007.

4. Clemente Fusero states that the affair began just days after Giulia Farnese's marriage to Orsino Orsini on May 21, 1489, which would be her fifteenth year. See Clemente Fusero, *The Borgias*, tr. Peter Green. New York: Praeger, 1972. pp. 148–49.

5. Guicciardini, 1969. p. 442.

6. Mallett, 2005. pp. 139–40.

7. Anthony Majanlahti, *The Families Who Made Rome*. London: Chatto and Windus, 2009. p. 128.

and would continue throughout Alessandro's life: the size and magnificence of the palace growing in proportion to his advancements in the Church.

The intelligence and ability of Alessandro Farnese soon led to his appointment as the dean of the College of Cardinals. He was both the archpriest of the cathedral of St. John Lateran and cardinal bishop of Ostia at the time of the Sack of Rome in 1527–28, an event that had a profound effect on him, a portent perhaps of the greater tragedy of the division of Christendom.

Despite the fact that he held many ecclesiastical positions simultaneously (in reformer's eyes the corruption of "pluralism") he was full of reforming zeal and wished to address the charges of the Lutherans and their theological differences directly. Recognizing how well-suited Alessandro was to the challenging times in which the Church found itself, the conclave that followed the death of Clement VII in 1534 quickly elected him as pope. He was already sixty-six years old, and the conclave was confident his reign would not be long: there would soon be time to deliberate more carefully. How wrong they were: Alessandro Farnese would enjoy the longest pontificate of the century, 1534–49. The name he chose for himself was Paul III.

In a sincere attempt both to project his desire for fundamental reform of the Church and as an invitation to the Lutherans to engage in serious discussion, Paul considered summoning a General Council of the Church. One was indeed duly called in 1536 for Mantua but came to nothing. However, his commission to identify abuses in the Church and offer instruments of reform proved more useful. This *Consilium de ecclesia emendanda* of 1536 was drafted by nine of the most respected senior members of the Church, all characterized by a desire for reform, learning, and piety. It was a remarkable document that even attracted the attention of the Protestants in Germany, as it was intended to do.[8] Unfortunately, the duel between the king of France, Francis I, and the Habsburg emperor Charles V, together with the final apostasy of Henry VIII of England, derailed the reform program, as did the opposition of the Curia and many clerics who had benefitted from the abuses identified for correction.

Despite these obstructions, Paul continued a more measured policy of reform of central institutions and appointed pious reformers to the Sacred College. He also tried to steer a middle course between the Habsburgs and Valois. Yet, he was still a man of his age and one driven by dynastic ambitions. So it was that Paul himself broke canon law by making his fourteen- and sixteen-year-old grandsons cardinals; detached territory from the Papal States in Italy for his son Pier Luigi, who became duke of Parma; and engaged in marriage alliances and other attempts to cement his family among the rulers of the peninsula.[9] Indeed, attempts at reform were abandoned for a time because it seemed as if the emperor might defeat the Protestants militarily. In addition, new religious orders,

8. Kenneth R. Bartlett and Margaret McGlynn, eds., *The Renaissance and Reformation in Northern Europe*. Toronto: University of Toronto Press, 2014. pp. 114–20; also Partner, 1979. pp. 213–14.
9. Partner, 1979. pp. 34–35.

like the Jesuits, recognized by Paul in 1540, appeared to offer solutions to the loss of Catholic adherents to the new sects.[10]

In 1542 Paul established the Roman Inquisition as a means of enforcing orthodoxy and rooting out heresy. True, there had been regional inquisitions, such as that in Spain (1478), and most bishoprics had inquisitors in their employ but now there was a central office which would determine from Rome who or what was heterodox and impose penalties on those convicted of unauthorized thought or action. Now, after 1542, holding certain ideas could lead to serious consequences. Owning—or even knowing the content of—certain books was subject to discipline. Allowing logic—or even rhetorical hyperbole—to imply principles or ideas that were not specifically sanctioned could result in trial.[11]

It was the beginning of the end. There was now a chilling effect on the openness of dialogue and relative freedom of ideas that had both given rise to and sustained the energy of the Italian Renaissance. In effect, Paul III's Roman Inquisition began to sap the intellectual momentum of the Renaissance in Italy. The dynamic civilization characterized from the time of Petrarch by the quest for individual self-knowledge, based on the ideas and models of classical antiquity, was now threatened by the need to impose religious uniformity. Petrarch's concept of the dignity of man was consequently subject to sharp scrutiny, and conformity was increasingly required.

The Council of Trent

The Council to reform the Church ultimately met in 1545 at Trent, then an independent ecclesiastical principality under the shadow of the Habsburgs. It would continue until 1563, although with some interruptions and a good deal of friction, especially between the Italian and ultramontane clerics and between those with more sympathy with the French than the Imperial factions. Nevertheless, the Council was of the greatest importance for a renewed Roman Catholicism, establishing Roman Catholic doctrine, liturgy, and practice until the second half of the twentieth century.

Many reforms were indeed introduced, especially regarding clerical discipline and education. But many of the decrees reflected the Roman Church's wholesale rejection of the Protestant position: good works continued to play a necessary role in salvation, not faith alone; the traditions of the Church were accepted as part of the faith, rejecting biblical sources alone (*sola scriptura*); the pope was accepted as the vicar of Christ on earth, and his position was in some ways even stronger to ensure a unified opposition to the Protestants; Medieval theologians were accepted as guiding doctors of the Church; and

10. John W. O'Malley, *The Jesuits: A History from Ignatius to the Present*. Lanham, MD, and London: Rowman & Littlefield Publishers, 2014. pp. 1–54.
11. Thomas F. Mayer, *The Roman Inquisition: A Papal Bureaucracy and Its Laws in the Age of Galileo*. Philadelphia: University of Pennsylvania Press, 2013. pp. 9–75.

the Latin vulgate was identified as inspired by the Holy Spirit and the only acceptable version of scripture.

Trent also rejected the simplification of religious ritual and sites, instead advocating the sensual beauty of churches and liturgy. This was important for the maintenance of Italian Renaissance artistic production and practice, as the Church remained a powerful patron, in fact an even more generous source of commissions. The workshops that had developed in most major Italian centers to serve the market for art and architecture received a richer bounty, allowing for the brilliance of Renaissance painting, sculpture, and building to be sustained or enhanced. In this, the visual culture of the Renaissance remained, even if the intellectual openness and vigor declined. In fact, in architecture, new models were officially sanctioned.[12]

Trent also reinforced and spread the purposes identified by Ignatius Loyola and his Society of Jesus (or Jesuits): preaching, teaching, and missionary work. Thus, large hall churches with no side aisles were constructed so that the faithful could easily hear the sermon and see the rituals of the mass unobstructed. These churches reflected the design of the Gesù in Rome, the mother church of the Jesuit order, and were extravagantly decorated, serving symbolically as the waiting rooms of paradise. Indeed, paradise was often a theme of the ceiling frescoes projected in skillful trompe l'oeil illusionism, particularly as practiced in the next century by that Jesuit genius Andrea Pozzo (1642–1709).

Paul III as Patron

In addition to supporting reform, Paul III was also one of Renaissance Rome's great patrons. On his election in 1534 he honored the commission begun by Clement VII to Michelangelo to fresco the altar wall of the Sistine Chapel with an image of the Last Judgment. How different this image (completed in 1541) is from the vault painted from 1508–12! The classicism and physical beauty of the ceiling's figures are in stark contrast with the dark, suffering, tortuous, elongated characters on the altar wall: the images of the damned are frightening, and Michelangelo's self-portrait as the flayed skin of St. Bartholomew sends a clear message. The decoration of the vault and the painting of the west wall were, after all, separated by the Reformation and the Sack of Rome.

Michelangelo's love of the naked body remained, although it was strongly criticized by Papal Master of Ceremonies Biagio da Cesena. Biagio won in the end, as Michelangelo's young and respected colleague, Daniele da Volterra (1509–66), was required to paint over the nudity of his mentor's wonderful figures in 1565, the year after Michelangelo's death. This was a consequence of Trent as well, as nudity was condemned in religious art. Alas, the younger man would forever be known by the embarrassing nickname of "the pant-maker" (il braghettone).

---

12. John W. O'Malley, *Trent: What Happened at the Council.* Cambridge, MA: Belknap Press of Harvard University Press, 2013.

While Michelangelo's painting was subject to mutilation, his architecture enjoyed greater respect. Paul III convinced the sculptor and painter after the death of Sangallo in 1546 that he could assume responsibility for the rebuilding of the basilica of St. Peter. Because of that, we have to this day Michelangelo's magnificent dome. It was also Paul who commissioned Michelangelo to restructure the ancient Capitoline Hill, the Campidoglio, in Rome (1536–46).[13]

Restructuring the Campidoglio was a project worthy of Renaissance attention. It had been the site of the great temple of Jupiter Optimus Maximus Capitolinus from the earliest days of the ancient city. It overlooked the forum and was flanked by the ruins of the Tabularium, the ancient record repository of Rome, from whose arches prominent Romans had reviewed triumphs. In Medieval times it was the center of civic government. It was there that Cola di Rienzo had proclaimed himself tribune and summoned delegates for the unity of Italy. But by the 1530s, it was a jumble of ruined buildings, fallen stones, and ancient memories—memories that Paul wanted to revive and repurpose to reinforce his position.

In 1536 Charles V was to enter Rome, leading an army that consisted to some degree of the very soldiers who had sacked the city in 1527–28. Paul wanted a symbol of Rome's recovery and of papal power, reflecting his dual authority from St. Peter and Constantine. So Michelangelo created the Campidoglio we now know: eventually with two parallel classical palaces flanking the city hall with a new façade, adorned with ancient sculptures of Roma (actually Minerva) and river gods. At the center he placed the equestrian statue of Marcus Aurelius, the only life-sized bronze mounted figure to survive from antiquity in the city. It was moved from St. John Lateran to become the focus of this new space representing papal authority and patronage. In so doing, Paul also redirected the orientation of the Capitoline from the forum to the city, achieved by Michelangelo's grand staircase, the *cordonnata*.

When Paul III died in November of 1549 he had enjoyed not only a long but also a remarkably successful pontificate. For a young man who received preferment, despite his then dissolute life, he proved a very worthy successor to St. Peter. He left the Roman Church, the city, and Italian culture stronger and more beautiful. And he will always be associated with Trent, the formation of the Jesuits, and the work of the late Michelangelo. Moreover, Paul, who always characterized himself as a Roman, also re-established the deep connection between the papacy and the city. His love of pageantry, tournaments, and carnival endeared him to the common citizens, as did his personal charity, such as providing dowries for poor girls of good birth.[14] That said, we cannot omit the fact that he was also responsible for the Roman Inquisition, the tipping point that signaled the decline of Renaissance thought.

---

13. Partner, 1979. pp. 170–75; Majanlahti, 2009. pp. 138–74.
14. Signorotto and Visceglia, 2002. pp. 46–48; Partner, 1979. pp. 105, 194–95.

Julius III

Julius III (r. 1550–55), Paul's successor, had in many ways a distinguished early career as a diplomat and papal governor of Rome, one celebrated for his administrative skill. During the Sack of Rome, he suffered terribly, having been imprisoned and tortured, barely escaping with his life.[15] Nevertheless, he acquiesced to the Imperial request to reconvene the Council of Trent in 1551 over French objections, in fact accepting an alliance against Francis I. However, in 1553 he made his own peace with the Valois and the proceedings of the Council were again adjourned. Thereafter, he did little either for Church reform or papal politics outside of his narrow interests in Italy and his personal obsessions in Rome.

The nature of these obsessions fell into two categories: the first gave Rome another, wonderful papal residence, designed by the most talented architects and artists of the mid-sixteenth century; the other was a scandalous relationship with a young teenage boy, a largely illiterate, but beautiful, street urchin he had picked up when a cardinal in Parma. First, let's consider the Villa Giulia.[16]

It is not a coincidence that Julius's withdrawal from his earlier interests in Church reform and international diplomacy ended in 1553. That was the year in which his elegant, classically inspired villa was completed (it was begun in 1551). Julius chose the site not far outside the Flaminian gate because it was very close to Rome while still offering the pleasures of a *villa suburbana*, with extensive gardens. Access to the Tiber also permitted him to arrive by water from the Vatican Palace.[17] The most celebrated artists of his time contributed to its design. Vignola made the initial plans, later aided by Giorgio Vasari and Bartolommeo Ammannati. By tradition—and with some convincing evidence—Michelangelo was consulted as well. The result is one of Renaissance Italy's most beautiful buildings with its gardens, nymphaeum, painted passages, and space for the display of ancient sculpture. Julius spared no expense on either his villa or his entertainments, something that was not lost on those in the Protestant or Catholic camp that sought reform.

His greatest pleasure centered on a young boy named Fabiano who had filled odd positions in the pope's household, including that of the keeper of his pet monkey; however, it was universally accepted that the boy was his catamite.[18] There has always been a great deal of innuendo about the sexual proclivities of the successors of St. Peter; the scurrilous attacks on the Roman Church that flowed from Protestant presses was never more poisonous than in the sixteenth century. In some instances, these charges were

---

15. Partner, 1979. p. 38.

16. For a description and analysis of the villa, see David Coffin, *The Villa in the Life of Renaissance Rome*. Princeton: Princeton University Press, 1979. pp. 150–74.

17. Coffin, 1979. pp. 175–76.

18. Eamon Duffy, *Saints and Sinners: A History of the Popes*. New Haven: Yale University Press, 2006. p. 215.

patently unfair, as in the example of Pope Leo X de'Medici. Regardless of his interests before ordination (he only became a priest on his election as pope), Leo's life appears blameless thereafter. There were lurid stories about Paul II, Sixtus IV, and Julius II, but there is little incontrovertible evidence that any of these popes engaged in even a small fraction of the libidinous practices attributed to them. On the other hand, this was not the case with Julius III.

Members of the Sacred College and prominent clerics, even the Venetian ambassador and the celebrated French poet Jean du Bellay (his cousin was a cardinal in Rome and du Bellay a member of his household) discussed this uncanonical relationship frankly;[19] and Julius did nothing to silence the rumors. The urchin, Fabiano, was thought to have been about fifteen when he was brought into the household. Later, he was adopted by Julius's brother and his name changed to Innocenzo (Innocent!) del Monte. Once Julius was elected pope, he took the extraordinary step of naming this boy a cardinal, despite the fact that he was only marginally literate and still in his teens. Julius showered Innocenzo with rich benefices, much to the disgust of the Scared College and those who sought fundamental reform in the Church. The shocking relationship was a terrible scandal in the age of the Council of Trent and the struggle with Protestant Europe, especially as the boy cardinal could in theory one day be elected pope.

Paul IV

Julius's successor, Marcellus II, reigned for only three weeks in 1555 before dying,[20] after which the See of St. Peter was occupied by Paul IV Carafa (r. 1555–59), a pope whose prejudices, toxic personality, and vendettas contributed greatly to the decline of the Renaissance in not only Rome but all of Italy. Carafa was a Neapolitan noble, known for his vicious hatred of heresy and Jews, as well as of the Spanish.[21] He had no interest in the culture of the Renaissance or classical learning. Humanism offered him no pleasure, and he saw humanist ideas as threats to orthodoxy, so the Roman Curia lost much of its attraction for those scholars seeking employment in the Church without taking holy orders. For Paul IV, there was no Renaissance, except in places he wished to see it suppressed.

Rather, he was devoted to Medieval scholastic thought, personal asceticism, and rigid control of ideas. He was the pope who enacted the harshest measures against the Jews of Rome, creating the enclosed ghetto in the city, allowing only a single synagogue,

---

19. It was the poet Du Bellay who was said to be the author of the epithet that emerged on Pasquino, asking why if the pope had made his monkey keeper a cardinal, why not the monkey? See Partner, 1979. p. 203.
20. Despite his brief reign, Marcellus achieved some measure of immortality through Giovanni Pierluigi da Palestrina's *Missa Papae Marcelli* (*Pope Marcellus Mass*), probably composed in the early 1560s after the pope's death.
21. Partner, 1979. pp. 214–15.

and forcing Jews to wear distinctive dress. They were restricted in what professions they could practice and were forbidden to leave the ghetto at night. And, in a twist of his bigoted dagger, he declared that all action against them had to be paid for by the Jews themselves.[22]

On the other hand, Paul was an equal opportunity bigot, for he was no more charitable toward his fellow Christians. He hated heresy and Protestantism: it only took the suspicion of being a reformer to merit the pope's vicious reprisals. He had been a fanatic inquisitor, having been one of the strongest proponents of the Roman Inquisition of 1542. Even when he was elected pope, he continued to serve in that office, moving the Church against some of the most revered and respected reforming cardinals in the Sacred College, such as Giovanni Morone (whom he imprisoned) and Reginald Pole, Queen Mary's cousin and archbishop of Canterbury.[23] He went so low as to hide in the bedroom of a dying senior cleric to hear whether there was any hint during extreme unction of his suspected heresy. If there was, he intended to refuse the cleric burial in consecrated ground. He filled the prisons of the Inquisition with many perfectly innocent men and women. And, most destructively, in 1559 he introduced the Index of Forbidden Books (*Index Librorum Prohibitorum*).

This index was a compilation of books which could not be owned or read by Catholics, a list that was reissued, much strengthened, in 1564, and which grew inexorably until it contained thousands of titles.[24] Naturally, all of the works of the Reformation were included, but so, too, were the texts of Desiderius Erasmus, Niccolò Machiavelli, and Michel de Montaigne. It had a chilling effect on publication, driving authors, editors, and translators to go to extraordinary lengths not to offend or risk condemnation: ultimately self-censorship proved as effective as the Inquisition. Even the great initiators of Renaissance literature did not escape. Giovanni Boccaccio, that great friend and contemporary of Petrarch, saw his *Decameron* bowdlerized when the priests or monks in his stories who behaved uncanonically were redefined as "students"—a social group to whom any licentious actions could be reasonably attributed. Paul's reach was long: the Index was abolished only in 1966.

When the fanatical old pope died in 1559, the city exploded in a riot of jubilation. The prisons of the Inquisition were stormed and the prisoners freed. The statue just recently erected to him on the Campidoglio was defaced, including with the addition

---

22. Paul saw Judaism as a disease to be contained, like plague; hence, his motive for the establishment of the Ghetto of Rome (1555) was to create a quarantine area. His bull stated that the Jews of Rome "were to be confined so that they might be cured of the disease of Judaism . . . and arrive at the true light of the Catholic Faith." Quoted in Partner, 1979. pp. 43–46. See also Kenneth Stow, *The Theater of Acculturation: The Roman Ghetto in the Sixteenth Century*. Seattle: University of Washington Press. 2001. p. 40.

23. Stinger, 1998. pp. 329–30.

24. Alison Brown, "Rethinking the Renaissance in the Aftermath of Italy's Crisis," in Najemy, 2004. pp. 262–63.

of the special hat that he had made Jews wear in order that they be easily identified. The statue was then decapitated and tossed into the Tiber.[25] In fact, Paul IV was so reviled in Rome that his very body had to be safely hidden in Vatican chapels because the mob wanted to desecrate it. It was hastily buried, and then only in a temporary grave as the mob went to his family's church to burn it down rather than see the hated pope honorably installed. Members of his Carafa family, whom he had advanced through nepotism—one sin he clearly did not abhor—were targeted, eventually leading to their trial and, in two prominent examples, executions. Certainly Paul IV vied with Adrian VI for the title of the most despised pope of the century.[26]

Alternating Perspectives: 1559–85

The next quarter of a century saw a similar pattern of point–counterpoint in the election of popes—one the antidote to the other. Paul IV's successor was the elderly, irenic, learned, experienced, and respected Cardinal Giovanni Angelo de'Medici, a very distant relation to the Florentine family but Milanese by birth.[27] He took the name of Pius IV (r. 1559–64). Immediately, he pardoned all of those Romans who had rioted on the death of Paul, and he punished his predecessor's family as a signal that the hated Carafa influence was now over forever.[28] Unlike his predecessor, he not only had a deep respect for classical learning but wanted once more to restore Rome to its natural grandeur.

Most significantly, he reconvened the Council of Trent in 1562, preparing for what would be the last sitting of this great Council. The final session of Trent was a difficult piece of diplomacy, given that the political divisions in Europe had become complex after the 1559 Treaty of Cateau–Cambrésis, which effectively recognized Habsburg hegemony in Italy and much of Europe. The challenge was to find final decrees of the Council that both France and Spain could adhere to and that recognized the absolute authority of the pope in matters of the Catholic religion. In this he was remarkably successful. Indeed, Pius IV's pontificate illustrated that the principle of papal theocratic monarchy had been firmly established, whether for good or evil, depending on the policies and personalities of the popes themselves.

Pius IV's patterns of patronage were not deep; nevertheless, he did leave lasting monuments in the city and the Vatican. He invited Pirro Ligorio to construct the elegant, small villa or casino (completed 1562) on the grounds of the Vatican Gardens. It was a

---

25. Partner, 1979. pp. 46, 203.
26. Miles Pattenden, *Pius IV and the Fall of the Carafa: Nepotism and Papal Authority in Counter-Reformation Rome.* Oxford: Oxford University Press, 2013. pp. 8–33.
27. Pattenden, 2013. "The Family of Pius IV," Appendix II, p. 138. It is not altogether correct that there was no relation between the Florentine and Milanese Medici because the *stemma* (coat of arms) of the two families was virtually identical (the Milanese Medici did not display the *fleur-de-lys*).
28. Pattenden, 2013. pp. 34–135.

most creative way of returning to that classical ideal of *rus in urbe* (the country within the city) with that perfectly proportioned villa built within the confines of the Apostolic Palace itself.[29] It was also Pius who commissioned the aged Michelangelo to construct (1563–64) the church of Santa Maria degli Angeli (more correctly Santa Maria degli Angeli e dei Martiri) within the Baths of Diocletian.[30] The impressive volume of the former bath's *frigidarium* (cool room) was transformed by Michelangelo into a marvelous Christian basilica dedicated not only to the virgin and attendant angels but also to those Christian martyrs who were believed to have died in its construction during the reign of that persecuting emperor. A monk had experienced a vision of their torment and pressured the pope to honor their sacrifice. The results apparently pleased Pius because after his death at the end of 1565 his tomb was placed in the basilica.

His successor, Pius V (r. 1566–72), was in some ways a return to the harsh, ascetic, uncompromising world of Paul IV. Pius was a Lombard, Michele Ghislieri, a Dominican.[31] Pius IV appointed him grand inquisitor for the Christian world; and even after his election as pope he attended sessions of the Roman Inquisition, to the point of staying to witness the torture of suspected heretics. As a signal of his sympathy with his still-hated predecessor, he exhumed the corpse of Paul IV in 1566 and had it interred in the Carafa Chapel in Santa Maria Sopra Minerva in a fine tomb created by Pirro Ligorio, but destroying in the process part of Filippino Lippi's frescoes. He also shared Paul's virulent anti-Semitism, expelling all Jews from the Papal States, except for the ghetto in Rome and the port of Ancona, and there only because their services were useful. Rome needed the highly skilled Jewish physicians, musicians, and pawnbrokers, just as the Adriatic seaport required merchants with connections to the East and bankers.

And as with Paul, Pius V's hatred of Protestantism was pathological. It was he who excommunicated Queen Elizabeth I of England in April 1570. Nor would he permit any compromise with the Huguenots in France, thereby helping create the environment that culminated in the infamous St. Bartholomew's Day Massacre (August 24, 1572), which occurred a few months after his death. That slaughter of Protestant nobles in Paris, who had been invited to a royal wedding, was one of the most horrendous events of the French Wars of Religion.

There was no touch of the humanist about Pius V. It was as though the Renaissance had passed him by. For example, he hated the "pagan" sculptures displayed in the Belvedere courtyard and ordered that they be removed.[32] He was a Dominican theologian,

---

29. Coffin, 1979. pp. 267–78.

30. McGregor, 2005. pp. 101–2.

31. Simona Feci, "Pio V, papa, santo," in *Dizionario Biografico degli Italiani*. Vol. 83. Rome: Istituto della Enciclopedia Italiana, 2015; Simona Feci, "Pio V," in *Enciclopedia dei Papi*. Rome: Treccani, 2000. III, pp. 160–80.

32. Nicola Cortwright, *The Papacy and the Art of Reform in Sixteenth-Century Rome: Gregory XIII's Tower of the Winds in the Vatican*. Cambridge: Cambridge University Press, 2003. pp. 33–34.

with a purely scholastic perspective: as a sign of his retrograde thinking, he raised that earlier Dominican Thomas Aquinas to the status of a doctor of the Church. And, his efforts in regulating the liturgy established the rite practiced in Catholic churches until the twentieth century.

Detesting not only Jews, Protestants, and heretics, Pius was equally determined to halt the expansion of the Islamic Ottoman Empire. At least here he had substantial support. His good name was secured when his call for the creation of a Holy League against Islam in 1571 led to the crucial victory of a massive international Christian fleet at the Battle of Lepanto. This spectacular victory was of enormous significance, putting a stop to Ottoman expansion and raising Catholic confidence in the Church and its head. In a miracle that decided his nomination for saintly status, Pius declared the Christian victory at the very moment the outcome of the battle became clear—this, despite the fact that he was in Rome at the time and had none of the modern means of instant communication at his disposal to have known the victory for a fact. Consequently, Pius was canonized in 1712 as Saint Pius V. Few who actually lived under his rule would have credited this honor.

Pius's death in 1572 produced a pope who was something of a compromise: Ugo Boncompagni, who took the name Gregory XIII (r. 1572–85). A celebrated legal scholar, he was late to the Church but had been recognized by previous popes for his diplomatic skills, intelligence, and personal rigor. Consequently, in May of 1572 he was elected in an astonishingly brief conclave that lasted just one day.[33]

Gregory's policies were to struggle against Protestantism and heresy, not through punishment and fear but through example, education, and missionary work. In fact, Gregory had a far more open mind than some of his immediate predecessors. In particular, he enjoyed a real interest in science and geography. In part, this facilitated his ambition to convert non-Christians in the newly discovered territories of the world to Catholicism and to win back Protestants in Europe. He sent missions to China, India, and Japan, and established schools where he trained local boys and sent missions of conversion to rulers in Africa and Asia; and he received their delegation in return in Rome. In short, Gregory had a curiosity about the world and the place of the Church within it. This interest in cartography found a perfect focus in his Gallery of Maps in the Vatican palace.[34]

---

33. Cortwright, 2003. pp. 9–18.
34. For a broader discussion of cartography at the time of Gregory XIII, see Mark Rosen, *The Mapping of Power in Renaissance Italy: Painted Cartographic Cycles in Social and Intellectual Context*. Cambridge: Cambridge University Press, 2014.

Ignazio Danti and the Renaissance of Mathematics and Geography

The Gallery of Maps is a remarkable space—a long gallery with forty frescoed maps of the regions of Italy, most with their chief cities depicted in perspective and at a point of historic importance. The frescoes were commissioned in 1580 and completed in just eighteen months by a group of painters directed by Ignazio Danti. Danti is one of the most interesting polymaths of the sixteenth century and is far too little known. Born in Perugia, he entered the Dominican Order at nineteen and devoted himself not only to theology but also to mathematics and geography. His family had produced a number of artists, so he was already adept at drawing and painting, but his true love was science.[35]

In 1562 Danti left his native Perugia for Florence where he lived in the Dominican house of Santa Maria Novella, teaching mathematics and science and creating for Grand Duke Cosimo I a series of geographical maps and globes for the Palazzo Vecchio, as well as designing several scientific instruments. A dispute with Cosimo's successor, Grand Duke Francesco I, resulted in his departure for Bologna in 1575, where he became professor of mathematics at the *Studio*. Pope Gregory XIII had several plans that required someone of Danti's immense talents and knowledge, so Danti was invited to Rome.

Danti's first task was to collaborate on the design of the Gallery of the Maps.[36] Visitors today swarm through the corridor, stopping only briefly to examine the maps because they are intent on reaching the Sistine Chapel which lies just beyond. But the magnificent frescoes are a tour de force deserving close examination. They focus on Italy and are drawn with a bird's-eye view of Rome. As a result, modern notions of north at the top and south at the bottom simply don't apply. The corridor runs nearly four hundred feet in length with visitors asked to imagine the floor as the Apennines—the mountain range that divides the peninsula into east and west. The forty frescoes—twenty on each side—depict the regions of Italy with astonishing accuracy and charming detail.[37]

Much can be said about this representation of Italy and the surrounding Mediterranean. The 1580s were an age of discovery and cartography, an attempt to chart the European knowledge of the world that was growing daily with voyages of discovery, voyages which left records for a more perfect knowledge of the details of the earth's surface. But it was also the age of papal power and the Counter-Reformation. Knowledge is power, and the power of the Church over Italy is reflected in these maps: they indicate that Italy is the center of the world because of the authority of the Roman pontiff whose perspective is the point of view and in whose palace they are recorded.

---

35. Cortwright, 2003. p. 14.
36. Rosen, 2014. pp. 10–11, 13, 15 et passim.
37. See Roberto Almagià, *Le Pitture murali della Galleria delle Carte Geografiche*. Vol. 3. Vatican City: Monumenta Cartografica Vaticana, 1952.

Much the same can be said about the other task given to Danti by Gregory XIII: the reform of the calendar. The old Julian calendar, created in the first century BC by Julius Caesar, had become disassociated with the solar year and hence the important religious rites of the Church, such as Easter. Who better than a pope with an interest in science to reform a pagan calendar 1600 years in existence? The control of time is something that all powerful institutions or individuals aspire to achieve. It is for this reason that the French revolutionaries declared 1792 the Year One in their new calendar, or the Italian fascists deemed 1922 the Year I of the *Età Fascista* (EF). Gregory had the ambition to do the same. It was not only the need for religious ritual to be consonant with the solar year but also the establishment of a Catholic universe in which the pope decided how time would unfold—both on earth and in heaven, as symbolized by his two keys.[38]

The search for a reformed calendar was therefore a major task, and Danti was appointed pontifical mathematician and part of the commission to determine the new calendar, with the German Jesuit astronomer Christopher Clavius and the Italian mathematician Luigi Lilio (or Giglio).[39] An observatory, the Tower of the Winds (*Torre dei Venti*) or Gregorian Tower, was built between 1578 and 1580 into the Cortile del Belvedere in the Vatican palace so that precise readings could be made, including by means of a meridian designed by Danti. The results were the promulgation of a new and improved calendar in 1582. It was science and observation that permitted those around Gregory to record the physical shape of Italy and the Mediterranean and the correct movement of the heavens so that a calendar could correctly predict the date of Easter and govern Time—both divine and human. The Gregorian calendar, as we know it to this day, has become Gregory's lasting memorial.

Danti was named bishop of Alatri in 1583 and wrote a number of extremely important scientific books including one on the use of the astrolabe and other instruments, another on mathematics, as well as a translation of Euclid. Despite his failure to devise a plan to move the Vatican obelisk to allow the rebuilding of St. Peter's (this undertaking would have to wait until the reign of Sixtus V and Domenico Fontana), he was honored as a brilliant practicing scientist as well as an orthodox Catholic thinker whose belief in and knowledge of science did not conflict with his faith. Consequently, in the relief on the base of Gregory XIII's tomb in St. Peter's Ignazio Danti appears, honored with his benefactor at the center of Catholic Christendom.

---

38. Cortwright, 2003. pp. 28–40.
39. Ugo Baldini, "Christoph Clavius and the Scientific Scene in Rome," in G. V. Coyne et al., eds., *Gregorian Reform of the Calendar: Proceedings of the Vatican Conference to Commemorate Its 400th Anniversary, 1582–1982*. Vatican City: Pontificia Academia Scientiarum, 1983. pp. 137–70; Gordon Moyer, "Aloisius Lilius and the *Compendium Novae Rationis Restituendi Kalendarium*," in Coyne et al., 1983. pp. 171–88.

A Renaissance Pope of the Counter-Reformation

Gregory XIII's papacy was a triumph of intellectual endeavor entirely suited to humanist values. Besides his interest in science, Gregory XIII's desire to educate the clergy led to his building the Collegio Romano, the Jesuit seminary in Rome, as well as several other institutions of higher studies.[40]

Gregory also strove to improve the city of Rome itself,[41] enlarging the Quirinal palace and completing Michelangelo's plans for the Palazzo Senatorio on the Capitoline. He constructed the Via Gregoriana to better link Santa Maria Maggiore with St. John Lateran. And, to adorn the city and make it healthier, he improved the Acqua Vergine aqueduct, bringing water to Piazza Navona through two fountains—visible to this day— designed by Giacomo della Porta.[42] And, of course, work continued on St. Peter's. The drum for the dome was completed during his pontificate. He also commissioned the Gregorian Chapel in St. Peter's, named not for himself but for St. Gregory of Nazianzus whose relics were transferred to that richly decorated space. Eventually, however, the chapel also held his tomb.[43]

When he died in 1585, Gregory XIII left a remarkable legacy. He can be celebrated as a Renaissance pope in so many ways, as he balanced the demands of his religious policy with his broader interest in the culture, science, and philosophy of this world. He set a precedent, one that would reach into the next reign: the pivotal age of Sixtus V.

40. McGregor, 2005. pp. 289–90.
41. Cortwright, 2003. pp. 18–25.
42. McGregor, 2005. pp. 238–39.
43. Cortwright, 2003. pp. 25–27.

**Illus. 21.1 Baldassare Peruzzi, Antonio da Sangallo, and
Giacomo Barozzi da Vignola. Villa Farnese, Caprarola.**

The unsettled situation in Rome at the turn of the sixteenth century impelled Cardinal Alessandro Farnese, the future pope Paul III, to construct a fortress on his family estates near Viterbo, about fifty kilometers north of Rome. Alessandro had been raised to the Sacred College by Alexander VI Borgia as a consequence of the aged pope's liaison with Farnese's young sister, Giulia. The election of Julius II in 1503, the Borgia's hated enemy, suggested that a place of refuge would be wise, so Cardinal Alessandro called the architects Baldassare Peruzzi and Antonio da Sangallo to begin work on the villa on the hill above Caprarola in 1504.

The situation proved less dangerous than feared, so the fortress was never completed but served as the basic structure for a splendid pleasure palace re-commissioned in 1556 by another Cardinal Alessandro Farnese, the grandson of Pope Paul III. The architect was Giacomo Barozzi da Vignola who worked on other nearby villas, as well as the papal palace. The result is a huge palace, with five stories and exquisite gardens and staterooms. Of these, the *Room of the World Map* or *Sala del Mappamondo*, illustrating the known world in 1574, and the *Room of the Farnese Deeds*, a propagandistic narrative of great moments in the family's history painted by Taddeo Zuccari, are the most renowned.

Illus. 21.2 Giacomo Barozza da Vignola, Giorgio Vasari, Bartolommeo Ammannati, and Michelangelo. Villa Giulia, 1551–53. The Nymphaeum, Rome.

Julius III Del Monte (r. 1550–55), the pope whose enmity drove Cardinal Alessandro Farnese to finish his villa at Caprarola, used the same architect, Vignola, and a team of Florentine masters—among whom were Vasari, Ammannati, and Michelangelo—to construct the most elegant sixteenth-century villa in Rome, just outside the Flaminian Gate (*porta del popolo*). It was modeled on ancient Roman villas and was celebrated for its luxury, its classical ornamentation, and its access to the Vatican Palace by water.

Illus. 21.3 Michelangelo, *The Last Judgment*, 1536–41. Apostolic Vatican Palace, Altar Wall of the Sistine Chapel, Rome.

The Last Judgment was initially commissioned by Pope Clement VII de'Medici, but he died before significant work could begin. Nevertheless, Paul III Farnese continued the contract. In this vibrant, dynamic image, Christ is modeled on the statue of Apollo and is accompanied by Mary, Saints Peter and Paul, and the communion of saints being received into paradise at the last trumpet. Michelangelo painted his self-portrait as the face of the flayed skin of St. Bartholomew (held below Christ's left foot). The damned are consigned to hell, with a classical allusion to the boatman Charon transporting them over the river Styx.

At the far right at the bottom is a man with ass's ears being crushed by one serpent while another gnaws on his genitals. This is a portrait of papal Master of Ceremonies Biagio da Cesena, a prig who pestered Paul III to have the nudity covered as he believed it was inappropriate in the papal chapel. Michelangelo exacted his revenge by portraying da Cesena as Minos, judge of the underworld and the mythical king who was punished by the gods for his recalcitrance.

After Paul III's death, Paul IV Carafa, a most uncompromising, fanatical pope, sided with Biagio da Cesena. He stopped Michelangelo's pension and demanded that the painter cover the nudes in *The Last Judgment*, a demand the aged Michelangelo simply ignored. Paul often stated that he wanted the vault of the Sistine painted over, as he hated its pagan nudity. Fortunately, he did nothing about it.

Illus. 21.4 Pasquale Cati (1520–1620), *Pope Pius IV de'Medici Affirms the Decrees of the Council of Trent,* **1588. Santa Maria in Trastevere, Altemps Chapel, Rome.**

Pope Pius IV de'Medici (r. 1559–65) was committed both to Church reform and to papal theocracy. At its conclusion, Pius affirmed the decrees of the Council of Trent (1545–63), but also issued the famous bull, *Benedictus Deus* (1564). This critical document stated that only the papacy could interpret and enforce the decrees of Trent, a clear rebuke of the old Conciliarist principles that had arisen first at Constance. Anyone who attempted to interpret or define Trent without explicit papal approval would be subject to excommunication.

This image shows the pope presiding over the end of the Council, with his arms and name prominent on the dais in front of the assembled clergy. In the foreground is Ecclesia (the personification of the Church wearing the triple papal crown), with the elements of the Eucharist, supported by Faith, Charity, Wisdom, and other virtues applicable to the entire world (the globe) and all peoples. Heresy is shown as defeated and the faithful armed against its return.

**Illus. 21.5 *Gregory XIII and the Revision of the Calendar,* 1582.
Archivio di Stato, Siena. Tavola della Biccherna numero 72.**

Gregory XIII (r. 1572–85) was a remarkable man who challenged the popular view that the late Renaissance Church was altogether hostile to science, geography, astronomy, and mathematics. He reformed the calendar, ordered the construction of an astronomical observatory, and commissioned Ignazio Danti (1536–86) to decorate the Hall of Maps.

This image shows Pope Gregory presiding over an explanation of the astronomical—and astrological—research that informed the new calendar. On the table are books needed for this work, together with a Ptolemaic armillary sphere. This model of the heavens placed the earth as the center of the universe rather than the sun. The spherical metal ribs surrounding the earth allowed for astronomical calculations to be made.

The image comes from the painted wooden book covers which protected the official accounts of the republic of Siena (*Tavolette di Biccherna*). These were often painted by very celebrated artists and consequently constitute both an artistic and a cultural history of the years between the thirteenth and eighteenth centuries.

Illus. 21.6.a Giorgio Vasari, *The French King Charles IX Justifies the Massacre of Protestants (Huguenots) to the Parlement of Paris, August 1572.* Apostolic Vatican Palace, Sala Regia, Rome.

Philip II of Spain was said to have laughed publicly for the first and only time in his life on hearing the news of the Saint Bartholomew Massacre in which thousands of prominent French Huguenots—Calvinist Protestants—were slaughtered. It was in this context that, at the very beginning of his pontificate, Gregory XIII tarnished his reign for posterity by having a *Te Deum* sung and a medal struck to commemorate the 1572 massacre. Subsequently, however, he was more open to dialogue with the Protestants, moderating the Church's call for the overthrow of Queen Elizabeth of England, for example, and insisting that English Catholics still had the responsibility to obey her in matters other than those of faith.

Although much of Europe was appalled by the brutal murder of innocent Calvinist men and women, the papacy commissioned a fresco by Vasari in the Sala Regia of the Apostolic Palace celebrating the event. It is important to note, however, that Gregory wrongly believed that the massacre resulted from a plot by the Huguenots to overthrow the Catholic royal house of Valois. For him, the atrocity represented a victory for Catholicism over its enemies. That is why it shares the room with Vasari's other great fresco depicting the triumph over the Ottoman Turks in the Battle of Lepanto, 1571.

Illus. 21.6.b Gregory XIII's Bronze Medal Celebrating the St. Bartholomew's Day Massacre (August 23–24), 1572. Engraved on the obverse side is in Latin Gregory XIII, Pontifex Maximus, year 1 (1572); on the reverse is Slaughter of the Huguenots, 1572.

**Illus. 21.7 Ignazio Danti, *Hall of the Geographical Maps*,
1580–83. Apostolic Vatican Palace, Rome.**

The architect of the Hall of the Maps was Ottaviano Mascherino (Ottaviano Nonni, 1536–1606, called *Il Mascherino*). It was this hall that connected Gregory's astronomical observatory, *The Tower of the Winds*, with the Apostolic Palace. The intention was that members of the Curia would travel through the geography of the earth before entering into a vision of the heavens.

The topographical detail by Ignazio Danti is remarkable, using color to define mountains, plains, shores, forests, and towns. Close observation reveals charming historical details, such as ships from the papal fleet at sea; Hannibal with his elephants confronting the Romans in Lombardy; and, significantly, the papal Curia returning to Rome from Avignon after the Babylonian Captivity.

CHAPTER 22
THE END OF THE RENAISSANCE IN ROME

Ironically, the Renaissance ended in many ways in Rome, not with the horrific Sack of 1527, but with the remarkable pontificate of Sixtus V. True, he was a great builder, like Julius II or Sixtus IV, but in no way did he share their appreciation of the ancient city as a witness to humanist scholarship and learning. On the contrary, he consciously set out to wipe Rome clean of its pagan memories and to exorcize its monuments, viewing classical humanism as a threat to Christianity. He outright rejected the notion that the Roman Church sustained the culture and authority of the classical world. Consequently, a perspective that had flourished from the time of Petrarch was now considered abhorrent and profane.

In fact, Sixtus V was a mass of contradictions both as a cardinal and as pope. He was of the humblest birth yet exercised an imperious nature. He was not a gifted or careful scholar, yet he worked on the most difficult texts, even to the point of commissioning a new version of the Vulgate. He had few books and showed little interest in them, but he not only established a papal printing press but also commissioned the construction of a wing dedicated to the Vatican Library. He had little knowledge of or even interest in art and architecture, yet he became a major builder. He despised paganism and wanted the ancient monuments of Rome repurposed as Christian symbols, an obsession that resulted in the loss of some of the city's antiquities but also the rehabilitation of others. He was a devout Franciscan, and hence dressed and ate simply and avoided a luxurious court, while simultaneously he commissioned one of Rome's most elaborate papal burial chapels to house his remains. He sincerely considered the needs of the city by rebuilding the ancient aqueduct of Alexander Severus, constructing straight streets and paving others, and establishing an office to control the price of grain; but he was unable to end banditry, despite draconian punishments; and he raised papal taxes in the countryside and in Rome itself when he needed cash.

Despite these inconsistencies, Sixtus V proved a great pope for late Renaissance Rome and accomplished more in the five years of his reign (1585–90) than most others, regardless how long they held the throne of St. Peter. So it is necessary to investigate the remarkable age of Pope Sixtus V Peretti.[1]

---

1. Torgil Magnuson, *Rome in the Age of Bernini: From the Election of Sixtus V to the Death of Urban VIII.* Vol. 1. Stockholm: Almqvist & Wiksell International, 1982.

Felice Peretti

Felice Peretti was born to a family of poor farmers in Grottamare in the Marches in 1521.[2] Despite his poverty and lack of privilege, he entered the Franciscan Order, where his natural talents were recognized, leading to studies at the universities of Bologna and Ferrara. In 1547 he was ordained a priest, after which he embarked upon a career as a preacher, achieving great acclaim for his sermons. This resulted in his appointment as abbot of a succession of monasteries and led to his role in the Inquisition in Venice (*Tre savi sopra l'eresia*) as a representative of the Roman Inquisition. His abilities and his implacable confidence, as well as his obvious and sincere piety and devotion to Catholic orthodoxy, led to his appointment to the Sacred College as a cardinal in 1570 by Pope Pius V.

Felice was ambitious as a scholar, but his impatience and lack of true erudition clouded his reputation. For example, when he was a cardinal, he worked on the letters of St. Ambrose, intending to produce a new edition. However, he saw that some of Ambrose's biblical quotes did not correspond with the text of the translation in the Vulgate. So, in an ill-advised move, he replaced Ambrose's original passages, made directly from the Septuagint, with those from the Vulgate. This superficial foray into Biblical scholarship then motivated Peretti to begin a new edition of the Vulgate, an edition which he rushed into print after his election as pope, and an edition that was so full of errors it had to be suppressed by his successor, Gregory XIV.

These unfortunate actions characterized Sixtus's strengths and weakness: he was exceptionally confident in his own abilities, even in confronting highly technical editorial and linguistic matters that he really did not fully understand. They also illustrated his impatience: everything had to be done quickly and immediately, leaving no time for sober reflection or review.

Sixtus V

In the conclave of 1585 Felice Peretti was elected pope, choosing for papal title the name of Sixtus V. Unfortunately, all of the characteristics he had displayed as a cardinal returned with even greater force as bishop of Rome, and the many contradictions of his personality were magnified. He accepted no restrictions, accepted no traditional limits on his actions, and his imperious character insisted that huge undertakings be accomplished quickly, even when they were considered by the most thoughtful and intelligent minds of the Renaissance to be impossible.[3]

This trait was perhaps most clearly announced through his decision to move the Vatican obelisk at the very beginning of his pontificate. This large standing needle of red

---

2. Renato Canestrari, *Sisto V*. Torino: Società Editrice Internazionale di Torino, 1954.
3. Irene Polverini Fosi, "Justice and Its Image: Political Propaganda and Judicial Reality in the Pontificate of Sixtus V," *Sixteenth Century Journal*, 24 (1993), pp. 75–95.

granite, eighty-four feet high and weighing more than 350 tons, had been set up by the emperor Caligula in the racecourse that he had constructed near the base of the Vatican Hill. It was believed that St. Peter had been crucified in the racecourse and buried beside it in a pagan cemetery, so it was on this site that the original basilica of St. Peter had been built by Constantine.

By the time of the Renaissance, this was the only ancient obelisk still standing—a fact that owed more to the rather marshy subsoil that absorbed any seismic movement than to the belief that God kept it standing on purpose to honor St. Peter's martyrdom. When Julius II decided to demolish the old basilica of St. Peter and replace it with a huge new church, it was obvious that the obelisk would have to move. Michelangelo and Antonio da Sangallo, who were both chief architects of St. Peter's, had stated categorically that it was impossible to lower the obelisk, move it along uneven terrain, and re-erect it on a new plinth without its sustaining irreparable damage. But Sixtus did not let such advice interfere with his plans.

After wide consultation and a competition among engineers to plan the repositioning of the immense obelisk, Sixtus chose the plan of Domenico Fontana. Fontana had developed a complex system of scaffolding, pulleys, and ropes to lower the obelisk, which would then be moved to a purpose-built causeway to slide the huge object along in a wooden cage on rollers (called his *castello*, or castle). Once it was in position, he planned to re-erect it with the efforts of hundreds of horses and sailors from the papal fleet who had been trained to pull with equal force in unison—a skill necessary at sea for hoisting large sails.

The entire process took thirteen months.[4] Finally, when the obelisk was to be raised in the piazza on September 10, 1586, Sixtus made an extraordinary declaration. Knowing that huge crowds would gather to witness the erection of the obelisk, he ordered that anyone watching this technical marvel who made the slightest sound would be summarily executed: he wanted to ensure that those pulling on the ropes were free to concentrate and that no noise would be permitted to startle the hundred horses necessary for the elaborate operation.

Needless to say, the tension in the piazza was extraordinary. Hundreds of collective breaths were held. But, in the unnatural silence as the sailors pulled on their ropes, the resulting friction caused the hemp to smoke. It soon appeared that the ropes would break into flame, weakening them to the point that the obelisk would fall and shatter. A courageous sailor from Genoa, Benedetto Brasca, then disobeyed the code of silence and screamed, "Water on the ropes" (*acqua alle funi*). Comrades appeared hastily with

---

4. Fontana created a book to describe his feat: Domenico Fontana, *Della trasportazione dell'obelisco vaticano, Del modo di tenuto in trasferire l'obelisco vaticano et delle fabbriche fatte da papa Sisto V.* Rome: Domenico Basa, 1590. Fortunately, it is available in facsimile editions, and the original text, with all of the illustrations, is available electronically (https://archive.org/details /gri_33125008662708).

buckets of water, dousing the fire. The operation then continued until the obelisk was securely upright and in place.[5]

The city was jubilant and Sixtus well satisfied. Contrary to his orders, the Genoese sailor was not executed but, rather, given a monopoly on the selling of palms for Palm Sunday in perpetuity. This was a lucrative sinecure indeed! As for Fontana, his relief was extraordinary. It was never a sure thing that his scheme would work, so as a precautionary measure he had kept ready a relay of fresh horses to help him flee Rome and Sixtus's wrath if the project had failed.

Sixtus V as City Planner

Sixtus, with his imperious and impatient nature, had an overarching plan for Rome and the papacy centered on his obsession with making the city once more *caput mundi,* rivaling the ancient Imperial capital in grandeur but one now dedicated to Christian rather than pagan power.[6] He also, as a consequence, wanted his papacy to appear like the rule of a benevolent emperor, mixing grand structures with public convenience—all, of course, with his name attached. It was for this reason that he set the bronze figures of the apostolic martyrs Peter and Paul atop the ancient columns of Trajan and Marcus Aurelius—on display to this day. But he didn't stop there. Instead he drove a concerted effort to recover and erect other ancient obelisks—but always in locations particularly associated with Christian sites and ritual.[7]

Sixtus's new urban plan was remarkably ambitious. A series of new, straight, wide streets were to replace the Medieval alleys and narrow roads that still characterized the city. These were to radiate out from Santa Maria Maggiore, which was not only the site of Sixtus's family chapel but also the location of his family's villas on the Esquiline. There were many reasons to pursue this plan. One was the rapidly changing means of transport where carriages began to replace litters and where larger carts were needed to supply the growing population. The other was to encourage pilgrims within the city to navigate it more efficiently, encouraging the population and services to spread beyond the crowded and still insalubrious *Abitata.* While there was a great need, like so many urban planning projects, most of these streets were proposed but never realized.

---

5. This phrase, *acqua alle funi,* subsequently became aphoristic in Italy. It is uttered when action or courage in the face of dangerous, or legal, impediments is required.

6. Helge Gamrath, *Roma sancta renovata: Studi sull'urbanistica di Roma nella seconda metà del sec. XVI con particolare riferimento al pontificato di Sisto V (1585–1590).* Rome: L'Erma Di Bretschneider, 1987; M. Fagiolo and M. L. Madonna, *Roma di Sisto V. Arte, architettura e città fra Rinascimento e Barocco.* Rome: De Luca Editori d'Arte, 1993.

7. For a description of Sixtus V's "exorcism" of the obelisks, see Pamela Jones, *Altarpieces and Their Viewers in the Churches of Rome from Caravaggio to Guido Reni.* Aldershot, UK: Ashgate, 2008. pp. 40–41.

To facilitate this expansion of Rome, Sixtus rebuilt the third-century aqueduct of Alexander Severus. The work was extremely difficult and very expensive, but by 1589 water was pouring from a huge new *mostra*—the technical name for a fountain at the end of an aqueduct. Dubbed the *Fountain of Moses*, the *mostra*, however, was poorly received, as the figure of Moses (in the somewhat stylized likeness of Sixtus) was awkwardly composed. Worse, the very long dedication carved above was a rather blatant celebration of the pope himself. In a further act of self-promotion, Sixtus renamed the aqueduct that fed the fountain, calling it the *Acqua Felice*, which literally means "happy" or "fortunate water" but equally references his birth name, Felice.[8]

Sixtus's plan for Rome was to build *Roma Felix* (or *Roma Felice*), a city fortunate in its papal sovereign and renewed Christian mission—that somewhat awkward portrait of Moses by Lionardo Sormani and others notwithstanding. To Sixtus's mind, Rome would indeed be a "happy" metropolis. This epithet may sound a bit ingenuous to us, but the fountain was a tremendous tonic for the city. It provided fresh water and hence allowed for population growth on the Esquiline and Quirinal hills, areas that had previously been partly abandoned.[9]

Equally welcomed were Sixtus's commission of a fountain for the nearby Largo Santa Susanna and the justly famous Quattro Fontane—the Four Fountains—which grace the corners at the intersection of two major streets—the present Via del Quirinale and the Via delle Quattro Fontane. Conveniently, these fountains were close to the Quirinal palace, a building favored by cool breezes in summer, situated on the hilltop called Monte Cavallo (after the horses of Castor and Pollux, the Dioscuri, from the Baths of Constantine that once stood on the Quirinal Hill). Sixtus took advantage of his own urban renovation and expanded the palace, later adopting it as the summer residence of the papacy.[10]

Sixtus's desire to rebuild Rome as a Christian city rivaling the ancient metropolis focused not only on repurposing ancient monuments but also on constructing new ones. The ancient Lateran Palace, which had been the residence of the bishop of Rome since the time of Constantine, was so derelict that it was not worth repairing. Sixtus, consequently, had his architect Domenico Fontana plan a new structure that would adjoin the cathedral and connect with the Piazza which held the baptistery and the newly re-erected obelisk.[11]

Fontana's task was complicated by the fact that there were Christian elements within the old Lateran Palace that had to be preserved, particularly the Sancta Sanctorum; that

8. McGregor, 2005. pp. 238–39.
9. McGregor, 2005. pp. 250–51; Stefano Sandano, *Renovatio Christiana: The Counter Reformed Patronage of Pope Sixtus V at The Holy Steps in Rome (1585–1590)*. CreateSpace Independent Publishing, 2013. pp. 19–40.
10. McGregor, 2005. pp. 244–45.
11. Corinne Mandel, *Sixtus V and the Lateran Palace*. Rome: Istituto Poligrafico e Zecca Dello Stato, 1994.

is, the chapel of St. Lawrence that had been a private papal chapel since the Middle Ages. Also, there were the Scala Santa, the steps which Constantine's mother, St. Helena, was said to have brought back from Jerusalem. They were believed to have been in the praetorium of Pontius Pilate, the very stairs that Christ had climbed to be judged by that Roman proconsul. Sixtus ordered Fontana to solve the problem of their preservation, and the result is the freestanding building of the Scala Santa, where even modern pilgrims ascending the central staircase progress on their knees to discover at the summit the reconstructed Sancta Sanctorum. Once again Fontana proved his ingenuity and practicality.[12]

Sixtus, as might be expected, continued work on St. Peter's, and it was under his pontificate that the basilica was finally closed through the essential completion of the dome.[13]

However, the church that benefitted most from Sixtus's patronage was Santa Maria Maggiore. Not only did he order a burial chapel of considerable size constructed for himself and his family, but he also transferred the body of Pope Pius V (who was not yet canonized) to the chapel. A splendid kneeling figure of Sixtus by Fontana dominates his tomb; and the chapel itself is conspicuously ornate.

The Observant Pope

Sixtus's devotion to the basilica's most cherished relic, the *presepe*, that is, the crib of Christ, was sincere. He arranged for a crypt beneath the altar to be made so that it could be worshipped and connected to the service of the mass. Other churches were rebuilt as well, including part of Santa Sabina on the Aventine Hill and San Girolamo degli Schiavoni. However, in making these improvements, he also stripped Rome of one of its ancient treasures, the Septizonium, the gate—or fountain—built by Septimius Severus early in the third century to announce the beginning of the Appian Way at the foot of the Palatine. Sixtus ordered it be destroyed, its stones being reused for the Lateran Palace, the bases of obelisks, and most especially his chapel in Santa Maria Maggiore.

There was no doubt as to Sixtus's piety and commitment to traditional Catholicism and papal authority. He himself led cardinals and high members of the Curia to hear mass at various churches, especially on their saint's day. These "stational masses" became popular with Sixtus because, it was suggested, he could personally experience how easy or difficult it was to navigate Rome and how his various urban plans were developing.[14]

---

12. Christopher L. C. Ewart Witcombe, "Sixtus V and the Scala Santa," *Journal of the Society of Architectural Historians*, 44 (1985), pp. 368–79. Sandano, 2013. pp. 41–80.
13. Henry Millon, "Michelangelo to Marchionni, 1546–1784," in Tronzo, 2005. pp. 103–4.
14. Pompeio Ugonio in his *Historia delle stazioni di Roma* (1588) credits Sixtus for restoring the early Christian tradition of visiting the stational churches during Lent and Easter. He lists forty-five different churches for these processions, but as some are visited twice, the total came to fifty-four! Jones, 2008. pp. 19, 38.

He was abstemious in his personal life, although the Villa Montalto (later pulled down to construct Rome's railway station) was growing ever grander, with its gardens and ancient statues, becoming in fact known as the Palazzo delle Terme, as it was adjacent to the Baths (*Terme*) of Diocletian. In the tradition of many of his predecessors, Sixtus provided a similar villa to his sister, Camilla, as well as raising members of his once humble family to high status in Rome.[15]

Nepotism aside, Sixtus was concerned with the poor and their necessities of life. He had constructed the Ospizio dei mendicanti in 1587, a place where the indigent poor could go to be fed and find work. Located near the Ponte Sisto, close to the Tiber, it eventually could house about two thousand poor. He created the Congregation of the Abbondanza in the same year, endowing it with sufficient funds to purchase bread cheaply to be resold to the poor. He ensured that the Acqua Felice would always be maintained by establishing a commission to care for it. He attempted to increase grain production and reduce the risks of disease in summer—the lethal Roman malaria—by draining parts of the Pontine Marshes.

Sadly, despite these measures, Sixtus in the end was largely unsuccessful in accommodating the poor. The problem of poverty in the city was simply too great to be solved in such a short pontificate.

Small industries, such as textiles, were encouraged, especially nascent silk production. In fact, in 1586 he issued a regulation that all uncultivated land had to be planted with mulberry trees for silkworms. However, his reign was not long enough to produce any real advantage. And, as is universally to be expected, he ran into hostility from the noble landowners who hardly wanted the Holy See interfering with their property.

Support of Knowledge and Learning

We have seen that Sixtus himself was not really much of a scholar, but he admired knowledge and saw learning as one of the sure defenders of the faith. So he commissioned Fontana to build a new wing across the immense Cortile del Belvedere, designed by Bramante for Julius II. This enormous enclosed space between the two wings of the Vatican palace was a lovely sequence of parterres, ramps, and stairs, following the grade of the Vatican Hill. Previously it been used for jousting, tournaments, festivities, even bear baiting. Now it was bisected by the Library Wing to house a large, purpose-built structure—the Apostolic Vatican Library.

The institution itself might have been founded by Nicholas V and Sixtus IV, but it was Sixtus V who gave it a magnificent home. The entire program took just thirteen

---

15. The Peretti family did, however, further Sixtus's ambitions, especially his sister, Camilla, who benefitted significantly from her brother's position. See Kimberly Dennis, "Camilla Peretti, Sixtus V, and the Construction of Peretti Family Identity in Counter-Reformation Rome," *The Sixteenth Century Journal*, 43 (2012), pp. 71–101.

months. The halls, painted by Sixtus's favorite painters, Cesare Nebbia and Giovanni Guerra, and an army of assistants,[16] celebrated the themes of the Councils of the Church, the libraries of antiquity, and the inventors of alphabets. These all referenced Sixtus's incontrovertible belief that the word became flesh and that word was now invested with the bishop of Rome. He also had painted on the library walls his "works," including his urban plan, the drawings for the Lateran Palace, and other significant commissions.[17]

Not only the Apostolic Library but also the university benefitted. Sixtus was a major benefactor of the Sapienza. In an extraordinarily practical move, he raised professors' salaries with the stated purpose of attracting better talent and contributing to the Sapienza's international reputation. He restructured its weak administration, permitting its expansion. And, he allowed for fifty students from his home region of the March of Ancona to be educated at his expense in the Collegio di Montalto.

Sixtus was also the founder of the Vatican Press, not with a humanist's eye to publishing classical texts, but rather with the intention of reversing the tide of Protestantism. He brought a skilled printer from Venice to manage the presses and used scholars from the university and texts from the Vatican Library to ensure that saints' lives, papal decretals, patristics, canon law, theology, and Church histories were all readily available.

To accomplish this, he employed philologists and editors and he patronized the great Cesare Baronio (1538–1607). Baronio (or as Latinized, Baronius) had wisely dedicated the first volumes of his magisterial five-volume Church history, the *Annales Ecclesiastici* (*Ecclesiastical Annals,* 1588–1607), to Sixtus. In recognition of this he was given a subsidy for the remaining research and for his later work on the Roman martyrology (1586). The enormous influence of this scholarship was such that Baronio was named a cardinal and later beatified and is even now in the process of canonization.[18]

The Legacy of Sixtus V

What a remarkable set of achievements in a pontificate that lasted a mere five years! In so many ways, Sixtus reshaped Rome and completed the institutionalization of Renaissance style and content in the city. His famous impatience and refusal ever to be told that something was impossible led to truly astounding feats, such as the moving of the Vatican obelisk and the building and decoration of the Vatican Library in just over one year.

On the other hand, Sixtus's vision was limited by obsession with orthodoxy in the Church and hostility to Protestantism. In this he was not alone, but where he did diverge from earlier Renaissance popes was in his lack of interest in classical humanism and the

---

16. For Nebbia and Guerra's ability to coordinate large numbers of painters for Sixtus, see Rhoda Eitel-Porter, "Artistic Co-Operation in Late Sixteenth-Century Rome: The Sistine Chapel in S. Maria Maggiore and the Scala Santa," *The Burlington Magazine,* 139 (1997), pp. 452–62.
17. Grafton, 1993.
18. For Baronio (or Latinized as Baronius), see Cyriac K. Pullapilly, *Caesar Baronius, Counter-Reformation Historian.* Notre Dame: University of Notre Dame Press, 1975.

humanist culture of the Renaissance. He was a theologian—and not a very good one—and his interests were to subvert the ancient city to his dream of a Christian capital. Not only was there vandalism, such as the destruction of the Septizonium and the placing of Peter and Paul on the columns of Marcus Aurelius and Trajan, but there was even subversion in his plans to make Rome again the *caput mundi*. The obelisks were excavated and re-erected not as ancient monuments but as pilgrims' markers. The urban plan was not to allow the ancient city to be more accessible, but, rather, to sacrifice a great many Roman remains to widen and straighten the streets that were built in his reign.[19]

These are the reasons for suggesting that the Renaissance in Rome ended with the remarkable pontificate of Sixtus V. He was a great builder. But, unlike Julius, he did not see himself as the successor to Caesar and St. Peter: he was the successor only to St. Peter. He might have continued to wear the red shoes of a Roman emperor, but his mission was to be only the successor to the Prince of the Apostles, greater than any pagan emperor. He set out consciously to wipe Rome clean of its pagan memories and in so doing rejected the view established by Petrarch that classical humanism was no threat to Christianity.

---

19. J. A. F. Orbaan, "The Destruction of the Septizonium," in *Sixtine Rome*. New York: Baker and Taylor, 1911. pp. 232–80.

Illus. 22.1 Domenico Fontana, Cesare Nebbia, Giovanni Guerra, et al., *The* *Sistine Hall of the Apostolic Library,* 1587–88. Apostolic Vatican Palace, Rome.

Sixtus V had several purposes in mind when he commissioned Domenico Fontana to construct the Library Wing of the apostolic palace across Bramante's vast Cortile del Belvedere. First, he wanted a large purpose-built modern repository for the books and objects that had accumulated in the Apostolic Vatican Library since its inception under Nicholas V. This new library wing would permit scholars greater access to more texts which could be used to reinforce the faith and confront heresy, particularly Protestantism. Second, he wanted to end the tradition of using the Cortile del Belvedere for secular, often inappropriate activities, such as jousts. These he saw as detrimental to the divine mission of the papacy. Third, he wanted a cultural legacy which would associate his reign with great and continuous intellectual foundations of learning and religious orthodoxy. This third impetus determined to a great degree the decorative program, featuring as it does the celebration of writing and the book, including a visual history of libraries, the Councils of the Church, and the creators of alphabets.

A small army of painters coordinated by Cesare Nebbia (ca. 1536–ca. 1622) and Giovanni Guerra (1544–1618) completed the decorations in just thirteen months. It was an astounding feat, but one which the imperious pope demanded, as he wished to see the library finished before his death.

Illus. 22.2 Cesare Nebbia, Giovanni Guerra, et al., *The Erection
of the Relocated Obelisk of St. Peter by Domenico Fontana*, 1586.
Apostolic Vatican Library, Hall of Papal Archives, Rome.

The obelisk that presently stands in front of St. Peter's was the first obelisk Sixtus ordered to be repositioned.

Most architects, including Michelangelo, thought it would not be possible to move the huge granite needle, transport it up a rather steep grade, and then re-erect it without damage. But, Sixtus insisted it be accomplished and ordered his engineer–architect, Domenico Fontana, to accomplish the relocation. So, Fontana invented a complex machine for the operation, as it is pictured here.

Obelisks had been a signature of Imperial Rome from the time the emperor Augustus brought the first of them from Heliopolis in Egypt to adorn the spina (or central boulevard) of the Circus Maximus, following his victory over Marc Antony and Cleopatra in 31 BC. Over the intervening years, multiple obelisks had been raised, toppled, and eventually lost to the Renaissance city, most having been victims of earthquakes. Sixtus directed his scholars to locate where these monuments had been and to excavate those sites in order to uncover the structures. So it was that the Circus Maximus obelisk was restored and moved to the center of the Piazza del Popolo. There it serves both as a welcome to the city for those pilgrims from the north who entered through the Flaminian gate (Porta del Popolo) and as a visual marker for the *Tridente*—that is, the trident of three streets that converge on the Piazza (now the Via del Corso, the Via Babuino, and Via Ripetta).

An obelisk from the mausoleum of Augustus was set up in front of Sixtus's favorite church, Santa Maria Maggiore (also, not coincidentally, the site of his funerary chapel). A second obelisk from the Circus Maximus—the tallest in Rome—was moved to the basilica of St. John Lateran. Significantly, each of these tall needles served as signposts for pilgrims, defined a new urban plan, and celebrated Christianity. All were marked with new inscriptions on their bases commemorating their sacral repurposing, and all were subject to an exercise of exorcism to ensure that no pagan aura remained. This was especially important for the Vatican obelisk as it was improbably believed that the ashes of Julius Caesar were kept in the bronze ball on the top. Ancient statues and memorials were thus deliberately reassigned to celebrate the Christian and papal dispensation.

And, to those familiar with the traditions of antiquity, the connection between heaven and earth symbolized by the obelisks was not representative of the divinity of a pagan emperor but of Christ's vicar on earth: the bishop of Rome.

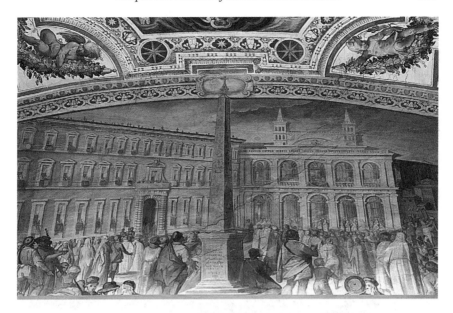

Illus. 22.3 Cesare Nebbia, Giovanni Guerra, et al., *The Lateran Palace, Benediction Loggia and Lateran Obelisk,* 1585–88. Apostolic Vatican Library, Hall of Papal Archives, Rome.

As part of his plan for the rebuilding of Rome as a Christian capital of a Catholic empire, Sixtus V ordered Domenico Fontana to reconstruct the derelict Lateran Palace, shown here in a contemporary fresco in the Vatican Library. Fontana was also responsible for relocating the obelisk you can see in the foreground. The tallest in Rome, the obelisk had been carved circa 1400 BC in Karnak, Egypt. More than seventeen hundred years later, it was brought to Rome by the emperor Constantius (the son of Constantine the Great, r. 337–61) and set on the *spina* (central boulevard) of the Circus Maximus. Sixtus had the obelisk excavated in 1587, repaired, and transported to this important site.

Altogether, Sixtus moved one standing obelisk (St. Peter's) and re-erected three others: the one above on the Piazza San Giovanni; the Flaminian obelisk (1589) on Piazza del Popolo, the first one brought to Rome by Augustus and set up in the Circus Maximus after his defeat of Marc Antony and Cleopatra at Actium in 31 BC; and the Esquiline Obelisk (1587) from the Mausoleum of Augustus, moved to the apse end of the basilica of Santa Maria Maggiore, where Sixtus V is buried.

Illus. 22.4 Tommaso Laureti, *The Triumph of the Christian Religion,* 1582–85. Apostolic Vatican Palace, Room of Constantine (*Sala di Costantino*), Rome.

This image is displayed on the ceiling of the last of the *Stanze* or Rooms of Raphael, the *Room of Constantine*, painted by the artist's workshop after his death (1520) to replace a wooden ceiling from the time of Pope Leo X de'Medici. The pictorial program in the room is a highly propagandistic celebration of the Emperor Constantine's recognition of Christianity.

Although the image on the ceiling invokes the theme of the room, it can also be seen to symbolize the end of the Renaissance in Italy. At the very center, a statue of Mercury—the god of eloquent speech and communication—lies shattered, thrown off its altar, only to be replaced by the crucifix. Supporting this central image are depicted the eight regions of the Italian peninsula and the three continents of Asia, Africa, and Europe. The message is clear: Christianity through the Roman Church will rule Italy and the whole known world.

Two centuries earlier, Petrarch had initiated a world of human dignity and agency, validating the experiencing of life on earth and the value of classical, even pagan antiquity. What Petrarch never imagined when he wrote that "words mirror the soul" was that the principle could and did lead to the desire to control both words and souls. And when he spoke of the need for eloquence, good words, and good style, his intention was to use clarity of speech to permit individuals to identify good over evil, reflecting our natural human dignity. Petrarch, then, left much to personal choice and agency, believing in the innate goodness of mankind, even those born before Christ.

After the Italian Wars, the Sack of Rome, and the Reformation in all its forms, the papacy in Rome could no longer tolerate such freedom. What is good is manifestly not clear, and souls can be lost through sophistry or false prophecy masquerading as reform. Petrarch's dream, then, expired in Rome during the sixteenth century and was by the end of that century superseded by enforced catechisms of truth that could not be debated or ignored, except at the greatest peril. If the Italian Renaissance had been born among Florentines and germinated in Florence, it went to Rome to die, a casualty of events that challenged the very concept of the dignity of man and the efficacy of human reason, creative genius, and eloquent words.

CONCLUSION

Beginning with Petrarch, the Italian Renaissance was a period of great energy, remarkable experimentation, and optimistic celebration of human capacity and individuality. But as we've seen, these years of promise came to a melancholy end with savage conflict, the Roman Inquisition, the Index of Prohibited Books, and the loss of economic pre-eminence. Nevertheless, this in no way means that the Renaissance in Italy did not contribute fundamentally to the evolution of Western culture in a great many ways: it was not just an isolated—if brilliant— moment in history, fascinating to study but irrelevant to modern life. In fact, it has had profound consequences for our institutions; our patterns of thought and seeing; and our conception of what it is to be an individual in a community, and how our ability to create pervades every aspect of the human condition.

The ideas of human autonomy in this world and the validity of individual experience, principles first delineated by Petrarch, in many ways were the preconditions of the modern world. The power of personal self-creation to connect an inward perception of self with its outward manifestation gave us the concept of individual worth, the platform on which so many Western ideas were formed. Individuality and its value, individual and collective human rights, and the belief that an individual can create something which would be of value to him or herself and to others: these are legacies of the Renaissance.

The validity of individual human experience had to be accepted before there could have been a Scientific Revolution. If you do not accept the results of your own observations, then how can these be offered to others to test independently? Without the invention of linear perspective, could the cartography of the voyages of discovery have been possible? Placing objects in space with a rational means of establishing the relationship among them is a primary method for reproducing what the eye sees. The obsession with correct anatomy and physiognomy gave us the perfection of anatomical studies found in the notebooks of Leonardo da Vinci and the *De Fabrica Humani Corporis* of Vesalius. In other words, the contributions of Copernicus, Galileo, Vesalius, and Mercator, together with the compilers of herbals, and botanical and zoological compendia, owed their methods and to a degree their motivations to the Italian Renaissance, whose questions about mankind and the world prefigured their own.

The humanist dedication to clarity of thought and the use of precise language in both Latin and the vernacular, together with their application in rhetoric, provided the vocabulary for the externalization of thought and the clear definition of ideas and advice which we assume, however hopefully, to be the foundation of modern education and politics. The humanist system of education, based on classical authors and languages, was not an antiquarian fossilization of thought, even if it did on occasion decline into that unfortunate category. Rather, it was the means of determining the precise significance of words and ideas in context, looking for models of clear thinking and expression. Textual editing, philology, and comparative stylistics, then—the essential tools of the humanist—revealed the strengths and weaknesses in texts, and hence ideas, and uncovered interpolations and lacunae and showed that what mattered was the intention of the author and the integrity of the material. When Petrarch wrote that we could be of use to the souls of others through our words, he meant that good words expressing good thoughts would have good consequences. Democracy and public affairs in general assume these things, and the evidence of their perversion in recent times reflects how vigilant we must be to maintain this humanist dedication to truth, clarity, and shared values.

These values permeated the literature of the Renaissance. Petrarch invented the sonnet sequence to explore his love for Laura and that emotion's complex significance in his life. His formula became a standard method that lasted over half a millennium. Shakespeare, Sidney, Daniel, Spenser, Joachim Du Bellay, Elizabeth Barrett Browning, and John Berryman, poets from the Renaissance until the twentieth century, all wrote in the fashion of Petrarch because, like painting, these sonnets allowed the poet and hence the reader to experience something profoundly human with which we can identify and from which we can ideally benefit. Love, loss, pain, and the deep mines of an emotional life can be explored and shared through words: this is humanism at work—still at work, just as Petrarch had hoped.

Similarly, when we travel to Europe or visit an art gallery or museum why are we attracted to the rooms displaying Renaissance material? Why do Botticelli, Leonardo, Raphael, Michelangelo, and their contemporaries provide a very generally accepted concept of the beautiful, the elegant, the numinous, or simply the human? The reason is that the art of the Italian Renaissance was a vocabulary of humanism and humanist values. We identify with the color, composition, figures, symmetry, and deep meaning of these works, even if we do not altogether understand the iconography that underlies them. The Sistine Chapel, the *Stanze* of Raphael, the *Mona Lisa*, and the *Birth of Venus* are part of humanity's legacy, extending beyond the Western tradition into the aesthetics of all peoples. They speak to us as human beings, regardless of origin: this is the value of humanism and the Italian Renaissance.

When you walk down the street in almost any European or American city you will see even the legacy of classical architecture, a style that has in fact spread around the entire world, even to those places that had no early contact whatsoever with the cultures of ancient Greece and Rome. The humanist adoption of classical design and style in building resulted of course from the same imperatives that drove them to acquire the texts and ideas of those great civilizations. But, as with writing, this knowledge was applied to the needs and circumstances first of the Italian Renaissance, and then of other places and times. Why do beaux arts banks remind us of the Pantheon, or palatial estates and many schools and universities of the villas of Palladio? The highly intellectual content of these buildings, their symmetry, and especially their harmony define the values of those who will occupy them, with deep reference to "eternal" principles, such as harmony, and aesthetic and intellectual significance. Vitruvius and Alberti believed that built structures influenced the characters and actions of those who inhabit them. So, we still hope that studying in a building designed in Palladian style will link us to a shared past and culture and give us—through a kind of osmosis—clarity of mind and speech. It is not an accident that Thomas Jefferson accepted this in his plans for both his own home, Monticello, and the buildings of the University of Virginia.

The Italian Renaissance, then, is a living concept, an idea, animated by styles and knowledge and forms still very much with us. These constitute a vital part of our collective culture in the West and a vehicle for inclusion among other cultures. Humanism is not an historical relic of an age long past: it remains the essence of what is human in a common humanity. The Renaissance past is not prologue; rather, it still operates. For this reason the Italian Renaissance will never lose either its attraction or its significance.

BIBLIOGRAPHY

Abulafia, David, ed. *The French Descent into Renaissance Italy, 1494–95: Antecedents and Effects.* Aldershot, UK: Ashgate, 1995.

Ackerman, James S. *Palladio.* London: Penguin, 1991.

Acton, Harold. *The Pazzi Conspiracy: The Plot Against the Medici.* New York: Thames and Hudson, 1979.

Ady, Cecilia. *A History of Milan under the Sforza.* CreateSpace Independent Publishing Platform, 2015.

————. *Pius II: Æneas Silvius Piccolomini, The Humanist Pope.* London: Forgotten Books, 2016. Reprint of 1913 edition.

Alberti, Leon Battista. *On the Art of Building in Ten Books.* Translated by Joseph Rykwert, Neil Leach, and Robert Tavernor. Cambridge, MA: MIT Press, 1991.

Almagià, Roberto. *Le Pitture murali della Galleria delle Carte Geografiche.* Vol. 3. Vatican City: Monumenta Cartografica Vaticana, 1952.

Ames-Lewis, Francis. *Isabella and Leonardo: The Artistic Relationship between Isabella d'Este and Leonardo da Vinci, 1500–1506.* New Haven: Yale University Press, 2012.

————. *The Early Medici and Their Artists.* London: Birkbeck College University of London, 1995.

Apuleius, Lucius. *The Tale of Cupid and Psyche.* Translated by Joel C. Relihan. Cambridge, MA, and Indianapolis: Hackett Publishing Company, 2009.

Azzolini, Monica. *The Duke and the Stars: Astrology and Politics in Renaissance Milan.* I Tatti Studies in Italian Renaissance History. Cambridge, MA: Harvard University Press, 2013.

Baker, Nicholas Scott and Brian Jeffrey Maxson, eds. *After Civic Humanism: Learning and Politics in Renaissance Italy.* Toronto: University of Toronto Press, 2015.

Baldassari, Stefano, ed. *Dialogi ad Petrum Paulum Histrum.* Studi e Testi: Istituto Nazionale di Studi sul Rinascimento. Florence: Olschki, 1994.

————. *Coluccio Salutati: Political Writings.* Translated by Rolf Bagemihl. The I Tatti Renaissance Library 64. Cambridge, MA: Harvard University Press, 2014.

————, and A. Saiber, eds. *Images of Quattrocento Florence.* New Haven: Yale University Press, 2000.

Baldi, Bernardino. *Vita e fatti di Federigo di Montefeltro, Duca di Urbino: Istoria di Bernardino Baldi.* 2 vols. Edited by G. Rosmini. St. Albans, VT: Wentworth Publishing, 2016. Reprint of 1824 edition.

Baron, Hans. "Cicero and the Roman Civic Spirit in the Middle Ages and Early Renaissance," *The Bulletin of the John Rylands Library,* 22 (1938).

————. *The Crisis of the Early Italian Renaissance.* Princeton: Princeton University Press, 1966.

————. "Franciscan Poverty and Civic Wealth as Factors in the Rise of Humanistic Thought," *Speculum,* 13 (1938).

————. *Petrarch's Secretum: Its Making and Its Meaning.* Cambridge, MA: Medieval Academy of America, 1985.

Bartlett, Kenneth R. "Platonic Perfection amid Political Failure: The Text and Context of Castiglione's *Cortegiano*," *Memini: Travaux et Documents,* 6 (2002), 170–212.

————, and Margaret McGlynn, eds. *The Renaissance and Reformation in Northern Europe.* Toronto: University of Toronto Press, 2014.

Bassetti-Sani, F., ed. *The Earliest Lives of Dante.* New York: Frederick Ungar, 1963.

Baxandall, Michael. *Painting and Experience in Fifteenth Century Italy.* Oxford: Oxford University Press, 1988.

Bazzotti, Ugo. *Palazzo Te: Giulio Romano's Masterwork in Mantua.* London: Thames and Hudson, 2013.

Becker, Marvin. *Florence in Transition.* Baltimore: Johns Hopkins University Press, 1967.

Bedini, Silvio A. *The Pope's Elephant.* London: Penguin Books, 2000.

Bentley, Jerry. *Politics and Culture in Renaissance Naples.* Princeton: Princeton University Press, 1987.

Benzoni, Gino. "Federico da Montefeltro, duca di Urbino," in *Dizionario Biografico degli Italiani.* Vol. 45. Rome: Istituto della Enciclopedia Italiana, 1995.

――――――. "Lodovico Sforza, detto il Moro, duca di Milano," in *Dizionario Biografico degli Italiani.* Vol. 66. Rome: Istituto della Enciclopedia Italiana, 2006.

Bergin, Thomas, ed. *Selected Sonnets, Odes and Letters of Petrarch.* New York: Appleton-Century-Crofts, 1966.

Bernardini, Maria Grazia and Marco Bussagli, eds. *Il '400 a Roma: La Rinascita delle arti da Donatello a Perugino.* Geneva–Milan: Skira, 2008.

Bertelli, Sergio, ed. *Italian Renaissance Courts.* Translated by M. Fitton and G. Culverwell. London: Sidgwick and Jackson, 1986.

Bible of Borso d'Este Facsimile Edition of Modena, Biblioteca Estense Universitaria. Mss. Lat. 422 and Lat. 423. Modena: Franco Cosimo Panini Editore, 1997.

Black, Jane. *Absolutism in Renaissance Milan: Plenitude of Power under the Visconti and the Sforza 1329–1535.* Oxford: Oxford University Press, 2009.

Black, Robert. *Humanism and Education in Renaissance Italy: Tradition and Innovation in Latin Schools from the Twelfth to the Fifteenth Century.* Cambridge: Cambridge University Press, 2001.

Blondin, Jill. "Power Made Visible: Pope Sixtus IV as 'Urbis Restaurator' in Quattrocento Rome," *The Catholic Historical Review*, 91 (2005), pp. 1–25.

Bo, Carlo. *Il Palazzo Ducale di Urbino.* Novara: Istituto Geografico DeAgostini, 1982.

Bonoldi, Lorenzo. *Isabella d'Este: A Renaissance Woman.* Translated by Clark Lawrence. Rimini, Italy: Guaraldi/Engramma, 2015.

Bourne, Molly. *Francesco II Gonzaga: The Soldier-Prince as Patron.* Rome: Bulzoni, 2008.

Boutin, Lisa. "Isabella d'Este and the Gender Neutrality of Renaissance Ceramics," *Women's Studies*, 40 (2011), pp. 23–47.

Breisach, Ernst. *Caterina Sforza: A Renaissance Virago.* Chicago: University of Chicago Press, 1967.

Brezzi, Paolo and Maristella Lorch, eds. *Umanesimo a Roma nel Quattrocento.* New York and Rome: Columbia University and L'Istituto di studi romani, 1984.

Brown, Patricia Fortini. *Art and Life in Renaissance Venice.* New York: Abrams, 1997.

Brucker, Gene A. *The Civic World of Early Renaissance Florence.* Princeton: Princeton University Press, 2016.

Brugi, Biagio. *Gli Scolari dello studio di Padova nel cinquecento.* Padua: Drucker, 1905.

Bruni, Leonardo. *History of the Florentine People.* 3 vols. Translated by James Hankins. The I Tatti Renaissance Library. Cambridge, MA: Harvard University Press, 2003–2007.

Bruzelius, Caroline. *The Stones of Naples: Church Building in Angevin Italy, 1266–1343.* New Haven: Yale University Press, 2004.

――――――, and William Tronzo. *Medieval Naples: An Architectural & Urban History, 400–1400.* New York: Italica Press, 2011.

Burchard, Johannes. *At the Court of the Borgia.* Translated by Geoffrey Parker. London: The Folio Society, 1963.

Burckhardt, Jacob. *Civilization of the Renaissance in Italy.* 2 vols. Translated by S. G. C. Middlemore. New York: Harper & Row, 1958.

Burke, Peter. *The Fortunes of the Courtier: The European Reception of Castiglione's* Cortegiano. University Park: Penn State Press, 1996.

Burns, J. H. and Thomas Izbicki, eds. *Conciliarism and Papalism.* Cambridge: Cambridge University Press, 1998.

Caggese, Romolo. *Roberto d'Angiò e I Suoi Tempi.* Florence: Bemporad, 1922.

Campbell, Stephen. *The Cabinet of Eros: Renaissance Mythological Painting and the Studiolo of Isabella d'Este.* New Haven: Yale University Press, 2006.

_____. *Cosme Tura: Painting and Design in Renaissance Ferrara.* Boston: Isabella Stewart Gardner Museum, 2002.

Canestrari, Renato. *Sisto V.* Turin: Società Editrice Internazionale di Torino, 1954.

Cappelli, Guido. *Per l'Edizione critica del'De principe'di Giovanni Pontano.* Naples: Edizioni scientifiche italiane: Istituto nazionale di studi sul Rinascimento meridionale, studi, 7, 1993.

Cartwright Ady, Julia, ed. *Baldassare Castiglione, the Perfect Courtier: His Life and Letters, 1478–1529.* 2 vols. London: Forgotten Books, 2017. Reprint of 1908 edition.

_____. *Beatrice d'Este, Duchess of Milan, 1475–1497: A Study of the Renaissance.* London: J. M. Dent & Co., 1905.

Cassirer, Ernst, Paul Oskar Kristeller, and John Herman Randall Jr., eds. *The Renaissance Philosophy of Man: Petrarca, Valla, Ficino, Pico, Pomponazzi, Vives.* Chicago: University of Chicago Press, 1948.

Castelli, Patrizia, ed. *In supreme dignitatis . . . : Per la storia dell'Universita di Ferrara 1391–1991.* Florence: Leo S. Olschki, 1995.

Celenza, Christopher. *Petrarch, Everywhere a Wanderer.* London: Reaktion Books, 2017.

_____. *The Intellectual World of the Italian Renaissance.* Cambridge: Cambridge University Press, 2018.

Chambers, David and Brian Pullan, eds. *Venice: A Documentary History.* Toronto: University of Toronto Press, 2004.

Chastel, André. *The Sack of Rome, 1527.* Translated by Beth Archer. Princeton: Princeton University Press, 1983.

Chiappini, Luciano. *Gli Estensi.* Varese, Italy: Dall'Oglio, 1967.

Christiansen, Keith. *Andrea Mantegna, Padua and Mantua.* New York: George Braziller, 2000.

Ciappelli, Giovanni. *Fisco e società a Firenze nel Rinascimento.* Studi e testi del Rinascimento europeo 36. Rome: Edizioni di Storia e Letteratura, 2009.

Ciceri, Angelo. *The Duomo of Milan.* Milan: Veneranda Fabbrica of the Duomo of Milan, 1965.

Cipolla, Carlo M. *The Monetary Policy of Fourteenth Century Florence.* Publications of the UCLA Center for Medieval and Renaissance Studies, 17. Berkeley and Los Angeles: UCLA Press, 1982.

Clarke, Paula C. *The Soderini and the Medici: Power and Patronage in Fifteenth-Century Florence.* Oxford: Clarendon Press, 1991.

Coffin, David. *The Villa in the Life of Renaissance Rome.* Princeton: Princeton University Press, 1979.

Cole, Alison. *Italian Renaissance Courts: Art, Pleasure and Power.* London: Laurence King, 2016.

Cordaro, Michele, ed. *Mantegna's Camera degli Sposi.* Milan: Electa, 1993.

Cortwright, Nicola. *The Papacy and the Art of Reform in Sixteenth-Century Rome: Gregory XIII's Tower of the Winds in the Vatican.* Cambridge: Cambridge University Press, 2003.

Cosenza, Mario and Ronald Musto, eds. *Petrarch, The Revolution of Cola di Rienzo.* New York: Italica Press, 1996.

Cosgrove, Denis. *The Palladian Landscape: Geographical Change and Its Cultural Representations in Sixteenth-Century Italy.* University Park: Pennsylvania State University Press, 1993.

Coyne, G. V., et al., eds. *Gregorian Reform of the Calendar: Proceedings of the Vatican Conference to Commemorate Its 400th Anniversary, 1582–1982.* Vatican City: Pontificia Academia Scientiarum, 1983.

Croce, Benedetto. *History of the Kingdom of Naples.* Translated by F. Frenaye. Chicago: University of Chicago Press, 1970.

Crum, Roger J. and John T. Paoletti, eds. *Renaissance Florence: A Social History.* Cambridge: Cambridge University Press, 2006.

Cummings, Anthony M. *The Lion's Ear: Pope Leo X, the Renaissance Papacy, and Music.* Ann Arbor: University of Michigan Press, 2012.

da Bisticci, Vespasiano. *Renaissance Princes, Popes and Prelates.* Translated by W. G. and E. W. Waters. New York: Harper & Row, 1963.

———. *The Vespasiano Memoirs: Lives of Illustrious Men of the XVth Century.* Translated by W. George and E. Walters. Toronto: University of Toronto Press, 1997.

D'Amico, John F. *Renaissance Humanism in Papal Rome.* Baltimore: Johns Hopkins University Press, 1983.

D'Ancona, Paolo and Cesare Gnudi. *The Schifanoia Months at Ferrara.* Milan: Edizioni del Milione, 1954.

Davis, Robert C. *Shipbuilders of the Venetian Arsenal: Workers and Workplace in the Preindustrial City.* Baltimore: Johns Hopkins University Press, 2007.

Dean, Trevor. *Land and Power in Late Medieval Ferrara: The Rule of the Este, 1350–1450.* Cambridge: Cambridge University Press, 2002.

Decembrio, Pier Candido. *Vita di Filippo Maria Visconti.* Edited by Elio Bartolini. Milan: Adelphi Edizioni, 1983.

De'Grassi, Giovannino and workshop. *The Visconti Hours* (Biblioteca Nazionale Centrale di Firenze). Introduction by Millard Meiss and Edith Kirsch. New York: George Braziller, 1972.

D'Elia, Anthony F. *A Sudden Terror: The Plot to Murder the Pope in Renaissance Rome.* Cambridge, MA: Harvard University Press, 2011.

de Mazzeri, Silvia Alberti. *Beatrice d'Este duchessa di Milano.* Santarcangelo di Romagna: Rusconi, 1986.

de'Medici, Lorenzo. *The Complete Literary Works of Lorenzo de'Medici.* Translated and edited by Guido A. Guarino. New York: Italica Press, 2015.

de Mesquita, D. M. Bueno. *Giangaleazzo Visconti, Duke of Milan (1351–1402): A Study in the Political Career of an Italian Despot.* Cambridge: Cambridge University Press, 2011.

Dennis, Kimberly. "Camilla Peretti, Sixtus V, and the Construction of Peretti Family Identity in Counter-Reformation Rome," *The Sixteenth Century Journal*, 43 (2012), pp. 71–101.

Dennistoun, James. *Memoirs of the Dukes of Urbino, Illustrating the Arms, Arts and Literature of Italy, 1440–1630.* 3 vols. London: Bodley Head, 1909.

Derbes, Anne and Mark Sandona, eds. *The Cambridge Companion to Giotto.* Cambridge: Cambridge University Press, 2004.

De Roover, Raymond. *The Medici Bank: Its Organization, Management, Operations, and Decline.* Forward by Thomas Cochrane. Whitefish, MT: Literary Licensing, 2011.

d'Este, Isabella. *Selected Letters.* Edited and translated by Deanna Shemek. Tempe: Arizona Center for Medieval and Renaissance Studies, 2017.

Draper, W. H. *Petrarch's Secret, or the Soul's Conflict with Passion (Three Dialogues Between Himself and St. Augustine).* CreateSpace Independent Publishing Platform, 2015. Reprint of 1911 edition.

Duffy, Eamon. *Saints and Sinners: A History of the Popes.* New Haven: Yale University Press, 2006.

Dunstan, A. J. "Paul II and the Humanists," *The Journal of Religious History*, 7 (1972–73), pp. 287–306.

Eitel-Porter, Rhoda. "Artistic Co-Operation in Late Sixteenth-Century Rome: The Sistine Chapel in S. Maria Maggiore and the Scala Santa," *The Burlington Magazine*, 139 (1997), pp. 452–62.

Epstein, Steven A. *Genoa and the Genoese, 958–1528.* Chapel Hill: University of North Carolina Press, 1996.

Fagiolo, M. and M. L. Madonna. *Roma di Sisto V. Arte, architettura e città fra Rinascimento e Barocco.* Rome: De Luca Editori d'Arte, 1993.

Falkeid, Unn. *The Avignon Papacy Contested: An Intellectual History from Dante to Catherine of Siena.* Cambridge, MA: Harvard University Press, 2017.

Farinella, Vincenzo. *Alfonso I d'Este, le immagini e il potere.* Milan: Officina Libreria, 2014.

Feci, Simona. *Enciclopedia dei Papi.* Rome: Treccani, 2000.

_____. "Pio V, papa, santo," in *Dizionario Biografico degli Italiani.* Vol. 83. Rome: Istituto della Enciclopedia Italiana, 2015.

Finlay, Robert. *Politics in Renaissance Venice.* New Brunswick: Rutgers University Press, 1980.

Finley, M., Denis Mack-Smith, and Christopher Duggan. *A History of Sicily.* New York: Viking Penguin, 1987.

Fiore, F. P., ed. *Francesco di Giorgio alla corte di Federico da Montefeltro.* 2 vols. Florence: Olschki, 2004.

Fontana, Domenico. *Della trasportazione dell'obelisco vaticano, Del modo di tenuto in trasferire l'obelisco vaticano et delle fabbriche fatte da papa Sisto V.* Rome: Domenico Basa, 1590.

Fosi, Irene Polverini. "Justice and Its Image: Political Propaganda and Judicial Reality in the Pontificate of Sixtus V," *Sixteenth Century Journal*, 24 (1993), pp. 75–95.

Franceschini, Gino. *I Montefeltro.* Milan: Dall'Oglio, 1970.

Frommel, Christoph Luitpold, ed. *Michelangelo's Tomb for Julius II: Genesis and Genius.* Los Angeles: The J. Paul Getty Museum, 2016.

Frugoni, Arsenio. *Il Giubileo di Bonifacio VIII.* Edited by Amedeo De Vincentiis. Rome and Bari: Editori Laterza, 1999.

Fudge, Thomas A. *The Trial of Jan Hus: Medieval Heresy and Criminal Procedure.* Oxford: Oxford University Press, 2013.

Furlotti, Barbara and Guido Rebecchini. *The Art of Mantua: Power and Patronage in the Renaissance.* Los Angeles: The J. Paul Getty Museum, 2008.

Fusco, Laurie and Gino Corti. *Lorenzo de'Medici, Collector of Antiquities: Collector and Antiquarian.* Cambridge: Cambridge University Press, 2006.

Fusero, Clemente. *The Borgias.* Translated by Peter Green. New York: Praeger, 1972.

Gamberini, Andrea, ed. *A Companion to Late Medieval and Early Modern Milan: The Distinctive Features of an Italian State.* Leiden: Brill Academic Publishing, 2014.

Gamrath, Helge. "The History of a Success in the Italian Renaissance: The Farnese Family, c. 1400–1600," *Analecta Romana Instituti Danici*, 24 (1997), pp. 93–111.

_____. *Farnese: Pomp, Power, and Politics in Renaissance Italy.* Rome: L'Erma Di Bretschneider, 2007.

_____. *Roma sancta renovata: Studi sull'urbanistica di Roma nella seconda metà del sec. XVI con particolare riferimento al pontificato di Sisto V (1585–1590).* Rome: L'Erma Di Bretschneider, 1987.

Gardiner, Eileen and Francis Morgan Nichols, eds. and trans. *The Marvels of Rome: Mirabilia Urbis Romae.* New York: Italica Press, 2008.

Gardner, Edmund Garratt. *Dukes and Poets in Ferrara: A Study in the Poetry, Religion and Politics of the Fifteenth and Early Sixteenth Centuries.* London: Forgotten Books, 2017. Reprint of the 1903 edition.

Garin-Llombart, Felipe V. "Alessandro VI a Roma: Cultura e Committenza Artistica" in *I Borgia. Catalogo mostra Palazzo Ruspoli Fondazione Memmo Roma 3 ottobre 2002–23 febbraio 2003.* Milan: Electa, 2002.

Giacommetti, Massimo, ed. *The Sistine Chapel: Michelangelo Rediscovered.* London: Muller, Blond and White, 1986.

Gill, Joseph. *The Council of Florence.* Cambridge: Cambridge University Press, 2011.

Goldstone, Nancy. *The Lady Queen: The Notorious Reign of Joanna I, Queen of Naples, Jerusalem, and Sicily.* London: Walker Books, 2009.

Goldthwaite, Richard A. *The Building of Renaissance Florence: An Economic and Social History.* Baltimore: Johns Hopkins University Press. 1980.

————. *The Economy of Renaissance Florence.* Baltimore: Johns Hopkins University Press, 2011.

————. *Wealth and the Demand for Art in Italy, 1300–1600.* Baltimore: Johns Hopkins University Press, 1993.

Gouwens, Kenneth. *Remembering the Renaissance: Humanist Narratives of the Sack of Rome.* Leiden: Brill, 1998.

Grafton, Anthony. *Leon Battista Alberti: Master Builder of the Italian Renaissance.* Cambridge, MA: Harvard University Press, 2002.

Grafton, Anthony, ed. *Rome Reborn: The Vatican Library and Renaissance Culture.* New Haven: Yale University Press, 1993.

Grendler, Paul. *The Universities of the Italian Renaissance.* Baltimore: Johns Hopkins University Press, 2002.

Grubb, James. *Provincial Families in the Renaissance: Private and Public Life in the Veneto.* Baltimore: Johns Hopkins University Press, 1996.

Guicciardini, Francesco. *The History of Italy.* Translated by Sidney Alexander. New York: Macmillan,1969.

Guicciardini, Luigi. *The Sack of Rome.* Edited and translated by James McGregor. New York: Italica Press, 2008.

Gundersheimer, Werner. *Ferrara: The Style of a Renaissance Despotism.* Princeton: Princeton University Press, 1973.

————. "The Patronage of Ercole I d'Este," *The Journal of Medieval and Renaissance Studies,* 6 (1976), pp. 1–18.

Hankins, James. "The Dates of Leonardo Bruni's Later Works (1437–1443)," *Studi medievali e umanistici,* 6 (2007), pp. 1–51.

————. *Plato in the Italian Renaissance.* Leiden and New York: E.J. Brill, 1994.

————, ed. *Renaissance Civic Humanism: Reappraisals and Reflections.* Ideas in Context 7. Cambridge: Cambridge University Press, 2000.

————, John Monfasani, and Frederick Purnell Jr., eds. *Supplementum Festivum: Studies in Honor of Paul Oskar Kristeller.* Binghamton, NY: Medieval and Renaissance Texts and Studies, 1987.

Herlihy, David V. and Christiane Klapisch-Zuber. *Tuscans and Their Families: A Study of the Florentine Catasto of 1427.* New Haven: Yale University Press, 1989.

Hibbert, Christopher. *The House of Medici: Its Rise and Fall.* New York: William Morrow, 1975.

Hook, Judith. *The Sack of Rome.* London: Palgrave Macmillan, 2004.

Howard, Peter, ed. *Creating Magnificence in Renaissance Florence.* Toronto: Centre for Reformation and Renaissance Studies, 2012.

Humfrey, Peter, ed. *The Cambridge Companion to Giovanni Bellini.* Cambridge: Cambridge University Press, 2003.

Il Ducato Visconteo e la Repubblica Ambrosiana (1392–1450). Storia di Milano. Vol. 6. Milan: Fondazione Treccani degli Alfieri, 1955.

Infessura, Stefano. *Diario della Città di Roma di Stefano Infessura.* Edited by Oreste Tommasini. Rome: Forzani e tipografi del senato, 1890.

Isaacson, Walter. *Leonardo Da Vinci.* New York: Simon and Schuster, 2017.

Jacob, E. F., ed. *Italian Renaissance Studies.* London: Faber and Faber, 1960.

Johnson, Eugene J. S. *Andrea in Mantua: The Building History.* University Park: Pennsylvania State University Press, 1975.

Jones, Pamela. *Altarpieces and Their Viewers in the Churches of Rome from Caravaggio to Guido Reni.* Aldershot, UK: Ashgate, 2008.

Joost-Gaugier, Christiane L. *Raphael's Stanza della Segnatura: Meaning and Invention.* Cambridge: Cambridge University Press, 2002.

Kemp, Martin. *Leonardo da Vinci: The Marvellous Works of Nature and Man.* Oxford: Oxford University Press, 2006.

Kent, Dale. *Cosimo de' Medici and the Florentine Renaissance: The Patron's Oeuvre.* New Haven: Yale University Press, 2000.

_____. *The Rise of the Medici: Faction in Florence, 1426–1434.* New York: Oxford University Press, 1978.

Kent, Francis W. *Princely Citizen: Lorenzo de'Medici and Renaissance Florence.* Edited by Carolyn James. Turnhout, Belgium: Brepols, 2013.

Kiesewetter, Andreas. "Luigi d'Angiò" in *Dizionario Biografico degli Italiani.* Vol. 66. Rome: Istituto della Enciclopedia Italiana, 2006.

Kirkham, Victoria and Armando Maggi, eds. *Petrarch: A Critical Guide to the Complete Works.* Chicago and London: University of Chicago Press, 2012.

Kirkham, Victoria, Michael Sherberg, and Janet Levarie Smarr, eds. *Boccaccio: A Critical Guide to the Complete Works.* Chicago: University of Chicago Press, 2013.

Kirsch, Edith W. *Five Illuminated Manuscripts of Giangaleazzo Visconti.* Philadelphia: Penn State University Press. 1991.

Kohl, Benjamin G. and Ronald G. Witt, eds. *The Earthly Republic: Italian Humanists on Government and Society.* Philadelphia: University of Pennsylvania Press, 1978.

Krautheimer, Richard. *Rome, Profile of a City, 312–1308.* Princeton: Princeton University Press, 1980.

Kruft, Hanno-Walter. *A History of Architectural Theory.* New York: Princeton Architectural Press, 1996.

Landucci, Luca. *A Florentine Diary from 1450 to 1516.* Translated by Alicia de Rosen Jervis. London: J. M. Dent and Sons, 1927.

Lane, Frederic C. *Venetian Ships and Shipbuilders of the Renaissance.* Baltimore: Johns Hopkins University Press, 1992.

_____. *Venice: A Maritime Republic.* Baltimore: Johns Hopkins University Press, 1973.

L'Antico ospedale di Santo Spirito dall'istituzione papale alla sanità del terzo millennio. Atti del Convegno internazionale di studi. Rome: Il Veltro Editrice, 2001.

Larner, John. *Italy in the Age of Dante and Petrarch, 1216–1380.* London: Longmans, 1983.

Laskowski, Birgit. *Piero della Francesca.* Cologne: Konemann, 1998.

Lee, Egmont. *Sixtus IV and Men of Letters.* Rome: Edizioni di Storia e Letteratura, 1978.

Lev, Elizabeth. *The Tigress of Forli: Renaissance Italy's Most Courageous and Notorious Countess, Caterina Riario Sforza de'Medici.* Boston: Houghton, Mifflin, Harcourt (Mariner Books), 2012.

Levey, Michael. *Florence, A Portrait.* Cambridge, MA: Harvard University Press, 1996.

Lockwood, Lewis. *Music in Renaissance Ferrara 1400–1505: The Creation of a Musical Center in the Fifteenth Century.* Oxford: Oxford University Press, 2009.

Looney, Dennis and Deanna Shemek, eds. *Phaethon's Children: The Este Court and Its Culture in Early Modern Ferrara*. Medieval and Renaissance Texts and Studies. Tempe: Arizona Center for Medieval and Renaissance Studies, 2005.

Lubkin, Gregory. *A Renaissance Court: Milan under Galeazzo Maria Sforza*. Berkeley and Los Angeles: University of California Press, 1994.

Luzio, Alessandro. *Mantova e Urbino: Isabella d'Este ed Elisabetta Gonzaga Nelle Relazioni Famigliari e Nelle Vicende Politiche; Narrazione Storica Documentata*. London: Forgotten Books, 2018. Reprint of 1893 edition.

Machiavelli, Niccolò. *Diplomatic Missions (1498–1527)*. Translated by Christian Detmold. CreateSpace Independent Publishing Platform, 2015.

_____. *History of Florence and of the Affairs of Italy from the Earliest Times to the Death of Lorenzo the Magnificent*. New York and London: W. Walter Dunne, 1901.

_____. *Opere*. Edited by M. Bonfantini. Milan: Ricciardi Editore, 1954.

Madden, Thomas F. *Venice: A New History*. London: Penguin Books, 2013.

Magnuson, Torgil. *Rome in the Age of Bernini: From the Election of Sixtus V to the Death of Urban VIII*. Stockholm: Almqvist & Wiksell International, 1982.

Majanlahti, Anthony. *The Families Who Made Rome*. London: Chatto and Windus, 2009.

Mallett, Michael. *The Borgias: The Rise and Fall of the Most Infamous Family in History*. Chicago: Academy Chicago Publishers, 2005.

_____. *Mercenaries and their Masters: Warfare in Renaissance Italy*. Barnsley, UK: Pen and Sword, 2009.

_____, and John Hale. *The Military Organization of a Renaissance State: Venice c. 1400–1617*. Cambridge: Cambridge University Press, 1984.

_____, and Christine Shaw. *The Italian Wars, 1494–1559: War, State and Society in Early Modern Europe*. New York: Pearson, 2012.

Manca, Joseph. *Cosme Tura: The Life and Art of a Painter in Estense Ferrara*. Oxford: Clarendon Press, 2000.

_____. *The Art of Ercole de' Roberti*. Cambridge: Cambridge University Press, 1992.

Mancini, Girolamo. *Vita Di Lorenzo Valla*. London: Forgotten Books, 2018. Reprint of 1891 edition.

Mandel, Corinne. *Sixtus V and the Lateran Palace*. Rome: Istituto Poligrafico e Zecca Dello Stato, 1994.

Marcigliano, Alessandro. *Chivalric Festivals at the Ferrarese Court of Alfonso II d'Este*. New York and Bern: Peter Lang, 2003.

Martellotti, Guido. "Gasparino Barzizza," in *Dante e Boccaccio e altri scrittori dall'Umanesimo al Romanticismo*. Florence: Leo S. Olschki, 1983.

Martines, Lauro. *April Blood: Florence and the Plot Against the Medici*. Oxford: Oxford University Press, 2004.

_____. *Fire in the City: Savonarola and the Struggle for the Soul of Renaissance Florence*. Oxford and New York: Oxford University Press, 2007.

_____. *Power and Imagination: City-States in Renaissance Italy*. Baltimore: Johns Hopkins University Press, 1988.

Marton, Paolo, Manfred Wundrum, and Thomas Pape. *Palladio: The Complete Buildings*. Cologne and London: Taschen, 2008.

Mattei, Francesca, ed. *Federico II Gonzaga e le arti*. Europa delle Corti/159. Rome: Bulzoni Editore, 2016.

Matthews, L. and P. Merkley. *Music and Patronage in the Sforza Court*. Turnhout, Belgium: Brepols, 1999.

Mayer, Thomas F. *The Roman Inquisition: A Papal Bureaucracy and Its Laws in the Age of Galileo*: University of Pennsylvania Press, 2013.

McGregor, James. *Rome from the Ground Up*. Cambridge, MA: Belknap Press of Harvard University Press, 2005.

Michelet, Jules. *Histoire de France, Vol. 7, XVI siècle, La Renaissance*. Paris: A. Lacroix, 1874.

Miglio, Massimo, Francesca Niutta, Diego Quaglioni, and Concetta Ranieri. *Un Pontificato e una Città: Sisto IV (1471–1484)*. Rome: Istituto Storico Italiano per il Medio Evo, 1986.

Minnich, Nelson H. *Councils of the Catholic Reformation: Pisa I (1409) to Trent (1545–63)*. London: Routledge, 2008.

──────. *The Renaissance Papacy 1406–1565*. Harlow, UK: Longmans, 2011.

Molfino, Alessandra and Mauro Natale, eds. *Le Muse e il Principe: Arte di Corte nel Rinscimento Padano*. Modena: Pannini, 1991.

Molho, Anthony. *Marriage Alliance in Late Medieval Florence*. Cambridge, MA: Harvard University Press, 1994.

Mollat, Guillaume. *The Popes at Avignon, 1305–1378*. Translated by Janet Love. London: Thomas Nelson, 1963.

Moore, Frances. *Historical Life of Joanna of Sicily, Queen of Naples and Countess of Provence, with Correlative Details of the Literature and Manners of Italy and Provence in the Thirteenth and Fourteenth Centuries*. 2 vols. London: Forgotten Books, 2017. Reprint of 1824 edition.

Muir, Dorothy Erskine. *A History of Milan Under the Visconti*. London: Methuen, 1924.

Mullins, Edwin. *The Popes of Avignon: A Century in Exile*. New York: BlueBridge Books, 2011.

Musto, Ronald G. *Apocalypse in Rome: Cola di Rienzo and the Politics of the New Age*. Berkeley and Los Angeles: University of California Press, 2002.

──────, ed. *Medieval Naples: A Documentary History, 400–1400*. New York: Italica Press, 2013.

Najemy, John M. *A History of Florence, 1200–1575*. Oxford: Blackwell, 2006.

──────, ed. *Italy in the Age of the Renaissance, 1300–1550*. Oxford: Oxford University Press, 2004.

Nauert, Charles G. Jr. *Humanism and the Culture of Renaissance Europe*. Cambridge: Cambridge University Press, 2006.

Norwich, John Julius. *A History of Venice*. New York: Vintage Books, 1989.

O'Brien, Emily. *The "Commentaries" of Pope Pius II (1458–1464) and the Crisis of the Fifteenth-Century Papacy*. Toronto: University of Toronto Press, 2015.

O'Malley, John W. *The Jesuits: A History from Ignatius to the Present*. Lanham, MD, and London: Rowman & Littlefield Publishers, 2014.

──────. *Trent: What Happened at the Council*. Cambridge, MA: Belknap Press of Harvard University Press, 2013.

──────, Thomas M. Izbicki, and Gerald Christianson, eds. *Humanity and Divinity in Renaissance and Reformation: Essays in Honor of Charles Trinkaus*. Leiden: Brill, 1993.

Orbaan, J. A. F. *Sixtine Rome*. New York: Baker and Taylor, 1911.

Osborne, June. *Urbino: The Story of a Renaissance City*. Chicago: University of Chicago Press, 2003.

Pade, Marianne, ed. *The Reception of Plutarch's Lives in Fifteenth-Century Italy*. 2 vols. Copenhagen: Museum Tusculanum, 2007.

──────, Leene Waage Petersen, and Daniela Quarta, eds. *La corte di Ferrara e il suo mecenatismo, 1441–1598: Atti del convegno internazionale. Copenaghen*. Modena: Panini, 1990.

Palladio, Andrea. *The Four Books on Architecture*. Translated by Robert Tavernor and Richard Schofield. Cambridge, MA: MIT Press, 1997.

Pardi, Giuseppe, ed. *"Diario Ferrarese dall'anno 1409 sino al 1502 di autori incerti"* in *Rerum Italicarum Scriptores*, 2nd ed. XXI:V, pt. 7. Bologna: 1928.

Partner, Peter. *Renaissance Rome 1500–1559: A Portrait of a Society*. Berkeley and Los Angeles: University of California Press, 1979.

Pattenden, Miles. *Pius IV and the Fall of the Carafa: Nepotism and Papal Authority in Counter-Reformation Rome*. Oxford: Oxford University Press, 2013.

Pernis, Maria Grazia and Laurie Schneider Adams. *Federico da Montefeltro and Sigismondo Malatesta: The Eagle and the Elephant*. New York: Peter Lang, 1997.

_____. *Lucrezia Tornabuoni de'Medici and the Medici Family in the Fifteenth Century*. Bern and New York: Peter Lang, 2006.

Petrarch, Francesco. *Petrarch's Book Without a Name (Liber Sine Nomine)*. Translated by N. P. Zacour. Toronto: Pontifical Institute of Medieval Studies, 1973.

Piccolomini, Aeneas Silvius (Pius II). *Commentaries*. Edited by M. Meserve and M. Simonetta. Cambridge, MA: Harvard University Press, 2004.

Pico della Mirandola, Giovanni. *Oration on the Dignity of Man: A New Translation and Commentary*. Edited by Francesco Borghesi, Michael Papio, and Massimo Riva. Cambridge: Cambridge University Press, 2012.

Pietrangeli, Carlo, ed. *Il Palazzo Apostolico Vaticano*. Florence: Nardini Editore, 1992.

Poliziano, Angelo. *The Stanze of Angelo Poliziano*. Translated by David L. Quint. Philadelphia: Penn State University Press, 2005.

Polizzotto, Lorenzo. *The Elect Nation: the Savonarolan Movement in Florence, 1494–1545*. Oxford: Clarendon Press, 1994.

Portoghesi, Paolo. *Rome of the Renaissance*. Translated by Pearl Sanders. London: Phaidon, 1972.

Puaux, Anne. *La Huguenote: Renée de France*. Paris: Hermann, 1997.

Pullapilly, Cyriac K. *Caesar Baronius, Counter-Reformation Historian*. Notre Dame: University of Notre Dame Press, 1975.

Puppi, Lionello. *Palladio*. Milan: Electa, 1973.

Pyle, Cynthia Munro. *Milan and Lombardy in the Renaissance: Essays in Cultural History*. Rome: La Fenice, Istituto di filologia moderna, Università degli studi di Parma, testi e studi, nuova serie, studi, 1, 1997.

Queller, Donald E. and Thomas F. Madden. *The Fourth Crusade: The Conquest of Constantinople*. Philadelphia: University of Pennsylvania Press, 1999.

Quillen, Carol. *The Secret by Francesco Petrarch*. Boston: Bedford/St. Martin's, 2003.

Rabil, Albert Jr., ed. *Renaissance Humanism, Volume 1: Foundations, Forms, and Legacy*. Philadelphia: University of Pennsylvania Press, 1988.

Raggio, Olga. *Federico Da Montefeltro's Palace at Gubbio and Its Studiolo: Italian Renaissance Intarsia and the Conservation of the Gubbio Studiolo*. 2 vols. New Haven: Yale University Press, 2000.

_____, and Antoine M. Wilmering. *Lo studiolo di Federico da Montefeltro*. Milan: 24 Ore Cultura, 2008.

Ramsey, P. A., ed. *Rome in the Renaissance: The City and the Myth*. Binghamton, NY: Medieval and Renaissance Texts and Studies, 1982.

Reiss, Sheryl and Kenneth Gouwens, eds. *The Pontificate of Clement VII: History, Politics, Culture*. London and New York: Routledge, 2005.

Richter, Jean Paul, ed. *The Notebooks of Leonardo Da Vinci*. 2 vols. Mineola, NY: Dover, 1970. Reprint of 1883 edition.

Robert of Clari. *The Conquest of Constantinople*. Translated by Edgar Holmes McNeal. New York: Columbia University Press, 2005.

Robin, Diana. *Filelfo in Milan: Writings 1451–1477*. Princeton: Princeton University Press, 1991.

_____. "Reassessment of the Character of Francesco Filelfo," *Renaissance Quarterly* 36 (1983), pp. 202–24.

Robinson, James Harvey, ed. and trans. *Petrarch: The First Modern Scholar and Man of Letters.* New York: G. P. Putnam, 1898.

————. *Readings in European History.* Boston: Ginn and Company, 1904.

Rocke, Michael. *Forbidden Friendships: Homosexuality and Male Culture in Renaissance Florence.* Oxford: Oxford University Press, 1998.

Roeck, Bernd and Andreas Tönnesmann. *Federico da Montefeltro. Arte, stato e mestiere delle armi.* Translated by S. Accornero. Turin: Einaudi, 2009.

Rollo-Koster, Joelle and Thomas M. Izbicki, eds. *A Companion to the Great Western Schism (1378–1417).* Leiden: Brill, 2009.

Rondinini, Gigliola Soldi. "Filippo Maria Visconti, duca di Milano," in *Dizionario Biografico degli Italiani.* Vol. 47. Roma: Istituto della Enciclopedia Italiana, 1947.

Roscoe, William. *The Life and Pontificate of Leo X.* 4 vols. London: Henry Bohn, 1846.

Rosen, Mark. *The Mapping of Power in Renaissance Italy: Painted Cartographic Cycles in Social and Intellectual Context.* Cambridge: Cambridge University Press, 2014.

Rosenberg, Charles M. *Art in Ferrara during the Reign of Borso D'Este (1450–1471): A Study of Court Patronage.* Ann Arbor, MI: University Microfilms, 1974.

————. *The Court Cities of Northern Italy: Milan, Parma, Piacenza, Mantua, Ferrara, Bologna, Urbino, Pesaro, and Rimini.* Cambridge: Cambridge University Press, 2010.

————. *The Este Monuments and Urban Development in Renaissance Ferrara.* Cambridge: Cambridge University Press, 1997.

Rowdon, Maurice. *Lorenzo the Magnificent.* Chicago: Regnery, 1974.

Rubinstein, Nicolai, ed. *Florentine Studies: Politics and Society in Renaissance Florence.* London: Faber & Faber, 1968.

————. *The Government of Florence under the Medici (1434 to 1494).* Oxford: Clarendon Press, 1966.

————. "Lorenzo de'Medici: The Formation of his Statecraft," in *Lorenzo de'Medici: Studi.* Edited by Gian Carlo Garfagnini. Istituto nazionale di studi sul Rinascimento, Studi e testi, 27. Florence: Olschki, 1992.

Ruffo-Fiore, Silvia, ed. *Niccolo Machiavelli: An Annotated Bibliography of Modern Criticism and Scholarship.* New York: Greenwood Press, 1990.

Runciman, Steven. *The Sicilian Vespers: A History of the Mediterranean World in the Later Thirteenth Century.* Cambridge: Cambridge University Press, 2012.

Ryder, Alan. *Alfonso the Magnanimous: King of Aragon, Naples, and Sicily 1396–1458.* Oxford: Clarendon Press, 1990.

————. "Giovanna II d'Angiò" in *Dizionario Biografico degli Italiani.* Vol 55. Rome: Istituto della Enciclopedia Italiana, 2001.

————. *The Kingdom of Naples Under Alfonso the Magnanimous.* Oxford: Oxford University Press, 1976.

Sakellariou, Eleni. *Southern Italy in the Late Middle Ages: Demographic, Institutional and Economic Change in the Kingdom of Naples, c.1440–c.1530.* Leiden: Brill, 2011.

Salmi, Mario, ed. *The Complete Works of Raphael.* New York: Raynal-William Morrow, 1969.

Salutati, Coluccio. *On the World and Religious Life.* Translated by Tina Marshall. Introduction by Ronald G. Witt. The I Tatti Renaissance Library, 62. Cambridge, MA: Harvard University Press, 2014.

Salvemini, Gaetano. *Magnati e popolani in Firenze dal 1280 al 1295.* Florence: Carnesecchi e figli, 1899.

Sandano, Stefano. *Renovatio Christiana: The Counter Reformed Patronage of Pope Sixtus V at The Holy Steps in Rome (1585–1590).* CreateSpace Independent Publishing Platform, 2013. pp. 19–40.

Savonarola, Girolamo. *Apologetic Writings.* Translated by M. Michèle Mulchahey. The I Tatti Renaissance Library, 68. Cambridge, MA: Harvard University Press, 2015.

_____. *A Guide to Righteous Living and Other Works.* Translated and edited by K. Eisenbichler. Toronto: CRRS, 2003.

_____. *Selected Writings of Girolamo Savonarola on Religion and Politics, 1490–1498.* Edited and translated by A. Borelli and M. Passaro. New Haven: Yale University Press, 2006.

_____. *The Triumph of the Cross.* Edited and translated by John Proctor. London: Sands and Company, 1901.

Scotti, R. A. *Basilica: The Splendor and the Scandal: Building St. Peter's.* New York: Viking-Penguin, 2006.

Sgarbi, Vittorio. *Francesco Del Cossa.* Milan: Skira, 2007.

Shaw, Christine. *Julius II: The Warrior Pope.* Oxford: Blackwell, 1993.

Signorini, Stefania. *Poesia a corte: le rime per Elisabetta Gonzaga (Urbino, 1488–1526).* Pisa: ETS, 2009.

Signorotto, Gianvittorio and Maria Visceglia, eds. *Court and Politics in Papal Rome, 1492–1700.* Cambridge: Cambridge University Press, 2002.

Simon, Kate. *A Renaissance Tapestry: The Gonzaga of Mantua.* New York: Harper & Row, 1988.

Simonetta, Marcello. *The Montefeltro Conspiracy: A Renaissance Mystery Decoded.* New York: Doubleday, 2008.

_____, Jonathan J. G. Alexander, and Cecilia Martelli. *Federico da Montefeltro and His Library.* Vatican City: Biblioteca Apostolica Vaticana, 2007.

Singleton, Charles. *The Book of the Courtier: The Singleton Translation: An Authoritative Text Criticism.* New York: W. W. Norton, 2002.

Skinner, Quentin. *Machiavelli: A Very Short Introduction.* Oxford: Oxford University Press, 2002.

Smith, Christine and Joseph F. O'Connor. *Building the Kingdom: Giannozzo Manetti on the Material and Spiritual Edifice.* Arizona Studies in the Middle Ages and the Renaissance, Vol. 20. Turnhout, Belgium: Brepols, 2006.

Smith, Denis Mack. *Federigo da Montefeltro.* Urbino, Italy: Quattroventi, 2005.

Solerti, Angelo. *Vita Di Torquato Tasso.* 3 vols. Turin: Loescher, 1895.

Speroni, Ernesto. *Congiura. Mors acerba, fama perpetua.* Milan: Lampi di Stampa, 2006.

Stinger, Charles. *The Renaissance in Rome.* Bloomington: Indiana University Press, 1998.

Stivini, Odoardo. *Le Collezioni Gonzaga: L'inventario dei beni del 1540–1542.* Edited by Daniela Ferrari. Milan: Silvana, 2003.

Stow, Kenneth. *The Theater of Acculturation: The Roman Ghetto in the Sixteenth Century.* Seattle: University of Washington Press, 2001.

Stump, Phillip H. *The Reforms of the Council of Constance (1414–1418).* Leiden: Brill, 1994.

Sutton, Kay. "Giangaleazzo Visconti as Patron: A Prayer Book Illuminated by Pietro da Pavia," *Apollo: The International Magazine of Arts,* 372 (1993), pp 89–96.

Syson, Luke. *Leonardo da Vinci: Painter at the Court of Milan.* London: National Gallery London, 2011.

Tafuri, Manfredo. *Venice and the Renaissance* Translated by Jessica Levine. Cambridge, MA, and London: MIT Press, 1989.

Tamalio, Raffaele. "Isabella d'Este, marchesa di Mantova," in *Dizionario Biografico degli Italiani.* Vol. 62. Rome: Istituto della Enciclopedia Italiana, 2004.

Tavernor, Robert. *Palladio and Palladianism.* London: Thames and Hudson, 1991.

Thibault, Paul. *Pope Gregory XI: The Failure of Tradition.* Lanham, MD: University Press of America, 1986.

Thompson, David., ed. and trans. *Petrarch: A Humanist Among Princes: An Anthology of Petrarch's Letters and of Selections from His Other Works*. New York: Harper & Row, 1971.

_____, Gordon Griffiths, and James Hankins, eds. and trans. *Humanism of Leonardo Bruni: Selected Texts*. New York: Renaissance Society of America, 1987.

Tabacco, Giovanni. *The Struggle for Power in Medieval Italy: Structures of Political Rule*. Translated by Rosalind Brown Jensen. Cambridge: Cambridge University Press, 1990.

Trinkaus, Charles. *In Our Image and Likeness: Humanity and Divinity in Italian Humanist Thought*. Chicago: University of Chicago Press, 1970.

Tronzo, William, ed. *St. Peter's in the Vatican*. Cambridge: Cambridge University Press, 2005.

Tuohy, Thomas. *Herculean Ferrara: Ercole d'Este (1471–1505) and the Invention of a Ducal Capital*. Cambridge Studies in Italian History and Culture. Cambridge: Cambridge University Press, 1996.

Valla, Lorenzo. *The Profession of the Religious and Selections from The Falsely-Believed and Forged Donation of Constantine*. Translated and edited by Olga Zorzi Pugliese. Toronto: CRRS, 1998.

Van Der Wee, H. *The Growth of the Antwerp Market and the European Economy*. Dordrecht: Springer, 1963.

Vasari, Giorgio. *The Lives of the Painters, Sculptors and Architects*. Translated by Gaston De Vere. Everyman's Library. New York: Knopf, 1996.

Vaughan, Herbert M. *The Medici Popes (Leo X. and Clement VII)*. London: Methuen, 1908.

Villani, Giovanni. *The Final Book of Giovanni Villani's New Chronicle*. Translated by Matthew Thomas Sneider. Kalamazoo: Western Michigan University–Medieval Institute Publications, 2016.

Viroli, Maurizio. *Niccolo's Smile: A Biography of Machiavelli*. Translated by Antony Shugaar. New York: Hill and Wang, 2002.

Vivanti, Corrado, ed. *Niccolò Machiavelli, Opere*. Turin: Einaudi-Gallimard, Biblioteca Della Pleiade, 1997. Online edition http://machiavelli.letteraturaoperaomnia.org/machiavelli_decennale_primo.html.

Watkins, R. N., ed. *Humanism and Republican Liberty*. Columbia: University of South Carolina Press, 1978.

Weinstein, Donald. *Savonarola and Florence: Prophecy and Patriotism in the Renaissance*. Princeton: Princeton University Press, 1970.

_____. *Savonarola: The Rise and Fall of a Renaissance Prophet*. New Haven: Yale University Press, 2011.

Weiss, Roberto. *The Renaissance Discovery of Classical Antiquity*. New York: Humanities Press, 1973.

Welch, Evelyn. *Art and Authority in Renaissance Milan*. New Haven: Yale University Press, 1996.

Westfall, Carroll William. *In This Most Perfect Paradise: Alberti, Nicholas V, and the Invention of Conscious Urban Planning in Rome, 1447–55*. University Park: Pennsylvania State University Press, 1974.

Wilkins, E. H. *Life of Petrarch*. Chicago and London: University of Chicago Press, 1961.

_____. "On Petrarch's Ep. VI, 2," *Speculum*, 38 (1963), pp. 620–22.

_____. *Petrarch's Eight Years in Milan*. Cambridge, MA: Medieval Academy of America, 1958.

Wills, Gary. *Venice: Lion City: The Religion of Empire*. New York: Washington Square Press, 2001.

Winspeare, Fabrizio. *La Congiura dei Cardinali Contro Leo X*. Florence: Olschki, 1957.

Witcombe, Christopher L. C. Ewart. "Sixtus V and the Scala Santa," *Journal of the Society of Architectural Historians*, 44 (1985), pp. 368–79.

Witt, Ronald. *In the Footsteps of the Ancients: The Origins of Humanism from Lovato to Bruni*. Leiden: Brill Academic Publishing, 2000.

_____. *Hercules at the Crossroads: The Life, Works, and Thought of Coluccio Salutati*. Durham: Duke University Press, 1983.

Wooton, David, ed. and trans. *Machiavelli, Selected Political Writings*. Indianapolis: Hackett Publishing Company, 1994.

Wright, John trans. *The Life of Cola Di Rienzo*. Toronto: Pontifical Institute of Mediaeval Studies, 1975.

Zak, Gur. "Boccaccio's Fiammetta and the Consolation of Literature," *MLN*, 131 (2016), pp. 1–19.

_____. *Petrarch's Humanism and the Care of the Self*. Cambridge: Cambridge University Press, 2010.

Zevi, Bruno. *Biagio Rossetti: architetto ferrarese, il primo urbanista moderno europeo*. Turin: Einaudi, 1960.

IMAGE CREDITS

Except where noted below, all images are in the public domain.

1.2 Caracas1830/Wikimedia/CC BY-SA 2.5 Generic.

1.3 Sailko/Wikimedia/CC BY-SA 2.5 Generic.

2.1 Sailko/Wikimedia/CC BY-SA 3.0 Unported.

2.3 RicciSpeziari/Wikimedia/CC BY-SA 3.0 Unported.

3.2 Sailko/Wikimedia/CC BY-SA 3.0 Unported.

3.3 Yair Haklai/Wikimedia/CC BY-SA 3.0 Unported.

5.1 Daderot/Wikimedia/CC BY-SA 3.0 Unported.

8.1 Ugo franchini/Wikimedia/CC BY-SA 3.0 Unported.

10.5 Valerie McGlinchey/Wikimedia/CC BY-SA 2.0 UK: England & Wales.

11.1 Nicola Bisi/Wikimedia/CC BY-SA 3.0 Unported.

11.2 Diego Baglieri/Wikimedia/CC BY-SA 4.0 International.

11.3 Sailko/Wikimedia/CC BY-SA 3.0 Unported.

12.5 Sailko/Wikimedia/CC BY-SA 3.0 Unported.

13.3 Gillian Bartlett.

13.4 Gillian Bartlett.

13.6a Sailko/Wikimedia/CC BY-SA 3.0 Unported.

13.6b Didier Descouens/Wikimedia/CC BY-SA 4.0 International.

14.3a Dogears/Wikimedia/CC BY-SA 3.0 Unported.

14.3b Marcok/it.wikipedia.org/CC BY-SA 3.0 Unported.

14.4 Marcok/it.wikipedia.org/CC BY-SA 3.0 Unported.

15.2a Berthold Werner/Wikimedia/CC BY-SA 3.0 Unported.

16.1 Sailko/Wikimedia/CC BY-SA 3.0 Unported.

16.2a Justin Ennis/Wikimedia/CC BY-SA 2.0 Generic

17.1 Jean-Marc Rosier from www.rosier.pro/Wikimedia/CC BY-SA 3.0 Unported.

18.2 Gobbler at wikivoyage/Wikimedia/CC BY-SA 3.0 Unported.

18.4 Sailko/Wikimedia/CC BY-SA 3.0 Unported.

21.1 Livioandronico2013/Wikimedia/CC BY-SA 4.0 International.

21.2 Mongolo1984/Wikimedia/CC BY-SA 4.0 International.

21.4 Anthony M./Wikimedia/CC BY-SA 2.0 Generic.

21.7 Владимир Шеляпин/Wikimedia/CC BY-SA 3.0 Unported.

22.1 Michal Osmenda/Wikimedia/CC BY-SA 2.0 Generic.

22.2 Jean-Pol Grandmont/Wikimedia/CC BY-SA 3.0 Unported.

22.3 Jean-Pol Grandmont/Wikimedia/CC BY-SA 3.0 Unported.

INDEX